Conversations with Erskine Caldwell

Literary Conversations Series

Peggy Whitman Prenshaw
General Editor

Conversations with Erskine Caldwell

Edited by
Edwin T. Arnold

University Press of Mississippi
Jackson and London

Copyright © 1988 by the University Press of Mississippi
All rights reserved
Manufactured in the United States of America
91   90   89   88   4   3   2   1
The paper in this book meets the guidelines for permanence and durability of the Committee
on Production Guidelines for Book Longevity of the Council on Library Resources.

Library of Congress Cataloging-in-Publication Data

Caldwell, Erskine, 1903-
    Conversations with Erskine Caldwell / edited by Edwin T. Arnold.
        p.   cm. — (Literary conversations series)
    Includes index.
    ISBN 0-87805-343-3 (alk. paper).   ISBN 0-87805-344-1 (pbk. : alk.
paper)
        1. Caldwell, Erskine, 1903-   —Interviews.   2. Authors.
American—20th century—Interviews.   3. Southern States in
literature.   I. Title.   II. Series.
PS3505.A322Z463 1988
813'.52—dc19   87-27682
                                                                    CIP

Books by Erskine Caldwell

The Bastard. New York: Heron Press, 1929.

Poor Fool. New York: Rariora Press, 1930.

American Earth. New York: Scribner's, 1931. Revised edition, New York: Duell, Sloan & Pearce, 1950. Parts I and II, "Far South" and "Farthest East," reprinted under title *A Swell-Looking Girl.* New American Library, 1950.

Tobacco Road. New York: Scribner's, 1932.

God's Little Acre. New York: Scribner's, 1933.

We Are the Living: Brief Stories. New York: Viking, 1933.

Journeyman. New York: Viking, 1935. Revised edition, 1938.

Kneel to the Rising Sun and Other Stories. New York: Viking, 1935.

Some American People. New York: McBride, 1935.

Tenant Farmer. New York: Phalanx Press, 1935.

The Sacrilege of Alan Kent. Portland: Falmouth Book House, 1936. Originally Part III of *American Earth,* "In the Native Land."

You Have Seen Their Faces, text by Caldwell, photographs by Margaret Bourke-White. New York: Viking, 1937.

Southways. New York: Viking, 1938.

North of the Danube, text by Caldwell, photographs by Margaret Bourke-White. New York: Viking, 1939.

Jackpot; The Short Stories of Erskine Caldwell. New York: Duell, Sloan & Pearce, 1940.

Trouble in July. New York: Duell, Sloan & Pearce, 1940.

Say, Is This the U.S.A.?, text by Caldwell, photographs by Margaret Bourke-White. New York: Duell, Sloan & Pearce, 1941.

All Night Long: A Novel of Guerrilla Warfare in Russia. New York: Duell, Sloan & Pearce, 1942.

All-Out on the Road to Smolensk. New York: Duell, Sloan & Pearce, 1942. Published as *Moscow Under Fire: A Wartime Diary* in London: Hutchinson, 1942.

Russia at War, text by Caldwell, photographs by Margaret Bourke-White. New York: Duell, Sloan & Pearce, 1942.

Georgia Boy. New York: Duell, Sloan & Pearce, 1943.

A Day's Wooing and Other Stories. New York: Grosset, 1944.

Stories by Erskine Caldwell: Twenty-four Representative Stories. New York: Duell, Sloan & Pearce, 1944.

Tragic Ground. New York: Duell, Sloan & Pearce, 1944.

A House in the Uplands. New York: Duell, Sloan & Pearce, 1946.

The Caldwell Caravan. Cleveland & New York: World, 1946.

The Sure Hand of God. New York: Duell, Sloan & Pearce, 1947.

This Very Earth. New York: Duell, Sloan & Pearce, 1948.

Place Called Estherville. New York: Duell, Sloan & Pearce, 1949.

A Woman in the House. New York: New American Library, 1949.

Episode in Palmetto. New York: Duell, Sloan & Pearce, 1950.

Call It Experience: The Years of Learning How to Write. New York: Duell, Sloan & Pearce, 1951.

The Humorous Side of Erskine Caldwell, edited by Robert Cantwell. New York: Duell, Sloan & Pearce, 1951.

The Courting of Susie Brown. New York: Duell, Sloan & Pearce/Boston: Little, Brown, 1952.

A Lamp for Nightfall. New York: Duell, Sloan & Pearce/Boston: Little, Brown, 1952.

The Complete Stories of Erskine Caldwell. New York: Duell, Sloan & Pearce/Boston: Little, Brown, 1953.

Love and Money. New York: Duell, Sloan & Pearce/Boston: Little, Brown, 1954.

Gretta. Boston: Little, Brown, 1955.

Gulf Coast Stories. Boston: Little, Brown, 1956.

Certain Women. Boston: Little, Brown, 1957.

Claudelle Inglish. Boston: Little, Brown, 1958.

Molly Cottontail. Boston: Little, Brown, 1958.

When You Think of Me. Boston: Little, Brown, 1959.

Men and Women: Twenty-two Stories. Boston: Little, Brown, 1961.

Jenny By Nature. New York: Farrar, Straus & Cudahy, 1961.

Close to Home. New York: Farrar, Straus & Cudahy, 1962.

The Last Night of Summer. New York: Farrar, Straus, 1963.

Around About America. New York: Farrar, Straus, 1964.

In Search of Bisco. New York: Farrar, Straus & Giroux, 1965.

The Deer at Our House. New York: Collier, 1966.

Miss Mamma Aimee. New York: New American Library, 1967.

Writing in America. New York: Phaedra, 1967.

Deep South: Memory and Observation. New York: Weybright & Talley, 1968. Published as *In the Shadow of the Steeple.* London: Heinemann, 1966.

Summertime Island. New York & Cleveland: World, 1969.

The Weather Shelter. New York & Cleveland: World, 1969.

The Earnshaw Neighborhood. New York: World, 1971.

Annette. New York: New American Library, 1973.

Afternoons in Mid-America: Observations and Impressions, text by Caldwell, illustrations by Virginia Caldwell. New York: Dodd, Mead, 1976.

The Sacrilege of Alan Kent. Illustrated by Alexander Calder. Galeric Maeght, 1976.

The Black & White Stories of Erskine Caldwell. Selected by Ray McIver. Atlanta: Peachtree Publishers, 1984.

With All My Might. Atlanta: Peachtree Publishers, 1987.

Editor of:

The American Folkways Series, 25 volumes. New York: Duell, Sloan & Pearce, 1941-54.

Contents

Introduction   ix

Chronology   xvii

Erskine Caldwell's Initial Novel Out Next Month
   Portland Evening News   3

Caldwell Sorry for Critics: Author Feels
   Mayor Has Insulted Them   *Ashton Stevens*   5

Erskine Caldwell Has Seen the Faces
   of the Czechoslovakian People   *Eugene Gordon*   7

A Talk with Erskine Caldwell   *Robert van Gelder*   11

Who's Who in Darien: Erskine Caldwell   *The Darien Review*   15

Erskine Caldwell's Lesson From Russia:
   America May Lose War   *PM's Weekly*   23

New England Literary Tour: Erskine Caldwell's Connecticut Home
   Is A Place of Beauty and Charm   *Alice Dixon Bond*   26

Caldwell Returns to Hollywood   *Ezra Goodman*   32

America's Most Censored Author—An Interview
   with Erskine Caldwell   *Publishers' Weekly*   34

Erskine Caldwell at Work   *Carvel Collins*   38

Sex, Sin and Society Through the Eyes
   of Erskine Caldwell   *Guccione*   52

Erskine Caldwell   *Roy Newquist*   58

"Sex Was Their Way of Life": A Frank Interview
   with Erskine Caldwell   *Morris Renek*   66

Caldwell Assays Sales of Novels   *Harry Gilroy*   81

An Interview with Erskine Caldwell   *Alan Lelchuk*
   and Robin White   83

Erskine Caldwell: Down South Storyteller   *Jack McClintock*   103

The Art of Fiction: An Interview with Erskine Caldwell
   Donald Lewis and *Richard Wertman*   109

An Interview in Florida with Erskine Caldwell   *Richard B. Sale*   120

Interview with Erskine Caldwell   *Jac Tharpe*   138

Caldwell's Little Acre   *John Dorschner*   148

Erskine Caldwell: A Georgia Boy Returns Home
   Helen C. Smith   156

"A Writer First": An Interview with Erskine Caldwell
   Elizabeth Pell Broadwell and Ronald Wesley Hoag   160

The Art of Fiction LXII: Erskine Caldwell   *Elizabeth Pell Broadwell*
   and Ronald Wesley Hoag   179

Erskine Caldwell on Southern Realism   *Ronald Wesley Hoag*
   and Elizabeth Pell Broadwell   200

An Interview with Erskine Caldwell   *Michel Bandry*   205

Fifty Years Since Tobacco Road: An Interview
   with Erskine Caldwell   *Richard Kelly and Marcia Pankake*   218

Portrait of an American Primitive: A Conversation
   with Erskine Caldwell   *D. G. Kehl*   233

A Good Listener Speaks   *Kay Bonetti*   244

Erskine Caldwell's Little Acre: A Portrait of the Irascible, Maverick
   Author at Home   *Kent Biffle*   252

Erskine Caldwell at Eighty-One: An Interview
   Marilyn Dorn Staats   257

Interview with Erskine Caldwell   *Edwin T. Arnold*   265

Erskine Caldwell: The Final Chapter   *Charles Trueheart*   297

Index   306

Introduction

Erskine Caldwell, among the most public and controversial of American authors, was also among the most often interviewed. In the 1930s, following the success and scandal of his books *Tobacco Road* (1932) and *God's Little Acre* (1933) and the long-running Broadway dramatization of *Tobacco Road,* which played from 1933 to 1941, he was often approached for his views on the economic and social conditions of the South, the development of southern literature, and, inevitably, the role of censorship in American society. During this period he gave few substantive interviews, preferring to address these questions through special correspondence to newspapers and magazines such as *The New York Times,* the *New York Mirror,* the *New Leader,* and the *New Republic;* through commissioned articles such as his controversial 1935 *New York Post* series on poverty in the South; or through the books, fiction and nonfiction, themselves.

The first major interviews began to appear near the end of that decade. Despite all the publicity surrounding his work, Caldwell, a personally reticent man, had maintained a low profile and kept his distance from celebrity. He had lived in the small town of Mount Vernon, Maine, although he was often separated from his family as he escaped to New York, California, Georgia, and other locations to do much of his actual writing. However, by 1938 his life had changed. He was divorced by his first wife, Helen, as a result of his association with Margaret Bourke-White, whom he had met in 1936. Together, Caldwell the writer and Bourke-White the photographer made an attractive and adventurous couple as they travelled about, recording their impressions of America and Central Europe in a series of popular and timely books. They made good copy, and their romantic image was conveyed in numerous newspaper features, of which the articles in *The Darien Review* (1940) and *The Boston Herald* (1942) serve as examples. This reputation was confirmed on their trip to Russia, where, when Germany invaded, they acted as witnesses to history, reporters to America on the war that lay ahead. Caldwell, especially, became an ardent spokesman on the courage of the Russian people and stressed America's need for wartime preparation. His pronouncements made in interviews such as those selected from *The Daily Worker* (1939) and *PM's Weekly* (1942) illustrate the authority he held in the early days of World War II. For a time he joined other celebrities on war bond tours, and in Hollywood he was considered the film industry's resident expert on wartime Russia.

Following the war, however, Caldwell retreated once again from the public eye. He and Margaret Bourke-White were divorced in 1942, and he too quickly entered into an unhappy marriage with June Johnson, a young student at the University of Arizona. Already a wealthy man because of his work in Hollywood, the success of the play *Tobacco Road* (both on Broadway and in road-show companies that performed throughout the country), and the healthy sales of his books, he now multiplied his earnings through an arrangement with Victor Weybright and the recently-established New American Library, which brought out his work in paperback form. Inevitably, perhaps, as his sales in this medium increased, his reputation suffered.

In the decades to follow, he normally spent several months of each year on tour—to promote his books at paperback sales conventions, to lecture at colleges, to serve abroad as a speaker for the United States Information Agency—and he was interviewed by innumerable local newspapers and student publications. There was a great deal of redundancy in the questions asked, and Caldwell often responded in kind, with pat, rote answers. As he said in a 1968 interview with Jack McClintock, "I get tired of talking about myself and I get bored. . . . You find yourself saying the same things over and over. So I usually don't have interviews the rest of the year, except in exceptional circumstances." On occasion, however, significant interviews which went beyond the routine did occur, such as Carvel Collins's 1958 *Atlantic Monthly* piece, Morris Renek's 1964 discussion with Caldwell in *Cavalier,* or the Lelchuk and White 1967 *Per/Se* interview. Examples such as these show Caldwell engaging in conversation rather than performing for the press, and he is often revealing in his frankness.

James Korges's 1969 monograph *Erskine Caldwell,* published by the University of Minnesota Press, and Richard B. Sale's 1970 interview, published in *Studies in the Novel* in 1971, marked a renewal of scholarly interest in Caldwell which has continued until the present time. In one sense, age gave him and his work a dignity and respect not previously accorded. Caldwell himself seemed more willing to talk at length, to look back on his career, to discuss his ideas and views. While he in no way regained his previous fame, he was again recognized and celebrated as an American original, one who had influenced the development of American literature. Elizabeth Broadwell and Ronald Hoag's extensive and rewarding 1980 interview, portions of which appeared in *The Paris Review* and *The Georgia Review* in 1982 and in *The Mississippi Quarterly* in 1983, illustrates the kind of thorough, knowledgeable interest shown in Caldwell in the last years of his life.

Erskine Caldwell was never an easy or comfortable interviewee, although he was generally a gracious one. He considered the interview as one of his responsibilities as a professional writer: an author should try to sell his books, and if the selling often involved public relations events and repetitive questions from newspaper reporters—and later from inquisitive academics—then that was simply part of the job. When I interviewed Caldwell in March 1986, approximately a year before his death, he had recently finished his autobiography *With All My Might.* "You can ask me anything you want," he told me as we began. "There are things I can't remember, but I will answer to the best of my ability." There were indeed times when he could not recall certain events. "That's so far back in my memory that I cannot see through the dimness of it," he replied to one of my questions. On other occasions he would redirect the question or respond with a routine answer or an episode fresh in his mind from writing the autobiography. He was usually unwilling to discuss what he considered private or personal matters about his life or his art, deflecting these inquiries with "Oh, I'll leave that up to you" or "Well, I've discussed that in my book" or sometimes a smiling silence. He forever denied having any "statement" to make, any point of view to propound. As he told the *Washington Post* reporter Charles Trueheart in one of his last interviews, "I'm not going to talk about anything unless I'm asked, because I have nothing to say," a disclaimer reflected in many of the interviews.

And yet he often had a great deal to say, for his writing was motivated by serious and universal concerns. As he explained to Robert van Gelder in 1940, "I try to hold up a mirror to nature in the South—and to my own nature, to human nature. I don't say that lynching is evil or that cruelty is bad. But by showing people as they are cruel, and by showing their victims, by showing people oppressed to hopelessness and impoverished to hopelessness—perhaps in that way I'll have some effect on many lives." In my own interview with Caldwell, he espoused the same idea in discussing *Tobacco Road*. "I couldn't think of anything else to do except to write what my conscience told me about these people who were suffering. I thought other people could help somehow, either by medical aid or by food—something. What else could I do but write about it?" Thus, Caldwell could at times be passionate in his views, especially on social issues, although he preferred to maintain a more detached stance. "I'm a writer, not a crusader," he would say. "I leave the crusading to others."

There was always a good deal of repetition in the questions Caldwell was asked during his sixty years as a publishing writer. "I just never give the same answer twice," he once joked, but the fact is that he usually took the interviewing process seriously and prided himself on his forthrightness and honesty. He did, of course, sometimes contradict himself, and there are obvious inconsistancies found among his answers. For example, he told Robert van Gelder in 1940, "I've been an unwilling witness at a number of lynchings," but in that same year a reporter from the *Darien Review* noted that Caldwell "has never seen an actual lynching, but he has been there right after one in time to 'still see the body hanging from a limb.' " And as late as 1982 he could maintain, "I only witnessed one lynching in my life. But I had read about and I had heard about . . . many other instances of violence of that nature." Other accounts of his youth and years as a beginning writer are also sometimes open to question; he could tell an episode in various ways and was not above romanticizing the life of the struggling author in either his autobiographical writings or interviews to make a good story. But even when myth-making was involved, it was generally good-natured and sometimes even slightly self-mocking. Especially towards the end of his life he spoke of his youth in a rather wry and understated manner. "I was just a young punk," he once said with a grin. In later years, he would not "praise" himself, but he was confidently aware of and satisfied with his accomplishments. Although one might sometimes question the "facts" in Caldwell's statements, there was almost always a "truth" to be found in them.

On the other hand, Caldwell was usually consistent in his comments on the writing itself. In 1929 he remarked that "today's fiction writers [are] more interested in presenting character studies, type descriptions, than in producing a good story, and [I have] attempted to get away from this trend in [my] first published novel." In his 1964 interview with Roy Newquist he remembered, "When I began writing, all those years ago, I was more interested in the content of a story than I was in any technical derivations of a story or a novel. . . . All I wanted to do was to tell a story, to tell it to the best of my ability—better, I hoped, than anyone else could tell that particular story. . . . So, when I wanted to write a story, and tried to write it, I was writing for myself—not for a million people—because I had to please myself first." "I am the reader," he told Marilyn Dorn Staats in 1984. "Anybody else who comes along is welcome to read what I am reading."

He was, he claimed, not interested in *plot*: "I've never known exactly what a plot is because I wouldn't know how to do one if I saw it. What I try to do is to help people themselves furnish the entire basis of a story." The story, the work of fiction, had to come from the imagination. "I like to imagine something and to write it because I do not consciously write realism," he explained to D.G. Kehl in 1982. "To me, realism is something that is photographic, we'll say, something that's fixed, something unchangeable, something that exists like a rock or a tree. What I try to do in my writing is to create something that does not exist and make it real. To me, that's the ultimate aim of fiction: to create something that has never existed before."

In other comments on his writing, Caldwell sometimes gave the impression that the act of creation could be for him a rather mechanical or even passive experience. As he told Elizabeth Broadwell and Ronald Hoag regarding his characters, "I have no influence over them. I'm only an observer, recording. The story is always being told by the characters themselves. In fact, I'm often critical, or maybe ashamed, of what some of them say or do. . . . But I have no control over it." He described to Carvel Collins his writing process: "I never have any big ideas to build up with notes and things of that sort. Actually I only have one idea at a time. It may be a very small idea that you can express in ten words. I start from that and see what happens. The way I like to do is not to have any preconceived notions about the idea, but to see what happens. . . . Then I get a sheet of yellow paper and put down the first sentence. Then I see what happens in the second sentence and go on from there. That's about the only method I have."

As a young writer, Caldwell liked to suggest that he rarely revised his work. He told Robert van Gelder that he wrote "as it comes to me; I can't change it." For example, in his autobiography *Call It Experience* and often in interviews he described having written *God's Little Acre* in a kind of white heat. "Now with *God's Little Acre* I dropped the sheets on the floor as I went and didn't pick them up until I had finished," he told Broadwell and Hoag. "Then I put them together and that was the book. No revision." He always maintained that his editors rarely made changes in his finished typescripts, that "I've never wanted anybody to tell me to change anything or to take anything out. And no one ever has." Such colorful statements helped to underscore Caldwell's image as a rather artless and instinctive writer, although manuscript evidence, at least from the first part of his career, challenges these assertions. *God's Little Acre,* for example, was extensively rewritten, and books such as *Journeyman* or *Trouble in July* were carefully edited by others. These comments also overshadowed Caldwell's other statements on writing which emphasized the care he took in constructing his work. "My wastebasket always holds more than my folder does anyway," he told Carvel Collins. "Oh, I might have two or three pages worth keeping at the end of the day," he later explained to Broadwell and Hoag. "And that's a lot, you know; three pages is a lot. I probably write forty or forty-five total to get those three I can keep. And it is not unusual to sit at a typewriter all day and end up with nothing. But if you get up, you know you'll have nothing. . . . [And] usually when the book is finished, I rewrite the whole thing anywhere from six to a dozen times because I'm never satisfied."

At least one critic has dismissed the importance of Caldwell's interviews, finding them to be of little help in a study of his work. And certainly Caldwell maintained a protective mask which baffled all who knew him and which hid the complexity inside. But, despite certain repetitions and standardized answers, despite obvious omissions or evasions, and despite an occasional exaggerated naivete or simplicity, Caldwell's interviews should be of interest to any reader or student of American literature. These "conversations" present an overview of writing in the twentieth century. Never far removed from the social, political, and cultural events of the time, they remind us of our history and of one man who, in his own way, both shaped and recorded aspects of that history.

Arranged chronologically according to the time each was given rather than published, the following interviews are reprinted in their entirety. In some cases punctuation has been silently amended for clarity's sake, and minor corrections requested by the interviewers have been made in the Broadwell and Hoag *Paris Review* interview and in the Marilyn Dorn Staats *Arizona Quarterly* interview.

For their assistance and cooperation in bringing these interviews together and for allowing me to spend three memorable days with them for my own interview in 1986, I would like to thank first of all Erskine and Virginia Caldwell.

I also want to acknowledge the support of the National Endowment for the Humanities for research travel made in the course of my work. Support was also given by the English Department, the Cratis D. Williams Graduate School, and the College of Arts and Sciences at Appalachian State University: my gratitude in particular goes to Dr. Loyd Hilton, chairman of the English Department; Dr. Joyce Lawrence, dean of the Graduate School; and Dr. J. William Byrd, dean of the College of Arts and Sciences.

For help in research and location of many of these interviews I want to thank Philip N. Cronenwett, curator of manuscripts, and the staff at Baker Library, Dartmouth College, Hanover, New Hampshire; J. Larry Gulley and the staff in the Special Collections Division, the University of Georgia Libraries, Athens, Georgia; and Robert A. Hull, Manuscripts Department, Alderman Library, the University of Virginia, Charlottesville, Virginia. My thanks also to Martha Kreszock and staff of the InterLibrary Loan Division of Belk Library at Appalachian State University, Boone, N.C. Their work and assistance is much appreciated.

For advice and further assistance in collecting and preparing the manuscripts I would like to thank Dr. William C. Griffin of the Interdisciplinary Studies Department, A.S.U., Dr. Jerry Williamson, editor of *The Appalachian Journal*; Dr. James L.W. West of Pennsylvania State University; Janet Welborn and Shannon Taylor of the English Department, A.S.U.; and Elizabeth and Matthew Arnold. I am also grateful to the interviewers, editors, and publishers who have given me permission to reprint their works.

It should be noted that many foreign interviews were done with Erskine Caldwell over the years. Caldwell criticism in France, Poland, Japan, Italy, Russia, Romania, and elsewhere has treated him with a seriousness not always found in America. These works remain to brought together, translated, and studied as a supplement to this collection.

This book is dedicated to my mother, Jean Darden Arnold, and to the memory of my father, Edwin T. Arnold, Jr., M.D.

ETA June 1987

Chronology

1902 or 1903   Erskine Preston Caldwell born on 17 December in
               White Oak, Coweta County, Georgia, the only child of the
               Reverend Ira Sylvester Caldwell and Caroline Preston Bell
               Caldwell. [As a student at the University of Virginia,
               Caldwell listed his year of birth as 1902 and later changed
               it to 1903, the date he held to in later life.]
1903-18   Ira Caldwell's job as Secretary of the Associate Reformed
               Presbyterian Church Home Missions Board keeps the
               family moving throughout the South. Caldwell lives in
               Prosperity, S.C.; Timber Ridge and Staunton, Va.;
               Charlotte, N.C.; Bradley, S.C.; Ybor City, Fla.; Fairfield,
               Va.; Atoka, Tenn.; and finally Wrens, Ga., where the
               family settles in 1918. Caldwell attends several years of
               school in Staunton but is basically educated by his mother,
               a former teacher. While in Atoka in 1917, he works for a
               brief time as driver for the YMCA, transporting soldiers
               from Millington army base to nearby Memphis. Based on
               this experience, he attempts his first work of fiction, "A
               Boy's Own Story of City Life," which described the
               denizens of Beale Street.
1918-20   Caldwell attends Wrens High School but does not
               graduate. During this time he works as a driver for a local
               doctor and the county tax assessor and later shovels
               cottonseed at a local mill. He also accompanies his father
               on calls throughout the region. These experiences
               introduce him to the people and surroundings of East
               Georgia, where many of his books will be set. He also
               begins to write for the local paper, *The Jefferson Reporter*,
               and then serve as a "string" correspondent for nearby
               newspapers such as the *Augusta Chronicle* and the *Macon
               Telegraph*.
1920-22   Caldwell attends Erskine College, a Presbyterian school in
               Due West, S.C., from which his father had graduated. He

plays football, spends much of his time traveling to nearby cities, and makes a poor showing as a student. In the Spring of 1922 he is jailed for nine days in Bogalusa, Louisiana, suspected of being an I.W.W. labor agitator.

1923-25   He attends the University of Virginia on a United Daughters of the Confederacy scholarship, his income supplemented by work in a local poolhall. Caldwell is an "in-and-out" student with time spent in Washington, D.C., and Pennsylvania. In the Summer of 1924, he lives in Philadelphia, where he takes economics classes at the Wharton School of the University of Pennsylvania. In the Fall, he moves to Wilkes-Barre, where he works as a stockboy for the S.S. Kresge Company and tries out for semi-professional football in the Anthracite League. In the Spring of 1925 he returns to Charlottesville. On 3 March, he elopes with Helen Lannigan, the daughter of the U.Va. track coach; they are married in Washington, D.C.

1925-27   Still two years short of graduation, Caldwell withdraws from the University of Virginia and moves to Atlanta to work as a reporter on the *Atlanta Journal* while he pursues a career as a professional writer. First child, Erskine Preston, is born. Caldwell often said that he and Helen moved to Atlanta in 1925 and that he worked at the *Atlantic Journal* for a year before moving to Maine. However, he was again enrolled at the University of Virginia in the Fall of 1926, his address given as Box 197, Ivy Road Boarding House. In fact, he received grades for the first term of 1926-27. He seems to have gone to Atlanta in 1925 and then returned to UVa in 1926 for the Fall term before going on to Maine in 1927, an explanation in keeping with his comments to Carvel Collins in 1958 that he "went to work on a newspaper in Atlanta and then went back to college again."

1927-28   Caldwell, his wife and child, move to Mt. Vernon, Maine, to live in the Lannigan vacation house ("Greentrees"). Caldwell gives himself five years to become a published writer and devotes his energy to writing and book reviewing. In 1928 he opens Longfellow Square Bookshop at 666-A Congress St. in Portland, Maine, stocked with review copies and run by Helen and a friend, Marjory Morse. His second son, Dabney Withers, is born.

1929   In March, his story "Midsummer Passion" is accepted for publication in *The New American Caravan*. Other stories are published in numerous "little magazines" of the day. *The Bastard,* a short novel, is published in a limited edition by the Heron Press. The book is banned in Portland, his first brush with censorship.

1930   In March, his stories "The Mating of Marjory" and "A Very Late Spring" are accepted by Maxwell Perkins for publication in *Scribner's Magazine,* a sign to Caldwell of his success as a writer. Emboldened by his accomplishments, he applies, unsuccessfully, for a Guggenheim Fellowship, and on 4 July burns much of his unpublished material and his collection of rejection slips. His second novel, *Poor Fool,* is published in a limited edition by Rariora Press. Scribner's proposes to publish his first collection of stories, under the title *American Earth*. With the advance royalties, Caldwell travels to California and then to Georgia, where he is inspired to write the story of impoverished sharecroppers.

1931   *American Earth* is published. In New York City, Caldwell writes *Tobacco Road,* which is immediately accepted by Perkins. Caldwell then begins work on a novel set in New England. He lives for a time at Sutton Place, run by Nathanael West, with whom he becomes friends.

1932   *A Lamp for Nightfall* is refused by Scribner's. Caldwell moves to Viking Press. During the summer, he writes *God's Little Acre*.

1933   Viking publishes *God's Little Acre* and his second collection of stories, *We Are the Living*. Caldwell is hired as screenwriter by MGM and spends Spring and Summer in Hollywood. His only daughter, Janet, is born in May. *God's Little Acre* is deemed obscene by the New York Society for the Suppression of Vice, resulting in a notable decision by Magistrate Benjamin E. Greenspan who rules in the book's favor after it is defended by over sixty writers and critics. In September, Caldwell receives *The Yale Review's* award for fiction for his story "A County Full of

Swedes." On 4 December, the play *Tobacco Road*, written by Jack Kirkland, opens at the Masque Theatre in New York. It will run for seven-and-a-half years, 3,180 performances, before it closes on 31 May 1941, making it the longest-running play in the history of the New York stage at that time.

1934   Caldwell works on a novel and collection of short stories. In June he returns to Hollywood for several months at MGM.

1935   *Journeyman* is published by Viking in January. He spends the first three months of the year traveling in the South with his father and writes a series of controversial articles for the *New York Post* depicting subhuman conditions among the rural poor. *Tenant Farmer* and *Some American People,* both published by small presses, examine the subject in more detail. *Kneel to the Rising Sun* is published by Viking.

1936   Caldwell teams with photographer Margaret Bourke-White for a photo-journalistic book of impressions of the South. They travel together during the summer. In October Caldwell separates from Helen and moves to New York.

1937   *You Have Seen Their Faces* is published by Viking.

1938   *Southways,* another collection of stories, is published by Viking. Caldwell is divorced from Helen. In the Summer he and Bourke-White travel to Czechoslovakia to record this country on the brink of war.

1939   Caldwell and Bourke-White are married on 27 February. *North of the Danube* is published by Viking in April. Caldwell moves to Duell, Sloan & Pearce and starts work on the *American Folkways* series while Bourke-White goes to England on assignment for *Life.*

1940   *Jackpot,* a collection of seventy-five of his stories, is published with brief introductions to each written by Caldwell. *Trouble in July,* hs first novel in five years, is also published. Caldwell and Bourke-White travel throughout the country preparing their third collaboration, a celebration of America and its people.

1941   *Say! Is This the U.S.A.?* is published. Caldwell and Bourke-White go to China and Russia, reaching Moscow in May. On 22 June, the Russian-German War begins, and they are among the few correspondents there to report on the German attack. Caldwell makes broadcasts for CBS Radio and writes for *Life* and the newspaper *PM.* They return to America by way of England in October. Film version of *Tobacco Road* is directed by John Ford.

1942   Caldwell's experiences in Russia result in several books, both fiction and nonfiction, the most notable being *Russia at War,* his final work with Bourke-White. While his wife continues on war assignments for *Life,* Caldwell is called to Hollywood to write the screenplay for *Mission to Moscow,* a propaganda film for which he receives no credit. He works on and off in Hollywood for the next two years. His separation from Bourke-White ends in divorce and shortly after, on 21 December, he marries June Johnson, a 21-year-old student at the University of Arizona.

1943   Caldwell publishes *Georgia Boy,* which he would sometimes deem his single best work. He and June settle in Tucson. Her unwillingness to travel and her growing dependence on psychoanalysis cause increasing strain within the marriage.

1944   Caldwell publishes *Tragic Ground,* a return to the harsh naturalism of *Tobacco Road.* His fourth child, Jay Erskine, is born. Ira Sylvester Caldwell dies.

1945-50   Caldwell becomes known as "The World's Most Popular Novelist," largely because of the phenomenal sales of his works in paperback. In 1947 he travels to Europe for the first time since World War II. He continues writing on his "cyclorama" of southern life, publishing a novel a year. His critical reputation suffers as his popularity grows.

1951   *Call It Experience,* his "informal recollection of authorship," is published.

1952-56   Duell, Sloan & Pearce is bought by Little, Brown. Caldwell continues to publish a book a year. In 1953, *The Complete Stories of Erskine Caldwell* appears, a comprehensive but not definitive collection of his work in the short story. He separates from June Johnson and moves to Phoenix. Later, Caldwell returns to Europe to

	check on his publications there. He and June are divorced in 1956 and Caldwell moves to San Francisco.
1957	Caldwell marries Virginia Moffet Fletcher, who has worked as his secretary. They honeymoon in Europe.
1958	Film version of *God's Little Acre* is directed by Anthony Mann and is named one of the year's best by *Time* magazine.
1959	The Caldwells travel to England, Turkey, Greece, and Russia; they spend time with the John Steinbecks on the trip.
1960	They go to Japan, where Caldwell is honored for his work. Caldwell moves to Farrar, Straus publishing company.
1961	Caldwell becomes a speaker for the United States Information Service in Europe and Asia. He and Virginia make five tours over the next few years.
1964-68	Caldwell turns more toward nonfiction and autobiography. *In Search of Bisco* is published by Farrar, Straus & Giroux in 1965, but they refuse Caldwell's next book *In the Shadow of the Steeple,* his meditation on religion and his father. The book is published in England in 1967 and in America, under the title *Deep South,* in 1968. Both *In Search of Bisco* and *Deep South* are considered among Caldwell's best nonfiction works. In 1967 Caroline Bell Preston Caldwell dies. After Caldwell is diagnosed as having emphysema, he and Virginia move to Dunedin, Florida.
1968-74	Caldwell continues to tour for USIF and serves as writer-in-residence at Dartmouth College, which holds the most extensive Caldwell collection. In 1972, a blocked artery almost results in the loss of his left leg, and Caldwell gives up his heavy smoking. After his release from the Mayo Clinic, he serves as a judge at the Cannes Film Festival. His final novel, *Annette,* is published in 1973. In 1974 he and Virginia prepare to collaborate on a travel book, but Caldwell must undergo surgery for cancer of the right lung.
1975	The Caldwells resume research on their travel book. In the spring they go to Poland. Upon their return, Caldwell undergoes surgery of the left lung.

1976   Caldwell makes his final European tour for USIF.
             Afternoons in Mid-America, with illustrations by Virginia
             Caldwell, is published.
1977-84   The Caldwells move near Scottsdale, Arizona. In 1978,
             Caldwell is honored on his seventy-fifth birthday at the
             University of Virginia. He continues to serve as a
             Montgomery Fellow at Dartmouth. In 1981 he is awarded
             the Republic of Poland's Order of Cultural Merit. In 1982
             he is honored by the Erskine Caldwell Literary Society in
             Japan. In 1983 he is given the Republic of France's
             Commander of the Order of Arts and Letters. In 1984 he
             is elected to the select fifty-chair body of the American
             Academy of Arts and Letters.
1985-87   Caldwell works on his autobiography. In May 1985, he is
             honored at the University of Georgia at the *Roots in
             Georgia* conference. In September 1986, he begins
             chemotherapy treatment for a recurrence of lung cancer.
             With All My Might is published in March 1987. On 11
             April 1987 Caldwell dies at home in Paradise Valley,
             Arizona.

Conversations with Erskine Caldwell

Erskine Caldwell's Initial Novel Out Next Month

Portland Evening News/1929

From *Portland Evening News*, 24 September 1929, p. 15.

October will bring to patrons of the most utterly modern type of fiction, a novel and at least two short stories from the pen of a Portland man. For Portland claims Erskine Caldwell, founder of the Longfellow Square Book Shop.

The novel, entitled *The Bastard,* is Mr. Caldwell's first. It is the story of Southern people in their typical atmosphere, but the author remarked that he has introduced no distinct types in his characters. He said he considered today's fiction writers more interested in presenting character studies, type descriptions, than in producing a good story, and he has attempted to get away from this trend in his first published novel.

Mr. Caldwell is well acquainted with the locality represented in his story. For several years he was a member of the editorial staff of the *Atlanta Journal,* the largest daily south of Philadelphia. He remarked that several well known writers of today "got their starts" on that paper, but he hastened to add that he had no expectations of this fact assuring him equal success.

The two short stories are "Midsummer Passion" and "Tracing Life With a Finger" which are to appear in *The New American Caravan,* the third of the *Caravan* collections, published by Macaulay. The *Caravans* are compilations of short stories, poems and articles of an essayistic variety of younger contemporary writers. Many of these writers receive their first public introduction through these collections.

The New American Caravan is expected to be more interesting and more important than the first or second, and is likely, according to Mr. Caldwell, to be the monthly choice of one of the more important book clubs.

Mr. Caldwell is also a contributor to *Transition,* the exceedingly modern (in a distinguished way) monthly of short articles of varied sorts. The monthly, although known to all literary folks, is not widely read, but has fathered the careers of a great many of the finest writers of today. Ernest Hemingway, popular writer, and James Joyce, author of the daring *Ulysses,* which was published about ten years ago, are but two of the well known literary figures to prove their first merits through *Transition.* Mr. Caldwell admits that *Transition* furnished the basis for his novel *The Bastard.*

The Longfellow Square Book Shop was begun slightly less than two years ago and has already won the reputation of one of the finest in the State. Mr. Caldwell founded the shop, but leaves it in the hands of his wife the greater part of the time.

Caldwell Sorry for Critics:
Author Feels Mayor Has Insulted Them
Ashton Stevens/1935

Unidentified article found in Erskine Caldwell's Scrapbooks. It
likely comes from *The Chicago American,* for which Stevens was
a columnist at this time. The play *Tobacco Road* was ordered
closed by Mayor Edward H. Kelly on 22 October 1935.

Erskine Caldwell had said he would meet me at my club yesterday at
3. But I turned up there without really expecting him. On my way I
learned that Mayor Kelly had abruptly discovered, after it had run
eight weeks at the Selwyn, that Mr. Caldwell's *Tobacco Road* is not a
nice play, and had closed the show. So I fancied that Mr. Caldwell
would be too busy with attorneys, managers, actors and front-page
journalists to remember our assignation for a highball.

But there he was at the third chime of the clock, reminding me of
the punctual and imperturbable A.H. Woods that time the pineapple
tossers blew out the front of Al's newly built Woods Theater just a
couple of minutes before our tryst at the Blackstone, but without
causing Al to cancel his friendly date.

Mr. Caldwell, who looks like six feet of retired footballer, was as
calm as his writing isn't. Never, I take it from the biographies, a gabby
man, he, nevertheless, at once talked readily and charmingly about
many things, none of which bore the remotest relationship to the
black ribbon with which the mayor had just decorated the Selwyn
door.

He was, for all that he has written about the backward Southerner,
a Southern gentleman first and an insulted author quite a while
afterwards. He was the most hospitable guest I ever entertained.

It was I who finally brought up the subject and in so doing
discovered that Mr. Caldwell, in the tactfulness of a fine heart, was
brooding more on my sorrows than on his own—not my sorrows
alone, but those of all Chicago drama critics. It was now a delicate
situation, he intimated, for those reviewers who are presumed to be
able to protect their readers from evil plays. Their mayor had publicly

humiliated them, repudiating their reports on the human earthworms that squirm in the saffron soil of *Tobacco Road.*

But, in the comforting opinion of the author of the veracious book from which the suppressed play was made, the people would in the end vindicate the downtrodden Chicago critics who had tried to uphold the freedom of the stage. No arbitrary one-man censorship could long silence the ardent voice of Truth in Drama and Truth in Criticism. We critics had been badly mauled by a mayor, but our wounds would heal, our loyal readers would not desert us.

Mr. Caldwell left me not without a little hope. I began to think. Perhaps, I thought, it was that catch-line, that double-barreled catch-oath uttered so unemotionally but so tellingly by Henry Hull's Jeeter Lester, which had soured the good Christian mayor on the show. Perhaps the imprecation could be changed and *Tobacco Road* given another chance—changed, say, to "By-gum-by-Wriggley!"

Erskine Caldwell Has Seen the Faces of the Czechoslovakian People

Eugene Gordon/1939

From *The* (NYC) *Daily Worker,* 17 January 1939, p. 7.

"Mr. Caldwell is on his way in from Darien, Conn., and will be at the Hotel Roosevelt about 4 o'clock. He said he'd meet you there."

But I had never seen Erskine Caldwell. Perhaps she could tell me what he looked like?

"Well," considered the voice on the phone, "he's a large man—somewhat over six feet, I should say. Sandy-haired. Young-looking. And freckled. And—oh, yes—retiring. Likes to get off to himself and sit in corners."

I possessed also some additional details from a portrait drawn earlier by a friend named Henning. Edgar Henning, now a taxi driver, was the first stage manager of *Tobacco Road.*

"We'd invited Caldwell down from Maine to give us some pointers about the characters. Henry Hull, who was the Jeeter Lester in those days, asked Erskine what Jeeter's age was and what he looked like, and so on. Caldwell answered just those questions but said nothing else. He was awfully shy. But he had never seen a play in rehearsal before and got a big kick out of it."

When *Tobacco Road* was ready for its Broadway opening, Henning heard from Caldwell again. The laconic note from Mt. Vernon, Maine, asked whether they couldn't reserve two second-night seats—in the balcony!

Having searched for freckles and sandy hair on a shy six-footer shrinking in a corner, we—a hotel porter and I—finally came upon such a person in the semi-basement coffeeshop with the cherry blossom photo-murals.

"Erskine Caldwell?"

He was. He was hiding behind a plate of mashed potato and baked pork sausages shriveled to the size of brown lead pencils. He himself was more brown than ruddy—as his hair was more brown than sandy. He wore a brown suit of rough texture.

7

So here was the author of *Tobacco Road, God's Little Acre, Kneel to the Rising Sun* and *Can You See Their Faces* [sic]. In a few minutes he was telling about what he saw and heard in Czechoslovakia, whence he had recently returned.

"But I'm saying all that in my new book," and smiling, stopped.

"Perhaps you might give us something—some odds and ends—that didn't get into the book, yet are significant. There must be some."

Silence. . . . "Oh, yes. Several things. . . ." Silence, while he ate, slowly. His features are rough-hewn rather than chiseled, square rather than rounded. Presently he was talking freely, even if lengthy pauses intervened.

"Well, I might tell you something about my new book. Perhaps it'll suggest some question you would like to ask me. . . . It's called *North of the Danube,* and will be brought out in February by Viking Press. It's a book of sketches about the peoples—get that carefully—the peoples—of Czechoslovakia. It's illustrated with photographs by Margaret Bourke-White."

"Must be somewhat like the book you did on the South—*You Have Seen Their Faces?*"

"Yes, it is.

"It's divided into four sections, each named after one of the four provinces—Bohemia, Moravia, Slovakia and Ruthenia. . . . Ruthenia has now been renamed Carpatho-Ukrania—and deals with the lives of the peoples of that country—our travels among the various nationalities. . . . How they lived, what their outlook was, how they worked. Before Hitler came to power. . . .

"Speaking of the way the Czechoslovakians acted before and after the invasion—these facts are interesting. There used to be a sort of book union or guild, something like the Book of the Month Club here in the United States. It was called, I believe, 'People's Culture.' It published mostly foreign titles—books from the Russian, the French, the German, English—including even *Tobacco Road.*"

"Why 'even *Tobacco Road*'?"

He made a vague, depreciating gesture.

"Well, when the fascists came in, this 'People's Culture,' which had existed solely to acquaint the masses with the literature of other countries, was destroyed. Dangerous organization."

"How about the Czech theatre?"

"Used to have what they called 'The Liberated Theatre,' devoted to satire—and mostly of an anti-fascist nature. Well, you can imagine what happened to that. The people had a high degree of political intelligence—exceedingly high."

"Were you able to observe the progressive effect of the fear of fascist invasion upon the people's minds? To notice, as the weeks and months passed, how this dread foreboding grew upon them?"

Caldwell drained his cup and pushed it and the plates away. He lighted a cigarette, smiling briefly. "I tell all that in my book. . . . But I can say this. There was a growing nervous tension. Of course the people felt that the Nazi attack was inevitable. . . . They never had any faith in the French ruling class—that is, most of the people felt sure that France wasn't going to help them. Everybody was surprisingly well informed of what was happening in Europe's chancellories. . . . And—"

"How about the Soviet Union? How did they seem to feel about her?"

"I was going to say that the Czech people were as confident of the good will and the friendship of the Soviet Union as they were of the French government's perfidy. Traveling as we did in and out of the country, we were in a most favorable position to judge the situation from all angles. . . ."

The Czech people—all the various nationalities that made up the nation—were like a great peaceful neighborhood. And the Germans were perhaps the best treated of them all—the obvious reason being that Hitler must be given no excuse to attack.

Strangers noticed growing tension among the people as anti-Czech propaganda increased. Refugees were being welcomed from Austria, Hungary and Germany. Karel Capek—Caldwell pronounced it 'Chapek'—made despairing radio appeals to his people to maintain courage, although who was more courageous? To refrain from any act which might serve as tender to the smoldering flame. But raw nerves had already been shredded and exposed through months of rigid self-discipline and unnatural restraint. The terrifying physical and mental strain undergone by the 48-year old progressive author of R.U.R. accelerated his death.

In Vienna, once, Erskine and his party visited a refugee camp, curious to see the kinds of persons driven out by fascist hatred. From Berlin there had come the "full-blooded 'Aryan' mother with her flaxen-haired child of six." Her crime? Her husband was fighting for democracy in Spain. There were Catholic priests, Socialists, Communists. . . . Germans, Austrians, Poles, Czech, Slovaks, Africans. . . .

"The point is that not only the Jews suffer when fascism comes. Those who do not swallow the fascist poison and die from that, die from fascist violence. Here's something that'll interest you. In the refugee camp in Vienna I saw two Negroes—Africans who had been driven out of Germany. One of them was from Senegal—a boxer. He had a beautiful wife and child. He wanted to come to the United States. He asked us about getting in touch with Joe Louis—thought he might come here and get a job among Louis's trainers."

Did Caldwell, perhaps, see a lesson for the people of the United States in what happened to peaceful, democratic little Czechoslovakia?

"Yes. Let our people beware of and fight against the infiltration of anti-democratic propaganda. If our people could see what is happening in the fascist countries they would not need to be told to prize and cherish their democracy. They would hold on with such desperateness to what they have that nothing short of total annihilation could shake them loose."

When Caldwell said that, he was in no sense the timid wood violet shrinking from passersby; he was a serious-minded lover of humanity. And he let it be understood, as we were about to part, that he intended more than ever to set an example for his fellow writers.

"We *must* use our talents to destroy the artificial barriers of race and national prejudices; we writers *must* bring the people together so they will *know* one another. Our people are essentially democratic. . . ."

A Talk with Erskine Caldwell

Robert van Gelder/1940

From *The New York Times Book Review,* 31 March 1940, pp.
18, 20. Reprinted in Robert van Gelder, *Writers and Writing* (New
York: Charles Scribner's Sons, 1946), pp. 34-37, Copyright © by
The New York Times Company. Reprinted by permission.

The story is that in the early days of the record-breaking run of
"Tobacco Road," Erskine Caldwell, from whose novel the play had
been taken, came down from Maine to have a look at the
performance. But every time he went into the theatre the laughter of
the audience drove him out. The laughter—golden to the
commercial-minded—sent him wandering the streets in rage.

Questioned about this, Mr. Caldwell said—not complacently, but
not sadly, either—that all this if it happened, happened a long time
ago. "Seven or eight years, wasn't it?" A play that runs that long can
wipe out a considerable amount of woe. It probably is true, said Mr.
Caldwell, that he found the laughter provoking. "I don't write things
that are supposed be funny. But if people want to laugh at what I
have to say, that is up to them. There's nothing I can do about it, and
nowadays I've found that out."

As for wandering the streets in a rage, there would have been
nothing new in that. "I was cooped up in this town when I wrote my
first novel. My room was in one of the houses torn down to make a
place for Radio City. When I lived there they were making sample
drillings and doing some preliminary work and I'd come out about
three o'clock in the morning, pick up a loose board that workmen
had left lying around, and go to Fifth Avenue, where I'd bang a
lamppost with the board. Other times I'd pick up loose bricks and
crack them together until they broke. That's one reason I live in the
country. I need exercise."

When he is working on a novel he spends much of his time
chopping wood and cutting down brush and digging ditches. He is
tall, unusually well built, with sizable, very capable-looking hands,
and he keeps his hands busy while he broods about his work. He

11

spends about a year thinking a novel before he does any writing at all. No notes; no outlines. He has made only one note in his life. That was for a name that he considered using, but eventually he threw the note away.

He writes "as it comes to me; I can't change it." When he wrote *God's Little Acre,* he ripped the pages from the typewriter and threw them on the floor; never looked at them again. Someone else gathered them up and sent them off to the publisher. His new book, *Trouble in July,* just published by Duell, Sloan & Pearce, was, in a sense, rewritten. That is, he typed a manuscript copy and made changes in phrasing. There were no structural shifts, however.

When he finishes something he likes to have one person agree that it is all right. When he gets an agreement the story or novel goes out for sale. His wife, Margaret Bourke-White, the photographer, does most of the first reading.

He has written 125 short stories, 100 of which have been published. Most of the stories and all the novels concern life in the South. He is not trying to do a "Southern panel" but he is trying to cover the various aspects of the Southern scene that seem most important to him. "But not a planned cycle—nothing like that."

His novels and stories crackle with violence. In one an old man falls into a pigpen and is eaten by the hogs; there are lynching scenes and scenes of torture; people are burned with turpentine and the tails of dogs are sliced off for sport; heads are crushed and bodies mutilated.

"Well," says Caldwell, "it is a violent country. I've seen a man beat a mule to death because the sun was hot and he was tired and tense, sick of the endless sameness of his life. I've been in a barnyard at the end of a day in the cotton fields when the boss came over to ask why a mule was lame. A Negro explained that the mule had stepped in a rabbit hole. The boss beat the Negro unconscious—knowing the Negro couldn't fight back. I've been an unwilling witness at a number of lynchings."

Caldwell first tried his hand at writing when he was eight years old; went to work in the fields when he was nine. The son of a country preacher, "and maybe you know how country preachers are paid," his view of the world always was "economic." He did not go to school until he was sixteen; then he had a year of high school and moved on into a prep school, where he paid his way by playing football. He played semi-pro football also, and football earned his way for a year at the University of Virginia.

The fact that his position was center and that he weighed only 98 pounds when he started playing football for a living is perhaps a pretty good scale to indicate the strength of his determination. Ninety-eight-pound centers have a rugged time on the football field. Caldwell still wears the marks of his career in sports.

Cutting loose from the university and from a newspaper job that he held for a time in Atlanta, he set out to live by writing.

He decided to settle in Maine, for a number of reasons. One was that there he could view the South from afar, an aid to perspective. Another, he thought the life there would be simple and cheap. Another, he anticipated that his neighbors would let him alone while he worked.

"I suppose it is all right to save up a thousand dollars and then go off somewhere to write a novel. That wasn't possible for me, and I'm not sure that I wasn't better off. I never let other people or extraneous things interfere with me at all. They could turn off the lights and cut off the water—it couldn't be helped. I wanted to work at writing and I did. I never have let any one influence me or turn me aside."

The best writing, he believes, is the work of people who are moved, driven by life—not the manipulators of life. Theodore Dreiser and William Faulkner "dig their stories out of life with both hands."

He feels sorry for the people who go to writing classes—sorry for them because he believes they are wasting their time. "The important thing is to live first, have something to write about. If you have enough to say, you'll say it all right."

Though in his own work he concentrates on the South, he roams the rest of the country and believes that there are great areas alive with material that have been too long neglected. Our literature is not yet all plaster and niches; all life today has a place in it, and if writers would realize that, our books and magazines would be far more exciting than they are.

As for his own reception in the South—"they still write editorials against me every now and then; but I think that what I'm doing is having its effect." He is not, he says, an evangelist or crusader; he doubts that much good can be accomplished by preaching.

"I try to hold up a mirror to nature in the South—and to my own nature, to human nature. I don't say that lynching is evil or that cruelty is bad. But by showing people as they are cruel, and by showing their victims, by showing people oppressed to hopelessness and impoverished to hopelessness—perhaps in that way I'll have some effect on many lives."

Who's Who in Darien:
Erskine Caldwell
The Darien Review/1940

From *The Darien* (Conn.) *Review*, 5 September 1940, pp. 1-2.

Ranking as one of the most important modern writers living in the East, Erskine Caldwell of Point O'Woods Road, Darien, is one of the most modest and unassuming men that one could wish to meet. Tall and vigorous, with a large, big-boned face, and sandy, close-cropped hair, he is quiet and soft spoken. His voice has a pleasant, natural Southern drawl—completely unlike that affected by the sweet young things who "you-all" their way East.

Mr. Caldwell, himself, is a contradiction. A serious student of Mr. Caldwell's work, who reads his sordid, macabre studies of the "poor whites" of the South, might expect to find him a somber, gloomy individual, but this definitely is not the case. His home is called "Horseplay Hill," which is a far cry from *Tobacco Road* and *God's Little Acre.* Neither is there anything of Jeeter Lester about Mr. Caldwell.

He talked to the writer of this article in the living room of his attractive home. The decorations of the room are modern, but simply done in excellent taste, and the room has an abundance of light. Mr. Caldwell was dressed in a blue slack suit and was very much at ease—much more so, in fact, than his interviewer. He slumped back in his chair, inhaled luxuriously on his cigarette and told the reporter to "shoot" his questions.

Mr. Caldwell answered everything he was asked readily enough, but he seemed to have a little trouble with his dates. He was born in the village of White Oak, Coweta County, Georgia, in 1903. "I've got to give you the name of the county," he said, "because there are two or three White Oaks in Georgia." He laughed at the suggestion that the village was as large as Darien. "It was so small it didn't even have a post office." Railroad men call places like White Oak whistle stops.

The author is the son of the Rev. and Mrs. Ira S. Caldwell who now

live in Wrens, Georgia, where Mrs. Caldwell teaches in the high
school. The Rev. Mr. Caldwell is now secretary of the Presbyterian
Church there, a position he has held for some years and which has
entailed a great deal of traveling.

Mr. Caldwell was scarcely the child of well-to-do parents. "When
my father was minister in White Oak he had a salary of about $300 a
year. That's not very much for a man with a family," he said.

Asked about his education and literary background, he said that
his education was "informal" and, although he has attended one
junior college and two colleges, he was not "encumbered" with a
college degree or diploma. As for his literary background, Mr.
Caldwell admitted that it was not thorough—that he was not steeped
in Shakespeare or "good" literature. In school and college he was
always interested in unrelated subjects like economics or sociology in
preference to courses in English and American literature.

Because of the peripatetic nature of the Rev. Mr. Caldwell's calling
as secretary of his church, after leaving White Oak, young Erskine's
education was obtained at scattered points in the South. He first
attended grammar school at Atoka, Tenn., and after that he went to
high school in Wrens. At 16 he entered Erskine Junior College in Due
West, S.C., and in between the ages of 18 and 22 attended the
University of Virginia at Charlottesville, Va., for two years and the
University of Pennsylvania, Philadelphia, for two years.

Between his educational spasms Mr. Caldwell did a large amount
of traveling on his own and probably knows his own country much
better than most people. "I held hundreds of jobs and I went all over
the country," he said. In his school vacations he roamed the country,
stopping here a month, there a week, talking to people and seeing
things that were strange to him. In 1920, when he was 17, he went to
Mexico. He traveled alone, going to Monterey, Chihuahua and any
point of interest that struck his fancy. Here and there he picked up
companions and for a while moved about with them. In 1922 he
took a ship to British Honduras and roamed that country pretty
thoroughly. Mr. Caldwell has done a lot of roaming and says today
that he would rather travel than do anything else.

"I'd just get the urge to go and I went. I guess I was restless. No, I
didn't do it with the idea of getting source material for my books. I
was just curious. I'd get the urge to go out and see them take in the
wheat crop in Montana and I'd go. I wasn't idle during all this

wandering. I always had a job of some sort as I bummed my way out to somewhere. I worked as a roustabout in a circus, I washed dishes, I dug ditches. I went to the Texas Panhandle; I went to Seattle—wherever there were things I wanted to see. That was it."

Timidly the *Review* reporter asked what his family thought of all this, in view of the fact that his father was a minister, that he was so young and irresponsible etc., etc. Mr. Caldwell smiled broadly and said: "They let me do as I wanted. I figure they thought that I knew what I was doing." It was a good answer.

He continued his roamings about the broad United States for some years, at first splicing his ventures between terms at the University of Virginia and the University of California. For a while he worked for a Tennesee construction company and then went back to his education, giving no thought to literature. Mr. Caldwell began to write at a fairly early age, but thought there was nothing unusual about that. "I just wrote because I felt like it," he said, "just as some men carpenter or whittle, or paint pictures. Most of the stuff I threw away."

In his meanderings Mr. Caldwell spent some time in Eastern Pennsylvania and, while in Wilkes-Barre, he played professional football with the Anthracite League. At the time he was a stock clerk in a Kresge store there and a football "toughie" between hours. He played center, and today he looks as though he could still get in there and give the boys a run for their money. "We didn't get paid as they do today," he admitted ruefully, "but it was good experience."

Besides being a truck driver, among 100 odd other things, Mr. Caldwell has also been a newspaperman. He worked for two years (1926-1928) as a reporter for the *Atlanta Journal*. He was leg man, office boy and general factotum. He adds, too, that this was the job he held the longest.

He first began the serious writing of short stories about 1924 and it took him five years to crash the literary markets. Admitting that it was a long and discouraging process, he said that he stuck at it anyway. "I used to write whenever I had any free time between jobs as I went about the country. I collected a trunkful of rejection slips, but I guess I lost them somewhere. I wanted to save them."

His first published stories appeared in 1929 in *Scribner's Magazine*. They were called "A Very Late Spring" and "The Mating of Marjorie." After his initial success with the short story, he turned to the novel, and in 1931 turned out *Tobacco Road*. After the furore raised by its publication it sold well and he was made. It was also made into a long-run and lucrative play. Having made his reputation as a writer, it was only natural that he should go to Hollywood. He went the following year. Since that time he has been there twice at three-year intervals and each time stayed over six months.

The first picture he ever worked on was *The Wicked Woman,* in 1932. This picture introduced the lovely German star Mady Christians, and was a terrible flop. (Miss Christians has since succeeded on the Broadway stage and during the last two seasons has played the role of Hamlet's mother in *Hamlet* with Maurice Evans.) In his other visits Mr. Caldwell has worked on the M-G-M "Crime Does Not Pay" series and other pictures.

Asked pointblank what he thought about Hollywood and if all the things that were said about it were true, Mr. Caldwell was not too morbidly biting in his answer. "Most of the things they say about it are true, but it could be a lot worse," he said. "It's like a tremendous factory where things have a natural tendency to get confused now and then. They hire you as a writer. You work for months on a story and they never use it. It just drops out of sight and no one talks about it. Of course, you get paid."

At this point Mrs. Caldwell (Miss Margaret Bourke-White), one of America's finest photographers and current head of the photographic department of the new newspaper *PM,* entered the room. She had just returned from New York, to which she commutes daily. Gay and humorous, the lovely Mrs. Caldwell was a great help to *The Review* reporter in interpreting and enlarging the cryptic replies of her husband. She sat on a stool near his feet and watched him closely as he talked about himself.

The author stated that his love of wandering remained with him and that he and Mrs. Caldwell had just returned from Mexico where they witnessed the bloody election period, during which many people were killed. He explained that he had much fondness for New England and had written about it—he did not write exclusively about the South. He had a house in Mount Vernon, near Augusta, Me., where he lived for five years from 1932 to 1937 between visits to Hollywood. A very adaptable man, Mr. Caldwell says, "I like it in New England; I like it in the West; I like it in my own South." He is cosmopolitan in attitude, but in an unworldly way, differing very much from the tired manner of Somerset Maugham. Mr. Caldwell has not been everywhere and he has not seen everything. Still a very young author, he has kept his restless eagerness.

Returning from a Hollywood trek late in 1936, Mr. Caldwell made a deep swing through his own Southland, accompanied by Miss Bourke-White. The result of their trip, which lasted well into 1937, was the deeply-moving and incisive book, *You Have Seen Their Faces*—text by Erskine Caldwell, photographs by Miss Bourke-White. The book told in pictures and in simple, unemotional words the story of many "Tobacco Roads." It was a documentary study of misery, poverty and bad living conditions.

In 1938 the harmonious collaboration was repeated with the book, *North of the Danube,* which was written following a trip to Europe in the spring of that year. The book was a prelude to the abortive Munich peace. It showed the life of the peasants in the regions north of the Danube. A simple study of their habits, work and life, it showed how these contrasted with the selfish grabbing hatreds of the Munich overlords.

Mr. Caldwell took his house in Point O'Woods in November of 1938. Mrs. Caldwell said that one of the main factors of choice was the presence of a big rock near the house which immediately appealed to Mr. Caldwell as an ideal place on which to write.

It was left to Mrs. Caldwell to tell about the marriage of the author and the photographer. They were flying to the West Coast in a private plane and decided to get married on the way out. Miss White picked the site of the ceremony because of its pretty name. They borrowed the pilot's map and when her finger fell on Silver City, Nev., she knew it was "their" town. But Silver City was such a small town that it didn't have a minister of its own, and they stopped in Carson City, Nev., and picked one up and flew on to the bridal hamlet. "It was very romantic," said Miss Bourke-White: "we were married in an old, deserted church that hadn't been used in two years. We had to get somebody to open it. For our honeymoon we chose Hawaii."

The next question was inevitable: How did they like Darien? Both were quick in saying that they liked it very much. They like their house. Mr. Caldwell likes to chop down bushes around "Horseplay Hill," and invariably when Mrs. Caldwell came home from "a hard day at the office," she discovered that her husband had attacked the very bushes she wanted kept. The town of Darien appealed to both of them because it was small—and, well, there was "just something about it."

It was equally inevitable that some reference to *Tobacco Road* should be made. The play, dramatized from the novel by Jack Kirkland, has been running for more than five years. Mr. Caldwell believes the success of the play is deserved. Asked whether the picture of filth, squalor and human horror and degradation it gives should be taken as tragedy or comedy, the author said that it was up to the theatre-goer to decide. They could take it as they wished. If they wanted to cry, all right; if they wanted to laugh, all right. Mr. Caldwell didn't care so long as they did see it.

Mrs. Caldwell laughed at the question. "When Erskine didn't know me very well," she said, "he took me to see *Tobacco Road,* and I didn't know just how to take it. I was in a quandary and I kept looking at him. I was afraid he'd be hurt if I laughed."

The author has seen all the actors who have taken the role of Jeeter Lester, but has no real preference between Henry Hull, James Barton, Will Geer and all the others who have played it. He admits, however, that Hull, who first had the part, set the pace for the others.

Most of Mr. Caldwell's novel[s] depict conditions in the South and are to many people sordid. *God's Little Acre, Journeyman* and his recent *Trouble in July* all deal with people and events that many readers find shocking. A realistic novelist, who is unsparing in incisive dialogue and detail, he is not for thin-skinned people. With this in mind the author was asked what he had to say about persons who found his work shocking and revolting beyond measure and not fit for decent people to read. Mr. Caldwell said that he didn't care what people thought. He wrote what he wrote and if people didn't like it that was all right, too.

Mr. Caldwell has never seen an actual lynching, but he has been there right after one in time to "still see the body hanging from a limb." Mr. Caldwell does write from actual experience—that is, he knows what he is talking about. In telling all the horrible things about the South that he has, Mr. Caldwell has not been writing exposes.

"I represent the people," he explained. "I'm just like a Congressman asking for a WPA appropriation. I am citing facts, telling what there is, what exists, what these people are facing. The South is as good as any other part of the country and the people I write about are just as good as anybody in the South, or the North, for that matter."

Mr. Caldwell stated that he favored the anti-lynching bill that has been discussed in the Senate so many times, and that has never been passed. He said that it hinged on the old theory of States' rights and that was the sticker that made the bill so hard for the South to swallow. The author loves his home country and thoroughly understands it and the people who live there. He was quick to defend charges that his books smeared the region.

His latest book came out at the end of last week. It is called *Jackpot* and is a collection of all his short stories over a period of years, plus eight or ten new ones. "And it's a beauty, too," said Mrs. Caldwell looking at her husband with obvious pride. The book is published by Duell, Sloane & Pierce [sic].

Mr. Caldwell's books have been translated into the Japanese, Norwegian, Danish, Swedish, German, French, Italian and Russian. Copies of these translations adorn the walls of his library and it goes without saying that he is a widely and internationally read author. *Tobacco Road* has been produced in London and Oslo, and road companies are continually touring the South. The play is not unpopular in that section, as one might think. Mr. Caldwell said it had done very well there.

Since *Tobacco Road,* in 1931, he has published 15 books, two of them having been collaborations with his wife. His favorites among his own work are "My Old Man," a short story, and *God's Little Acre,* among his novels. As for having a favorite author, no. He likes something in each work of the modern novelists, but he has no definite favorite. He likes Hemingway, Steinbeck, Faulkner and many others, but he will not be pinned down to a definite favorite. Among his sports and hobbies are swimming (the Caldwells have their own pool), watching football games and attending the theatre. His favorite sport, as stated before, is traveling.

Like every author and celebrity, he gets his share of crank and fan letters, but assuredly he has a novel way of dealing with them. He throws away the fan letters and saves the mean ones. These he calls "pan" letters and frames the most malicious that come in the mail.

Mr. Caldwell was modest when he described his writing habits. "I'm really a very lazy man. I don't do much writing. In the old days I used to write all the time and stay up all night, but I don't do that any more."

Mrs. Caldwell sniffed at this lacksadaisical account. "He writes continuously when he gets absorbed," she said. "Sometimes I come home to find him all hunched up over a typewriter. He doesn't even hear me. Long periods go by when he doesn't write, but then suddenly he gets to work. Something ferments inside and gets ready to come out."

Mr. Caldwell smiled and let his wife do the talking. "He likes to sit on the big rock and write. Our cat sits on his papers to keep them from blowing away. He never reads or writes over anything he has written. 'Written is written' for him. It stays on paper just as it came out of his mind."

A little grey kitten about five weeks old, which ranged the room during the interview, rubbed against Mr. Caldwell's leg and mewed. "That's not the one who sits on my papers," he said. "This is a new addition to our family."

The interview was at a close, and *The Review* reporter left with the conviction that Mr. and Mrs. Erskine Caldwell were two of the nicest people one could possibly meet and that Darien was lucky to have them in residence on "Horseplay Hill."

Erskine Caldwell's Lesson From Russia: America May Lose War

PM's Weekly/1942

From *PM's Weekly,* 22 February 1942, pp. 6-7.

"Would you rather have a temporary dictator," demanded Erskine Caldwell, "or be completely subject to Hitler?"

It was [not] a rhetorical question. For Caldwell was in Russia on June 22, the day Hitler's legions crashed into the Soviet lines, and he was in America on Dec. 7. So he knows what happens when a blitz strikes. He knows, too, what kind of effort is needed to stop one and that America is a long way from making that effort.

A great deal of Mr. Caldwell's eloquence on how to stop a blitz is contained in *All-Out on the Road to Smolensk,* his latest book, which came out Wednesday. The book is an account of what he saw of the Nazi-Soviet war from June to October.

It's the other part of the story, the part about the lessons we should have learned from Russia, and haven't, that Caldwell is concerned about right now.

"You can't make it too strong how I feel about the lackadaisical Americans," he says. "And it's the duty of the government to wake them up if they won't wake up themselves. The means can't be too harsh. If the President isn't strong enough, we ought to have a dictator to do it. We won't have a democracy in the end, anyway, if we don't wake up."

In Russia, when the invasion began, Mr. Caldwell found, it took just 24 hours for the people to recover from their shock and to start pulling together; to start carrying into resolute action their resolve that Hitlerism must perish; to start training civilians in air raid precautions and fire-fighting; to start getting a second army into training in the Urals; to start plans for moving factories out of the war zone. The result was that the Russians were able to take most of the edge off the Germans' initial superiority, and were able to make a quick comeback.

"But here," says Caldwell, "We have a war on and we go along the street and you'd think it was July, 1925. I wouldn't be surprised if the United Nation group got beaten before the end of the year. We don't realize how fast this sort of thing moves. A rolling army like Hitler's can swallow nations in a few hours. We think of 1943-44. They think of 3 p.m. to 5 a.m.

"Love of our country is universal. Under our veneer we feel it as strongly as the Russians do, but we aren't conscious of it. We've lived on the fat of the land so long we can't feel through that protective layer.

"The time is almost over when we will be able to do anything. A few of us take first-aid classes. Quite a few of us have been called into the Army. But the rest of the people don't know it. They don't know it's war time and that the greatest army in the world can invade this country, without a doubt.

"You may be sure that Hitler isn't sitting down and waiting for us to get armed. The Japanese attack proved that. They jumped in when they knew we weren't ready and Hitler isn't going to wait until 1944, as Congress says, when we'll be fully armed. Germany is much stronger than she was, and is going to get stronger all the time. They didn't lose anything in Russia. The Germans don't retreat; they draw back. If they don't start a spring offensive in Russia, they will start one somewhere else.

Caldwell is angry because he can still go around in civilian clothes.

"I think guys like me should be called up right now," he says, "should have been called up two months ago. If we had a lot of strong guys like MacArthur around the country now to take over the situation and put us in a state of siege—to haul guys like me out of civilian clothes and put us on a drill field—we'd have something. We would be able to meet Hitler and the Japs on equal terms when they try to come up through Mexico and down through Canada."

We need an army of 10,000,000 men, like the Russians have, and need it quick, Caldwell says. We need an immediate halt on non-essential production—we won't ever have any of the things we want if we lose the war.

"Sure, I think we can learn a lot from the Russians," Caldwell concludes emphatically. "And I'm not advocating Communism. I'm just being realistic. What their political system is doesn't really matter.

They have demonstrated and proved something, while we sit back on the fact we're a democracy and must do things such and such a way. Would you rather," he repeats, "have a temporary dictator or be completely subject to Hitler?"

New England Literary Tour:
Erskine Caldwell's Connecticut Home
Is A Place of Beauty and Charm

Alice Dixon Bond/1942

From *The Boston Herald,* 13 July 1942, p. 5.

"God's Little Acre" can now be found in Darien, Connecticut. Great trees surround it and lovely gardens; a swimming pool reflects the tranquil sky and a low white house faces the curving road. To the right of it, a field of gay tiger lilies, placed with studied abandon, lends color to the grey rocks which flank the path. It is a place of beauty and of complete peace; a place of recreation and gracious charm.

Two of the world's famous people live here: Erskine Caldwell, writer, and his wife, Margaret Bourke-White, great artist of the camera.

The place reflects them both. Mr. Caldwell is a lover of the sun. He lives out of doors whenever possible, taking his typewriter to the top of one of the many grassy slopes, proping it against a rock and then doing his writing. Everywhere there are trees and lovely vistas.

Margaret Bourke-White planned the grounds as well as the house, and both have that natural beauty which is the result of careful thought and a gay and discriminating imagination.

We entered the house from the side, through Mr. Caldwell's study, a practical room, simple in line and color. It opens into a long hall leading to kitchen, dining room and porch. Beyond is the living room, which is one of the most striking and unforgettable rooms I have ever seen. The walls are lined with murals taken by Miss Bourke-White of the Bohemian forest in Czechoslovakia.

As one would expect with people who have looked upon the world as their front yard, the house is filled with treasures gathered from far places. Icons from Russia and Ural Mountain wooden bears; a magnificent copper tray from Syria and some beautiful horses from Czechoslovakia are but a few, while star fish from Wake Island and

Japanese fishing-ball floats add a touch of reality to the aquarium beside the front door.

At luncheon, we ate off plates designed by Rockwell Kent and drank from wooden glasses made from redwoods of California. The ashtrays were tiny fish with yellow faces, pink bodies, pink tails and purple fins, while the place mats were of exquisite Syrian embroidery.

From where I sat I could see the most unusual object in the front hall. It looked like a plant, yet resembled nothing that ever grew on land or sea. They let me guess for a while, and then disclosed the secret. Seems that when Margaret Bourke-White took some of her magnificent pictures for the telephone company they gave her a short piece of steel cable, opened at one end, the separated wires springing in shaggy profusion like the fluffy head of a giant flower, complete with stem. They call it their cable plant, and so it is.

In Russia, Mr. Caldwell said, a banquet usually lasted about five hours, invariably beginning with vodka followed by many wines, including champagne. One of the most delicious dishes he has ever tasted is chicken a la Kiev, which consists of white meat of chicken "all in one piece, folded over with butter on the inside and then fried." The butter permeates the whole, and the result is ambrosia.

He and his wife were in Russia most of last year, each one getting material for a new book and studying the country and the people with unabating zeal. He wrote *All-Out on the Road to Smolensk* three different times: first in Russia, where he forgot to get the censor's seal and so had to leave it; then in England, which he left so unexpectedly that there was no time to get the censor's approval, and finally in America, where he wrote the book as we know it.

He was a little bit tired of the whole thing by that time, even though the form and content had changed a good deal in the numerous writings. In England, the volume even took the form of a diary and was called *Moscow Under Fire*.

Erskine Caldwell is a meticulous and exacting worker. He could keep a story for 10 years and work on it every week and still not be satisfied.

Son of a Presbyterian minister, he was born in Georgia and after a more or less desultory formal education got himself a job on the *Atlanta Journal*. He wanted to write intensely, however, and nothing he did pleased him.

Finally, he decided he had better "just chuck everything" and go away and write. He went to Maine and cut wood and raised potatoes so that he could live and wrote and wrote and wrote.

His first published story appeared in *The New Caravan* in 1929. After the publication of *God's Little Acre* in 1933, he wrote: ". . . . I am ashamed of *Tobacco Road* now, and if I'm not ashamed of *God's Little Acre* inside of the next six months, I'll never be able to write another book."

Apparently he was, for fortunately, the books are still coming.

His new novel, to be called *All Night Long,* will be published by Duell, Sloan and Pearce next October and will have Russia as background.

Tobacco Road played in New York seven and a half years, and a road company has pleased the public for nine months of each of ten years. There were several years even when two or three companies were touring the land. Believe it or not, the reprint of the book has sold over a million copies.

From Maine, Erskine Caldwell went to Hollywood to do script writing. Then came travel, more Hollywood, and then the remarkable books which he and his wife did together, she supplying the pictures and he the text. They are interpretations as well as recordings: *You Have Seen Their Faces, North of the Danube,* and *Say, Is This the U.S.A.?*

We were sitting on the screened-in porch while he talked of his recent Russian experiences. Seven kittens of assorted shapes and sizes kept tumbling over each other and us as he spoke of the tremendous impression which the Philippines had made on him. He spoke also of the avid interest which the young people, not only the writers, showed in all that was going on in outside countries. They were all essentially alive and eager for all that life could give them.

Persistence, steady and unabating, as well as a good deal of luck finally got them to Russia. They found Chungking a Spartan city, and were glad to leave it, although they had to come back to it again against their will.

While they were flying over the Gobi desert, a terrific sandstorm blotted out the world below them and the sun overhead, wrapping them in complete darkness. The pilot suddenly put the ship into what seemed like a nose dive and the floor of the Gobi desert rushed up to meet them. In what seemed like a second, they found themselves bumping over the rough ground. Unfortunately, they had landed near a military air field, and almost immediately they were surrounded by soldiers while two six-footers guarded the plane's door with fixed bayonets.

They were in a German-made plane, without any identifying symbols. So the soldiers were taking no chances. They were locked in for six hours with no ventilation whatsoever, and with the temperature hovering between 95 and 100 degrees. Lunchtime came and went. They had a few hard crackers and a small water jug, which helped a little.

At last an officer appeared, and they were herded into trucks, lined up outside and guarded by soldiers, still with fixed bayonets. After a 10-mile drive they came to a desert castle with a high wall around it. Inside, soldiers and their families lived together in perfect accord, surrounded by numerous cows and chickens. Here they spent the night and the next morning were on their way again.

Traveling was precarious, to say the least. A month before they had arrived in China, an American plane had been shot down by the Japs, had landed in a river, and as the passengers were swimming toward the shore, they had been machinegunned, and the girl hostess and one pilot had been killed.

A Russian airplane hostess never does much hustling, apparently. The Caldwells found theirs sitting peacefully in the rear of the plane selling the things the passengers wanted.

"In Russia," he went on, "nothing is free. If you go to the station to tell someone good-bye, you have to pay to get in. There is an entry charge for the free parks.

"It is a strange country, yet I was genuinely interested, in spite of passing irritations. For instance, there is a definite and unswerving rule that no one can wear an overcoat in a public building. You have to check it, and you have to pay for the checking.

"In a theater, the coat room is the largest room in the building. It looks like a clothing store. Once I had a very severe cold and refused to take off my coat when we entered the theater. They sent for the manager. We talked. I insisted, he commanded, but I finally won my point. I think that I am probably the only person in the new Russia who ever sat through a performance with his overcoat on."

The feeling that the Russians have for the Germans is far deeper than hatred, he thinks.

"Hatred," he said, "is brought up by a contemporary event. Their feeling has a longer range. The Russians' greatest national hero is Alexander Nevsky who, 150 years ago, drove the Germans out of the Ukraine. A film [was] made of this great event and launched with much pomp and ceremony.

"When the Germans became their allies, they insisted on the withdrawal of the film."

Eisenstein, the great Russian producer, gave the Caldwells a private showing of it. "When you see this in the theaters," he said, "you will know that the pact no longer exists."

Of course it is shown everywhere now.

"Ever since Nevsky's time," Mr. Caldwell continued, "the Russians have hated the Germans, hated them implacably and with bitterness. Twenty-three years ago, the Germans occupied the Ukraine for the second time."

"We were there a year ago, just a month before war started," Mr. Caldwell said. "We were visiting collective farm 106. It was a great place of 100,000 acres. The chairman of the farm took us to dinner, and over the caviar and roast duck (yes, that's what we had), I asked why they called the place 106.

"His reply was indicative of a universal feeling. 'Because we do not want to forget. When the Germans came, 106 of our people were killed defending our farm. We will remember that!'

"Now, for the third time, the Germans are advancing, and those same Russian men and women have vowed to fight as long as life lasts. We Americans are apt to lose sight of the long generative part of the Russian character.

"There is no parallel between Hitler and Napoleon. The Russians hated the Germans long before Napoleon. They never hated his army as they do the Germans. The Russo-German pact was a shrewd move in order to give themselves an ample preparatory period. The day after the Munich pact, Russia began preparing, although the world did not know it. By the time the war started, they knew how to decontaminate both water and air from gas."

Mr. Caldwell knew that the war was coming as soon as he reached Russia. The arrogance of the Germans was simply terrible. They would buy up all the theatre seats allotted to the hotel so they would not have to suffer any British or Americans beside them!

The whole story of what he said and did and thought; what he observed and came to know is in his excellent volume, *All-Out on the Road to Smolensk.*

It is a full, uncensored and extraordinary story by a man who is completely fearless. Perhaps that word characterizes him as well as any. Tall, good-looking, deceptively quiet, he is an intensely alive individual, who grasps life firmly and who has the power to translate it for the rest of us.

Caldwell Returns to Hollywood
Ezra Goodman/1942

From *The New York Herald Tribune*, 13 September 1942, VI, p. 3.

HOLLYWOOD.—Erskine Caldwell, Hollywood's foremost authority on the Soviet Union, is as indigenously American as his novel *Tobacco Road*. He is a tall, bronzed Southerner with a shock of corn-yellow hair and a slow drawl. Caldwell now is engaged in extracting a screen play for Warner Brothers from former Ambassador Joseph E. Davies's *Mission to Moscow,* while Metro-Goldwyn-Meyer has purchased the film rights to his forthcoming novel about Russian guerrilla warfare, *Vengeance of the Earth [All Night Long]*. Hollywood discovered Russia and Caldwell almost simultaneously, and everybody concerned seems happy about it.

Since Caldwell's arrival in the cinema city in mid-July he has been examining the private papers and diaries of Davies and going through other source material preparatory to beginning work on the screen play.

"The screen play will stick to the spirit and letter of the book," he said. "The problem is only one of organization and selection. *Mission to Moscow* covers a lot of ground and there is a wealth of material in it. As the adaptor, I am confronted with an embarrassment of riches. I will say, though, that the picturization will follow the diary closely. It will be the honest, plain-talking account of an American Ambassador in Soviet Russia. Names will be named and facts and figures respected.

"More than thirty Russian personalities, ranging from Molotov and Litvinov and Timoshenko, will figure in the film. There will be references to leading events of recent Russian history, such as the famous trials and other high points of Soviet internal affairs, as they relate to world affairs. This is not going to be a soft-soaping job, but a fair and square depiction of our great ally. The purpose of this picture, as of the book, is to promote mutual understanding and confidence between our two nations and so aid the Allied cause."

Would the picture contain any of that staple Hollywood ingredient, romance?

Caldwell smiled. "You can't eliminate romance," he said. "It is a part of life, isn't it? And this picture will be a realistic one."

Caldwell has been in the film capital before, working at various studios. He wrote several "Crime Doesn't Pay" short subjects. "I've had my break-in here," he said, "and now that I've got that over with I can settle down to work."

His first and only trip to Russia was made last year with his photographer-wife, Margaret Bourke-White. They were there for seven months. The initial Caldwell book inspired by Russia's great battle was *Moscow Under Fire*. This was followed by *All-Out on the Road to Smolensk*. His fictional *Vengeance of the Earth [All Night Long]* will be published early in October.

Caldwell reports that almost the entire Russian film industry now is devoted to propaganda films and war documentaries, but that several fiction films like Sergei Eisenstein's new production on the life of Peter the Great are being shown. "The Russians," he said, "have a strong dramatic impulse. Their theater, opera and ballet are all very good. And their films are powerful and realistic productions, rooted in an earthy tradition.

"The screen is the greatest medium for the promotion of international understanding and amity. One picture is worth a thousand words, and the screen speaks primarily through images. A motion picture transcends the barriers of language and culture that divide the nations. The exchange of films among the Allies is an invaluable instrument of propaganda."

America's Most Censored Author—
An Interview with Erskine Caldwell
Publishers' Weekly/1949

From *Publishers' Weekly* (14 May 1949), pp. 1960-61. Reprinted
by permission of R. R. Bowker Company.

Georgia-born Erskine Caldwell has, in the years since the
publication of *Tobacco Road* in 1932, achieved an international reputation for his realistic portrayal of life in the
American South. His active life has included periods as a
cotton picker, stage hand, professional football player,
book reviewer, screen writer, and war correspondent. He
is now touring Europe.

"After 16 years of being mildly harassed by censors, I am sometimes
sorry that I ever wrote or heard of *God's Little Acre*," Erskine Caldwell
said in an interview with *PW* on the question of an author's approach
to the problem of censorship, "but if people can still get excited about
it after 16 years, I am encouraged to think it must take a pretty good
novel to create so much interest."

Mr. Caldwell, who was on the point of leaving for a two months'
tour of Europe, feels deeply disturbed about the nature and extent in
America of the censorship of books for alleged violations of public
decency. "I don't feel personally bitter about it," he said, "nor do I
feel any animosity toward the judge who must do his job. But
censorship, in cases where obscenity or salaciousness is not clearly
defined or evident, is now a basic threat to the freedom of the press,
and to writing and reading in general. Sooner or later it can touch
everyone."

Mr. Caldwell believes that every writer of any consequence bears
constantly in mind the importance of restraint and decorum. He
wants to do a good job, and, moreover, be universally acceptable. "If
he lends himself to material obviously tainted in any way with

obscenity or sacrilege," Mr. Caldwell said, "he is the exception." All writing is penalized, he believes, when these exceptional authors cause isolated incidents of suppression. "When the author reads about these cases, his work is bound to be affected. He may crawl into a hole, cutting himself down to mouse size, and try to anticipate the various objections which may arise in different parts of the country. Finding a solution to this problem," he continued, "is of extreme importance to the writer. It is perhaps the most harassing phase of American life; he comes to feel that he must limit his interest and the scope of his ability.

"A really objectionable book," Mr. Caldwell declared, emphatically, "rarely survives. It feeds on itself—just as magazines which appeal to offensive sensationalism rarely last—and is inevitably consumed by its own salaciousness. Competition among books is so keen that a book has to be universally acceptable in order to endure."

As to the underlying causes for the efforts to suppress certain books, now occurring with increasing frequency, and as an explanation of why Philadelphia may attempt to ban a book cleared in Boston, Mr. Caldwell feels that one reason is the geographical magnitude of America. "Regionalism prevents America from having common standards of taste and interpretation. What may be acceptable speech or behavior in one area may not necessarily be accepted in another. We maintain great regional pockets, and a writer is bound to offend the sensibilities of people somewhere. For example, none of my books has ever been publicly charged in the South, although there are many instances in the South and elsewhere of unofficial banning by librarians. Perhaps, all in all, they understand me better in the South. *Tobacco Road*, as a play, was subjected to it in Atlanta, as well as in New York, Oklahoma, and in other places, but that involves visual presentation, which must be analyzed in a different way."

Mr. Caldwell feels greatly concerned about the effect of book trials on the bookseller and publisher, as well as upon the writer. When a book is impounded by local authorities, Mr. Caldwell feels it becomes a public responsibility. "The bookseller should certainly not be held responsible; bookselling is a public service, not primarily a money-making enterprise with profit the sole motive."

The present method of handling censorship cases which arise in

various cities throughout the country is also harmful to the public, Mr.
Caldwell believes, because it creates sensationalism completely out of
proportion to the facts involved. "The sensational aspects are
overplayed in a public trial, and people are unusually attracted by
them. Some other method must be worked out."

Mr. Caldwell is keenly aware of the difficulties in evolving a new
formula. He feels that some of the individual public officials who take
it upon themselves to act on the basis of a complaint, which anyone
can make, may do so intelligently and thoughtfully. But to insure that
there is no misuse of the courts, he suggests that a representative
group of the city's lawyers, doctors, educators, and churchmen act as
a panel to consider the book before it is actually brought into court.
He recognizes the fact that in some communities such a group, if it set
itself up as a self-appointed "morals committee," might well
constitute more of a threat to free expression than the system they
replace, but he believes that as a cross-section of prevailing standards,
it would be inherently less arbitrary.

Of primary and immediate importance, however, is, he believes,
coordinated action on a national scale. There should be a national
conference of all groups concerned with the threat of censorship to
investigate the cause of it, consider ways and means to check the
abuses of free expression not already adequately controlled, and
develop a theory which would lead to a solution on the existing
problem. The issue must be faced cooperatively, Mr. Caldwell
believes, because "the United States is in the unique position of
having a great, world responsibility for the freedom of writing and
reading."

Erskine Caldwell is the author of more than two dozen books. His
publisher, Duell, Sloan & Pearce, estimates that approximately
20,000,000 copies of his books, in all editions, have been distributed
in the United States alone. He has been subjected to more
censorship than any other author in America. His publisher's share in
defending, with other publishers, the two most recent actions in
Philadelphia and Boston, has amounted to several thousands of
dollars—"an out-of-pocket expense a publisher now can ill afford,"
said Cap Pearce, "except in that a suit successfuly defended
advances the cause of free expression."

Conscientiously gauging the effect upon his work of more than ten
attempted bans in the past sixteen years, Mr. Caldwell said that it

had, of course, been harmful, but, in a way, challenging, since "you renew your confidence in your own philosophy and principles of writing. I have," he concluded, "been called indecent, communistic, reactionary, and sacrilegious—but I have never been called a plagiarist. And if the time ever comes when I am called that—without a smile—I'll really get angry."

Erskine Caldwell at Work
Carvel Collins/1958

From *The Atlantic Monthly,* 202 (July 1958), pp. 21-27. Copy-right © 1958 by the Atlantic Monthly Company. Reprinted by permission.

Erskine Caldwell had consented to be interviewed at his home on Twin Peaks in San Francisco immediately follow-ing last Christmas, when the film made from his phe-nomenally popular *God's Little Acre* was in the final stages of cutting and preparation for release in the spring. *God's Little Acre* has sold over eight million copies—more than any other novel written in our century. Other Caldwell novels—*Tobacco Road, Journeyman, Tragic Ground,* and *A House in the Uplands*—have sold between three and five million copies apiece in their American editions alone; and more than forty million copies of his books have been sold altogether.

A tall, ruggedly built man of quiet amiability and con-trolled force, Mr. Caldwell greeted me in a room where broad windows opened on a staggering view. Below was the city; to the left, the Golden Gate and the Pacific; to the right, the Bay with its bridges. Mr. Caldwell pointed out several institutions, such as the University of California on the Berkeley slopes, Alcatraz, and—far below—that fa-mous observation post, the Top of the Mark. It was easy to understand why he kept the blinds closed on similar win-dows in his adjoining workroom.

A prolific writer, Erskine Caldwell has published more than twenty-six volumes, his most recent novel being *Certain Women,* issued last fall. A new novel, *Claudelle Inglish,* will appear next January. To keep up this steady production of a volume almost every year, the author works for months at a time on a nine-to-five schedule, six days a week. But having broken off gun-fire typing in his workroom to join Mrs. Caldwell and their visitor, he was cordial and unhurried and showed no irritation at the interruption of his writing.

38

Question: Have you any opinion why *God's Little Acre* has sold more copies than any of your other novels?

Answer: Well, for one thing, I think maybe it's not a pessimistic story, you might say, as *Tobacco Road* is. *God's Little Acre* has more humor to it, more lightness. Maybe it's not as depressing as *Tobacco Road*. And maybe it's a better book. I don't know.

Q: Are you able to have considerable control over the conversion of *God's Little Acre* into the film?

A: The script is by Philip Yordan, but he has talked with me about it and I have made suggestions. I've waited now about twenty-five years to find the right combination of circumstances, because I never wanted to sell *God's Little Acre* to a studio. Once you sell a book to a studio it is completely out of your hands. In the present arrangement I have one-fourth voice because I am one of the partners.

Q: From what you have seen of the film do you think it is closely related to your novel?

A: I think it will show the essence and the atmosphere of the novel. Naturally when you film any book you have to condense it. But the movie is based on the novel's central theme, which is the attempt by the leading character, Ty Ty Walden, to hold his family together under all circumstances, even though he himself is not setting a good example by digging for gold instead of farming the land. He is attempting to arrange what a family is supposed to do, I think, which is to stay together.

Q: Were there any special problems in making the film?

A: Well, we had a little trouble when we tried to shoot it in Georgia. Some people there became unhappy about it and instigated the idea that the book should not be filmed in Georgia because they were afraid some scenes might not show the cotton mills in a favorable light as to labor relations. So we abandoned the location in Georgia and shot the picture on location here in California.

Q: When *Tobacco Road* was made into a play did you have any control over it?

A: Until now I haven't had anything to do with dramatizations.

Q: Do any subjects appear often in your mail or interviews which suggest misunderstandings about your writing that you would like to discuss?

A: I don't have any complaints to make about anything. But a lot of people seem to be looking for something that I don't know is there. My principal concept of writing is to be a storyteller and nothing else. And once in a while I get the feeling that people think I'm trying to reform something or trying to change something. All I'm trying to do is make the story interesting to myself. People do write letters asking, "What does that mean?" Well, it doesn't mean a thing. There is no meaning to it. The only meaning you can get out of it is what you find yourself. And if it's bad, why then you can deplore it. And if you don't like it you can go out and do something about it. But I'm not going to do anything about it.

Q: On the other hand, you were speaking about Ty Ty Walden and said that *God's Little Acre* shows a man trying to do what you personally think the head of a family ought to do, hold it together. So though the novel isn't trying to reform anything, isn't a kind of meaning there?

A: Well, there is a meaning in every story. But whether I'm trying to sell that idea is something else. I'm just trying to portray it, to tell the story of it as I see it—in terms of the characters themselves. If the reader comes along and reads the story, he may get much more out of it than I got out of it, because he may be able to see in it things that I didn't see.

That's one trouble with censorship. When you try to control writing by censorship you forbid somebody from telling not what he is trying to but what other people are going to find in it. You are hemming in a writer when you censor him, saying use these words. I'm sort of like a doctor. I'm accustomed to all this stuff. In other words, if somebody got his leg mangled, I wouldn't get a violent stomach-ache and say I can't operate on that man because it's a terrible sight to see his mangled body. I'd go right ahead if I were a doctor and do the best I could. It's the same with a writer, I think. He's not interested in trying to be obscene, he's just trying to tell a story.

Q: And if the reader finds it obscene it's because of his limitations?

A: That's true. He's conditioned to think that such and such a thing is not acceptable in good society or in good speech; he has a block of some kind, I guess you'd call it. That is understandable. But it is the professional reformer and censor I'm talking about. I don't think the reader ever really objects to what you write, because I think the reader is more understanding of these things than the professional censor is.

Q: About your writing in general—do you have a story consciously in mind a long time before you actually begin writing it?

A: Well, everybody would have a different answer to that.

Q: That's why I'm asking yours.

A: [laughing] My answer would not be very enlightening to anybody, because I don't know it myself very well. I never have any big ideas to build up with notes and things of that sort. Actually I only have one idea at a time. It may be a very small idea that you can express in ten words. I start from that, I suppose, and see what happens. The way I like to do is not to have any preconceived notions about the idea, but to see how it works out. For that reason I don't make any notes at all. This may be a very poor plan, as I say. But the idea is the important thing with me. Then I get a sheet of yellow paper and put down the first sentence. Then I see what happens in the second sentence and go on from there. That's about the only method I have.

Q: It seems to have been enough. When working on a novel do you sometimes put the whole thing aside, turn to other work, and then come back to it later?

A: I don't like to stop in the middle of a novel, else I'd throw it away and start over again. My wastebasket always holds more than my folder does anyway.

Q: Each day?

A: Yes, as I'm writing along I throw away more than I keep. I have to do it over and over—maybe twenty times.

Q: Do you revise a novel much when you have it nearly done?

A: Well, that's hard to say. I'm never finished, it looks like. I may have written a thing ten times and then at the tenth time I decide the year's up. So that's going to be it. I give myself a year, and if I can do it in eight or nine months that means I have two or three months I can travel. Often I go at the writing seven days a week, from nine to five, for six months sometimes—you know—and make myself obnoxious to everybody by not going anywhere and not doing anything and not getting my hair cut and not getting my shoes shined. I have to be satisfied myself; I don't care what other people are going to think about it. If I get happy with it, then I don't want to quit.

Q: You don't have the reader in mind in the least?

A: No, no. I do it for myself. I don't know what a reader is, you know. He's somebody I can't visualize at all.

Q: With more than forty million, I see how you couldn't.

A: I only want to make it interesting to me. When the publisher says this line doesn't make sense or something, it does to me; so I tell the publisher, well, that's the way it is.

Q: So you never let criticism from editors lead you to make a revision?

A: Well, I never have yet. I always invite it but no one ever has made any suggestions other than about the ordinary typographical mistakes. It's not that I don't welcome criticism from a publisher or a reader or an editor, it's just that I think I know more about it than he does. If he can prove to me that I'm wrong, why I'm quite willing to acknowledge it and to try to make it more clear or to change the wording or something, but it never really comes up. I think the first novel I ever wrote set me on the track of thinking that maybe I could be my own editor. A long time ago when I wrote *Tobacco Road* I worked on it in my usual way, ten to twelve hours a day and seven days a week for eight or ten months, whatever it was, and when I got through with it I was satisfied. Of course, I didn't know anything about it—a novice writer, and I didn't know this or that about writing a novel—but it seemed to me to be all right. So I submitted it to Scribner's. Maxwell Perkins was the editor, and he had been reading some of my short stories. When he got this novel he wrote me a little note and said: "We want to publish it; we don't want to change anything." That gave me confidence, I suppose. I don't say that anything I have written since then has been perfect, by any means. I know it hasn't been. But I think he gave me confidence that I could do it and that I wouldn't have to get into the state where I would want to submit everything I wrote to someone and have him suggest and revise and rework.

Q: Do you write as much short fiction as you used to?

A: Well—no. I like to write short stories, and every once in a while I stop and write a few. I guess it was two years ago now, the last time I wrote a book of short stories. It was called *Gulf Coast Stories,* and I've written about two or three novels since then; so maybe I'll go another year or two and won't be able to hold out any longer and will go back and write a book of short stories again, because I like them. I don't think there is anything to compare with the short story. I think it's the best form of writing there is.

Q: What makes it better than the novel?

A: Well, I think you can tell as much in a story as you can a novel, but it's more difficult to do. It's hard to accomplish a good short story because you have to concentrate it so much. So I like the discipline of it.

Q: Then I'd think you would write poetry. It's one step farther on the same path, isn't it?

A: Yes, and I tried that too.

Q: Have you written much poetry?

A: No. No. I wrote it a long time ago. I was just a young punk. I'm fifty-four—somewhere in there—and I'd been trying to write short stories and hadn't done much with them. Then I started to write poetry, and I got pretty well wrapped up in it for about a year. I got a batch of it together, and of course nobody would publish the stuff. I decided to get an expert opinion; so I sent a batch off to Louis Untermeyer. He wrote back a little note to the effect that this poetry is no better and no worse than thousands of other young men in America write, and if you want my sincere advice I would advise you to change to another field of writing.

Q: Was he right?

A: [laughing] Yes, very much so. Everybody has to write poetry sooner or later. I got it out of my system early in life.

Q: How about nonfiction books? You've written a number; do you expect to do more?

A: It all depends. I like travel books. That's about the only nonfiction I like to do. I've written three or four, I guess, altogether; and I have one favorite: *You Have Seen Their Faces*. But *North of the Danube* is the kind of book I'd like to do a lot of if I had the time. I like Czechoslovakia and had been there half a dozen times off and on, I suppose; and the book is something like half fiction and half fact. That is my favorite type of nonfiction: travel sketches.

Q: I take it you really like to travel?

A: I do, yes. I'd like to travel all the time.

Q: Do you write on trips?

A: Not now. I don't even touch a typewriter. The only place I like to write now is at home; then I like to go at it all the time. I can't just

get out and walk around town or sit and play bridge or do any of
those things—they bore me to death and I make everybody
unhappy. They say, "Go away, go home, get away from me!"—you
know. So I like to work when I'm working, and when I'm not working
I like to travel.

Q: You've spoken about different kinds of writing; have you ever
written directly for the movies?

A: In a very minor way. My first introduction to movie life was a
long time ago. I was broke; so my agent got me a job at $250 a
week, which was a lot of money—and still is. But in those days, back
in the 1930s, $250 a week was a million dollars. So he got me a job
in Hollywood. Nothing of any importance.

Q: Did you feel about that kind of writing the way you feel about
fiction?

A: No. No. I have great respect for motion picture writing, but I
think you have to be attuned to it. My goal is to see the printed word
and nothing else; anything beyond that is sort of superfluous to me. I
like to see the form of the word, the shape of it, the way the lines
come out. That's really what I'm interested in, nothing else. I suppose
I like to experiment a lot, but with the printed word: the sight of it,
how short it can be. I like to contract the word and make it look good
to me.

Q: Was it any pleasure to see *God's Little Acre* shaping on film
instead of in printed words, since you had already put it into print?

A: Yes, it was—mainly because like an illustrated edition it
enhanced the book in some way, although of the two forms, if I had
to make my choice between a picture and the novel of it, I would still
choose the novel.

Q: Have you special favorites among your novels?

A: I'd hate to have to select one, or even half a dozen of them. But
I still have a feeling for a book I wrote which took me, I suppose, four
years altogether to do off and on. It was a book called *Georgia Boy,* a
series of sketches about a boy in Georgia growing up in company
with his mother, his father, and a Negro playmate of the same age—
growing up at that particular time in America when life was a little
more leisurely and there was not so much compelling action put
upon people.

Q: The sketches that make up *Georgia Boy* can stand alone as
short stories, can't they?

A: Yes.

Q: Did you think of them as parts of a unified book when you were writing them?

A: No. That's why it took such a length of time, I suppose, to do it. I would do one and then think of something else that would go with it. I remember writing that book all over: I wrote some of it in New York, some in Los Angeles, some in London, some in Moscow, and I wrote some of it in China.

Q: A moment ago you spoke of short story and novel and said the short story was harder to do. Maybe *Georgia Boy* is a combination of both?

A: Yes, it could be that it is the ideal form as far as I am concerned: it can be divided into parts and yet the whole put together is a novel.

Q: In *A Place Called Estherville* and some of the other novels, aren't you doing a different thing from what you did in *Tobacco Road* and *God's Little Acre? A Place Called Estherville* shows the pleasant Negro boy and girl in trouble, victims. It seems to me that novel presents an injustice you want people to notice. Not that you say how to reform it, but you obviously don't think the situation is good. And *A House in the Uplands* is the same, isn't it?

A: Well, I don't know. Where are you going to draw the line? For example, suppose you are writing about the dope habit. Anyone who wrote a book about the dope habit, wouldn't he naturally write in a way that would be a denunciation of it?

Q: I suppose so.

A: Well, that's the way I look at it. And I suppose, after living amongst it for so long, I have an unhappy feeling about the degradation of the Negro—a feeling that it is unhealthy too. But I don't know what I set out to prove in *A Place Called Estherville*. I don't know that I set out to prove anything—just to tell a story about what actually happened between whites and blacks in a small town in the South at that particular time.

Q: I suppose many people ask you how to be a successful writer.

A: Yes, and I don't know any way for a person to get to be a writer actually. First he has to want to be; second, he has to condition himself by practice and work, just as a doctor or a lawyer has to study and do case work and internship before he is qualified. Just studying and wanting are not enough. You have to practice it. Once you get your grip you know how to use words. I read dictionaries all the time and every book on words I can get, such as *The American Language* by Mencken.

Q: But you always keep coming back to the simplest word?

A: Yes, I try to find out how to squeeze it. Take a long word like "entertainment," for example. I don't like a word that length. It looks too long to me. But I wouldn't like the word "fun." So there you are, now I'm having trouble. So I have to get a word between those two that has the meaning I want.

Mrs. Caldwell: Erskine has every dictionary you can think of, practically, around the house, and there's never a word you ask him about that he doesn't know the best definition for.

Q: Even the long words he won't use?

Mrs. Caldwell: He knows all the big words, but he never breaks down and uses them in his writing.

Q: About your learning to write, did you consciously learn anything from others?

A: Sometimes I wish I knew myself, because I can't explain it very well. To begin with, I didn't read anything to speak of. I am not a reader. But after I had been in college awhile I became interested in writing. The thing that interested me most during the first two years I was in college was sociology, and I took all the courses I could. After two years I went to work on a newspaper in Atlanta and then went back to college again. By that time I was interested in writing after fooling around with the newspaper; so I took all the courses in English all the way up to the graduate school. I was hardly taking anything else but English at that time, and I began finding magazines and books in the library which I had never seen before. It interested me to see that people could write short stories and have them published. So I got the idea I should try it, and began writing stories.

Q: Did it take long to get your stories accepted?

A: Oh, yes. Certainly. I think it took about seven years to get something really published: Maxwell Perkins, the editor of *Scribner's Magazine,* took two or three short stories. By then I probably had a hundred or more stories and I don't know how many novels and what not, which I had been writing over the seven years. As soon as I got those first stories published in *Scribner's,* a general magazine, I made a big bonfire and burned everything I had. What I had done before was preliminary and practice; so I lit the bonfire and started over again at that point.

Q: What kept you going for seven years?

A: It's hard to look back and say what motivates something that long ago, except that I knew I wanted to write and I knew I would not be satisfied unless I accomplished it. I was going to do it just as I was going to make something to eat—you know, grow potatoes, or whatever it happened to be. I remember when I was living in the state of Maine that sometimes I would start in the morning and go through the whole day and night until the next morning before I would quit. You know, trying to get something that suited me.

Q: And you weren't thinking mostly about publication?

A: Oh, that was secondary at the time, because I was provided. I was cutting wood and raising potatoes, so I was provided and it wasn't a question of trying to make money. It was not decided that this was the way I was going to make my living. That wasn't the idea; the idea was that I had to get the story written the way I wanted it.

Q: I'd like to ask about your future plans if it isn't wrong to ask a writer such a question. Have you completed the series that includes *A Place Called Estherville?*

A: Yes.

Q: Have you any such series in the offing?

A: I have no other series in mind at the present time. I finished up what I considered that series about the South; and I have been writing the past two or three novels in general terms, I suppose you'd say, setting them in the middle of America.

Q: *Gretta,* for example, is such a novel?

A: *Gretta,* yes, that is one. And there is a more recent one called *Certain Women.* I'll probably write one or two more with that idea in mind. Then it will be something else. I don't care right now what it's going to be because I don't like to think about those things ahead of time. I like for them to come when they do come.

Q: Speaking of books in series, is the American Folkways Series completed?

A: Completed up through the twenty-three volumes with which I was concerned. I gave up my editorship about three years ago. It was just taking too much time, and I had completed what I set out to do.

Q: What drew you to be the editor of that series, with all the time it would take from your writing?

A: Well, you know, when you're young you don't care about time. It really doesn't matter. You can do anything you want to do, I suppose. In that particular stage I had time on my hands: I was only writing one or two novels a year and maybe twenty-five short stories and maybe going around the world, and I had plenty of time left. So I got the idea for the series, and when a publisher took it on I scurried around the country finding writers I thought were suitable to their regions.

Q: What was your original intention for the series?

A: It was to present segments of the country, individual regions, which were more distinct in those days.

Q: What about regionalism in fiction? If you set a novel along a tobacco road, you don't in any way think that you are chiefly trying to show the life in that particular region, do you?

A: No. I think what a writer wants to do and ought to do is use what he knows best. If he happens to know North Dakota, say, I think he should—and if he's a good writer, he will—write about North Dakota. Of course, commercial writing is something else. I don't know anything about it, but there is nothing you can't do with commercial writing. You can take any story and put it into any environment you want to for commercial purposes, but I don't consider that true writing. That's outside of my field.

Q: Does the fact that you are the American author most widely read abroad influence your writing at all?

A: Well, I look at it this way. To me people are the same everywhere, regardless of nationality or language, and if the story seems simple and clear and interesting in America, it's going to seem the same in other parts of the world. I don't write anything now that has dialect in it. I never try to make a phonetic word in print. I have nothing against it, it's fine and all right and a writer should do it if he wants to; but I don't think you can translate dialect. That's just an idea. There may be other reasons too, but that's one feeling I have about it.

Q: One difficult aspect of censorship which isn't just the usual concern with obscenity is the growing objection that many American writers widely translated abroad don't write happy stories showing us in a good light at all times. Have you any thoughts about that?

A: Well, I don't operate with that in mind, but I can understand it. Propaganda is one thing; you have the evidence of it in Russian literature, which is propaganda. I don't think Western life is in the frame of mind to accept writing as propaganda. I think the artist, the writer, is free to have self-expression. As long as that continues, I don't think that he should be handicapped by telling him he shouldn't write about certain things because of the effect that it might have somewhere else.

But when you come to have the misuse of writing, that's something else. For example, I remember that just preceding the war my agent had an offer from Germany to publish a book. The book was *Trouble in July,* which is the story of how a colored boy got into trouble, egged on by a white girl. At that time the Nazis were using such things in Germany to build up a hatred for America. We decided we did not want the book sold to Nazi Germany at that particular time. There was no pressure on us, just a private individual thing between the agent and myself. Unfortunately it developed later that the German publisher, or the German government, in some way bought the rights to the book from another language in a contrived manner. So the book was published in Germany, which was deplorable. Half a dozen times, I suppose, in the past two or three years certain countries have wanted to publish certain books and we said no, because there was the possibility that they might be used for propaganda.

Q: Do you supervise translations of your work in any way?

A: We usually take the advice of agents, who recommend the publisher and the translator. We have one master agent and then fifteen subagents around the world. The master agent in New York, Jim Brown, works through the others. Then it all comes here and Virginia has to worry with it and we have to make decisions. In the old days I wouldn't open a letter for six days but on the seventh day, which I took off from writing, I would go through all the paper work. But in the past eight or ten years it has reached the point where we have to do it every day—one of us, Virginia or I.

Mrs. Caldwell: That was interesting to me, because it never entered my head how much of that sort of thing was involved with writing.

Q: You must be at your typewriter much of the time too.

Mrs. Caldwell: Well, it certainly makes me feel more a part of what's going on.

Mr. Caldwell: One of our main troubles in the way of paper work and business is the pirating that is spreading out anew. In the old days it was quite common, then during the war years it died down. But in

the past two years we've been pirated in three countries where we
have no control.

Q: What book is pirated most?

A: *God's Little Acre,* I think.

Q: Have any of your works been made into movies outside the
United States?

A: Not to my knowledge.

Mrs. Caldwell: Did you show Mr. Collins *Molly Cottontail?*

Mr. Caldwell: No, I didn't.

Mrs. Caldwell: Well, I think he should see that side of your work
too.

Mr. Caldwell: It's a children's book to come out in the spring.

Q: Is it your first children's book?

A: Yes. It's actually a short story that has been revised for children.

Mrs. Caldwell: It was written originally from the point of view of
the boy who can't bring himself to shoot the rabbit, but now it's in the
third person.

Q: Are you going to adapt for children more of the things you've
already written?

A: No, I don't think so. I just wanted to see how it went. It was
Virginia's idea; so we give her credit for getting it done.

Q: Do many people not interested in becoming authors write to
you for personal advice?

A: Yes. People seem to think a writer knows something about
psychiatry, psychology, sociology, philosophy, and everything else. I
guess it's human nature to write to somebody for help. But I don't
know how to answer when someone asks, "Should I go back to my
mother because I am unhappy living in Peoria, Illinois?" They come
all the time, letters like that.

Q: Do you answer such letters?

A: Not if I can help it. I don't think we've answered one in a year,
now. Sometimes we turn them over to a doctor or to a minister. All
writers get letters like that—just a form of fan mail, I suppose.

Q: Do you reply to other kinds of letters at all?

A: If someone writes and says he likes a book, and it's a genuine
letter, I usually write back and say thank you for liking my book.

I think one of my greatest troubles is not being able to help people.
People are always wanting to know how to write and I don't know
what to tell them. People say, "Here is a story I wrote, all you have to

do is read it and tell me what's wrong so I can fix it up." Well, I don't know what's wrong with it. And I don't think a writer can rely on somebody else to help him to any extent. When you're starting—in college, for example—you can get direction toward how to do it yourself. But a writer can't really help someone who comes along with a story and says, "Please help me."

I think you must remember that a writer is a simple-minded person to start with and go on that basis. He's not a great mind, he's not a great thinker, he's not a great philosopher, he's a storyteller. I mean, that's the field I belong in; there are, of course, writers who have great minds, but I don't pretend to. I can't take the responsibility of saying that I know anything that anybody else doesn't know, because I don't. I have my own way of writing, which I don't recommend to other people. I do it my own way. I don't like other people to tell me to do it their way. I'm just completely obnoxious and hardheaded. And I can't help it. That's why I can't tell anybody how to write. I don't know how to do it; it was just a combination of trial and error and revision that finally came out as it did. It's not an exact science, as you know; you can't pin it down. All I can say is I like plenty of yellow second sheets. That's what I want in life: yellow second sheets—and typewriter ribbon and plenty of typewriters, too. I wear them out one or two every year; I dislike old typewriters, and I dislike ones that break down, and I dislike ribbons that get dim, and I dislike white paper. So you see I have my prejudices.

Sex, Sin and Society
Through the Eyes of Erskine Caldwell
Guccione/1961

From the London American, 23/29 March 1961, p. 7.

America's most widely-read author—his books have sold 62,000,000 copies in 27 languages—is noted as a man who thinks a lot, but says little. London American cartoonist Guccione broke through the silence barrier in a friendly interview with Caldwell at his London hotel.

"I have no favorite contemporary writers, except myself," Erskine Caldwell told me in his suite at the Savoy Hotel. "I am not a modest man . . . I can't afford to be."

The world's most widely read author—he has sold more than 62 million copies of his books—is a tall, tough, softly-spoken man with a face that could have been chipped from stone. He speaks freely about himself, his four marriages, his attitude to life, sex, and love, but he dismisses the subject of writing as "a thing you do . . . a thing you don't talk about."

"I was born in Georgia in 1903," he said. "My father was a Presbyterian minister. I am not a religious man, not in the ordinary sense. You could call me an agnostic. I have my own religion, my own beliefs, every bit as good, if not better, than those of organized religion."

Caldwell is a man with a set purpose in life. He writes because he "has to." Nothing could replace his need to express himself through the printed word. He has no other ambition, and never has had. At the age of 14 he knew he wanted to write. He read little and digested less. His ambition mounted as his experience increased, and his interest in people became an infatuation with humanity at large, a love affair which has never ceased and from which he has profited enormously as both a man and a writer.

"I was a reporter on the Atlanta Journal," he said, "but I quit in 1927. I was about 23 years old then and I badly wanted to write. I got busy, seriously busy. Seven years later I published a book of short stories called *American Earth*. It was my first success. The book sold 500 copies.

"I held a lot of jobs in those days. I was a milkman, milked cows, bottled the stuff and delivered it door to door. I drove a cab in Memphis, even drove an ambulance; I worked as a stone mason chipping tomb stones for a living. At one point I was chief cook and bottle washer at a railway station in Wilkes-Barre, Pennsylvania. It made me live with people, and I got to know them. I learned how to write from living . . . not from books."

Caldwell's personal philosophy bears all of the deceptive simplicity of his prose. To him, life is truth, and truth, however expressed, is its own justification.

"The people I write about are real people with real problems," he said. "I don't use sex as a gimmick or lever for success. I have written as much about sociology and economics as I have about sex. People are more interested in the sex side, therefore that side emerges most prominently.

"My characters are drawn from experience," he continued. "You couldn't write about human beings if you had never seen one. They live and evolve their own lives, their own habits and morals and attitudes within the framework of the story I provide."

Caldwell's penetration into the lives of real people is no less evident in fact than in the fiction he writes. He has a consuming interest in life around him, an interest in the ordinary people who "write" the great sagas of human experience. He travels the world two months out of every year. The remaining ten months he dedicates to work.

His hours are strictly routine. He writes from 9 to 5, seven days a week. The room in which he works is bare, consisting only of an uncluttered desk, a chair, typewriter and a waste basket.

"Unlike earlier times," he said, "when I used to work straight through the night. I have a routine now but one or two things still hang over from the past. I keep the shades down all day; can't stand the sun when I work. It's night all the time that way."

I asked Caldwell what he thought about women and the Thurber allegation that they would soon dominate all aspects of society in America.

"I don't agree with Thurber," he said. "It'll never happen in my

time, not if I have anything to do with it. I believe in a 50-50
relationship."

"And how do you feel about the popular European notion that
Americans are sexually frigid or inhibited," I said.

He smiled. "There's a basis for truth in that," he said. "I think it's
the result of religion. America is probably the most religious country
in the world. There are more Catholic, Protestant and Anglican sects
in the U.S. than anywhere else. Americans have a strong religious
background. They believe that everything they do is a sin. Therefore,
if they don't want to sin, they don't do anything."

"Marilyn Monroe is a fake; an automaton! I don't have anything
against her personally, but she can't act. Helen Hayes is a great
actress, been going for fifty some years. It's all a matter of personality.
I think sex appeal is really personality and you need personality to be
a success in life. It can be the way you dress or comb your hair or the
way you talk."

I asked him if he thought of Henry Miller as an artist or as a
pornographer, where, in fact, art ends and pornography begins.

"Miller is a great writer," he said. "I put him in a class with
Steinbeck or Faulkner. Writers are either pros or non-pros. I have no
sympathy for writers that fail. Miller has succeeded because he is
good. No, I do not think he is a pornographer. He knows how to
write a good sentence.

"Sex is an important ingredient in life. You use it to tell a story if
the story needs it. That is not pornography."

I knew he was reticent to discuss his work and I began by asking
which three, if all the books in the world were to be destroyed, would
he save if it was within his power to do so.

He thought for a moment. "I would save one," he said. "A blank
book with no printed words. Five hundred blank pages so that I
could write the only book worth saving myself."

"What about the Bible," I said. "Would you save that too?"

"What for!" he said.

"How about art in general," I asked. "How do you feel about the
European idea that America is culturally vapid or sterile."

"I don't agree with that," he said. "There is a basis for this type of
thinking but there is a lot going on to make up for it. I agree that we
don't have enough good writers and that there is not enough written
about America.

"Americans come to Europe to write about America. A lot of writers at home go on writing for years and never say anything about America. Today's writers want to turn out a best seller the first time and become disillusioned if they don't make it.

"There's no solid encouragement to new talent. If a man is good he becomes absorbed by Madison Avenue turning out public relations copy for $25,000 a year, or Hollywood or television for $50,000 a year. These big paying industries drain off our good talent as fast as we can produce it."

I asked him if he thought financial security was an obstacle to creative writing. "Positively," he said. "You've got to strive to pay the rent. If you're born with a million dollars you rarely have any time to think about anything but protecting your money.

"I made my first million by the time I was forty . . . through my work. I spent it fast. . . . With taxes the way they are today, it would probably take me about two years to make another million."

"Is emotional stability necessary to write well?" I asked.

"No," he said, "it's a detriment. A good writer has to be emotionally unstable. His work must go up and down, rise and fall. If he were emotionally stable all the time he would never get a chance to kick the dog around or pull a cat's tail."

"Do you think of yourself as being in competition with other writers, either living or dead?" I asked him.

"Everything in life is competition. I have to compete with myself. With the things I have already done and with the image I have already created. The more you write the harder it becomes because you become more critical of yourself."

"To what extent," I asked, "should a writer concern himself with the socio-political problems of the day?"

"No writer gains anything by walking up and down the street with a sandwich board around his neck, or physically protesting against something he doesn't agree with. He should write about it. I concern myself with these problems all the time but I write them down."

I asked him which among his books did he consider his favorite.

"*Georgia Boy,*" he said. "It is the most complete book I have ever written. It has everything, sociology, economics. It was first published in Britain over ten years ago. I believe it will hold up longer than any other book I have written or any other book anyone else has ever written for that matter! It goes into people more."

"How do you begin a book or a story? Do you follow any particular outline or work it out in your head first?"

"I begin with the first sentence. After that things take their own course. If I knew in advance how it would end I would get bored and never finish. Once the process of creation is over the story is dead."

"Have you ever had the desire to go back and rewrite or revise any of your books such as *Tobacco Road.*"

"No, *Tobacco Road* was contemporaneous with the time and period in which I wrote it. To make any changes now or bring it up to date would falsify and invalidate the revision."

"Does the reading public tend to classify writers according to the themes which they, the writers, take—such as sex, violence, crime, sociology, etc.?"

"Writers are like brands of cigarettes or gasoline. People get to recognize a particular brand. All gasoline is basically alike. If you want high octane in one field you read Henry Miller. If you want low octane in another, you read Faulkner. They're both good."

"Why do successful writers, such as Hemingway or yourself, withdraw from the company of other writers in later years?"

"I believe that writers withdraw from everyone, not only other writers. Talking things out is a waste of time. You can't be a talker and a writer at the same time."

"What would you call the essential difference between good writing and great writing?"

Caldwell paused for a moment and lit a cigarette. "That's a tough one," he said. "I don't know. It's beyond me. I suppose it has something to do with its effect on the reader; the greater the effect, the greater the book. Greatness survives. What is only quality today may be mediocrity tomorrow."

Caldwell has strong feelings about anything which comes within the sphere of his interest. Politics, as such, do not concern him. "I voted for Kennedy," he said. "I have no particular feelings about him. As far as I'm concerned running the country is his business and he can run it as long as he runs it the way I want him to."

But this tall, brash, chiselled figure of a man, this sometimes quiet, deeply sensitive, irreverent and yet thoroughly human individual has spoken to more people through the printed word than any other man of his time.

To many he is the greatest sociological writer ever to come out of America, to others he is a ribald and swaggering immoralist. But whatever the feeling to those people who read him, Erskine Caldwell is something strong and unforgettable, a giant among story tellers, an artist whose words are the colours and the wisdom of life and whose voice is the voice of the people.

Erskine Caldwell
Roy Newquist/1963

From *Counterpoint,* edited by Roy Newquist (Chicago: Rand McNally & Company, 1964), pp. 66-73. Copyright © 1964 by Rand McNally & Company. Reprinted by permission.

N. Erskine Caldwell occupies a strategic position in the world of American letters. He entered the scene, over thirty years ago, with the subtlety of a dynamite blast. Novels like *God's Little Acre* and *Tobacco Road* established the fact that poverty and deprivation were universal problems, not exclusively the sad issue of the big-city slum. Many of the established critics were shocked, but since jarring the establishment has been part of any innovator's career, shock alone could not pronounce Caldwell's fame.

The gaunt and disturbing picture of life among the underprivileged was the framework upon which Caldwell built his sensitive and searching stories embracing compassion, humor, and irony. A bold simplicity of style, matched with a clean and virile story line, has made major works like *Tobacco Road* and minor opuses like *The Last Night of Summer* readable, memorable, and even significant. But in talking to Mr. Caldwell, I'd like to move to the very beginning, so to speak—to his own story.

Caldwell: My life is really rather dull. It would not make a book, and I would hate to have to read my own biography. My life is not typical, yet it's not extraordinary; it's mostly just dull. What I mean by dull is that I'm a writer, and the only thing I like to do in life is write. I've been writing now for the past thirty or thirty-four years and I'll probably keep going a little while longer. This is the way I live and breathe and work and believe.

When I began writing, all those years ago, I was more interested in the content of a story than I was in any technical derivations of a story or of a novel. What I did was to start at the beginning, without any background as a writer, without any knowledge as a writer. All I wanted to do was to tell a story, to tell it to the best of my ability— better, I hoped, than anyone else could tell that particular story. So I began when I was about seventeen by working on a newspaper. I think I learned a great deal about life and writing in those years of apprenticeship on a newspaper. It was a small newspaper, what you might call an intimate newspaper, a weekly. But I learned that there can be a story in anything and everything. Anything will make a story because everything has meaning in itself, and that meaning is always applicable to life itself. If it happens to one person it could happen to a million persons. So, when I wanted to write a story, and tried to write it, I was writing for myself—not for a million people—because I had to please myself first. If I was not satisfied with that story I would throw it in the wastebasket. If it didn't appeal to me, how could it please the million?

I was concerned with perfecting my own writing to the extent that its meanings were obvious. Not only to me, but to that audience of a million. They had to find a meaning. I did not add philosophy, or significance, but felt that any story of human life would find its own level of significance. Every reader would find a different meaning because every reader finds what he's looking for. All I do is to furnish the mirror, a mirror the reader can look into. This way he can see what he's looking for. If he's looking for a philosophy of life he can probably find it in some way, or if all he wants is entertainment he can find that, too.

N. But along with "mirroring" there are elements of compassion so evident in works like *Tobacco Road* and *God's Little Acre* that I feel you must consciously dig to the heart of persons and the root of issues.

Caldwell: I think any work of fiction always has a basis in reality. We were just speaking of story content being a mirror—but actually, if we have to be serious about these things, we have to realize that fiction is more than entertainment. It is not a pastime, it furnishes something we can't get from life itself because fiction must concentrate, eliminate, add to life. People read to find out what they cannot find in their own lives or see around them. I don't claim to have any divine ability, I can't define any emotion or situation or thesis better than any other writer, but I can select my material with care and discrimination. In other words, I'm not interested in finding a plot on which to hang a story; I want to find out what elements of life move and motivate people. People make their own plot, if that's how the storyline must be defined. I've never known exactly what a plot is because I wouldn't know how to do one if I saw it. What I try to do is to help people themselves furnish the entire basis of a story.

If you are really deeply interested in people's lives and write about them, or even want to or try to write about them, they're going to furnish you with all the materials you spoke about a moment ago. You see, people themselves are compassionate by nature. Very few people—certainly not ordinary people like you and me, for example—have any great claim to being experts in psychology and psychiatry, and so on. What we do, what a serious writer tries to do, is to create people who have never really existed and make new people. These new people reflect everybody because they're composites of many persons. They are not re-created from life, like an extra-dimension photograph. In order to create something you have to make something which doesn't truly exist. In order to make this true and believable you have to know people themselves, and be able to believe in these people you're writing about. If you do not believe in them, if you think they're just characters to manipulate and turn into elements of plot, you end up with nothing. You have a book filled with words and nothing else. I think that all serious writing is something that's been created, that reflects people the author came to know and love and understand, with something of the author thrown in.

N. To turn to the physical processes of research—could you describe the travel that went into the backgrounds for your various southern novels?

Caldwell: I don't know whether you call it research or not. What I know is what I have done and seen and heard, and if this is research I'm guilty.

I grew up in the South and I happened to have been fortunate enough to live all over the South in my youth. I lived in every southern state, and I don't know how many towns and cities. When a person moves every six months or so from one place to another I suppose he gets a real cross-section of life by comparing life in Louisiana, for instance, with life in Florida. There are differences, and you recognize these differences if you have an opportunity to compare them, whereas if you live in just one place all your life you can't make such comparisons. I think that comparison has a great deal to do with understanding. No matter what the dialect is, or the racial characteristics might be, or their educational standards, you don't really recognize differences unless you can compare.

N. The states south of the Mason-Dixon line have produced a disproportionately large share of America's leading writers. Why do you suppose this has happened?

Caldwell: I don't know the real answer. In terms of my own experience, because this is all I can talk about, I think it's that the South—until after the Second World War—was an agricultural region. It was not an industrial area, with concentrations of population. Life is always elementary when you are scattered far apart. It isn't like a city slum, where you know people next door, above you, below you, on the street across from you. In a sparsely populated region, such as in any farming country, you have to go and look to find something to write about. You don't find it in your back door because beyond your back door is nothing but a cotton field. There's nothing in that cotton field—so you travel around. You find that people who live these isolated lives are more intense than people who live in an urban society. People in an urban society tend to become similar, they have the same interests and they do the same things and they talk the same jargon. In an isolated community people are individuals. This individuality stands out, it's there for the writer to grab. Because a writer needs individuals, not prototypes, both to stir him and to give him material that makes stories, the writer in the South has an advantage. You can find uniqueness, wonder what makes a person what he is, why he talks as he does, what his social attitudes are, his religious attitudes. These differences, these elements of uniqueness, flourish in isolated regions. To me that's why there has been and is so much material in the South.

N. To turn to a recent book, *The Last Night Of Summer,* I wonder if you'd describe how the novel was born and evolved.

Caldwell: The setting is deep in the Mississippi delta country. I lived in this delta country many years ago, and I go back there every year, sometimes twice a year. This particular region is one of my favorite spots between New Orleans and Memphis, the border of delta country.

You might say this particular story could have happened anywhere, yet in my own mind it could only happen where it did—not in North Dakota or California or New England or in Europe. It had to take place in this one particular region, where the people I wanted in the book really are, where this story could be created out of individual lives, where the conflict could arise. In the delta region the heat can be almost unbearable, sometimes, and emotional breaks in people seem to grow naturally from the pressures that build up in them during a really bad heat wave. Toward the end of summer, when the heat breaks in a really wild night of thunderstorms, emotions break wide open, too. All these elements to me could take place in just one locality, and *The Last Night Of Summer* had to happen in the Mississippi delta.

N. To switch to a totally different aspect of your writing, what sent you to Europe during the years before we entered the Second World War?

Caldwell: I've always liked to travel, having grown up that way since the age of five. I wanted to find more comparisons in life. A few minutes ago I spoke about comparing people in different localities to expose the character of persons. The Old World, in my opinion, was a good place to go to compare the differences between life in America with the outside world. The Old World produced the people who came here; people in this country are derivatives. I wanted to find out what characteristics had been brought to this country, and what had been sacrificed or altered or changed. I wanted to learn the true character of various European peoples.

N. At least one of your books treated the Soviet war effort in detail, didn't it?

Caldwell: I suppose everyone would have a different impression of what happened in wartime. It all depends on where you are, what you're doing, all given circumstances. It just so happened that I was in Russia at the beginning of the war. What struck me was the harrowing fact that what happened in Russia could have happened nowhere else at the time, may never have happened before, may never happen again. This was the attempted assault by a well-organized war machine against a people who were essentially unwarlike to begin with, and who were not prepared for it, and who were not even industrialized to any great extent. They could only, in essence, retaliate with their own bare fists. It was a question of survival, not right or wrong, not politics or theory.

But perhaps people who are subjected to aggression are going to fight a little harder than people who face a less tangible foe. The Russians had everyhting to lose, their lands and their lives, and no matter how overwhelming the odds were supposedly stacked against them they were successful in their opposition to Hitler.

N. To change to the purely theoretical for a moment—if you were to give advice to the talented youngster seriously interested in writing, what would that advice be?

Caldwell: I'd probably give the same answer I would if you asked the doctor how to go about being a doctor. He'd tell you to take an apprenticeship for ten or fifteen years to learn the profession of being a doctor. You have to learn the trade of writing. You can't walk in the door and say, "I'm going to be a writer." Get yourself a typewriter and paper and write out your story? It doesn't work that way. Hundreds and thousands of people have been disappointed in life because they think they have a good story, or they're good oral storytellers. They think all they have to do is write it down. But writing is not a re-creation of the oral at all, because the oral is something you don't have to worry about in regard to grammar. You can always make a little slip-up in English when you're speaking— just as I'm undoubtedly doing right now—but when you write it you have to know how to spell that word, you've got to know what that word means, and although you can use maybe half a dozen words to describe one particular thing you have to know which is going to be the best word to do the job out of that half dozen.

It's elementary, I think, to say that you must understand what you're dealing with. Words are tools or supplies or ammunition or the fruit of talent or whatever you might want to call them. But if you don't understand words, if you don't know the origin of a word, what its original meaning was and what its application is today, I think you are dangerously ill-equipped for the job of writer. You simply cannot become a good writer until you learn the tools of the business and the grammar. Anybody can learn to spell, I suppose, with the use of a dictionary, but it's the definition of words, the true meaning, and the implication of words that tell a real story.

N. How much rewriting do you do in the course of turning out a novel?

Caldwell: This is hard to say, because I never actually write a book, I rewrite a book. I wouldn't be able to set up rules for the process; everything varies. I might write one sentence that will stay put until the end, but I might go back and find an adjacent sentence that I don't like and I'll fool around with that sentence for a whole day before it comes out the way I think it should.

If you rewrite a book, say, ten times, I think you're most apt to have a good book than if you rewrite it two or three times. There's no limit to what you have to do to rewrite. It may take a whole year's time, simply to get a simple story where it should be, in a form that satisfies you.

So if I write a book ten times I think I've done rather well. If I write it fifteen times I think it's going to be a little better, so I write it sixteen times.

N. Do you have a definite schedule of writing hours?

Caldwell: Definitely. Just like everyone with a job, I follow a schedule. I like my work; if I didn't like it I wouldn't be doing it. I don't watch the clock in the sense that I put in two hours, or five hours, or seven hours, and then quit. I suppose I have worked ten or fifteen hours at a stretch, but as I've grown older I've gotten to the point where I say, "Well, I've got more time to do this, now, than I had twenty years ago, so maybe I'd better quit." So if the sun's going down and it's getting hungry time, I quit with just seven or eight hours under my belt.

The hours don't necessarily mean anything—it all depends on how much comes out of them. You may end up with only one page at the end of the day, or you may end up with fifteen pages. It's never merely a matter of gauging the words you write or the time you put in, but how successful you think you've been at the end of the day's work. If you're satisfied (and a writer has terrible problems satisfying himself) you've done a day's work.

N. What works have you in progress now?

Caldwell: I always have something to do. I've been writing a book during the last summer. My wife and I finished about 25,000 miles of travel for a series of travel sketches. This will be a book that should be finished up soon. It will be called *Around About America,* and it will be a book about American life today. Nonfiction.

N. In looking about you—at what is being written and published today—what do you think of the state of American letters?

Caldwell: I probably don't read nearly as much as you do, or a lot of people do. I've never been much of a reader—not because I don't like to read, but because I'd rather write than read. What I know about American writing is sketchy.

What I try to do is to read one book by every writer who has written as many as two or three books. I rarely read anybody's first book; I wait to see if he's going to do a second or a third. At this point I consider him a novelist or a short story writer, whatever he's attempting to do.

Of course, we constantly have trends, and even I notice these. But it isn't a matter of liking them—you live with them. If you were to say, "I only read Sir Walter Scott and I don't like these modern writers," you'd end up in a real bind.

I think that writing at the moment is comparable to other decades. It's different in one respect—we find a lot more sensationalism than we found even ten years ago, and a great deal more experimentation than we found then, but this is all to the good. Anything that's new might be good because it indicates an improvement over the old. Even if it isn't good, by itself, it means that an improvement is coming.

N. Do you feel that the writer has an obligation to the material he uses, on one hand, and to the public for which he writes, on the other?

Caldwell: I am single-minded enough to say that a writer is obligated first and only to his material. Giving the public what it wants is good business if you are selling chewing gum; fiction is an art, not merchandise, and readers are moved by a writer's talent and not by his salesmanship.

N. If it were possible to look back from the vantage point of 2064, how would you like the accomplishments of Erskine Caldwell judged?

Caldwell: I would not know what to think about this in 1964— certainly not in 2064.

"Sex Was Their Way of Life":
A Frank Interview with Erskine Caldwell
Morris Renek/1964

From *Cavalier* (March 1964), pp. 12-16, 40-42.

"The white race is the inferior race. This has always been apparent to me."

Erskine Caldwell's voice is clear, strong, and leisurely with a deep knee-bend of Georgian intonation with only a few words. His tall lanky appearance is that of a New Englander lean as his own prose, yet—like his own prose—given strength by understatement and a laconic directness.

This is Caldwell's shirt-sleeve appearance on first meeting a stranger. When comfortably eased in his chair and talking thoughtfully or listening to his quietly intelligent, attractive, dark-eyed wife, the slow gentlemanly confidence associated with a Southern style of living comes to the fore. This is the straight-guy mixture that is impressive: New England terseness with Southern ease and friendliness.

Firsthand experience with what he is talking about makes him thrifty with words. When he comes down hard on a statement, as he did with "The white race is the inferior race," he does it quite simply as though observation on this matter would exclude any need of further talk.

Combined with this pragmatism-based confidence is a straightforward way of listening that can give an interview the feel of conversation.

His first words, friendlily spoken, warned me of his sharpshooter's eye. "You're not going to question me about sex?" A good-humored smile radiated from his wife at this defensive flinch of her husband.

When I told Caldwell my intention was to use his writings as a background of the South from the plantation system to the present Negro revolution, he immediately became attentive in a serious way that black-jacked me to be at my best. A respectful silence broke on the room; I for the attention the Caldwells instantly gave me, and they for the magazine I represented.

Before leaving us to thresh it out, Mrs. Caldwell explained her husband's defensive move regarding sex with understandable abruptness. "He was talking with people from television last night."

A forgiving smile breached Caldwell's face as he gave me a sample of the TV question and answer exchange. "Why do you write about sex, Mr. Caldwell?" "Because it's there."

"This went on," his wife spoke with quiet charm, "for two hours."

When we sat down—and Mrs. Caldwell silently picked up her novel by a notoriously bland author, John Fuller, who is 3,000 leagues beneath her husband, and left us—I asked him if he were able to foresee this Negro revolution a generation ago when he started writing about the South. That's when he gave me his opening estimation of the races.

He went on to say, with his words coming at a thoughtful pace, "The Negro has strength. I don't only mean physical strength. He has strength of person." Then he stressed what he considered most important: "Personality; he has a strong personality."

"How did you meet Negroes?" I asked.

Caldwell: Instantly. The first ten years of my life were spent playing with Negroes and whites in the countryside.

Renek: Of Georgia?

Caldwell: In Georgia. From my earliest knowledge I knew the Negro was superior. The antipathy the white Southerner brings out is bad. Negro children grow up without prejudice to white, and I can say whites grow up without prejudice to Negro—until the age of ten. About that age is the turning point. At ten is when the Negro child realizes he's living in a hopeless white world, and he turns away and withdraws from social life. [The life went out of Caldwell's voice momentarily.] We're separated.

Renek: Beginning with the plantation system, there's no better character to start with than Jeeter Lester. I was surprised to find that *Tobacco Road*, this monumental best seller, only sold a few thousand copies when it came out.

Caldwell: In hardbound.

Renek: Yes. Was it too difficult even for the readers of the '30s to recognize the utter destitution of *Tobacco Road* as real?

Caldwell: It was a first novel [He nodded stoically.] You know how they throw out first novels? Bury them somewhere.

Renek: As for Jeeter, it's amazing all the history you packed so quietly into him. His grandfather owned the rich tobacco plantation just 75 years before we meet an illiterate Jeeter living near starvation on a tiny part of his grandfather's land that is not even his own. What happened to Jeeter's grandfather and father that they could be brought up on the land and know so little about preserving it?

Caldwell: There were no chemicals in those days. No one knew enough about the soil. Nobody thought of saving the land. There was just too much of it around. If the soil was depleted, you moved on to somewhere else. Land was so cheap they could afford to abandon it.

Renek: There's such a dense, mint-julep myth attached to the plantation owner's love of his land. Yet, didn't the plantation system pauperize the soil?

Caldwell: Yes. The soil that was the prime producer in the Civil War was depleted and eroded, and there were bankruptcies, and some went to the richer land in North Carolina. You must remember that these plantations were on sandhill country. The top soil was thin; it had a sandy base. They were growing cotton. Cotton was king. It was making fortunes. But the soil wasn't rich to begin with. In some areas of a state, the top soil might be no more than one inch deep.

Renek: I would think it didn't happen overnight. Didn't they see the soil eroding out from under their feet?

Caldwell: Life was easy for them.

Renek: What was their prime want from the slaves and the land?

Caldwell: To make as much money as fast as they could. It was all economics. You can't understand the South without economics.

Renek: Reading is vital to the life of a culture. Why was Jeeter allowed to become illiterate?

Caldwell: Education meant nothing. They didn't have all the schools you see in the South today. The schools were miles apart. Nobody wanted to walk ten miles to a school. The common man was illiterate.

Renek: In your writings, you mention that it was not only the Negroes who were deprived of a culture, but also the whites.

Caldwell: That's right.

Renek: How deliberate was this lack of education?

Caldwell: Of course it was entirely deliberate. An illiterate man can't read the law. He doesn't know what his rights are. Sign your X and get the hell out of here. They didn't want to encourage education.

Renek: I'll get back to education . . . religion . . . and even sex, if you don't mind. (Caldwell smiled.) But first, I want to trace the evolution of the plantation system. Where did the landowners go after they pauperized the soil and lost their slave labor? Did they stay on this eroded land?

Caldwell: They moved to the big cities: Augusta, Macon, Savannah, Charleston. And they moved their way of life with them. That's why you can still see in these cities these old mansions from the days they moved into the city. There are dozens of them in Macon.

Renek: The plantation system gave way to tenant farming?

Caldwell: Yes.

Renek: Did a middleman now move in to manage the land for them?

Caldwell: Yes. The tenant system was absentee landowner. The owner let out his land on shares.

Renek: What was the financial status of these former plantation owners now living in the city?

Caldwell: They were more affluent than ever.

Renek: Were they richer than when they were on their plantation?

Caldwell: Yes.

Renek: Were there any landowners who did not depend on slave labor to advance their fortune?

Caldwell: You had the land to make money from it. I don't recall any without slaves.

Renek: These gentlemanly, paternalistic Southern landowners, were they actually a robber-baron gentry of the soil?

Caldwell: You couldn't characterize them as robber barons. Psychologically, they were not so much robber as paternal. Life was so easy for them. They had so much money. There were not taxes to speak of. They looked on the sharecropper as their fathers had looked on slaves. This was the tradition that carried over from their fathers.

Renek: In a text and picture book of yours and Margaret Bourke-White, *You Have Seen Their Faces,* that I hope some publisher will reprint, you wrote: "Plantations produced numerous families of wealth who developed a culture that was questionable. The new [society] has concentrated the wealth in the hands of a few families who are determined that *no* culture shall exist." Were they against education on the grounds they could keep the price of labor down?

You mention in your novel, *A House in the Uplands,* that if the
Negroes and whites could read they would read the account books
and see how much they were being cheated.

Caldwell: As long as you kept a person ignorant, you could
automatically cheat him. He doesn't know his rights. He's afraid to
speak up. Put your X here and get the hell out. He couldn't hire a
lawyer. But it doesn't carry over to today what I said about the
account books.

Renek: In *You Have Seen Their Faces,* you also see the shacks
Negroes were forced to live in. The outsides are plastered like
billboards with all kinds of advertisements from curing piles to
chewing tobacco. The insides were wallpapered with newspapers and
magazines. What was behind this outdoor advertising madness?

Caldwell: The families living in these shacks didn't own them.
The owners allowed people to paint signs on the walls because the
advertisers shellacked the wall around the sign and saved the owners
from doing it. Or they'd give the owner a case of medicine for his
piles. The magazine wallpaper inside was protection against the
weather.

Renek: Were the owners that blind to these conditions or did they
find a shrewd way—a public image—to cover up their greed?

Caldwell: For the owners, this was the accepted way of life that
carried over from slavery. [They believed that] Negroes are inferior
people. That [belief] still carries over today and is the reason behind
racial trouble.

Renek: At first sight, it is amazing to know that Negro tenant
farmers were given the best land to farm.

Caldwell: That's right. The Negro was a harder worker. He
produced more. He was more conscientious about his work. He was
physically and personally stronger.

Renek: And he could be intimidated?

Caldwell: He could be driven more than the whites. And it was
easy to threaten, "I'll take your corn bread away from you." He had
no recourse to law.

Renek: Then, once tenant farming came in, there was absolutely
no basis for black-white accord because of the rivalry set up between
them?

Caldwell: It was economics. [Then matter-of-factly.] You have to
understand the farm owner had more respect for the Negro.

An unbelieving smile appeared on my face at this information, and I asked Caldwell, "The owner had more respect for the Negro than he did for the white?"

Caldwell straightened up to his full tall height in the chair to make himself undeniably clear. "Because the Negro was the harder worker. The white was called low-white or white trash. Both the Negro and the owner looked down on this low-white. The low-white was shiftless, drinking, and he was wasting away from lack of a proper diet. The white owner looked upon him as his no-account brother. And he encouraged this white man to be religious. Religion being a good opium to keep the people quiet."

Renek: That Harris plantation in the Delta country of eastern Arkansas paid its white sharecroppers in coupons. If the whites protested this type of coupon payment, they were thrown off the land, and a Negro family was moved into their place. Could black or white ever leave these farms legally?

A grim smile cat-walked briefly across Caldwell's face as the question brought him away from the luxurious hotel room high above New York to the intolerable conditions he had once known. Before he spoke, the smile was gone. His voice was not bitter or resigned, nor did it have any trace of the soap box, but was haunted by the sheer ghoulish injustice of it all as he spoke quietly.

Caldwell: The company store was owned by the landowner. The coupons could only be redeemed in the company store. If a farmer had money, he could buy items cheaper anyplace else. Negroes and whites paid twice as much by going to the company store. [Then a note of sadness] Never see a dime in money. Never see a dime in money all year 'round. The owners made profit everywhere. Too much profit, and their labor was free. Almost free. [Caldwell was quietly derisive about the goods sharecroppers received in lieu of money for their labor.] Flour. Corn bread. It was a terrible system.

Renek: Taking for granted the low educational level of the white tenant farmer, why, when he was sinking below the level of the Negro in some places of the South, didn't he rebel against the white landlord instead of the bedeviled Negro who was caught up in this system with him?

Caldwell: The white had to keep the Negro subservient. He can't let the Negro get ahead while he's growing weaker. That's the trouble you have in Birmingham. When you read about bombings of

Negroes by whites, these bombings are done by people everyone calls—including the whites—poor white trash. The white trash has resentment against the Negro moving ahead. As far as the white is concerned, the Negro must never move ahead and progress while he [the poor white] is getting worse and worse off. The reasons behind these bombings are economic, not social.

Renek: Does this hold true for the maniacal impotence of white lynchers? Did lynching give whites the cowardly hope that the Negroes would frighten and move out of the county and leave the better land for him to farm?

Caldwell: Exactly. That's what you have. Retaliation against the Negro coming up while they [the poor whites] were losing out economically.

Renek: It seems hard to visualize—having listened to what you said about the rural Negro—yet I get the impression from your writings that the city or town Negro in the South was even worse off than his country cousin; not as free, less happy.

The strong emphasis in Caldwell's voice told me my impression was correct.

Caldwell: City Negroes inhabit a kind of ghetto and still do. The white landlord makes no repairs. He does nothing for the Negro, who is at his mercy because the Negro can't buy property. The white man won't sell it to him because he's making too much money from him. He's making so much money on rents!

Renek: In *Tragic Ground,* there's a vivid picture of the uprooting that World War II brought to the rural families of the South. These white families from the hills are recruited to work in a war plant in town. When the war plant moves out, these hill people are left unemployed in strange surroundings. They never return home. How much of a factor is this old, war-plant population in the present tinderbox situation?

Caldwell: They're a residue of the old system resisting changes. They have the same heritage as tenant farmers. And, naturally, they're going to try to reinforce their heritage in the city.

Renek: Is it true about the boosters these war plants sent into the hills to recruit personnel? (Caldwell began smiling before I could finish the question.) Did these boosters recruit personnel by handing out a bottle of bourbon to the men and black lace drawers to the women to stir them up to come down to the city and live?

Caldwell's head leaned back and he laughed out loud as though he could still see the bourbon and the lace drawers changing hands. "Yes," he agreed with this picture. "They talked up the city as a nightclub, an all-day nightclub."

Renek: Was the chain gang another source of free labor for the South?

Caldwell: There wasn't much of a chain gang. There was a jail system. [He stopped at the thought of it.]

Renek: Didn't the law promote free labor? You keep the Negro down, in debt, don't educate him, work him hard for peas and old clothes and corn bread, and, if he rebels at these puny wages, you put him in jail and let him work for nothing.

Caldwell: Negro work gangs did all this road work in the South. The South got more road for less tax this way. It was a way the whites had of getting out of paying taxes legally. County commissioner needs more people on the road gang; he calls up the sheriff and tells him to round up more Negroes. If they want gardening work around their house, they call up the jail and tell them to send over some trusties who are Negroes.

Renek: What about those no account, low-whites? What was happening to them with the beginning of mechanization and fewer farm jobs and having to move to crowded cities?

Caldwell: Industry in the South started in North Carolina. The reason was because there was so much surplus labor in the small towns. It was all these whites who had left the farms. That's why these mills sprang up in these towns. They could get cheap labor for their cotton mills. It was always white. And it was always cheap because they had this large surplus of white men, women, and children to draw from. Before the child labor acts, children ten and twelve years old worked in the mills.

Renek: Did this long delayed mechanization raise the sharecropper to a more humane level of labor?

Caldwell: Mechanization displaced the sharecropper. He was no longer needed or wanted. It was all done now by scientific farming. That's when the students from agriculture colleges came down to get jobs on the farms and work their scientific methods. These college students became the new overseers. And the sharecropper had to move out to town.

Renek: Getting down to the basic black-white human relationship

in the South, would you say the relationship is really a triangle with
the white Southern woman a combustible third side?

(Mrs. Caldwell, by that miracle called woman's intuition or perhaps
by something as mundane as reminding her husband of an
appointment, entered the room at this point. Seeing us so seriously
engaged in conversation, she sat down a few feet from her husband
and went back to reading her book without saying a word.)

Caldwell: Combustible?

Renek: From both the white man's and the black man's side. (The
question was getting across and this imagery slipped out.) If we're
shooting pool. . . ."

The suggestion enlivened Caldwell. "Now you're talking my
language." He turned cheerfully to his wife. "Isn't he talking my
language?"

His wife nodded in agreement. She kept a smile courteously in her
cheeks, not wanting to break into our conversation, but finally gave
her quiet, though nonetheless enthusiastic, endorsement of the game.

I happily began again. "If we're shooting pool, the white Southern
woman is the side we have to bank our shots off."

Caldwell nodded "no" slowly. It was the first time in our
conversation he was hesitant. I could tell it was going to be the first
time we differed sharply on the very wording of the question itself. I
started again, this time giving him an illustration from his own works.
"In your novel, *Place Called Estherville*. . . ."

Caldwell: She's not combustible. A white woman is a wife.

Renek: But she can be a provocative wife. She can know just how
much she can get away with. Take Richard Wright's *Native Son*. . . .

Caldwell: I don't know. [He admitted slowly.]

Renek: Whenever sexual tyranny in the South is mentioned, it's
always the white man tyrannizing the Negro woman. What about the
sexual tyranny that exists in the white woman toward the Negro
man?

Caldwell: Why tyranny?

Renek: Call it aggression.

Caldwell: As a general rule, most of the intercourse is between
the white man and the Negro female.

Renek: There's a dramatic opening in your novel, *Place Called
Estherville,* where this spoiled, pretty, white girl is in bed egging on
this Negro servant boy, who knows damn well that if he's caught with

her it's his death. The white girl knows this, too. But she keeps tempting him, forcing the play. In the end, it turns out she got her thrill simply by torturing him in this sexual way.

Faced with this reminder, Caldwell harbored his thoughts for a moment. "The white woman can't afford it."

Renek: That's just it. She gets away with all she can.

Caldwell: [nodding "no"]: She can't afford it. If she has intercourse, she knows what color her baby is going to be. It's suicide. All the mulattoes are born of Negro women and not white women. Did you know that?

Renek: No. I didn't know it and I don't understand. Why not white women?

Caldwell: You never see a mulatto in a white family.

Renek: The white woman would hide it, wouldn't keep it, would lodge it some place, give it away. That's why they're not in white families.

Caldwell: [not convinced of this or at least not fully convinced] A Negro likes to lighten his skin. It's a sport. A throwback.

Renek: Are you saying that it may not be tyranny because the Negro woman may not be resisting the white man?

Caldwell: Negro women are not restricted by social status or inhibitions to have intercourse with white men.

Renek: What about the Negro woman who wants to resist?

Caldwell: The Negro woman was a servant, a laundress, a housekeeper. She couldn't get a job with status. Her job depended on her response. There was a certain threat. If she didn't respond, she could be thrown out of a job. If a family was dependent on her, the threat was implied. Once again, it's economics.

Renek: There are no sexual Hamlets in your stories. When a man gets the urge for a woman, nothing seems to stop him, and your women know this too. Is this recurrent theme your own basic outlook on sex?

Caldwell: It's an understanding of what I've seen.

Renek: If any group has a severe case of racial schizophrenia, it's the Southern white. In *Jenny By Nature,* the owner of a café throws out the light-skinned Negro girl who goes in hungry for a meal. After the owner has thrown her out on the street without serving her, he lowers his voice intimately and propositions her. And he's surprisingly quite subservient to her sexual prowess.

Caldwell: He's a captive of his race. He can't cater to her or he'd lose his business. He knows what his customers expect of him. When economics is not a concern, he can relate to her physically. If there were no economics, the barrier would wear away. It's the heritage we talked about.

Renek: Then, you believe, the whites and blacks can live—ideally speaking—together?

Caldwell: I'm not saying tomorrow. It takes time. But it will happen in the course of time. Just like the amalgamation of European races. [He pointed to himself.] I'm five different races. It's the economic barriers in the South that further racial prejudice. The same thing went on with the Irish in Boston. When the Irish came to Boston they were looked on as coming from a subcultural strata. But then John F. Kennedy from Boston was elected to the White House.

Renek: You dramatized the day-to-day helplessness this same Negro girl has to experience trying to get even an office job in a small town in the South. She continually turns away from those white employers who only want to know her sexual qualifications. The white woman must know what her husband is about. What sexual trump does she play?

Caldwell: She doesn't tolerate it. If the husband is fooling around, she resorts to outright divorce.

Renek: For all his outdoor talk of hunting and shooting, the Southern white man knows he can't out-primitive the Negro man. He never fights a Negro fair and square or man to man, but only gun to defenseless Negro. He covers up this cowardice with lame excuses of the Negro's inferiority. He belongs in some Molière play, except that you can't laugh at him. Is the hellhole bottom of this white man's hatred his own feeling of inferiority?

Caldwell: He has a fear of *becoming* inferior rather than of *being* inferior. He doesn't want the Negro to have a fine house when he can't. This means more to him than anything else. For this reason he must keep the Negro down.

Renek: You've written about Lolitas long before Nabokov came on the scene, and he's considered an avant-garde writer. Do you think this means that Tobacco Road country has been discovered to be everywhere, and that no kind of sophisticated gloss can cover it up?

Caldwell: The trend *appears* to be everywhere, but it is a wild-party trend. In those days, it was ignorance. A family has fourteen girls and wants to get rid of them as fast as possible.

Renek: Did these men and women on Tobacco Road enjoy their sex?

Caldwell: What?

Renek: Enjoy their sex. They're such great representatives of getting it while it's hot.

Caldwell: Sex was their way of life.

Renek: Did they enjoy this way of life? Were the women happier than most women because they could have it when they wanted it, and were the men happier than most men because they could take it when they pleased?

Caldwell: No.

Renek: There goes that marvelous myth of no repression.

Caldwell: Sex was their way of life in that they encouraged girls to be popular to save on the food bills. They wanted them out of the house. One less mouth to feed.

Renek: Their sexual way of life was based on economics?

Caldwell: [firmly] Everything in life is economics. I can't see anything that isn't economics.

Renek: When you brought these Georgia women out in print, you were censored. Do you still remember the furor started by the New York Society for the Suppression of Vice when it tried to ban *God's Little Acre?*

Caldwell: [standing up] It seems like a long time ago. It was the last of the censorship furors after Sumner died [John S. Sumner, secretary and attorney of the Society, who brought The Viking Press into court on an obscenity charge]. Times were changing. You can't stop communication. People became more familiar with books and magazines. In the 1940s, paperbacks came out.

Renek: What with the daring public sex symbols around today, do these backwoods Georgia women now look to Hollywood for the latest views of uninhibited sex?

Caldwell smiled and was amused by the question, even as he gave it serious reflection, and admitted, "It has come full circle."

Renek: Are there people left on Tobacco Road?

Caldwell: Some are still there. They go further and further back off the Road. There have also been less and less families living there because of education. The more education you have, the more the folkways evaporate. People become conformist. Industry brought it about. Individual farms went bankrupt. Industry came in and made money available to build schools.

Renek: Why did the church go along with this brutalizing of blacks and whites and provide the spiritual prop behind this inhumanity?

Caldwell: The church was in a binder. The church was these same people who were enforcing racial laws. The people were the church. Elders and deacons of the church were the same people behind the education of racial prejudice. The church was part of the system. Preachers preached what the elders and deacons wanted to hear.

Renek: In *Journeyman,* you have a prayer meeting with the women shaking orgiastically and the men prancing like stallions. Was their religious *coming-through* primarily a sexual release? One of the women goes through all the contortions of having an orgasm.

Caldwell: It was a social sexual release for these people. You have to understand the close proximity they were to one another in these small crowded churches. There was a holiday atmosphere. It was carnival in the guise of religion. The preacher came with no precepts of theology. And these meetings still exist. Religion was emotional. All emotional. Nothing intelligent. Nothing to do with Christ. They might say, "God is love" five hundred times. That would be the sermon, and they'd be working themselves up: "God is love. God is love. God is love."

Renek: What could have possessed the Negro to join this kind of church that was predicated on white superiority and his own inferiority?

Caldwell: The Negro joined this type of church because he liked music. You couldn't stifle a Negro's love for music. The church was an excuse to sing. That's where his spirituals and folk songs come from. And in church he could whoop up his joy in living.

Renek: When the Negro did make an active move for freedom in the last decade, it was in a profoundly un-Christian way. Dr. Martin Luther King, who has the word Christian in the title of his organization, wasn't giving unto Caesar what was Caesar's, namely the segregation laws.

King's followers were and are heroically passive. Their monumental courage is based on the belief that justice must be gotten here and now. No matter what you want to call it, this is a profound skepticism about the principle that justice is not of the earth but in heaven.

Caldwell: King has appeared at just the right time. He couldn't have come any sooner, for his people weren't ready for him. Now the Negro is getting an education. King can appeal to their intelligence and understanding. His ideas are converting them because he can now get through to them. Education is meeting education. His movement is non-Christian. I don't think the Negro is especially interested in being a Christian. Christianity is a white man's idea.

Renek: Does it hit you that, underlying this affirmative Negro revolution, the Negro has started too late?

Caldwell: It couldn't have happened any sooner. The Negroes weren't ready. They weren't getting an education. They didn't have their present poise. They didn't understand politics.

Renek: I was thinking about jobs. Automation means fewer jobs, not more. When the Negro is integrated, will he be integrated into the nightmare of smaller and smaller job markets?

Caldwell: The human race adjusts itself to economic systems. The Negro will adjust. If there are fewer jobs, he will create more of them.

Renek: It has been speculated about Dickens in recent years that what he really wanted was to write a novel about sex (Caldwell smiled at this irony), but Victorian society and his own reputation forbade any such probings. Do you have such a skeleton novel in your own closet?

Caldwell: I've always written what I wanted to write. I grew up with this attitude. I had no concept of writing other than living it, creating it. I go from one year to the next. See how it comes out.

Renek: One of the most terrifying short stories I've read is "Candy Man Beechum."

(Here Caldwell looked up and smiled broadly as it was obviously a favorite of his, too.)

Renek: Speaking of prophetic writings, you caught the senseless, lawless murder of Negroes by law. In "Saturday Afternoon," the whites lynch a Negro because he's making too much money by his intelligent way of growing cotton. And a boy is selling soda pop at the lynching. I know it's not expected to be in the province of a writer, but have you thought of any way out of this legalized madness?

Caldwell: It's the cruelty. The cruelty of the white man in the

South taking it out on the Negro. He needs something to do. He's trigger-happy. He can't shoot without liability. It's this combination of human cruelty, white prejudice, and his Southern heritage. Gradually this combination will evaporate due to TV, radio, magazines; especially education. We need a Peace Corps in the South. Yes we do. The older people have to die off. They can't be changed. When the older people die off, there'll be a completely different attitude. The older people make trouble by telling the young, "Throw rocks at that Negro." Education is coming to the South. You can't have prejudice in a democracy. If the South wants to be a democracy, Southern prejudice will have to go.

There was a general feeling of optimism as the interview ended, and we walked to the elevator. Mrs. Caldwell and I got into a conversation that touched on French existentialism and her husband's own writings. I said that the Faulkner revival after the war was partly due to the French seeing the chaos they had personally lived through already depicted in Faulkner's South. She agreed, and I added they could have gained this knowledge by reading her husband.

We carried on this conversation about violence in the South right into the crowded hotel elevator. Beyond Mrs. Caldwell's shoulder were two open-faced, conservatively dressed Negro men with conventioneer nameplates on their lapels. They were curious and pleased about our conversation and were instantly drawn to listen. But as soon as we mentioned the word Negro—highly favorable as it was—they turned away, and the light went out of their faces.

Caldwell Assays Sales of Novels

Harry Gilroy/1964

From *The New York Times*. 10 October 1964. Copyright © 1964 by the New York Times Company. Reprinted by permission.

Erskine Caldwell, the storyteller from the South who has a fair claim to being the most popular novelist in the world, stopped off in New York on business the other day to try to keep his literary income at $100,000 a year.

Mr. Caldwell, square shouldered from his football-playing days and with a look of country boy innocence, said over lunch, "I made my first million before World War II, but I don't think I'll ever make another."

He presented his pretty, dark eyed wife Virginia ("She's a good bookkeeper") and asked her the latest sales figure of his books. The total has passed 67 million, she replied.

The publication of his books in paperback covers, Mr. Caldwell said, has produced this enormous figure. "The paperback is the best thing that has happened to authors since the invention of the printing press," he added. "They couldn't subsist without it."

Paperbacks did not come into their own until the beginning of World War II and Mr. Caldwell credits royalties from the play made from his novel *Tobacco Road* for increasing his income when taxes were lower.

In 1945, the New American Library began to bring out Mr. Caldwell's books as paperbacks. "I was their first or second author," he recalled. "They've brought out 35 or 40 of my books in paperback."

A total of 18 of Mr. Caldwell's 44 books have sold more than one million copies. *God's Little Acre,* his most popular, was published in 9,280,122 copies up to June 30. His works have been published in 38 languages and more than 7 million copies have been printed abroad. "There is unfortunately quite a trade also in pirated editions," he observed.

Mr. Caldwell conducts dealings about his books through two agents, Elizabeth Otis of McIntosh and Otis in the United States and Laurence Pollinger in England. Subagents in 30 countries deal with Mr. Pollinger.

He added that his business affairs were handled by Arthur H. Thornhill, board chairman of Little, Brown & Company, Boston book publishers. Some years ago, Mr. Thornhill, at the author's request, bought up all rights on Caldwell books.

"He handles the business side," he declared. "When you own a property, you want it to yield something. Mr. Thornhill thinks it is a good idea to talk to Victor Weybright, chairman and editor in chief of New American Library, and find what his plans are for next year. So they get together, talk about re-issuing books with new covers adding 10 cents to the price to cover inflation and so on. Then it is put up to me whether I like it or don't."

Mr. Caldwell, who is 61 years old, turned from business to writing. He said he had brought to his hardcover publisher, Farrar, Straus and Giroux, a new book, *In Search of Bisco*.

He described it as a work of nonfiction that "deals with 50 years of my life in the Deep South in relation to the opposite life, which is the Negro life of the South." He added: "White life there has changed but Negro life hasn't changed—not in 50 years."

Mr. Caldwell has arranged a lecture tour beginning with a talk in the Library of Congress on Feb. 1. "After that," he said, "it will be back to the typewriter 7 days a week, 10 months a year. That is the other side of these business details."

An Interview with Erskine Caldwell
Alan Lelchuk and Robin White/1967

From *Per/Se* (Spring 1967), pp. 11-20

While the War on Poverty has stimulated a great deal of impersonal debate on the bureaucratic level, Erskine Caldwell has long been the sole spokesman for the individual reality of poverty as a measure of human existence. It has been the focus of many of his books such as *Tobacco Road* and *God's Little Acre,* and it continues to be the basis for the overwhelming international appeal of his work. We asked him about this at his home in the hills behind Berkeley, California, where the following conversation was recorded.

White: I understand that you were the son of a Presbyterian minister and spent most of your early life moving every six months around the South. Do you remember any incidents out of that period which you feel were of long-reaching consequence in your life?

Caldwell: The important thing from my standpoint was the fact that I gained all of my education in that environment. Of course, it was an informal education, and ever since then I have been dissatisfied with formal education.

White: In other words, you feel that experience itself is the best possible education?

Caldwell: Let me put it this way: I learned life as it surrounds a small town in a rural area of America, and I learned it through a country minister. In those days, a minister came more in contact with the raw ingredients of life itself than a doctor does nowadays, because a minister was everything: a sociologist, an adviser, psychiatrist, and so forth. People would break in on him at three in the morning because they had to get married before someone caught up with them; or they would be dying and want to be "saved" at the last minute, even though they had never been religious. And that's the way a minister's life went in those days of the old rural South.

Lelchuk: You describe going around with your father in *Call It Experience,* and he seemed extremely sympathetic to the plight of people less fortunate than he. To what would you ascribe that.

Caldwell: Part of it was due to the fact that he himself was poor and had grown up in a poor family and environment. He understood poverty in a way that an outsider who comes in to look at it cannot. So you might say that he was in the spirit of poverty because that's what he knew.

White: What sort of reception did your father generally receive in a South which was largely Baptist?

Caldwell: That's an interesting thing. You see, he belonged to a small, splinter church of the Presbyterian denomination. He was the minister of what is known as The Associate Reformed Presbyterian, which was basically a fundamentalist splinter group. So he was always looked upon as being a little off-brand. Then, as now, the big three among the Protestant churches in the South were Methodist, Baptist and standard Presbyterian. So his church was looked down upon as being very much of an outsider.

White: Did you ever find yourself in a position of rebelling against your father's religious views?

Caldwell: The thing was, he respected an individual's conception of life and never tried to influence me at all in regard to religion. Mostly he exposed me to it on the outside of the church. That is, there would be various groups in the congregation who would disagree about wanting to do this and that sort of thing; so I grew up very much aware of the various factions that exist in the church. But as far as church itself was concerned, when I got to be about sixteen or seventeen years old, he gave me the privilege of deciding whether or not I wished to attend any more. So I decided not to. And I took this as a liberal point of view, and I have had it *ever* since.

Lelchuk: While your father was intimately connected with religion and the everyday experience of poverty, I understand that your mother taught French and Latin. Did she then represent a more formal educational side of the family?

Caldwell: That's right. She never actually became a part of the religious environment. Not because she felt she was superior, I suppose, but because she had her own conception of life. She considered herself a teacher—and remained one up to her retirement.

Lelchuk: Did she encourage you to read books?

Caldwell: No, we had no books in our house. In the South in those days, you could barely live. You might have a newspaper and an occasional magazine, but you couldn't afford to buy books, and of course in the small towns there were no libraries. So my education was very sparse in that respect. I had no opportunity to read books at all.

Lelchuk: Where had your mother been educated?

Caldwell: At Mary Baldwin College in Virginia. Then she taught at a number of places and finally, many years later, went back to teaching in Georgia after going to the University of Georgia for her Master's. She taught in high school until she retired, and she's still living and still telling me how to write in the English language.

White: Returning to the idea of your being essentially independent at seventeen, was that when you left home and went around the country?

Caldwell: First I went to work at a small weekly newspaper in a town where I'd gone to high school for a couple of years—which was how I got into journalism, so to speak. Then I went to college for a year and after that took off for six months and went around the South.

White: You also played pro football. Where was that?

Caldwell: Wilkes-Barre, Pennsylvania. And it caught up with me many years later, because I got a broken nose that never healed. It developed cancer about five years ago, and I had to have surgery. So that's my scar from pro football.

Lelchuk: At the age of fourteen weren't you at one time captured in the mountains by moonshiners?

Caldwell: Yes, I was with my father. He was the cause of it; it was his fault. We were traveling in a car—it was unusual in those days to have one—and we were going through the Blue Ridge in Virginia. My father got thirsty and wanted a drink of water. So he saw a fellow sitting along the side of the road and got out and asked him for a drink. The fellow said, "Follow me," and took him down to a still. My mother and I were sitting in the car for five or six hours while my father kept saying he didn't want it out of a still, he wanted it out of a spring. But the guy thought he was a revenue agent and wouldn't let him leave all that day. So it wasn't a matter of being "held" captive: the guy just had a rifle and wouldn't let us go until he was convinced that my father was not a revenue agent.

White: This car of your father's interests me. What sort of a car was it?

Caldwell: He had so many cars—always bought every new one that came out, mostly Fords. The first car I remember his having was a white Ford that had three seats. Two were in front, and then in the rear where a seat would be today there was a tool box, and that had a little bucket seat on top.

Lelchuk: Looking back on yourself as a fourteen-year old, what would you say came out of that period?

Caldwell: Well, at that age you don't really know anything, and you're pretty dumb about life. What actually comes out of one's early years, I think, are impressions—lasting impressions of different types of humanity, the levels of humanity, of life that you come in contact with. You don't really think much about it at the time, except that you recognize the differences, whether they're physical, financial or educational. In that era there were great disparities. Even middle class people were very well off compared to the people who were the artisans, and the handimen and the washwomen, and the Negroes. So you get many deep impressions in that kind of life. There was probably more disparity then than now, because it's pretty well leveled off in some respects due to social security and pensions and whatnot, which did not exist in those days.

Lelchuk: In *Call it Experience* you tell of going with your father to Macon and asking Charlie Stevens about a job writing on the County . . .

Caldwell: No, Stevens was the editor and owner of the weekly newspaper in the small town where I lived. Macon was a big city fifty miles away, where I was trying to get a correspondent job on the daily newspaper.

Lelchuk: Well, you were with your father, and you met this man who said, "Oh, yes, I've seen some of the things you've been sending in, and what I recommend that you do is go back to your town and look for yourself and see for yourself."

Caldwell: That was Mark Ethridge, who later became editor of the Louisville *Courier-Journal.* He was then managing editor of the Macon *Telegraph.*

White: When did you go to work at the Atlanta *Journal?*

Caldwell: Let's see, I had been at the University of Virginia for a year, and then I left and got this job at the *Journal.* So I must have been around twenty or twenty-one.

White: And it was from Atlanta that you decided to go to Maine and write. Why did you pick Maine?

Caldwell: I'd never been any further north than New York, and I was curious about what life was like beyond that. I had no great desire to explore the West; I wanted to go north to get out of the South's way of life.

White: Was it in those few years in Maine that you wrote *Tobacco Road* and *God's Little Acre?*

Caldwell: No, *Tobacco Road* was written in New York. I'd been in Maine, and I'd saved up enough money to live in New York at $4 a week. So I went to New York for the winter, because the Maine winters are pretty tough. It gets to be 40 and 50 below, and I decided to go to New York where it was warmer to spend the winter. I had a $4-a week room—a bedroom they call it—in a brownstone right in the middle of where Rockefeller Center is now. And they were drilling all the time, night and day. So I got the rhythm of writing, I think, listening to those drills going all night long. They were making soundings for the pilings and whatnot for what was to be the foundation of Radio City or Rockefeller Center. All around the block, and I was right in the middle of it. Night and day. At least half a dozen of these sounding drills going on all the time.

Lelchuk: So you had gone to Maine, then, for the express purpose of writing, in order to become a writer?

Caldwell: Right. I wasn't doing any good in Atlanta because I couldn't get anything published. And I got unhappy about the newspaper business. I wanted to do my own writing and not what the city editor wanted me to write.

Lelchuk: What did your wife think of this decision suddenly to go to Maine to write?

Caldwell: Well, you know really, you don't know what a girl thinks very often. Either they go with you or they don't.

Lelchuk: She went?

Caldwell: She went.

Lelchuk: She stayed.?

Caldwell: She stayed.

White: So from Maine came *God's Little Acre,* and from New
York *Tobacco Road.* Had you published *American Earth* before you
decided to go to New York?

Caldwell: That was what gave me the money to get there. About
two or three hundred dollars, I think it was. Maxwell Perkins had
been buying some short stories for *Scribner's* magazine, so I
managed to accumulate enough money to live in New York six
months.

White: It must have been soon after the publication of *Tobacco
Road* or *God's Little Acre* that you found yourself no longer a
struggling writer but a prosperous one. How did that transition affect
you?

Caldwell: Well, for one thing I only got a few hundred dollars out
of *American Earth* and then *Tobacco Raod* didn't sell more than
maybe a thousand copies, so there wasn't much income out of that
either. Then when *God's Little Acre* came along a couple of years
later, the publisher thought it was a dirty book and didn't want to
advertise or promote it, so that, too, didn't make any money.

Lelchuk: How many years did you spend as a poor writer? I
mean the beginning ones—those in Maine. Were you there five
years?

Caldwell: It was seven years altogether, off and on.

Lelchuk: How did you support yourself?

Caldwell: By raising potatoes. If you can't do anything else in
Maine, you can always raise potatoes. And you can do everything to
a potato, you know—boil them, fry them, poach them. So I lived on
potatoes, and what I had left over I sold. You can sell them to anyone
who happens to come along, just like you can sell wood. I'd cut
wood in the winter and raise potatoes in the summer. Then I was
getting a little money from reviewing books. I was reviewing for a
Sunday book page and getting books—not getting paid for it, but I
could keep the books, and I'd sell those in Boston. About once a
month I'd take a load down to Boston and sell them to a secondhand
store. That's how I got the cash.

White: And that's still an honored practice among reviewers, isn't
it?

Caldwell: It should be. Because you don't really get paid for it, so
you might as well sell the books.

White: In time, though, you went to Hollywood to do some script-writing. Was that after *Tobacco Road* was dramatized?

Caldwell: Yes, I think production on that began around 1933, and I went to Hollywood around 1935.

White: Ever get to know any of the other writers who were there at the time?

Caldwell: No.

Lelchuk: Did you form any friendships during the twenties and thirties with some of the southern writers?

Caldwell: No. I didn't then and I don't now associate with writers, because I think writers are very dull people. Each has his own interests, and you just waste time talking. So I never knew any writers at all. But, come to think of it, I did know a chap in New York in those days, during the 30's, named Pep West—Nathanael West. He had a situation which was very helpful to me. He was assistant manager of a hotel that was going broke and had nobody in it because nobody could afford to live there: The Sutton, over on the East Side. So he took in quite a few writers like myself at a very reduced rate—something like $5 a week, I think— to keep the windows lighted at night to make it look like the place was doing business. So I got to know Pep West in New York during a period of several months when I lived at The Sutton. And then I saw him a few years later in Hollywood, where he also went the same time I did. And I got to know him, because there was a personality in Hollywood by the name of Stanley Rose. Stanley Rose had a bookshop on Hollywood Boulevard, which was a hangout for people like West and Saroyan—people who were trying to be writers and survive Hollywood at the same time and needed a place to go for common dissent. So I came to know West very well there, but that's the only person I can name as having known in Hollywood.

Lelchuk: Had West published *Miss Lonelyhearts?*

Caldwell: He had been publishing short stories. I don't know whether *Miss Lonelyhearts* was out then, but he had shown me some of his work while I was living at The Sutton. Later, I wrote a blurb for his book. I've forgotten what the book was now, or what the blurb was, but someone told me that he'd seen a blurb I'd written for one of his books.

Lelchuk: Did you like West's work?

Caldwell: Yes, I thought he was a fine writer. Of course, he was wasted in Hollywood, just like I was wasted. I couldn't do anything there.

White: For whom did you work?

Caldwell: I was at three or four studios—you'd be passed around, you know—at MGM, Warner's, 20th Century. I was one of the junior writers, but they paid about three or four hundred a week, which was real money in those days.

White: Do you remember any particular experience that you might say was exemplary of the time you were in Hollywood?

Caldwell: I was sent off on a location trip once, and I didn't know anything about the story or what was going on. No one ever told me anything. I was sent down to an island in the Gulf of Mexico, off New Orleans, for about a month. I couldn't find out what the story was; I didn't even know the name of it, or what they were shooting. All they were doing was going out and hiring a shrimp boat, and then they'd take pictures of it. That's all I ever saw them doing—just taking pictures of a shrimp boat. So I had no idea what was going on. And I got back to Hollywood about a month later, and the producer said, "Well, what do you think about the story?" And I said, "Well, what story?" I was out. I was fired. I still don't know what the story was. Of course, I was under contract for six months, and I had only spent a month, so I had five whole months to go on the contract. They showed me the door, and I went up to my office and sat there for five months. At the end of five months, a guy came in one day and took out my couch. Then I knew I was out. That's how you know in Hollywood that you're out: they take away your couch.

Lelchuk: Did you ever write a Hollywood novel?

Caldwell: No.

Lelchuk: Any reason why not?

Caldwell: I never appreciated Hollywood like some people do, I suppose. It was all so phony to me that I didn't want to get into the phony side of life. I was not interested in the satire of it; I was not interested in the humor of it. When I write something, I like to deal with real people in natural settings, and Hollywood is so artificial it never appealed to me.

Lelchuk: Did you like West's work about Hollywood?

Caldwell: Yes, because he was a confirmed satirist. He knew what

he was doing, and I admired that. But I couldn't do it, and I didn't
want to or try to.

White: What other writer's work have you especially liked?

Caldwell: I don't like any writer's "work," because I don't read
other writers that way. But I admire portions of the work of many
writers. That is, I read one particular thing by a writer. For example, I
was very much impressed by Faulkner's *As I Lay Dying,* which I think
is a superb book. What he did with it I don't think has been equaled
by any other American writer. Now what he did *other* than that, I
don't know. I just like that particular book of his.

Lelchuk: In reading your short stories, I am reminded of some of
Hemingway's techniques—such as the use of repetition to play down
an explosive situation. Have you ever found his stories appealing in,
say, a technical way?

Caldwell: No, not especially. I can't remember anything of his I've
read. I'm sure I read something. But I've never been interested in
how other people write, because I have my own ideas. Of course,
you can't grow up in an era without being influenced by the era itself.
I think that probably many writers in certain periods—whether the
20's or the 60's—have the same tempo, so to speak, because they
are the product of the times. It's not especially a conscious sort of
thing when writers write alike or about the same subject, but the fact
that there are shared conditions—economic, social and political—
makes for a certain tempo. Then, of course, you're always influenced
by something. I may be influenced by journalism because I like the
tightness of good journalism.

Lelchuk: Do you still prefer the short story partly for this reason?
Because of the economy of the form?

Caldwell: Yes, because I learned my writing in journalism. I *think*
I learned it—I hope I did. But if I learned anything, I derived it from
journalism. Because this guy would take his pencil and say, "That's
too much, strike that out. What's the story? What happened?" So
you'd get a concentrated attitude towards writing. Of course,
journalism changes from year to year and decade to decade. Some
of it gets real flowery, and maybe somebody will be influenced by
that. But for me, in my era, I think a lot of writers—Steinbeck,
Hemingway—were mainly influenced by journalism. One of the
newspapers I considered a real model in those days was the old New

York *World.* It had people like Lawrence Stallings and it was a whole
school of writing that may have influenced a lot of us.

Lelchuk: But do you still prefer the short story as a form?

Caldwell: I tend to change from one form to another. I haven't
written any short stories now for five or eight years. When I do them,
I like to do them in series. For instance, *Certain Women* and *Gulf
Coast Stories* were complete collections—in an environment. I like to
do them in a clutch, so to speak, not just isolated short stories. I have
to have a design for eight or ten or twelve, all in one field. Not about
the same people or same thing, but just an environment.

Lelchuk: Will you go back to writing a book of stories?

Caldwell: I'd like to. Right now I'm not, I'm trying to write a
novel. But maybe after this I will.

White: Since you form opinions of specific books rather than of
writers, can you think of another book aside from *As I Lay Dying* that
has especially impressed you?

Caldwell: I was impressed with the short stories of Sherwood
Anderson. I admired the way he could write a short story and get the
feeling of life into it. Not so much what he wrote about but just the
way he did it. I've always admired Anderson for that.

Lelchuk: Have you ever read Isaac Babel, some of whose stories
have qualities similar to yours?

Caldwell: No.

White: How about Mark Twain?

Caldwell: Never read anything by Mark Twain. But maybe
someday.

Lelchuk: Would you say that journalism is a preferred way of
learning?

Caldwell: You can't tell anybody to learn writing a certain way. A
person is going to gravitate into what he's going to do and how he's
going to do it. Some people may learn it through journalism, and
some people may learn it in a so-called "creative" writing class, as it's
termed these days. (I don't see how, but maybe some people can.) If
his interest, if what appeals to him, is journalism, sure, he can learn
that way. On the other hand, if he's an "intellectual" type, he may
feel superior to journalism and look down upon it. But I don't. I think
journalism is the greatest teacher there is. It has all the elements of
writing, the basis of writing. If you can't report something, how are
you going to write about it in a novel?

Lelchuk: This is somewhat tangental, but wasn't it in 1942 that you spent six months in Russia as a correspondent?

Caldwell: It was 1941. For nine months. In Russia and China combined.

Lelchuk: Did that lead you to read any Russian novels?

Caldwell: Well, now, you see, I get this Soviet magazine every month, in English. I look at it, but I don't get much out of it. It's too discursive for me. As for Russian writers, I don't read them. They don't interest me. Too much out of my field, maybe, and I don't comprehend it.

White: What of your experience in Russia? I have the impression that it was extraordinarily exciting for you.

Caldwell: I guess any war is when it really hits you.

White: But in this instance you seem to have gotten a grasp of people and place, almost as if your experience in the impoverished South had imbued you with a special sense of appreciation of poverty in Eastern European countries.

Caldwell: Of course it's a different type of poverty you find in Europe. You might call it almost "elegant." Not the same as our American poverty. Because they always have their wine, you know.

White: Do you feel that the sensitivity manifest in both your travel and war accounts might be responsible for the enormous interest in your works in the Eastern European countries?

Caldwell: In my limited knowledge of the world, I cannot find much difference in human life and human behavior from one nationality to the next. When you get to know people and see how they live, it's all the same. The style of clothing may be different, and the political philosophy may vary, but basically, socially and economically, it's all the same. The same race of people. We call it the human race. And maybe it's my view of that which accounts for the interest.

Lelchuk: Is the question of poverty, the question of human survival, one that you feel can be eternally written about and provides a kind of substance that a satiric novel about Hollywood would not?

Caldwell: Wasn't it a long-ago historian or writer who said, "The poor will always be with you?" Well, it hasn't changed in 2000 years, and I don't think it's going to change now, no matter how much the Great Society expands. There is always going to be poverty, and it has a leveling influence in life and among different peoples. I mean, if you could get the people of Vietnam together with the people of Mexico, I think they'd get along very well together and understand each other, because both of them live in the same poverty-stricken environment. So there's the tie, I believe. And of course wealth is artificial. It's been created. It's not natural. Just the cumulative effect of a lot of rich rabbits, or something. The normal, average person is a person who struggles to live; whoever and wherever he is, he has to struggle in some way to live.

Lelchuk: Would you say that someone growing up in affluence is cheated of an important experience?

Caldwell: Well, you see, he does not think so, because he does not know anything else. He lives in his own environment, and he thinks that's life. Of course, it's only a small part of life. But he's satisfied, and he's entitled to that, even if it isn't normal.

Lelchuk: Recently, Jean Paul Sartre said that he's made a mistake in his past books by not writing about common suffering, and that for any writer to speak for all mankind we must include that experience and deal with it. Is it possible then, that the trouble with western writers is that they are not looking at the important themes?

Caldwell: The affluence of America these days is not conducive to what I would call substantial writing anyway, because it's now all shock, and how loud you can shout, and how perverse you can be, which is just not basic to life. It's completely artificial, the writing is artificial—an attempt to interest somebody who is already jaded with these things. Your percentage of book readers is very small, and if a writer is going to cater to jaded tastes, he's got to be more loud and shocking all the time in order to hold his audience. Well, that sort of thing doesn't appeal to me. I don't think it's the purpose of writing. It should be the basic elements of life that you write about: how people live. You might not reach them all, but at least you can depict it. These real people might not be affluent enough to buy a book—even a fifty cent one—but they make life, and that's what's worth writing about.

Lelchuk: Does that express your purpose when you went to Maine to begin writing?

Caldwell: I wanted to write about life as I found it. And to find it you must know how people are living in other places, because if you stay in one environment all the time you can never compare what you understand. You have to find comparison somewhere, and in Maine I found it.

White: Have you ever thought about going to Vietnam and writing about the people's side of the situation there?

Caldwell: That's beyond me. I'm past the age. That's for the younger person.

Lelchuk: Would you ever recommend what Malraux did—going from a secure environment into a country where there is torment—as a way for a writer to escape his own limited perspective?

Caldwell: In my philosophy there is so much going on in America that's not being written about that you don't have to go somewhere else to find something. I could think of dozens of regions—and I believe in regional writing—where life right now in this great, big country could be fascinating to a writer but remains untouched.

Lelchuk: Could you name a few?

Caldwell: Look at the Mexican life along the border states from California through Texas. That's never been written about to any great extent or with much ability. There have been passes at it, but nothing solid. You see, the Mexican-American is living a very different existence because he's not accepted, and he's not rejected. He's border-line, just like the border states he's living in. Once in awhile people rise out of that element, but they're really not accepted and they don't want to be. They want to remain who they are. And then you get your wetback people, for example—the laboring class who live down in Imperial Valley the whole year around. They're not just seasonal workers. And they live in abject poverty. Along the Rio Grande through Texas it's the same way. So that's an element of American life that I think has been overlooked. And I think it's an important one, because the Mexican-American population makes up an important part of the economy and social and political life through Southern California, Arizona, New Mexico and Texas.

Lelchuk: Have you heard of a book called *The Children of Sanchez?*

Caldwell: Yes, but I haven't read it.

Lelchuk: It's written by an anthropologist in a novelistic fashion— five stories in first person—rather than data and statistics, and is perhaps better than most novels simply because the subject matter is so new and powerful.

Caldwell: There are many regions of America that might be

treated like that. As I say, I'm a great fan of regionalism. I think the
Cajon country in Louisiana also has a lot of possibilities for a writer.
The French bayou country. It's so different there from the way people
live only a hundred miles away. A little country of its own, with its
own language and customs. This has been very much overlooked. Of
course, things have been written about it, but it's never been done
well. A writer by the name of E.P. Donald, I think, wrote one book
about it a long time ago. He was the only writer who really knew the
so-called Evangeline Country, the Cajon.

Lelchuk: Why don't the young men who want to be writers think
in terms of these things?

Caldwell: Because mostly they get taken out into advertising,
radio and T.V.

Lelchuk: What about the very young writers, I mean. Is it that
they get grabbed up by the educational system and produce a certain
kind of novel that's meant for a "decadent" society, or the jaded
tastes that you spoke of?

Caldwell: The trouble with young writers these days is that they
mature too early. They get into a Creative Writing course, and they
learn from their instructor: Here's the great novel written last year,
why don't you do something like that? So they use that as a model to
stamp out another impression of the same old thing. These guys, who
are young and impressionable, get sidetracked from the real stream
of writing. All they do is imitate. They imitate, and they try to make it
a little more loud, shocking or something in order to get the attention
of the audience. Or else they go into advertising. They think: I can get
a thousand a month, so why try to write a novel? Same way with
television.

Lelchuk: So if a Zola, say, lived in America he might do just the
kind of thing you're suggesting.

Caldwell: If he didn't have his own personal integrity he would. I
think it's the fault of instruction that does it. I can't see that the
instructors are helping students when they try to get them published.
They try to get them to make money first. And that's not the whole
point of learning to write.

White: You feel that the publishing climate itself in the United
States today might have some inhibiting factors?

Caldwell: Very much so. You can't get a publisher to take a first
book unless there's some gimmick behind it. If he can't sell at least

5,000 copies, he's not going to touch it no matter *how* good it is. That's the economics of it.

White: What are some of the things that might be contributing to the enormous economic pressure that publishers face?

Caldwell: Ten or fifteen years ago, fiction was a commodity that was in great supply and great demand. The magazines were full of fiction. Publishers were publishing books of short stories. Every publisher had one or two books of stories on every seasonal list, and novels everywhere. Now you look at a publisher's list and you rarely see a book of short stories. There might be some reprints and anthologies, but very few books of short stories. You look at a magazine, and if you find one story in it you're doing well. So the publishers take the next easiest step, which is to put out non-fiction. They say it is in great demand, that everybody wants facts, they don't want fiction. Well, here's a bunch of books that came in the other day. From one publisher. All in reprint editions. There are about twenty-five books in the pile. I think if you find two novels there you're lucky. There are two or three mysteries, maybe two novels, and everything else is . . . stuff. So you see, they don't take a chance on a novel, but they'll take a chance on the non-fiction stuff. They'll take a chance on *any*thing that's non-fiction, because they think they're going to have a market for it. But a novel? Why, it might get bad reviews, and that's the end of it.

White: So you'd say, then, that one of the main contributing factors would be the increasing emphasis on non-fiction?

Caldwell: There are a lot of factors involved in why that is, too. For instance, your entertainment is coming out of television. It's all free to look at. So why pay to read fiction when you can sit there and look at free entertainment. That's one reason why fiction is in short demand: because there's so much competition from television.

White: Are the agencies playing any kind of role in the general market situation?

Caldwell: Oh, they just swim with the tide, you know. A publisher says, "I don't want to read any novels. Give me some good fact books, comic books, anything." And the agent tries to come up with the stuff.

White: Is this downward trend of fiction going to be an irreversible one in your opinion?

Caldwell: I don't think so. I think fiction will always survive and

will come back stronger, because when this gets over, when the
situation gets saturated with stuff, people are going to revolt and want
something different. I don't think this applies to Europe at all. I think
that in Europe, in my small knowledge of England, France and Italy,
for instance, fiction is just as strong as ever.

Lelchuk: Do you think it might take a very great young writer to
emerge to bring back the interest in fiction?

Caldwell: Maybe. But how is he going to emerge in the present
situation? On top of that, he's got to go to college (to keep from being
drafted, for one thing), and there he gets exposed to all this
pernicious influence of "creative" writing imitation. Some day
somebody's going to shoot me for saying that, but I've really got a tic
about it.

White: What about critics and criticism? Would you say they might
have something to do with the decline of fiction?

Caldwell: My estimate of critics is at a very low level, too. I don't
think there are very many critics in existence these days. Most of
them are superior personalities who are pushing a prejudice of some
kind. They pick up a trend, and they push it. They can't look at the
overall field of writing because they're too narrow in their opinions.
On the other hand, you have the reviewers, whom I respect. I have
always respected a reviewer. But not a critic. In the old days I think
there were many good critics who appreciated and had a wide field of
interest in writing—which they don't anymore.

Lelchuk: People like Malcolm Cowley, Kenneth Burke, Joseph
Wood Krutch?

Caldwell: They belong to that school.

Lelchuk: They all wrote about you, reviewing your books.

Caldwell: They wrote about *everybody*, They just didn't pick out
one or two and try to make an oracle of them, or God, or something,
as it happens now.

Lelchuk: Were they maybe reviewers first and critics second?

Caldwell: That's one way of putting it.

White: In this difference between the critic and the reviewer,
would you perhaps say that the whole area of reviewing itself might in
some way be contributing to the decline of fiction? That maybe the
reviewers, like the agents, are swimming with the tide?

Caldwell: The reviewer likes to be in good with the advertisement
department so he can be sure to get the advertising. Also, he wants

to get the books to review in order to hold his job. If he doesn't, he's going to get complaints from the upstairs' office: nobody's reading this page anymore because we don't have any advertising on it. These guys are really in a precarious position. Usually they have to have an outside moonlighting job to keep going. They have to teach, or something. Maybe have a college post and review on the side. There's just not much room for a reviewer in the present economy.

White: In other words, there is an actual, subtle, financial pressure brought to bear on the reviewers? a pressure of advertising money that can influence review opinion?

Caldwell: Well, let's say a reviewer has this job. Whatever he's getting for it, he's got to keep in good with the upstairs' office. If a publisher complains to his boss, saying "Why are you panning all my books?" that's bound to have an effect on the reviewer.

White: What about the over-concentration of the publishing industry in New York right now and its ability to bring this sort of pressure to bear on supposedly independent review opinion nationally? Isn't this somehow almost intellectually incestuous? in a way that might further contribute to the decline of fiction?

Caldwell: In my experience I do know that the day of the traditional individual publisher is becoming more limited as time goes on because of the mergers and concentration. It's eliminating the sort of publisher that Alfred Knopf used to be. Knopf was very much of an individual undertaking. Now he's combined with Random House, and that's out. As these things build up into larger and larger publishing enterprises, the individual has less and less to say. It's all becoming a reflection of what the business office of the combination says about the kind of books that are supposed to sell. Maybe they say, "We can't sell that. This is a book of short stories, and nobody buys a book of short stories. We can't take this out on the road." So all right, that has a repercussion right there.

White: That, of course, would be traceable to the sales staff and the retail outlets.

Caldwell: The salesman is on an expense account, and he's got to earn a certain amount of commission. With the hotel rate going up to $25 a day, he's really got to sell something in order to keep his job.

Lelchuk: But you didn't write for publishers. You wrote for yourself.

Caldwell: Yes, I wrote for myself, and I still do.

Lelchuk: Which is to suggest that if there's a decline of fiction it's because of a lack of great novelists rather than pressures on the publishing industry, that it's only the boy whose head is swelled with promises, or he's ambitious, or he wants to be successful, rather than he wants to write books.

Caldwell: Well, there's so much more to it than that, you see—so many facets and elements involved. Right now in France, for example, they say that unless you get an award or prize for a novel, you do nothing, nobody buys it. Well, they have twenty-five or forty annual prizes going on in France. So that's the only thing that matters to a publisher. He fills out the rest of his list, but he wants that one annual prize for such-and-such. That's what happens in one field. But this is *all* fiction. Here there's no inducement like that: after the Pulitzer Prize, what do you have?

Lelchuk: There are various publisher's prizes.

Caldwell: They are too limited and too few in comparison to the number of books that are published.

Lelchuk: Have you ever had an editor whom you've liked a lot? You mentioned Maxwell Perkins. Did you get to know him?

Caldwell: Not very much. He wasn't an easy person to know.

White: Are there any great editors coming up who would be in the category of a Maxwell Perkins?

Caldwell: There haven't been yet. I've known quite a few since Perkins, and there isn't anyone I'd put in that category.

White: And on that note we might leave the publishing industry and talk about the state of the South today. Al?

Lelchuk: Yes. In *Close to Home,* at the very opening of the book, which was in 1962 after a lot of the agitation and turmoil about Civil Rights had begun in the South, you have Native Honeycott saying that it makes no sense to hand the world over to the agitators and politicians because they just keep things in turmoil and start wars and make trouble for the ordinary people, who only want to live and let live. Don't you think that much of what's going on in the South is alleviating some of the problems of the unfortuante? According to this quote, the suggestion is that things are better off if they are left the way they are.

Caldwell: You have to understand that that quote was the attitude of a fictional character, which doesn't necessarily reflect the attitude of the writer. When you write about a created character, that's *his* opinion—the expression of somebody else who had that philosophy

about it. You take the average Southerner around 1962, and that's
the way he felt. Of course, his opinions are changing rapidly all the
time, due to the pressures of segregation and Civil Rights. It's
increasing in a ratio to the effectiveness of education. The younger
people are getting more of an education than Honeycott ever had,
having grown up in another era many years ago. The sense of
complacency is his. Well, maybe that's the attitude of a lot of people.
But as time goes on the general public outlook changes. Five years
from now you'll get a completely different attitude from the same
person, if he lives through this. He'll accept things more readily than
he would in 1962.

Lelchuk: So all the agitation that's been going on in the South
you feel has to be educational.

Caldwell: Yes. People learn from it. In the history of America,
there has always been progress. There's been no retrogression—
unless you want to call the John Birch Society a retrogression. But as
a general thing, American life progresses. And I don't mean
economic progress. I mean social progress.

Lelchuk: You don't feel emotionally ambivalent about the South
being torn in half?

Caldwell: Nobody can put time limits on a thing, saying this is
going to end on such-and-such a date. There are too many human
elements involved, and of course that makes for a certain distress.
But the older generation is dying off every minute of every hour of
every day, and the younger generation comes up every minute of
every hour of every day. And these new people are getting educated
in a different kind of way. Naturally they're getting a prejudice at
home, which carries over because prejudice survives from one
generation to the next. But it becomes lighter and less as time goes
on. You take a family where the mother and father are sixty years old
and have three children in their twenties. Well, the change of attitude
is so apparent there. And you find the same difference in any part of
the country. Right here in California you see it between the younger
and older generations. So five years from now there's going to be an
even greater acceptance of Civil Rights and a greater acceptance of
integration than there is right now. And in ten years it's going to be
even more so. It's a progressive kind of thing and will go on and on,
until eventually segregation is wiped out.

Lelchuk: If it is wiped out, what then?

Caldwell: As I say, you can change human nature up to a certain point. In other words, someone is always going to have a prejudice of some kind—a religious prejudice, or a color prejudice, or a social prejudice. But I think acceptance of human rights is going to progress from one day to the next. I don't think there's going to be any violent revolution about the whole thing anywhere. Of course, it looks like it every once in a while. You hear about it on television and in newspapers: riots here and there. But that is a passing phase.

Lelchuk: Will there come a day in the South when a situation will exist so that a book like *Close to Home* could end with the Negro maid staying with the native, ignorant southerner, who by then wouldn't be so ignorant, and social conditions would prevail that would permit them to live together?

Caldwell: I don't know how far you can go that way. I have seen white girls and Negro men, and vice versa, in the South on the street together two months ago, which you would not have seen five years ago. That's just a small trend. Whether they live together, I don't know. But at least when you see them walking along the streets together, that's a radical change from the old days.

Lelchuk: Even the consciousness of the Negro maid in *Close to Home* is, I think, a radical change from the consciousness of a Negro maid of, say, twenty years ago in the South.

Caldwell: When you compare, too, the lives of people in the South, you see the mixture of blood that is coming in the lightening of color among Negroes. It is so easy to recognize the vitality of this new breed of people, the people in between the white and black, these mulattoes and octaroons. And they are certainly going to have an effect. You can't escape it. They will be accepted because they are too vital. It's going to liven the whole civilization. It'll help in the other way, too, vastly of course. But I think you're always going to have a prejudice—the white and the black, the Jewish and the Christian, the Democrat and Republican. You're always going to have that going on. But you can socialize. Democrat and Republican don't have to get in a fight about it. They might vote differently, but they can socialize if they like each other. So, too, this medium that's going on—this color difference in the middle—is going to have a great effect. Because you're going to see more intermingling of the races. This has been the foundation of America anyway. And it is the foundation of the future.

Erskine Caldwell:
Down South Storyteller
Jack McClintock/1968

From *Florida Accent,* magazine section of *The Tampa Tribune* and *The Tampa Times,* 2 June 1968, pp. 8-9. Reprinted by permission.

DUNEDIN—If Erskine Caldwell were to sit on the colorful flower-print couch in the library of his house, and stretch out his arms to both sides as far as they would reach, which would be about six feet, the tips of his fingers would cover only about one-half of the span of the packed bookcase behind him.

The shelves are laden with copies of the various editions and translations of Caldwell's books. It is a large bookcase, for Caldwell has written and published a great many books—50 of them, to be precise.

There was *Tobacco Road* of course, which began to enrich our language in 1932. People would point at a row of dirt-bound shanties by the roadside and say, "Look, just like Tobacco Road." Before long they were saying, "Look, a tobacco road" and the term had become almost generic.

And there was *God's Little Acre,* one of the most famous novels in the world. It has sold more than 10 million copies in 40 languages, which may be a world record, and makes Caldwell's name familiar to peoples who never heard of such American folk heroes as Ronald Reagan or Rap Brown. Years ago, when Caldwell had published about 15 books, Murray Sinclair of the Associated Press wrote that he was "probably the world's most widely read living author."

The author is 64 now, even more widely read, and still writing. He finished his 50th book only a few months ago—a novel entitled *Summertime Island.* "It's the story of a fishing trip on the Mississippi many years ago," he says.

Much of Caldwell's writing springs from his experience of the Deep South, especially the rural south. His major novels do, and so does some of his non-fiction. A recent book, an informal study of Fundamentalism, is entitled *Deep South.*

103

Caldwell has only contempt for writers who play expert, but if there is a genuine expert on the American South in this century, it must be Erskine Caldwell. With him, old times are not forgotten.

"There's a deep heritage here that doesn't exist in other regions," he says. "It's not a nationalistic heritage, it's a social heritage—a great tradition of two things, of ancestry and of causes.

"The Civil War history background welds it together, makes it different from the rest of the country. And the climate is a big factor in keeping tradition alive: warm, semitropical, fertile, situated in a rain belt. The land, too: the fact that it is small holdings instead of large mechanized holdings as in the West, makes the South more . . . personal."

After some years in the San Francisco area, Caldwell has moved back to the South with his fourth wife Virginia, an attractive, pixie-ish dark-eyed brunette. The couple has bought a large house in an expensive new subdivision where the lots are all at least one acre in size, a fact which will sooner or later lead some precious wit to dub Caldwell's new homestead "Erskine's Little Acre." (If someone hasn't already, that is.)

Caldwell is in a position of real luxury today. He is not only materially successful, but artistically redeemed. If he were the type, he could say I-told-you-so, for Erskine Caldwell used to be referred to by a lot of people as that guy who writes dirty books. It has taken time, but mores are catching up with him and the others who insisted years ago upon writing about life—in all its aspects—as it really is and not only as prudes were willing to admit it is. There was a time—hard as it may be to imagine today—when writers were expected not to mention sex, for example, let alone make it funny sometimes. Caldwell did.

"I don't put it in to be banned," he said years ago. "Neither will I take it out to prevent a ban."

As a writer, he was telling it the way it is long before it became fashionable to phrase it that way. Yet, in four or five hours of conversation, Caldwell never used a so-called four-letter-word.

Erskine Caldwell doesn't look like a writer—a statement silly enough that it will probably amuse him! He once made a satiric talk to a group of aspiring young writers (it is reprinted in his book, *Writing in America*). In it he instructed them solemnly on how to assume a writer's Image, adopting a few harmless idiosyncrasies, perhaps an unusual haircut or a writer-type hobby. He concluded, in fact, that it is possible to spend so much energy and time creating your writer's image that you have no time or energy left for writing.

Caldwell himself resembles a retired Georgia farmer as cast for a naturalistic John Huston movie. He has bland blue eyes, a red face and reddened, freckled hands that have handled things heavier than typewriter keys. His gray hair is brushed straight forward and cut off short, almost like bangs—which may be a contrived idiosyncrasy or an elaborate, subtle Caldwell joke: One of those poses he mentioned in his speech to the writers happened to require bangs. He's a quiet man, almost shy. He laughs rarely but he means it when he does. When quoted and frozen on paper, some of his statements seem snappish, but they are invariably uttered in a gentle Georgia voice.

"I don't associate with writers," he says. "Writers are dull people. They're single minded. All they think about is self and work. Or they think they're experts on every subject you can think of." Caldwell's friends, he says, are journalists, TV and radio people, people in publishing and "the fringe professions."

He doesn't even believe that people should be encouraged to write. Not because he thinks there should be no writers, but because to become one is so difficult that only a driven soul will make it.

"Don't study law or medicine or business administration. Just learn to be a writer," he says in a wry drawl.

"Well, that's about the worst advice you can give anybody."

"My premise is to discourage it," he says. "If somebody has talent and you discourage it, they'll want to prove they have it."

Like most writers he gets pestered by hopefuls. "Some of them send a condensed biography or episodes from their life. 'I'll furnish all the rest of the material if you'll write it,' they say. These frustrated writer types who can't even write. . . . You can't take somebody else's story and write it. That's silly."

He asked that his address not be printed. Caldwell suffers other pests too, often women who want advice on their marital difficulties.

"They read something I wrote and they think it applies to them and that I know how to help them out," he says.

If there's anything Caldwell doesn't care for it is writers taking advantage of the rather common, if mistaken, belief among many readers that a writer is ipso facto an expert on everything. (The same belief is not uncommon among writers.)

"Writers are overrated as commentators on contemporary society," he says. "They have no qualifications to be leaders; they're storytellers."

For a long time Caldwell has been among those writers who considered storytelling a craft worth pursuing for its own sake, sufficient unto itself, without loading the thing down with mystical significance or selling it out in exchange for a buck.

Born in rural Georgia, the son of Presbyterian minister, Caldwell grew up in a household that was probably unusual for a writer. "We had no books," he says. "We had no money for books. It was no fault of my father's, just the fact that in that social environment—people today don't know what poverty is—there was just no opportunity."

When he was 15 he got his first book, Gibbon's *Decline and Fall of the Roman Empire*. He won it in a school geography quiz.

"That was the first book I remember reading cover to cover," he says. "I guess I was excited at winning that contest and getting this book, the first book I ever owned. I read it and reread it." He also remembers the old Tom Swift adventure series—*Tom Swift and the Electric Cannon* was one.

"I used to read those, every one I could get," he says. "They were an adventure and I may have been influenced. Because I have wanted to venture out ever since to see what the real world is like."

He ventured off to the University of Virginia, where he made a fortunate discovery in the library basement, one that made a difference in his life. The so-called "little" magazines of the day were printing a new kind of writing.

"They were written in a new style so much different from the style of the books in the big library upstairs," he says. "I became intrigued by writing. The books were remote from life as I saw it and was living it. I wanted to write about contemporary life, not about the past."

And he did. He had worked for local newspapers as a boy in high school and now he went to work for the *Atlanta Journal,* an experience he says he wouldn't trade for anything. He left after a while to write fiction, moving to Maine and living on an abandoned farm.

"I raised potatoes and cut wood," he says. "I kept eating and I kept warm. I got a few people sold on letting me review books. I was doing the Sunday books page in the *Charlotte Observer,* and got books by the bushel. Every few weeks I'd throw them on the back

seat of the car and take them down to Boston and sell them for a
quarter apiece. That's where I got my money."

He has also been, at various times, a cotton picker, stage hand, pro
football player and Hollywood film writer.

"Film-writing was not my medium," he says. "I had no ambition to
be a movie writer. But in those days they paid a lot of money and it
was a good thing to do. It gave you a lot of experience—which you
have to have to be a writer, I discovered," he added wryly, scratching
the side of his nose.

Caldwell had seen the bottom and he had come closer to the top
than most people ever do.

"From his numerous and fantastic jobs," said the *Encyclopedia
Britannica* article on him, "he not only gained an extraordinarily
broad experience of life in the U.S., but also developed an active
social conscience."

There have been critics who argue that Caldwell's work revealed
motives more akin to those of the reformer than the artist, that he
was trying to make the world over. Caldwell denies it, and close
reading of his work bears him out.

"I grew up in the Great Depression so I wrote about that," he says.
"Sure you protest about poverty, injustice. But that grew out of the
mood of the time.

"My interests are in social-economic subjects. Those are the basics
of life. Politics spring from that. I'm not a political person, and you
don't have to be a Democrat or a Republican to be interested in the
basics of life. You're going to find flaws—because they're there. So
that's a protest right there. But as far as agitating is concerned, no. I
let the material speak for itself."

Caldwell, in fact, maintains that the material often surpasses the
writer who is using it. "A novel has to have more than a superficial
knowledge of life. But the fact that a writer did it, doesn't mean he's
superior. The material must be. He doesn't even know what he's
doing sometimes. You can't create a new race of people, for
example, as in science fiction. You have to write about people as they
are. That's why I say a writer is no special person at all."

That time-sanctioned practice—now dying out—of dedicating one's
book to friends or wife or agent or publisher is, Caldwell believes,
absurd. A book should be dedicated to its own characters, the entities
which give it whatever life and value it has—even though the author
may not completely understand how he accomplished it.

Ego has a great deal to do with good writing of any kind. Any writer must believe he has something worth saying, worth saying as honestly as he knows how, and he must believe he is able to say it better and more originally than anyone else. If he has that conviction his writing is vigorous and truthful. Caldwell knows this, but he is just as aware of ego's limitations.

"You have to have confidence," he says, "but it can get out of control, out of hand. You think everything you do is good. But you've got to be your own critic, your own judge. You've got to have the backbone to throw that thing in the wastebasket when it isn't good."

"Some people don't like adverse criticism. I like it, it keeps you on your toes, keeps you sharp."

Traveling keeps you sharp too, and it is a special interest of Caldwell's. He has been a foreign correspondent in Mexico, Spain, Czechoslovakia, China, Mongolia and Turkistan, and a war correspondent in the Soviet Union (about which he also wrote a book) for *Life* magazine, CBS and the now-defunct newspaper *PM*.

"We usually get in one or two auto trips across America every year," he says, "and to Europe now and then. The people are a good comparison with Americans. The more you circulate. . . . "

His publishing contract calls for him to "circulate" for six weeks every year, a task he sometimes finds as onerous as some people find the pressure to circulate at cocktail parties. But he must travel about, lecture, sign autographs and promote his books. "I get tired of talking about myself and I get bored," he smiles. "You find yourself saying the same things over and over. So I don't usually have interviews the rest of the year, except in exceptional circumstances."

In a recent interview he was asked about his reading habits. He said: "Being a writer and a reader at the same time is a difficult occupation, because if you're going to read a lot you have to write less, and I'd rather write more and read less."

That is probably the difference between the would-be writers who get their kicks out of pestering the pros, and the pros themselves. Caldwell reads, but doesn't let it interfere with his writing. He lets nothing interfere with that. Hence, his advice for those aspiring writers.

"The only way I know of to get a book published," he says, "is to write a good one."

The Art of Fiction:
An Interview with Erskine Caldwell
Donald Lewis and Richard Wertman/1968

From *The University of Virginia Magazine*, CXXXII (November 1968), pp. 4-9, 24, 26.

On Homecomings Weekend, the new UVM "office" at 47 West Lawn took on a peculiarly literary atmosphere as Editor-in-Chief Donald Lewis and Literary Editor Richard Wertman spoke with Erskine Caldwell and questioned him about the art of fiction-writing. Mr. Caldwell, accompanied by his wife, stopped at the University in a gracious response to a summer UVM request for an interview. A prolific writer who has explored, in his fiction, many regions of this country and abroad, Mr. Caldwell is perhaps best known for two controversial works dealing with the South—*Tobacco Road* (1932) and *God's Little Acre* (1933).

Mr. Caldwell's career has consisted of a great variety of jobs, from mill working to semi-professional football. His chief source of livelihood for the main part of his life, however, has been writing. Now sixty-five years old, Mr. Caldwell continues to write. He is at present at work on a novel which he refuses to discuss, but which he hopes to finish by the new year. For the past four years, Mr. Caldwell has been on a professional lecture tour which has included stops at fifty to sixty colleges across the country. He offers colleges soliciting his service a choice of two titles, both of which actually denote the same lecture. Interestingly and ironically, the basic purpose of that lecture is "to show the hardships of writing and to discourage students from trying to become writers." Aspiring young authors, take note. At the time of this interview, Mr. and Mrs. Caldwell were en route from their home in Dunedin, Florida, to Dartmouth, where Mr. Caldwell would "walk the campus for a few weeks."

Mr. Caldwell attended the University of Virginia "on and off" for four years. He failed to take a degree here because he neglected to take "certain required courses" which failed to appeal to him. During the time he spent in

Charlottesville between 1922 and 1926, he anonymously
contributed a "few jokes" to the now-defunct *Virginia Reel*
(a humor magazine which has since been replaced by *The
Cavalier Daily*). Mr. Caldwell has never failed to give credit
to the University, and has in fact attributed much of his
success as a writer to "inspiring courses" he took while a
student here.

UVM: Mr. Caldwell, what is the basic intent of your writing?

Caldwell: I've always wanted to be a story writer, a story teller.
The only thing that interests me is the story itself. I have no message,
I'm not trying to prove anything, I'm not trying to change anything—
I'm trying to tell a story. I try to tell it as interesting as I can, but it has
to interest *me*. I don't care whether it interests *you* or not. If I were
trying to tell a story that would interest you, I would be so baffled that
I wouldn't know how to do it. I have to tell it so that I like it, and if I
like it, I'm willing for you to try to see if you like it. If you don't like
it—well, that's okay. My philosophy is that maybe half the people are
going to like what I do, and the other half won't. But as long as I like
it, I'm satisfied. I don't take reviews seriously. If I read them or if I
hear of them I say, "This is just one guy's opinion."

UVM: Have any basic changes taken place in your writing from
the days of *Tobacco Road* to the present?

Caldwell: There are really no basic changes. The only change is
in environment and in people, because I've moved around so much.
I've written about New England, I've written about the South, the
Midwest; once in awhile I've done something a little bit different, and
I've written a few novels in Europe—Russia and so forth. But that
was incidental; that wasn't the main theme of it.

I always have written and still try to write contemporaneously.
What I would write today would be the happenings of today, as of the
time of writing. They might be told in perspective, though, in what is
sometimes called a flashback. For a character always has a past. He
was born ten years ago or forty years ago or fifty years ago—so he
certainly has a past, and in order to write about this person as a
contemporary, you have to go back to some extent to indicate what
made him what he is today. I write about 1968 as I might have
written about 1948 or 1958 or as I might write about 1978. I write
about it as it is, but always with that historical background.

Recently I've written several novels that took place in the
Mississippi Valley, which interests me because I have a feeling for it.
What I'm going to do next, or what the change is going to be next, I
don't know. I'll wait and see. But that's the only change that I have.
The basic thing is always the story. The only change is in the locale of
a story.

UVM: Is it fair to say that you've maintained a simple,
straightforward style from the beginning?

Caldwell: I've always tried to write in the most simple style, and I
still do. I fail sometimes because I get carried away with enthusiasm,
and think maybe I have discovered a way to embellish something.
But that's so false with me that when I go back to revise it I always
strike it out and try to be simple. I don't think this is an age of
embellishment. I think this is an age of realism, simplicity, directness. I
appreciate the fact that another writer might have another conception
of present-day style, but what little I know from my reading, which is
very little, I haven't found any contemporary writer who has
improved on simplicity.

UVM: Do you find achieving this simplicity to be a difficult matter?

Caldwell: Simplicity itself, I think, is the most difficult thing there
is. Simplicity makes clarity; and if you want clarity, you're going to
have to work for it. It's not a gift; you're not born with it. I think I
started out in life with the idea that I was never going to use a word
that had more than three syllables—two if I could, but three if I got in
a jam. That sounds very peculiar—but you have to have some basis
of simplicity. If you can use a two- or three-syllable word in
preference to a four-, five-, or six-syllable word, by all means use the
shorter word. Because you will get that much closer to the meaning
of that word. The conjunctive putting-together of a lot of compounds
to make a word diffuses a word and makes it weak. That original
word is what you should seek and search for and try to grasp. Once
you get that, then you've got the meaning and got the clarity in your
writing.

UVM: To what extent do you attempt to employ symbolism in
your writing?

Caldwell: I don't think I try to do that consciously at all. Because
to me, in writing a story the story is implicit in itself. It's not something
that you devise and fashion to make a symbol, to make symbolism.
But symbolism may come out of this incident or story. I could not

consciously set out to make a theme symbolic of anything. I try to be implicit—and if the reader finds symbolism in it, well then, fine. I'm pleased that he did.

UVM: How difficult for you is the act of writing itself? How hard do you find it to get down to writing; how long does the creative process take?

Caldwell: We'll start talking about a short story first, because in my mind the short story is the origin of fiction. The first thing you write in life is a short story because you're not capable of writing a lengthy novel. You have to practice with the short story, you've got to perfect *it* first. In my experience, short story writing was the finest and best teacher I ever had, because it was something you could realize very rapidly. To write a long novel—three or four or five hundred pages—takes a year. Two or three years sometimes. You might do a short story in a week, you might do it in a month. You get a quick realization out of this fiction you're writing: you can see it more quickly, you can see it in a shorter period of printed space. And if you really like to write, as I do, you want to write as much as you can. And you're never satisfied because once you think you've perfected your story as much as you can, you immediately want to do the next one.

I don't know how many short stories William Saroyan has written, but in his early life there were times when he would write a short story a day. He learned he wasn't spending enough time on it, so he gave himself a week to write a short story. I had very much the same feeling about it, that I wanted to write as quickly as I could and then go on to the next one.

You *should* have learned something from short story writing by the time you try to write a novel. I say you *should*, maybe you don't. You have to realize that a novel is not a series of short stories. It's not a long short story. A short story is usually just one incident or maybe two related incidents. Whereas the novel encompasses many things, many incidents that you build right on top of another like you would build a brick wall. You put one right on top of another to reach the pinnacle you're trying to build. So what you learn in writing a short story you almost have to unlearn when you write a novel. Yet at the same time you've got that basis that you learned. Then you get a feeling of something bigger, something greater, and you know you're going to have to bring in more people or more events, more scenes and everything else that goes into the novel. It enlarges the idea of a fiction completely.

Of course, writing isn't always successful. There are many people who write these things and throw them in the wastebasket. I've thrown more short stories in the wastebasket, I suppose, than I've written for publication.

Now a novel . . . you know you're going to have to spend a year at it. At least I do, I give myself a year. I don't want to take *too* long because there's another book I know I want to write, and I don't want [to wait] too long to start the next one.

I start out working very slowly. I only work about six or seven hours a day, four to five days a week. At the end of two or three weeks I'm writing six days a week and eight hours a day. Pretty soon it's going to be ten to twelve hours a day, seven days a week. Then you find there aren't enough days in the week.

Once you get involved in a long piece you want to finish it, you want to perfect it. You don't want to waste it, and so you're never satisfied. I don't think any good writer is ever satisfied because he can always find his own defects. He can't always improve them, but he can see more defects than a critic can see in his work. You're always trying to improve, you've got to rewrite it, rework it, throw it away and do something differently to make it work. You have this conception in mind—it's not on paper, you can't put it down on paper, you can't make an outline. It's like a cloud up above, it's up there and you can't touch it, you can't see it; you can't even feel it but you know it's up there and you've got to get the essence out of that cloud whether it be sunshine or rain or drizzle or snow. But you can't get it on paper, you've got to get it in your mind, and then it's got to filter through you like you're filtering moonshine whiskey or something. You've got to filter it through yourself; it has got to come out of your emotions.

UVM: Do you find yourself doing a lot of revision, going through numerous copies of a short story before you find one you're satisfied with?

Caldwell: Yeah . . . yeah. Eight or nine, in fact. Not less than that, either. I'm working on a book right now—I don't want to talk about it—but it's typical of what I do. I might do one page fifteen or twenty times. Then I might still not be satisfied and I might have to go back to the page before that and do that one over. Because you have to reach way back to get what you want in the present page. You might have to go back a chapter or two. Or even start all over again.

UVM: Has it always been this way throughout your career?

Caldwell: No. When you're young, you're so intent, so sure, and have so much confidence in what you're doing that everything you write is great. You can't be bothered with self-criticism. You don't want any criticism from the outside, and you don't want to criticize yourself. As you grow older and get more experienced in life, you find more faults with what you do. The longer you've lived and the longer you write the more critical you become with yourself, the more you're dissatisfied with your work. I probably would spend twice as much time writing something now as I did fifteen or twenty years ago.

A lot of things change. I've tried various methods, various ways of writing things. Sometimes I'd go off and hole up in a cabin in the mountains somewhere and dig in for a month or so at a time and just stay there day and night. I've tried that—and I've tried working in various kinds of situations: in the city, in the country, everywhere. Nothing's ever the same; I like to move around. I like maybe to move into a motel, way off somewhere in another state, and to work there for awhile. Then go off to *another* town. Take a typewriter and yellow paper and end up doing things differently. I have nothing against people who can turn out a mystery story every month like a lot of them do—I admire those people, but *I* couldn't do it. I have to do something different all the time.

Either I want to write very rapidly or very slowly—write a draft out and put it away for a week and go back and do it over again. Write straight through or write a middle chapter and then go back to the third; or write a fifth chapter and then go back to the second. There are so many different combinations of ways of writing. The writer himself has to figure these things out; I don't think you can lay down any rules or regulations as to how it's done. Each writer has to figure out what suits *him*.

UVM: Mr. Caldwell, you've frequently been accused of obscenity. Precisely what part does sex play in your fiction?

Caldwell: Writing about sex is to me the same thing as writing about religion in a person's life—it's part of it. If you leave it out, if you shirk it, what you're doing is depriving yourself of this element of the story. You must write as a character is—it all depends on the character. I don't approve of a lot of things my characters do that I have to write about. I deplore their language sometimes, because I don't like profanity. But they have to do it, and I have to write about it.

If you're writing about someone's sex act, you have to write it as that character would carry it out. People become fanatical about a lot of things; so you can become a sex fanatic and write nothing but sex stories. Or you can switch around and write stories that are basically propaganda for a political system. Well, I don't. If I were going to do it, I'd do it, and be a fanatic about it, I suppose. Same way with sex, religion, politics. I do it just as it is—no more, no less than what the characters are doing.

UVM: What are your current reactions toward censorship?

Caldwell: I've only written one book that has actually been banned—in the state of Massachusetts; it was banned ten years ago. It couldn't be banned today. What is censorable today would have put a person in jail, would have cut his head off fifty years ago.

What has happened is a change in mores, so what we have now is a custom of freedom in writing. Censorship is negligible, it hardly exists. Maybe five or ten years ago, you can't write something; maybe now you can. Maybe in another five years you can't. These things go in cycles.

Personally, I disapprove of any kind of censorship, being a writer. I don't know if I were something else—a politician, a preacher, a professor—whether I might not have different ideas. But as a writer I don't approve of any form of censorship because I do my own censoring. Anything that I think is inappropriate for a character, I wouldn't write. Even if I thought it were going to lift up the sales of the book. It would be false.

UVM: You've given this University considerable credit for your successes as a writer. In what real ways did the University of Virginia contribute to your achievements?

Caldwell: As a student here I was very fortunate in the sense that I found what I needed and what I desired. I had a great desire to learn English, to learn how to use these simple words in two or three syllables. And I was very fortunate in my English courses in having good instructors and professors who gave me "inspiration." Also I was very fortunate in economics and sociology courses which I wanted and which to me were the bases of writing. If you study economics and sociology, then you're studying people. And what makes people is what makes stories. So you have this great variety in life to write about. My trouble in life is that there's so much to write about I can't do it all. I have to eliminate everything until I get to what I think is the greatest.

Any success I have had comes right out of what I call my University of Virginia background because this is where I got my education, and I got my education here because I had the opportunity to get inspiration out of these courses. Sociology inspired me more than music or drama or painting or anything else you can think of. All that was over my head. I was not educated enough to appreciate music or drama or poetry. I would go out to poor houses and insane asylums and places like that—I liked that.

UVM: Speaking of poetry, did you ever attempt any?

Caldwell: Everybody has, sooner or later in life. I wrote poetry, sure. I wrote a whole batch of it. I wrote—well, you can call it poetry, I suppose. It rhymed, with meter and everything. I had about fifteen or twenty pages of it, and I thought it was the greatest stuff that was ever written. I sent it to the man who at the time was probably the leading poet and critic in the country—Louis Untermeyer. Right back, it seemed to me the next day, he said in effect, "Forget it." And I did.

That's why I say everybody writes poetry—until he learns better.

Some people are tuned to different methods of writing—poetry, drama, essays, journalism. All that is in the field of writing, it's all legitimate. That's fine; that's what *they're* tuned to. What *I* want to do is write fiction. Just being a fiction writer takes everything there is. I don't think I could do anything else.

I do like journalism. I think that journalism is about the best instruction a fellow can get outside of a University. I think it is a much better field for learning than so-called "creative writing" courses. I can never quite figure out what they are or what they do for you.

UVM: Was it easy for you to become published and to gain a reputation?

Caldwell: It's not easy for anyone that I know of, and it certainly wasn't for me. I was writing short stories forever, it seemed to me, and sending them around to anybody who had a magazine. And nobody would publish them. That went on for such a long time that I wasn't ready to give up, but I certainly wasn't very happy about it by any means. I couldn't get any stories published in magazines that would pay anything. I wasn't writing to get paid; I was writing to get published, though. In those days there were a great number of so-called "little" magazines that published fiction and poetry but didn't pay anything. I ended up getting my first story published that way and it wasn't in the United States at all, it was in France. It was published then in the English language—about seven or eight years later. So that's how hard it is—seven or eight years of trying to get printed.

UVM: If you had had a more immediate success, do you think you might have "sold out"?

Caldwell: That might happen to anybody, if you had an immediate success. I didn't *want* immediate success. What I didn't like about a so-called "successful" novel was the fact that the author must have got the idea that he was pretty good; so he didn't have to improve himself or his writings. He was satisfied with what he had already done, so he didn't have any inspiration, or enough impetus to try to do better. So he may have repeated himself the next time. You can do that maybe two or three times . . . and then you're through. That's happened to a lot of people who write a very successful book. I had a sort of wish that I never wanted to have a best seller, because I'd seen what had happened to a lot of people who wrote one book and then they were done. I wanted to write all my life, I wanted to keep going.

One example was a fellow who was a very good friend of mine. He wrote one book which was a war book. When he wrote this book—I'm not going to mention his name or the title—it was a great success in the sense that it was, well, a "book-of-the-month club" choice and had a hundred thousand pocket sales, etc. He took in so much money that he thought he was so great that he didn't have to work at writing any more—he knew everything.

He said, "I'm writing another novel, and it's going to be just as good a money-maker as the other. I don't work in the daytime anymore. I go around and play golf, and do this, that, and everything. At night I have a good, fine dinner—the best dinner I can buy. Then I lie down on the couch and talk into a machine and write my book that way." Then, of course, he had a secretary who came in and transcribed these things.

He never got the book published and hasn't written a book since. And he was on relief the last time I saw him. So that's why I say I never wanted to write a best-seller. Of course, I don't know what I'd think right now . . . I might change my mind. But not in those days, not starting out. No. It's the worst thing that could happen to you.

UVM: The late William Faulkner once ranked you among the top five contemporary American authors. Would you care to do your own ranking as of today?

Caldwell: No. I don't read other people's work in that sense; I read so few. I only pick out half a dozen books a year to read. I don't keep up with it, so it'd be too much guesswork. I think that's the province of a critic, anyway. I'm not qualified to do that at all.

UVM: Have you done much classical reading of any variety?

Caldwell: No, no. You see, I like what I do, I like what I write. And I have to work at it so hard, so much, to make me like what I'm doing that I have no time to read somebody else. I might be influenced by someone else if I read someone else's work. I don't want to be influenced because I want to be my own influence. After I work on a book for seven days a week, eight or ten hours a day for eight to ten months, I don't want to see anything in print except a newspaper or something.

UVM: Do you ever re-read your own works after publication?

Caldwell: No, never have. I might be influenced by that if I did. I don't want to repeat myself. I want to do the next book as it comes at the time. There are so many influences in life that if you go back and read a book you wrote ten years ago you might say, "Well, it was a pretty good book, so I'll write another one like it." Or even unconsciously you might be influenced, even if you don't consciously try to imitate the earlier work. I don't want to be influenced. I want to write today the way I feel today about a thing.

UVM: Just how vital is personal experience in the art of fiction?

Caldwell: You could not write about anything you had not seen or experienced and do it authentically, or believably. What you write about has to be in part based on some personal observation or experience. But that's only the beginning of it. Then you have to bring imagination to that idea or experience. Reporting is not fiction; it's mere fact. What *actually* happened isn't, of course, going to be very interesting, anyway. You have to bring imagination into the basic reality to trap an emotion in it, to make it come alive.

The purpose of fiction is to create what does not exist. It has never existed before. You have to create it to make it real. And you don't create it, you can't create it, without imagination. Otherwise what you're going to have is just a photograph. You have to find a language which will translate a scene into an emotional quality which tells far more than just a photograph. You've got to make things more real than life itself. My whole theory is that fiction is more real than life.

UVM: When you begin a story, do you know what the eventual outcome will be?

Caldwell: It has to work out by itself as it goes. I never know how a story is going to turn out. I don't want to. I'd be bored by the whole thing if I knew.

UVM: Contemporary writers seem to a large extent preoccupied with the artist as protagonist. To what extent does the artist appear in your novels?

Caldwell: I did write a novel about a writer [*Love and Money*]. He was a no-good bum. I didn't do it with the idea of trying to prove that the artist was a great influence in life or had any great artistry. He was a writer, but he was just a bum. I have a low regard for writers and the mentality of writers. I don't think I'd waste my time trying to write a story about a writer with the idea that he might have any great philosophic ideas to impart to the world. I don't think the writer is a thinker; if he were a thinker he would be a philosopher, maybe, and have a good teaching job in a University. I don't think a writer has any qualifications to be an oracle of anything. The only thing a writer can do is write a story. If he tries to do anything else, he's a bum.

An Interview in Florida with Erskine Caldwell

Richard B. Sale/1970

From *Studies in the Novel*, 3 (Fall 1971), pp. 316-31. Reprinted in *Critical Essays on Erskine Caldwell*, edited by Scott Mac-Donald (Boston: G. K. Hall, Inc., 1981), pp. 279-93. Reprinted by permission.

Richard B. Sale, an editor of *Studies in the Novel*, interviewed Erskine Caldwell in Dunedin, Florida, on January 29, 1970. Erskine Caldwell's novels of rural Southern life have been critically and commercially successful for forty years. Although he has published many novels on the Southern theme, *Tobacco Road* (1932), is still his best-known work of fiction.

Sale: Mr. Caldwell, I have the impression that for a while your work was picked up by the Marxist critics as an illustration of their point. Then they turned you off when they felt it wasn't. Was that true in the late 1930s?

Caldwell: I wouldn't know the motivation behind that kind of attitude. What I do know is that when I was trying to write short stories and get them published in the little magazines of the day I had nothing to do with the so-called large circulation magazines; they didn't print my stories. But the little magazines did for a number of years. And to me it didn't matter what the motivation of the editorial policy was as long as they printed the story. So I was probably on both sides of the fence, the conservative and the liberal. I don't know if anybody ever gave me a great fanfare for writing along the Communist line. Maybe they did, but I wasn't aware of it. If I did write that way it was because it happened to be the way I was writing, not because I had any active motivation for it. I vote, but I vote for the man and not the party. That's been my policy. I wouldn't say I'm even a Democrat or a Republican at the present time, or have I ever been.

Sale: Does the Southerner represent a large part of your reading public?

Caldwell: Well, that's difficult for me to say; I don't know anything about the breakdown of the circulation of a book so much. Traditionally, of course, more people read books per capita in the North than they do in the South, so they say. But as for how you break those sales down, I really don't know.

Sale: Do letters from readers give you a general impression of reader reaction?

Caldwell: I don't know how to answer that because the kind of letters I get are really from students more than anybody else. I guess students these days are a little more sophisticated or open-minded or whatever you want to call it, and there seems to be no particular pattern to where they write from. Fifteen or twenty years ago, I would get what I call pan letters, pan letters which said, "Why do you write about the bad side of life in the South? Why don't you write about the good side of life in the South?" But that has died out completely. I guess that generation's died off or stopped reading or something. I don't remember getting anything like that recently because in recent years it's been mostly from students, and from no particular region. So I don't know who the other book readers are right now. I've never seen a typical book reader anyway. I don't know a typical Southerner. Maybe everybody's typical.

Sale: A few minutes ago you mentioned that country people used to be taken up with fundamentalist evangelical religion. It was true of many people throughout the country. Is anything around to give the people that temporary excitement that everyone seems to demand in some form or another? I have the feeling that those particular kinds of religious institutions are fading out. And if they're fading out, what's going to give people that emotional kick? What's going to give them all that sex and violence that they got from the church?

Caldwell: Of course, speaking lightly of that, it's always been my theory that all these country musicians and folk singers out of Nashville, the new generation of the old religious revival people in the back hills of the country, these people are all the younger generation that came out of the hills and down to Nashville. They're the country singers of the time and make more money than their fathers ever made back in the hills making moonshine or anything else. And, as you know, there might be a lot of good things coming out of that environment. We know all the present day popularity of Kentucky Fried Chicken.

Sale: Do these little churches or itinerant preachers still get the same number in their congregation or in their audiences or in their revival sessions as they did in the past?

Caldwell: They're getting bigger all the time. They're becoming more sophisticated. Billy Graham and Oral Roberts are the most successful ones.

Sale: Well, are they giving the people that same tremendous emotional kick that they had in a small, sweaty one-room church with the temperature rising?

Caldwell: I think there are two phases to that old-time revival back in the countryside. One was, of course, the emotional uplift due to rhythmical music and singing songs and preaching, but basically that emotionalism was stimulated by the fact that these people had something to do and were being entertained in a way. That was before the advent of television and before most of the picture shows. I think in the old days the people sought that out, immersed in it because it was entertainment. Now, of course, in keeping with the tempo of the times, these evangelists have to have a great stress upon music. In the old days a small organ would do but—

Sale: Now they have a minister of music.

Caldwell: Now they have to have a musical leader with a number of performers in the band or the orchestra or the choir or whatever it is, to make a lot of noise. Something else developed, the musical side of it, just as much as the old hell-fire preaching ever did. There's very little that people can preach against any more. When life becomes so sophisticated, it's hard to arouse anybody by preaching about sin. So you really have to sugarcoat the message with a lot of entertainment. I think entertainment probably is just as important as ever, even more so to attract a crowd. And they do attract the crowds. All up and down—I don't know about Texas, now—but all up and down this Atlantic side, revivals by traveling evangelists are still very much in vogue. They might have them in a convention center. I don't think they use any tents like they used to do, but they'll take over an armory or a school where they draw big crowds. But it's always with this musical accompaniment. That has a lot to do with it. The people still go.

Sale: It's just a more sophisticated replacement? The tradition hasn't vanished?

Caldwell: I don't know how much longer the religious grip is going to hold the old people, I mean to what extent. I guess it's going to stay because I notice that the collections I hear about in churches are still pretty good. As long as that money comes in, why, it's going to keep on. Of course, if the states begin taxing church properties and churches, making them pay a sales tax on collections, it might make a difference.

Sale: Let's talk a little bit about humor in your books. Some of the short stories that I read seemed to be strictly for fun, and most of your work has humor mixed with serious matters. Humor is a means of relief, a contrast to the serious matter of a novel or story. Do you consider humor as a device when you're putting a story together?

Caldwell: A question like that is a little bit baffling to me, because I don't know the reasons for these things. I only know what happens when you're doing a story. And I think if I had to find some excuse for this way of doing, say, a short story, I would answer that in life, maybe not in fiction but in life, there's always a balance there between tragedy and humor. The most tragic occurrence can also have its humorous aspects and vice versa. When you are telling the story of an occurrence that does have a tragic overtone or tragic burden, if you look beneath it or beyond it or to the side of it, there's always some humorous incident or some humorous aspect to that story or to that event. And I wouldn't know consciously how to go about doing it. All I would know is that it happened that way when the story was told.

The most serious incident could go to a tragic extreme; yet there's bound to be some light side to that whole affair. A man might be swimming for his life. He might be in danger of being drowned, and yet if he survives that tragedy, and does not drown but comes up on the shore, there's bound to be some reaction in which there's a light side to that great event in his life where he almost drowned. He would say something like, "I thought I was gonna die," or "I thought I was gonna drown." But what he was actually thinking about was something trivial which might be irrelevant to the whole idea. In other words what was going through his mind not only was the danger of being drowned but the thought of some humorous incident that had occurred or might occur.

Sale: A crab was pinching his toe.

Caldwell: Or something. Anything at all that would sort of balance that great tragic moment. So I think that's what life's like. I think that's real.

Sale: Whether you planned it to be that way or not, humor also heightens that crisis.

Caldwell: I couldn't explain it. It's just that it's the way it occurred to me. I don't know why or what, but it had to be that way. Otherwise it would not be satisfactory to me.

Sale: In the novel, *Close to Home*, there was a jarring juxtaposing of comedy and the most intense violence. What was your purpose there?

Caldwell: Well, you ask a question there that embarrasses me because I don't know why I do certain things. I have no forethought. It's just something that develops that way.

Sale: Were you happy with doing it that way?

Caldwell: Well, I had to be; otherwise, I would have thrown it in the wastebasket.

Sale: You wouldn't have sent it to the publisher?

Caldwell: When I'm not satisfied with something I throw it in the wastebasket immediately.

Sale: You've never been reticent about throwing things away?

Caldwell: No, I've got the biggest wastebasket in town. So that's the method I use to file an error. I try, and if there's an error, I throw it out. I have to be satisfied. If I'm not satisfied, I don't want anything more to do with that.

Sale: Can you recall any one particular published book that's given you more difficulty than any other?

Caldwell: Well, no. No. I couldn't. Because by the time I finish a book I'm sort of numb. I feel that if I've gone that far with it and this is what it says here now, it must be right; therefore I'm satisfied. But as for trying to analyze it, I couldn't do it. I'm just too numb with the idea because it's all been used. It's all been expended and there it is. I have to be satisfied page by page as I go, not with the end result but with the page result. One page may be done a dozen times, but I won't go to the next page until I'm satisfied with that page. I just have to go at it that way.

Sale: Has that always been your working procedure?

Caldwell: Yes.

Sale: You don't write a number of pages and then make serious revisions?

Caldwell: No, I like to see the page. I like to see the typewritten page the way it should be in a finished condition. If I have to cross out something or write something in, well, I'll go back and do that page over again to make it look better, to make it look more like print, rather than look like a sprawling mess or something. So I'll do it over maybe a dozen times because I might change one word or ten words or one sentence or take out half a dozen. But if it doesn't look right, if it looks messy, if it looks imperfect, I have to go back and do that page over on the typewriter to make it look clean and finished.

Sale: Have editors ever severely edited your work?

Caldwell: No, no. I learned early in life that that was not necessary. Maxwell Perkins was the first editor I ever knew and he published a number of my short stories in *Scribners* magazine, when *Scribners* was a respectable periodical. He was also book editor of Scribner's, and he also published a collection of my short stories in a book. The first novel I wrote after that was *Tobacco Road*. I remember very clearly that he wrote to me about it and said that he was going to publish the novel and that it wouldn't be necessary to change anything in it. So I took that to mean that revision could be done by the writer and not by the editor.

Ever since then I've gone on the principle that that's the way it is. Now if I make a mistake in grammar or something, I'm very happy to have it brought to my attention. If it escapes me and it escapes my wife, Virginia, who proofreads, copyreads, everything I do before I send it out, if it escapes both of us, I'd be very happy for an editor to say this is the wrong construction or something. But as for changing something, no. I say just forget it. Send it back. Nothing has ever been changed that I have written.

Sale: So there's never been any serious conflict between you and the publisher about revision?

Caldwell: No. I've moved enough from one publisher to another for various reasons but not for that reason. I've been with a half a dozen publishers in my life, but not because of any editorial difficulties. When I write something, that's the way it's going to be as far as I'm concerned. Whether somebody else likes it or doesn't like it

means nothing to me at all. That's the way it is. Not that I think I'm
perfect or anything of this sort, but I did the best I could and I don't
think anybody else could tell me how to do it any better. If anybody
else could think so, why hadn't I thought of it myself? So I wouldn't
take that kind of advice. Well, you know a lot of editors around these
publishing houses think they have to take a book apart to hold their
job or to get a lot of praise from the upstairs office. But you see that's
something that doesn't interest me at all, what their troubles are. I'm
only interested in what I'm saying.

Sale: Did you find Perkins to be an excellent editor?

Caldwell: Well, excellent in the sense that he never changed
anything. He gave me a lot of advice, nothing to do with the writing:
He said stay out of New York. And he would never take me to a
restaurant to eat, even for lunch. We'd go to a hamburger stand, hot
dog stand, stand up and eat.

Sale: What was the reason for this?

Caldwell: He said too many young writers come to New York and
eat very luxurious restaurant meals and they get the idea, they get the
feeling that this is the way it's going to be. Their ideas get warped
about being a writer. They think everybody's entitled to luxuries in
life, which is not true. Oh, he'd have a long talk about those things.

That was the best advice I ever had from him. I got out of New
York, too, and stayed out.

Sale: Yet you did some writing in New York. You stayed in New
York for some work, didn't you?

Caldwell: Yes, I went there to live because I didn't have anywhere
else to go. But I had nothing to do with the publishers at that time. I
was living unknown to people, publishers. I was just trying to write
stories. I did that off and on for a couple of years.

Sale: Have you ever had any problem finding a publisher since
you published *Tobacco Road*?

Caldwell: No. The reason I left Scribner's was because one of the
Scribner's people—someone by the name of Scribner, Junior or
somebody else, it had nothing to do with Perkins—didn't like a book
I had written. They took me in to their oak-paneled conference room
and gave me an hour of advice about writing. The duty fell on one of
the editors, who was not Perkins. He gave me a lengthy talk about
what I had written, how it was not suitable for the book readers who
bought Scribner's books, how many of these readers are very proper
elderly ladies who would be offended if they published a book of the

nature that I had written. And so he advised me to write another book with that in mind. I said, "No, thank you." And I walked across the street to the Viking Press and they published the book. That was the closest I came to not having a book published.

Sale: Back to the matter of humor. Randall Jarrell, in very warm praise of several of your works, said that one of the better things that he had seen in your humorous writings was the technique of understatement and repetition. Frequently, one of your characters will say something and then very quickly repeat it again and maybe a third, or fourth time. Is this to portray that character more clearly?

Caldwell: That's just the way he would act.

Sale: People just repeat themselves?

Caldwell: That's just his nature to say it. I couldn't. I wouldn't want to change his nature. I wouldn't want to edit the character, in that sense. I just have to do what these characters demand.

Sale: Do you work for an incantation effect by repeating key words of key statements several times? Is there some kind of magic to it?

Caldwell: Well, you see it's difficult for me to make a comment even on that. I always have to write this story about this person the way he is. And he's already formed himself or he is forming himself in my mind because I don't know who he is. I never saw him before. He's a new guy to me. So I have to go along with him whatever he may do. I might not approve of what he does. I might not like his language. He might be too vulgar to suit me, but I can't help that. He's already gone that far. You can't go back and start over with him, make him different. If somebody has certain characteristics, well, that's the way they have been growing in my mind, the way they're living, the way they are. So I have no control over these people.

Sale: Your main interest, when writing, is not the effect on the reader?

Caldwell: I don't do that intentionally. I don't know what my characters are going to do next, and that keeps my interest up in the book I'm writing. If I knew what they were going to do all the way to the end, I'd be too bored to go ahead and write the thing. Because then I would already know. Now these people have to expand or grow or be as they live from one minute to the next, from one day to the next. So I have no policy or method of doing these things about people. It's just what the people want.

Sale: You don't do any such thing as work out the structure of a novel and know what's going to happen in the last section of the book in advance?

Caldwell: I fear I wouldn't know how to make an outline. I wouldn't know how to make a progress sheet. I wouldn't know how to do anything like that.

Sale: No kind of interim plot outline?

Caldwell: Nothing. I don't have any notes. Nothing of that kind. I don't want them, because then you're restricted, you're constricted by what you've presupposed may happen. How do you know what's going to happen? How do you know who's going to come along? It might be a man or woman. It might be a giraffe or an elephant. How do you know what you're going to see when you walk out? So you're not going to sit here and write a story and say there's an elephant coming down the street. So you've got to wait and see what appears. Maybe it's going to be a horse. We don't know.

Sale: Do you make it a practice to notice the details of your surroundings, the sort of details of Georgia sharecropping, what farm gear looks like, what the harness for a team of mules looks like?

Caldwell: Well, let's put it this way. You see, everything, every piece of fiction, is based on experience.

Sale: Yes.

Caldwell: We're not considering science fiction, of course. The fiction we're talking about is based on experience, and the experience has to be in the mind of the writer. Now this experience is not necessarily something that you went out to find. It's not something you went out seeking. It might be something very casual at the moment but it might become momentous later if you recall it. So when you ask, do you see details when you're out somewhere, traveling around, going to the country, the answer is sure, you see everything. But it might make no impression at all at the time. No impression whatsoever. But in recollecting, you think, oh, I saw that tree that was bent over by a hurricane. It was falling on a house. I remember that now. But at the time, well, you see nothing. You look beyond that. It's just a flash as you go by, but you recall it. So everything is experience. Every writer has to have some kind of experience to write upon. But you don't go out looking for experience. If you go out and do that you're crowding it. It becomes too obvious and then it's authentic. So you don't have to go out and marry ten women in order to learn something about female characteristics. The mind has a recollecting ability to it and so it will recall something that's made some deep impression upon you earlier. It doesn't have to make a deep impression to begin with. The details of what you have experienced stay with you. You recall them, you recall them because one thing leads to another; it sort of snowballs, builds up, and first thing you know you have the whole clear complexion of certain conditions or circumstances or people.

Sale: What you've said over and over is that you are your only reader, that if the writing says what you want to say then you accept it.

Caldwell: I'm the reader. I don't know that I have any other readers.

Sale: You wrote somewhere that, if you are not your own satisfied critic, you don't deserve an audience.

Caldwell: Did I say that?

Sale: Not exactly; but you meant, I think, you were writing for yourself.

Caldwell: Yes.

Sale: And if you represent enough interests of other people, then they'll buy your books. They'll first accept your books and then buy them.

Caldwell: Well, of course, I never think of books being read by other people. I think of mine as being printed and bound, and that's as far as I go with a book. I don't consider who's reading a book or how many are. But I'm sort of pleased by someone who says he read such and such a book. And what pleases me most are the people who are *not* critics. They're not dilettantes. They're not people who are trying to put you on. It might be a bellboy in a hotel, somebody you meet in a bar, or just anybody who comes along. You know he's not trying to put you on; he wouldn't have said it if he hadn't read it. Of course, there's a lot of forced reading going on.

Sale: Are publishing patterns changing?

Caldwell: The impersonality of publishing is becoming very apparent and acute. Someone gave me a *New York Times*, yesterday, I guess it was, in which there's a piece about New York publishers running wild, playing musical chairs. That's no joke because what has happened as we know is that the corporate enterprises are taking over publishing, like RCA or Hertz Automobile Rental. They're buying up publishing houses. And the people in the

business, the editors, the presidents, are constantly moving the past
few years. As I say, I've been with many publishers in my time, and
I've noticed that the people I thought were in a publishing house are
not there today. They were there yesterday, but now I don't know
anybody there. The impersonality of publishing I think does worry a
writer who's been accustomed to having a sort of feeling of stability
with a publishing house. Now the younger generation of writers will
probably grow up being accustomed to this musical-chairs situation.

The younger generation will probably become accustomed to it
and expect nothing else, but the older generation to which I belong
will certainly become disconcerted every once in a while when the
guy you thought you knew who was in charge of everything
suddenly moves out and some guy you never heard of takes his
place. That's one of the trends or changes in publishing which is
probably going to continue the corporate idea of mixing up candy
companies and automobile rental companies and the publishing
house—making a conglomerate of it.

Sale: Did you begin your writing career by emulating other
writers? Any specific writer?

Caldwell: Well, all right, that's very easy to answer, if I can explain
myself about it. This is how it happened. You see I'd been in
journalism, sort of a country-style journalism, weekly papers and
what not, and I'd been the country string correspondent, covering
sporting news and what not. Every month you paste up a column.
You get two dollars for it. And so when I was in high school, I did
have maybe five or six string correspondent jobs in Augusta, Atlanta,
Savannah, Macon, all around in Georgia. I got out of high school and
was fortunate enough to get a scholarship to the University of
Virginia. That was my first window to the world.

When I got to Charlottesville, I discovered that there was a library
at the university. I hadn't anticipated finding a library. I thought a
library was a place where you had a lot of dusty old books,
dictionaries, and so forth. But this library had a basement room, a
very small room devoted to contemporary or current publications,
publications we now call the little magazines. They were experimental
magazines and they came from all over the U.S. There were some
from England. There seemed to be dozens of these small magazines
in existence which I'd never heard of before. I didn't recognize the
names of anybody who was writing these stories, and I still don't
know who they were. They were just guys writing short stories they

couldn't get published anywhere else, all experimental. I would read these things and I was amazed that all these people were writing stories and being published, and I thought I could do it better than they did. I started trying to write the kind of story that I would write or could write, not imitating what they were doing, but with the idea that they could be written. There were no names that I would recognize even now. That's how I got the idea that I should write my way rather than somebody else's way. I had no models to go by other than the fact that here were sort of offbrand names, guys who were writing and had succeeded.

Sale: So there were no big names to emulate?

Caldwell: Big names were selling their stories to the *Saturday Evening Post*, and I had no interest in the *Saturday Evening Post*. Oh, I read Octavus Roy Cohen, for example, about Negro life in Birmingham. I read one of his stories and it didn't interest me. It all seemed a fallacious kind of thing to do. Cohen was a big name in those days. His stories were all in dialect, and that immediately set me against writing anything in dialect. I've never written anything in dialect in my life. To me that bogus dialect is nothing. Real dialect should be in the rhythm of speech, not in the clipping off of letters, putting apostrophes and what not. I was convinced the way to go was in the rhythm of speech of the person talking.

Sale: I'm glad to hear you say that. You never play games with speech patterns.

Caldwell: That's something I learned.

Sale: You discovered that by reading people who write badly? Like Cohen?

Caldwell: Yeah, well, he's dead now, we can't say anything bad about him. But there were a lot of Negro stories written by white people in those days that try to imitate the sound of dialect which to me was completely false because to me that was not English. That was not the way it should be done. It should be done in the rhythm of speech. Well, that's what you asked and that's my answer.

Sale: I didn't know what you were going to say.

Caldwell: I know it might be fashionable to say I've been influenced by—I don't know—Thomas Hardy or Joseph Conrad or somebody.

Sale: Do you feel that you in any way helped in breaking taboos—barriers toward the acceptance of realistic fiction?

Caldwell: Not consciously, no.

Sale: I don't mean through planning, but as a matter of fact.

Caldwell: Well, I didn't even think of that, you see; I was only thinking of myself and not of the other people. Not what effect my writing would have on other people, but only the need to do it my way. And, so I had nothing to go by as an example of what to do or what not to do. I just did it my way. Now, if it's true that there is a universal Puritan tradition, possibly that influenced me a great deal in that I knew certain limits of conduct, training, or whatever there was in my environment. I knew certain concepts of morality, and that influenced me only to the extent that I stay within those limits.

Sale: So nothing was planned so far as breaking any barriers about what was accepted and what wasn't accepted?

Caldwell: No, because I was writing my own experience. My experience was the way it was, and you don't change those things to fit some concept. I'm pretty sure I would have known that certain things were offensive to other people because I had learned something in life. I didn't read the work of established writers. As I said, I didn't read any of those things at that time. I was only reading the experimental work. Well, that fitted in with my attitude of writing at that time. I was just going along with the trend, maybe, of writing as I felt I had the experience to write about. It was only later after I left college that I began reading books as a book reviewer. Then, of course, I read many books.

Sale: That's bound to have given you a pretty good picture of what was being published, wasn't it?

Caldwell: In a way, but I was not interested in anything I read, though. Those books did not interest me because I felt I could do better. Those books were always sort of second rate, and I reviewed them as such.

Sale: Of course: you were right about ninety-nine percent of the time, weren't you?

Caldwell: I had a lot of complaints from the editors of the papers I was writing for. "Didn't I ever like anything? Why was I always panning every book that came along?" I don't think I missed any masterpieces along the way.

Sale: You said in *Call It Experience* that you're primarily a writer of books rather than a reader of them. Have you any particular affinities toward practicing writers, people who are in the trade now? Have you read books in recent years that you thought highly of?

Caldwell: I do read a few books a year, maybe four or five. What has been my habit, I suppose for many years, is to read one work of a writer whom I have heard of as being worth reading. That's how I get to a book, and when I read one book by a writer, I'm satisfied. I don't have to read four of them to form an opinion. For example, we'll take some of my contemporaries like William Faulkner. I read one book of Faulkner which I liked very much. I thought it was superior and I still think it's a wonderful book and perhaps it's one of the least known that he's ever done. The title of the book was *As I Lay Dying*, which was not a sensational book. It was a solid book. So I formed my opinion of Faulkner just on that one instance, and I think I was right in forming that opinion. The same is true of other writers. One book only, that's all I read. I read one book of Steinbeck, for example. I read one book of Hemingway. I read one book of Dreiser; I read one book of Sherwood Anderson. Now when it comes to anybody since that bracket of time, I'm at a loss to pick out anybody that I consider in the same field with those writers that I've mentioned. Because I don't think contemporary fiction is as good as it was.

Sale: Why do you think so?

Caldwell: It could be that the novelists I mentioned were writing about a time that I am more familiar with. I don't know whether that's it or not. But they did leave a deep impression on me. On the other hand, the present fiction bothers me; it has taken a license that I think is not worthy of fiction, which I think is detrimental to fiction: that is the use of pornography.

Sale: Oh?

Caldwell: Because to me pornography is a dead end. And when you reach a dead end, you do not progress as a writer. What can you do next that is more pornographic than you have done? Basically, you see, pornography takes all the romance out of sex. It completely wipes it out as far as being romantic. To me life does have romantic elements. If you try to eliminate the romantic out of life, what have you got left except dullness and pornography? It can get pretty dull.

Sale: Has it been extremely frustrating to you to have been accused at times of producing pornography?

Caldwell: Well, of course, to me my work was not. It was only being what you might say romantic, not obscene or anything. It only bothered me to the extent that I thought it was unnecessary to accuse me of of these things. I did not think my work should have those labels at all. That's the only thing that's bothered me.

Sale: In *Call It Experience* you mentioned that you sometimes find a certain snobbishness among other writers who make a distinction between *artist* and *professional writer.* How would you describe yourself if you had to use one of those two terms?

Caldwell: Well I never thought of that in such a connection. Usually you think of a professional writer as being someone who does odd jobs and he's very professional at it. He can write something for a trade journal, or he can write a speech for the president of his company. That's usually what I would think of being a professional writer, but I'm just a writer with no adjectives in front of it. I am not artistic in a sense and I'm not professional in a sense, just because I work at it making a living. My occupation is writer, that's all. That's my occupation. An artist should be a painter or a sculptor or something.

Sale: There is artistry in words, I think.

Caldwell: Well, there's artistry in words, of course, but then you're getting very close to preciousness. You're writing style rather than content, and to me content is far more important than style. Anyone can probably spend a good part of his life working up a certain style, but then he has to make content conform to the style. Whereas I believe that your style will come out of your content, that the content will dictate the method, the style that you're going to write in. So I'm always a little bit suspicious of people who are stylists and who might be artists of the word and so forth. I'd rather be more content to be a common practitioner of content in writing.

I think if you set out to be a storyteller, that's more important than anything else. And that's what I still try to be, a storyteller in the written word. If you don't have a story, I don't know what else you've got in writing fiction. I don't know what else there is.

Sale: There is an element of heroism, something of a classical quality, in the characters of your early Georgia stories. More recent works, such as *The Last Night of Summer* don't seem to have that quality.

Caldwell: Well, I won't talk about the idea of their being heroic or classic. I don't know about that. But there were two different ideas involved there. *The Last Night of Summer* describes a situation in modern society. Society, I think, degenerates, and when it does degenerate, you don't have heroics because everything is taken for granted, that's the way it's going to be. Nobody's going to do anything about it, so go ahead and accept it as it is: a very dull existence. Whereas if you do put up a fight for something, why, then you do have an element of the ability to rebel and change something. I don't consider *The Last Night of Summer* to be an example of anything other than what it was. It's one of those dead-end things where nothing is ever going to get any better or worse than it was before. It's going to stay like it is. The people who are involved in that kind of situation are rather pathetic in the sense that they don't help themselves or they don't have the ability or the courage to help themselves. They just go ahead and live it as it is without taking any action about it. It's sort of contemporary in a way, you might say.

Sale: I guess that one of the definitions of hero is a rebel, a man who fights against conditions as they are, no matter how absurdly he does it.

Caldwell: As I see a hero, he doesn't always have to win; he can lose too, you know. But he can make an effort. With people who don't make an effort, you don't expect anything better than what they are or what they do. They don't have the courage to make an effort. In this particular book, in this particular story, the people had no ambition and no desire to do anything but what they did. They're willing to stay in their rut and live it out.

Sale: Have you finished the Georgia cycle do you think?

Caldwell: I don't know. I hope not. I don't know what will happen next.

Sale: What is in the works right now?

Caldwell: Nothing right now. I'm taking six months off, so on the first of March I'll have to get busy. Now, the two most recent books I did were set in Tennessee, *Summertime Island* and *The Weather Shelter*. They were Tennessee stories. Now, whether I will do any more in that area I don't know. I'll have to wait and see. I can't have another work which I've already decided upon. I've got no formula. I've got no outline. I have nothing. I've just got some blank paper there and I've got to put down the first words, the first paragraph. Then I'm going to see what happens after that.

Sale: Do you work from the assumption that people's sexual relations are sort of a core to everything else? Or am I misreading much of what I've read of you? Your novels suggest that the major

moves the characters make are traceable back to their sexual
impulses.

Caldwell: Well, of course, that's the motivating factor in life as
well as physical survival. First you've got to survive and then you
have this natural proclivity or this natural instinct. I would put it
number two. After number two, then you can build up a whole series
of motivations like social status and wealth and all. But I think
physical survival is your first. Your first instinct is to have something to
eat. Then nature takes over after that and you have this impulse, this
built-in impulse or sexual proclivity. It has a great influence on what
you do. And in order to support both of those two instincts, the
survival and the sexual thing, you have to produce some sort of
wealth.

Sale: I realize it is difficult to talk about much of the business of
writing.

Caldwell: Well, I will comment on anything that I know anything
about. But there are a lot of things that I don't know much about, so I
hesitate to make a statement or give an opinion on them. Writing is
one thing I know so little about that I get embarrassed by trying to
explain it.

Sale: Critics frequently know little about it, but they seem to be
perfectly willing to comment about it just the same.

Caldwell: I think that's an interesting subject. I wish I knew more
about it.

Sale: Do you agree that some people talk out their creations and
some people write them?

Caldwell: Yes. That's one thing I didn't like about Hollywood, the
idea that every idea had to be told to the producer or director or
whoever before you did anything. Well, to me what's said is already
gone. Why do it now? I never got along well in Hollywood for that
reason. Pre-made, prewrapped doesn't interest me. But there are a
lot of writers, I'm sure, who could explain themselves very clearly. A
fellow by the name of William Saroyan likes to talk, and he writes
too. He could be an actor, too. He could be all kinds of things.

Sale: Damon Runyon could talk.

Caldwell: I don't know how he ever got anything written. I only
knew him briefly. During that time all he would do was talk.

Sale: How do the react to the term "regional writer"?

Caldwell: I'm very much impressed by what I call regional writing because I think regional writing is much more important than trying to be universal or whatever the word would be for that, than trying to write the great American novel. I think the regionalist, if he knows what he's doing and can do it well, is a much more important writer than the big overall kind of thing where you write about something that might be applicable to all American life. There are still a lot of regions in this country that I think real fertile for writers. Even now I think they're real fertile. I keep on thinking of that Evangeline country in Louisiana between New Orleans and Lake Charles. To me it has always been very interesting, but I don't know enough French to get along with the people who live there. You have to know the dialect they use there to understand what they're saying. And the Indian reservations always interest me as a good fertile ground, too. There are a lot of things still around up in North Dakota, South Dakota, Utah, Colorado, which are very rarely done, very rarely written about. Apaches in Arizona.

Sale: There seems to be no particular home base, like the Georgia country, that lures you back.

Caldwell: No, because I like wherever I have traveled. At the time I'm living there; that's why I like it. I have no unpleasant feelings about any place, after having lived there. But I don't necessarily want to go back and live in the same place again.

Sale: Do you feel like that any of these places represented a sort of geographical ballast for your fiction writing?

Caldwell: Well, you see, I don't know how it affects other writers, but I like to see life in perspective, not so much in retrospect but in perspective. So I like to be away from what I'm doing, what I'm writing about. I like to be at a distance. But I like to go at all angles for that distance. In other words, go around the whole compass. Not, say, live in New Hampshire and look at it for a lifetime through a telescope. I would rather go from New Hampshire to North Dakota or into Oklahoma or Arizona. I like to go around the whole compass and keep that spot in mind as I move around so it gives me a perspective. I work on the theory that it does. And I like the process. I'm not exactly a Southerner or I'm not a Floridian; I'm not a Georgian; I'm not anything you can name or pin down because I have lived everywhere and I like everywhere I've lived. I started out when I was probably three or four years old moving around with my parents like that and I've never stopped. And I still like it.

Interview with Erskine Caldwell
Jac Tharpe/1971

From *The Southern Quarteryl*, XX (Fall 1981), 64-74. Reprinted by permission.

I interviewed Erskine Caldwell ten years ago, in August 1971, for the Mississippi Oral History Program at the University of Southern Mississippi. He was very pleasant throughout the two afternoon sessions, though he warmed somewhat on the matter of truth in art. I don't know whether he felt strongly or had often replied to such a question. I regret that I am unable in these excerpts to convey his personality as well as his opinions.

These remarks are published with his permission and that of the Oral History Program, and I am grateful to both for the privilege of the interview. Tapes as well as a transcript of the complete interview are available in the Cleanth Brooks Reading Room of the William D. McCain Library at the University of Southern Mississippi in Hattiesburg.

Question: Do you object to the use of the term social critic in describing you?

Caldwell: I've never had the ability to be a social critic. I'm only a storyteller. And what I do, or have done, and tried to do is tell the story of people and the life they live, which may produce some sermons in stones. I don't know whether it does or not. But I have not consciously and knowingly set out to be a social critic. It just happens that the life of people in the lower echelon does appeal to me, not because it's a curiosity but only because I have sympathy for life that is deprived. I grew up in the same way myself.

Q: You think of writing as working at a career?

Caldwell: When I say working, what I mean is that I have done many things like radio, television, journalism. But even beyond that, I like to take part in the distribution of what I do. I'll go to a sales convention with a publisher, for example, and spend a week there talking to people in the business, make a little speech to salespeople.

Or I'll go on a lecture trip. I did that for a couple of years because I felt I didn't have enough to do. I was writing books, of course, all the time; but then I would have three or four months in the year with nothing to do. So I went on lecture tours around the universities and colleges for about two years, spending two or three months at a time. So that's what I call working.

Q: *The Weather Shelter*, I gather, is proposing with some seriousness that miscegenation might be a solution to the whole racial problem. That is one of the reasons I wondered if you are a social critic.

Caldwell: It's not that I advocate anything of the sort. This amalgamation of races is a distinct possibility whether I have anything to do with it or not, or whether anybody else has anything to do with it. So if it is going to occur, that's nature's way, so to speak. I don't think anybody is going to change it by making any pronouncement or by criticizing it or by praising it. That's always been my feeling about the mixture of races, about the socializing between whites and blacks and others. Maybe it's going to end up where you have a race of people like Brazilians who claim that there is no racial distinction— that the white and the black in Brazil are all the same thing and that the shades of color between black and white make no difference whatsoever to the true Brazilian. Whether it's going to be, I won't be here to find out myself.

Q: Have you had objections to the rather intense move to integrate the South?

Caldwell: No, not as I understand what you say. I haven't been pressured in any way. I have had criticism from people who accused me of being in favor of integration, people whom I'd call professional Southerners, but nothing from the Northern point of view. People in the South have criticized me for feeling that nobody should be penalized for associating socially, sexually, economically.

Q: When you were writing back in the thirties, were you particularly conscious of your colleagues?

Caldwell: Well, you see, I never got associated with other writers. I still am not familiar with other writers personally. When I came out of Georgia, the Carolinas, Tennessee, there were no writers around. I didn't know any. I thought they all lived in New York or Paris or

someplace, which was true. There weren't any. The first writer I ever
saw probably was in New York. I had to go that far to see what one
looked like.

Q: Was he anyone we would know?

Caldwell: Well, I guess I could name a few people. Thomas
Wolfe, for example.

Q: You met him?

Caldwell: In New York. I think he probably had the same
experience. He had to go to New York to see a writer like me. I knew
quite a few writers in those days, in the thirties, in New York because
we had to associate in order to help each other out in the way of
survival. If someone knew a certain place you could go and get a
book review and get paid two and a half or five dollars that was
something to pass around.

Q: Would you just name the others who occur to you?

Caldwell: I don't know what their reputations are now. There was
a chap by the name of Robert Cantwell, who was writing novels in
those days, and now he's an editor of *Sports Illustrated*.

There was a fellow by the name of Charles Henri Ford, out of
Mississippi, who was in New York trying to scrape up enough money
to run a magazine, as I recall, and I think he—every time he'd get
enough money, he'd go back to Mississippi and get out another issue.

Who else can I think of right now? Norman McLeod. He was trying
to write a little magazine too. Everybody in those days either wrote
for a little magazine or tried to edit a little magazine. There were
dozens of them, dozens of them. That's how I got started getting
published. There happened to be a magazine in Paris called *transition*
that did it. That was the first one. That was the only way to get
published in those hard times.

Q: Were you aware of other figures who have become famous, like
Dos Passos or Steinbeck?

Caldwell: Well, not in those days, no. It was only later that I ran
into Steinbeck, and I ran into Faulkner, to name two. That was much
later. Not in the thirties, because in the thirties, I was either grubbing it
away in New York, trying to make enough to pay the room rent, or
else I was out somewhere else, like Maine, away from writers. So I
never got involved in the coteries of literature, so to speak. That's one
of the things Malcolm Cowley criticizes me for, for not associating
more with the élite in the field. Jokingly, of course, he's saying that.
Well, Cowley is a real good critic, no doubt about it, but I have no

inclination to move to Connecticut to live next door to him, just because he is a good critic, and become friendly with him. I'd rather stay miles, hundreds of miles, away from people than become obligated, in a sense, to be friends.

Q: Did you actually meet Steinbeck and Faulkner?

Caldwell: I got to know Steinbeck quite a while ago. Let's see, this was way back when he had a play on Broadway just about the time *Tobacco Road* was there. Our wives got to be friends, and they write occasionally now.

Q: Did you think he deserved the Nobel Prize?

Caldwell: Well, no. I remember I was in Yugoslavia when I heard about that, heard about them awarding the Prize to him, and someone asked me why he was given the award when there were other great writers about the world. Well, I think he deserved it in a way, but I was surprised at the time that other people were passed over.

Q: Would you feel that Hemingway or Faulkner deserved it more than Steinbeck?

Caldwell: Yes, I would say certainly Hemingway, because I think he had the ability to produce what other writers could not do. I didn't always like what he wrote. After he began writing novels, I sort of lost interest in Hemingway because I'm an aficionado of short stories. But just for his short stories, I would say he was deserving of any award. I never knew Hemingway. I knew one of his wives, who at one time was a correspondent in Europe when I was there, but I never had the opportunity to meet him.

As for Faulkner, I thought Faulkner was a choice that had to be made worldwide, for the fact that he had a lucidity, an ability to make clear through a very dark screen, make a clarity that you would never get just by a bland looking people or looking at life. You had to look through this screen.

Q: You admired Faulkner then?

Caldwell: Yes. He and I a lot of times were writing the same thing. I didn't know until it was too late, and he didn't know.

Q: When did you first become aware of Faulkner's work?

Caldwell: Oh, this was way early, way back in the thirties. I remember I was living in Maine at the time when some of his first books were done, and I read one of his first. What it was, I don't know. But this was way back in the early thirties.

We were once at a banquet in Paris when he was on the way back from receiving the Nobel Prize. He didn't say anything. Mostly the conversation around the table was in French, and I don't understand French. So I didn't know what was going on, and I don't think he knew either.

Q: After you read his first book, did you keep up fairly well with his career?

Caldwell: I know what it was. *As I Lay Dying*, which I thought was a great book and still do. Well, no, not especially. I would hear about him. People would talk about him in New York.

Q: Would you say that Faulkner's work is a true picture of the South?

Caldwell: Let's put it this way. You see, I don't think there is a true picture of any region, South or otherwise. It's the interpretation of truth or reality that really makes a work outstanding. It's the interpretation that the writer gives to it; and whether it's true to the South or not, I don't think really matters. That's not the point. The point is: What interpretation does he give of life in the South?

Did Faulkner write about life as it was? Sure he did. But it was not a reproduction of life. It was a creation of life, and therefore it was much sharper, much more true than the reality of it would have been. I think any great writer has that same ability.

Q: Do you remember what authors influenced you or those you would have been particularly conscious of when you started writing?

Caldwell: Probably the only writer that interested me was Sherwood Anderson. I read all the short stories of Anderson I could find, along with every other short story I could find in the little magazines. (I do remember Anderson had—I think it was *Winesburg, Ohio*.) Anyway, I got interested in the fact of writing, and I wanted to do the same thing. I wanted to be a writer. I wanted to tell stories.

Q: Had you wanted to be a writer before, or do you mean reading actually made you want to be one?

Caldwell: I'd wanted to, but I didn't know how to because I had never been able to go to writing school. I began reading magazines. I found a whole new world which was contemporary, up-to-date, rather than something out of the past. I had no interest in reading anything about the past. I wanted the present, and here it was in these small magazines.

That was my hardship in life, so to speak, to learn to write as rapidly as I could and the best I could under the circumstances. I think that's what influenced me to leave school, leave college, and go to work on newspapers, because I thought I had a better opportunity to learn to write on a newspaper than I would by staying in college, so I left.

Q: Does that mean that you consider you are self-taught as a writer?

Caldwell: Yes. I had accumulated so much. I think, in those prior years, living all over the South, that I had all the material I could use. I didn't have to be influenced. I didn't have to be inspired by anybody else, by a tall story of anybody else. I didn't know what these guys were writing or had written. It didn't interest me what de Maupassant had written; I wasn't interested in what he had done. I wanted to know what I was going to do, what I was trying to do, so that's why I say I never read books. I still don't read books.

What interests me as a writer is having an idea that's based on some solid, factual incident, but has no suggestion how it's going to end, what it's going to do in the middle, or anything of the sort.

In the South the small town is always alive, not only with gossip, but with stories and anecdotes and talk and conjecture about other people—next door, across the street, around the corner, on the other side of town. Then of course the more cohesive this life is, the closer they live together and the more intimate they are, the more they know about each other. All these things I think are conducive to Southern writing.

You contrast that with New England life where everything is remote. You can live in a rural area of Maine or New Hampshire and live across the road from somebody, and you may never know what the person's first name is even, or else you won't call him by his first name. You'll call him Mr. So and So as long as you live. That remoteness and that isolation are imposed by that life, whereas in the South there is no compulsion to be remote. The more friendly you are, the better you're going to enjoy yourself and the more friends you're going to make and so on.

The person who is raised in the Southern atmosphere, I think, has more freedom of feeling about life around him, and therefore he can project himself into other people better, to know what they are doing, saying, thinking or have done or might do in the future.

I think it opens up a little more for a writer to have been born and raised in a small Southern town. What it's going to be in the future, I

don't know, because the towns are getting larger, and there are very
few small towns left.

Q: Was it that kind of thing that made you like Sherwood
Anderson?

Caldwell: In a way, except that Anderson's attitude and approach
to the story were so much more interesting to me. He didn't have
that stiffness and tightness that a New England writer would have, for
example. He was more fluid; there was more activity in his words and
in his sentences and in his speech and dialogue. I had a feeling of
more activity and more life than I would find anywhere in, say,
Theodore Dreiser.

Q: Are you familiar with Dreiser?

Caldwell: No. I knew him when he was working in Hollywood,
and I was too. I only read one or two of his books in my whole life so
I don't know too much about him.

Q: Could you expand the comparison between you and Faulkner?

Caldwell: I haven't read enough of Faulkner to make any great
comparison of what he did with certain situations and things of the
sort, but I know he must have been dealing with the same kind of
people I was dealing with, all the way through. I don't know how
many books Faulkner wrote. I have no idea; I guess everything he
wrote was about Mississippi.

Q: Were you ever consciously sensationalistic in your writing?

Caldwell: No, no, because I never had any control over the things
I was writing about. It goes back to the fact that I never knew how
anything was going to end, so I couldn't consciously manipulate.

Sensationalism, if it existed, would have to come out of the people
and things themselves rather than being imposed upon the story. It
would have to be a logical outburst of the character. It would have to
be true to their nature, to whatever it was they were doing. If they
were cruel; then that was their nature, and I could have nothing to do
about it. I couldn't change their nature; otherwise, it wouldn't be true
to their character.

Q: Did anyone ever call you a Communist?

Caldwell: Yes, I was listed in the *Red Book*—what was the
name—the woman who got up this compendium of names? Dilling!
Mrs. Dilling. *The Red Network*.

Q: Was that because you were in Russia?

Caldwell: I don't know. I don't think so. No, that was before. That

was before Russia, I think. I think it all started because I went down
to Washington one day with Rockwell Kent, who called himself a
Communist. He had a project in mind that had something to do with
welfare. I was involved in a few things like that inadvertently, but I
was never deeply involved enough to contribute any money to these
causes and didn't get into any membership of anything. I was just on
the fringe of Communism, I suppose you would call it.

I did write short stories that were published in *New Masses*, which
in those days was considered violently Communist, and maybe it
was. I don't know. But that was about as close as I got to
Communism. Then I had gone to Spain during the Spanish civil war
and on the Loyalist side, which was labeled the Communist side.

I was interested in writing, and it just happened that in those days
around New York most writers were involved in some way in a
poverty program. The only people who were actually trying to raise
any money for people to survive on, writers especially, I guess, were
those Communist-affiliated or Communist-tainted groups.
I was involved just like anybody else around New York in those days.
Nobody ever asked me to join the Communist Party, and I never
paid any dues or anything of the sort. It was just in the atmosphere of
the time. I have a very good friend who was a Communist. Mike
Gold was sort of the leader of the young American writers in those
days. He was the editor of *New Masses*, I guess—one of the editors.

Q: Was there any particular ideological reaction associated with
your rebellion? Did you reject religion, for example?

Caldwell: Yes, I did. That was one thing I was going to say. When
my father, who was a minister, gave me the choice, he said it was my
privilege to decide whether I wanted to go to church or not. I chose
not to, and I told him so, and I didn't go. I didn't want to go and
didn't need to go.

I thanked him for giving me the privilege of making the choice, so I
never went back to church again after that. I didn't become violently
anti-religious or anything of the sort; it's just the fact that it doesn't
interest me to take part in it. Religion is fine for other people that
want to engage in it. They're welcome to it.

Q: Were you aware of Maxwell Perkins?

Caldwell: Yes, I was aware of him because he was real good to
me, in a way. He never helped me in any way as a writer other than
to publish some things I had written, but he was the only commercial

publisher, or the first commercial publisher, who ever did. So I did appreciate the fact that he saw something that he found publishable. These were short stories that interested him at the time.

I guess he had seen some I had written in little magazines, and that's how he got in touch with me—or the reason he got in touch with me—because he read some of my little magazine stories, which paid no money. So he comes along right in the middle of the depression and wants me to send him some short stories, which I did and which he paid for with money. Of course I was so encouraged and enthusiastic and grateful that I was almost like William Saroyan. I'd write a story a day and send it to him until he told me to quit— said he had enough—don't send anymore.

Q: Were you familiar with Nietzsche?

Caldwell: No, no. About the only philosopher, I think, who has ever influenced me is Henry Mencken. He was a little sharpster, you know. He was a little sharp boy, and I admired him because he was contemporary in a sense. I liked the way he presented his ideas, in modern dress, so to speak. I always admired Mencken.

I only knew him by correspondence. He had published some stories of mine in *American Mercury*.

He disregarded the conventions of life. He would throw out new ideas and reject whatnot; and I admired him for going up to Boston to sell *American Mercury* on the common and getting arrested. I thought that was a great publicity stunt, and he wasn't too dignified to do it. I admired him for doing that.

Q: Will you talk about what you are doing now?

Caldwell: I never talk about what I am doing. Once you have created the thought into words—put it into words—you have lost the whole essence of what you're doing, because then you cannot recreate the oral substance of it and put it into words. I don't want to talk about it, and I don't know myself what I'm doing most of the time. I have to wait and see what comes out on the printed page.

I never wanted to have a bestseller, because I hoped to keep on writing the rest of my life, and I didn't want to fade away at any point along the way. I don't expect ever to have a bestseller. Over a period of time, some of my books, over a period of fifteen, twenty years may have achieved the figure of what might be a bestseller.

Q: Korges persistently talks of you as having a comic vision or of writing comic scenes. Does this seem accurate?

Caldwell: I can only say that consciously I could not write anything that was comic or humorous, if you want me to use that word. To me, there is comedy in tragedy and tragedy in comedy; they are inseparable; they're interchangeable. It's like the old saying you hear sometimes, "I couldn't laugh for crying; I couldn't cry for laughing." To me, they are such interchangeable things that it's all one. It's life. It's a person's life that you are writing about, and he's going to have tragedy. He's going to have comedy in his existence. It's inescapable.

I wouldn't set out to try to write a comic or a tragic interlude. By the time I got halfway through the chapter I still wouldn't know whether the effect was going to be funny or sad.

Q: Are you acquainted with any figure you consider a neglected writer?

Caldwell: No. But I have always had a great admiration for a certain writer—to continue his work over a long period of time and to make it fresh and interesting over the years, and that's William Saroyan. He is what I would call a natural born writer. He has never lost the instinct, I think, that he had in the beginning.

Q: Could you name anyone else you consider a natural born writer?

Caldwell: I think Sherwood Anderson, by all means, would fit into that classification. I don't think I am influenced by the fact that I knew him slightly, because I admired his work long before I ever met him, and I have read him since, after having met him. I think he would be one of the candidates in my mind.

Caldwell's Little Acre
John Dorschner/1972

From *Tropic*, magazine section of *The Miami Herald*, 8 October 1972, pp. 16, 18, 20, 22.

Erskine Caldwell is writing in his study, and through the closed door come the staccato tap-taps of the typewriter, interrupting lengthy silences.

His fourth wife, Virginia, a gentle brunette with a down-home smile, has just shown me into the library. It is 4 p.m., and Erskine, she says, has been writing since 9 that morning. He will be done soon, she says. He always quits about this time of day.

The library has a fireplace, surrounded by scattered stacks of paperbacks, and a color TV in the corner, but the room is dominated by a 20-foot-long bookcase, crammed to the ceiling with books. All are the work of Erskine Caldwell. *Georgia Boy, Trouble in July, The Weather Shelter.* Each book is a different edition.

Virginia says she keeps track of the royalties, makes charts, adds the figures. He's written 50 books, sold 75 million copies and been translated into 40 languages—even Icelandic, Serbo-Croatian and Bengali. The Japanese alone have 53 editions out, and when the Caldwells travel abroad, she rummages through the bookstores searching for pirated editions to add to the shelves.

The typewriter tappings are rare. Four, five minutes of silence, then a rapid burst of maybe a half-dozen words, followed by more silence. At age 68, Erskine Caldwell is at work.

Deja-vu? No. Time-warp. His books—*Tobacco Road* and *God's Little Acre*—came out in 1932 and 1933. They were about the poor white South. Tobacco souring the land, the boll weevil wasting the cotton. Ramshackle shanties on forelorn dirt roads. People comically ignorant, pathetically trapped. Ty Ty kidnapping an albino to help him find gold on his Georgia farm. Ellie May trying to get a man in spite of her God-awful harelip. Will ripping the clothes off the beautiful Griselda while his wife Rosamond and sister-in-law Jill watch, aroused.

Tap-tap. Time-warp. Erskine Caldwell is writing. In suburbia. His house is a mere four years old, a one-story ranch style with three-car garage, screened-in swimming pool and self-lit doorbell button. It rests on an acre lot in a subdivision of Dunedin, Fla., once a lazy Gulf village, but now a booming city of 23,000, a bedroom suburb of the great green-bench megalopolis of St. Pete-Tampa. The neighbors are mostly Honeywell executives who in the evenings go to the well-lit baseball diamond to watch their sons in the Little League.

The typing stops, and within a minute Erskine Caldwell walks briskly into the library, says how-do-you-do, shakes hands and plops himself down in a chair, swinging a leg over the arm.

Yes, he's working on a novel. "I give it a year. What is it? You never know. If I knew how a book was going to end, I'd never finish it."

He says it will be his 50th book, but he said the same thing about *The Weather Shelter* (1969) and *The Earnshaw Neighborhood* (1971). He shrugs. "I always call it 50. Fifty is enough for any man.

"The writing is harder now. I keep getting more critical of my writing, and the writing keeps getting slower. When you're younger, you don't worry about it so much."

He stands and paces, clasping his hands behind his back. The hair is gray-white now, but the short-banged Caesar cut is still the same. That, along with the hooked nose and the erect carriage, give him an imposing patrician air.

Time-warp. He was born in the same 10-year-span as Faulkner, Hemingway, Dos Passos, West, Fitzgerald, and his name was once on a literary level with theirs. But it was the sex in his books that made him famous then, the same sex scenes that make him seem rather passe now. My father, at the University of Wisconsin in the 1930s, remembers the eternal little old ladies walking out of the play *Tobacco Road* when a character said, "Damn!" And I remember, in an Illinois high school in the early '60s, that all of us in Advanced English ran down to the library for *God's Little Acre*, the dirtiest book on the recommended reading list. What did Portnoy read?

He paces and jiggles the change in his pocket. Couldn't he stop writing and live comfortably on the royalties?

"Sure, you can always adjust yourself to what you have. You have to have a savings account—any writer has to. Either that, or marry a rich woman. I've been married four times, and they've all been poor girls. In more senses than one, they've been poor girls. Except the last one, of course." He shakes his head with a wry grin, gazing out the window, contemplating for a moment.

"All I know is that I have to write. If I didn't, I'd start kicking the cat around. Sooner or later, you're going to say you've done enough. But I wouldn't know what to do if I quit. I wouldn't have a job. Hobbies? I guess you could say travel is my hobby, but I don't know if that would be the same without writing."

He has lived in Dunedin for four years. Before that it was San Francisco, Arizona, Maine. "I've lived everywhere," he says without a trace of Southern accent, as he rearranges the tools beside the fireplace. He has not lived in Georgia since his early 20s. "I started traveling early in life, but at first I'd only go for a few months at a time."

He was born Dec. 17, 1903, in White Oak, Ga. "That's just a place name. There's no post office by that name, just a church where my father was the pastor. It's in Coweta County, a little south of Atlanta."

His father, a Presbyterian, was somewhat of a liberal maverick, and much of Caldwell's childhood was spent drifting through the small towns of the South as his father changed congregations. Each new church would bring a problem, like the time when Pastor Caldwell invited the black sexton to sit inside the church because of the winter chill outside. The elders frowned, and the Caldwells moved.

"My father sent me away from home the first time, just to get me going. It was during World War I, and he was imbued with patriotic fervor. I think he wanted to go himself, so he sent me. He found me a job as a driver with the YMCA for an Army camp in Tennessee. He wanted me to learn about the world."

Earning his own way, young Caldwell wandered in and out of three colleges. He was a storeroom clerk in the five-and-dime, a poolroom worker, orange juice stand operator, milkman and even pro-football player.

"I tried to be a pro, but I didn't last long. Before the NFL, they had regional professional leagues. In Pennsylvania, it was called the Anthracite League. All the coal towns were in it. I never made it to the regular season. In the training camp for the Wilkes-Barre team, I received a busted nose."

He keeps moving while he talks, pacing, looking, rearranging the paperback stacks with quick, crisp motions. "Finally, I quit college. Ran out of interest, for one thing. I wanted to get out and become a writer. I don't think I could have lasted anyway—I never was much interested in the educational side of life."

He worked briefly on the *Atlanta Journal*, then moved to Maine to sequester himself for five years while he learned the art of writing. "I was living on a farm, cutting wood, picking potatoes, reviewing books at 25 cents apiece."

It was Max Perkins, the famed editor who had worked with Wolfe, Hemingway and Fitzgerald, who gave Caldwell his big boost. According to legend, Perkins read some Caldwell stories, then called him on the phone and offered him two-fifty for two. Caldwell thought he meant $2.50 and said, "Make it three-fifty." Soon, he received a check for $350.

Is the legend true? Caldwell snorts and shakes his head with the wry grin. "Well, basically . . . True enough."

The stories appeared in the June, 1930, *Scribner's Magazine*, two tightly written tales about love and loneliness. Said the blurb under the headline: "Presenting for the first time in a general magazine, the work of one of the most talented of the new American writers. His milieu is the New England of today."

Well, the short stories were about New England, but Caldwell was working on novels about the South. The first two—*The Bastard* (1929) and *Poor Fool* (1930)—were published only in limited editions, and most readers and reviewers thought *Tobacco Road* (1932) was his first book.

"*Tobacco Road* was a slow starter. I love the idea of a slow starter. As a reviewer, I saw that the best sellers faded out quickly. I liked the idea of a book slowly building. I wanted to be a writer not for today, but for the ages." The next year, when *Tobacco Road* was produced on Broadway, the slow starter became a quick seller, and Erskine Caldwell's career was firmly launched.

In the library, the pacing is quicker now. We go outside to take some photographs. Would his wife mind posing, too? Hands clasped behind back, he goes looking for her in her art studio, part of the three-car garage. A stereo is playing softly, and on an easel sits a large, half-done abstract. "Virginia? Virginia?" She is not there.

He walks outside, over toward the neighbor's backyard. "Virginia? Virginia? I don't know where she could have gone to. Oh, there she is."

She is walking quickly up the driveway. "Virginia, the gentleman wants to take your picture."

The photo session is fast, Caldwell standing erect, hands behind back, asking: "Is that enough? Are you through?"

We wander back into the house and into his writing room. His

desk faces away from the window and toward a large nude oil
painting on the wall. An oversized, imitation-barrel wastebasket rests
beside the desk, filled with crumpled sheets of yellow paper. In a box
next to the typewriter is a thin stack of paper, his output for the day.

"I make it my profession to be a writer," he says, fingering a book
from a small bookcase. "I'm very serious about it. I do what suits me.
I don't care what the word-of-mouth has to say—or the critics. I do
what suits me."

The critics he says he ignores have both praised and condemned
him. Faulkner himself once listed Caldwell as one of the top five
contemporary writers, ahead of even Hemingway. (The list went
Wolfe, Faulkner, Dos Passos, Caldwell, Hemingway.) But after
Tobacco Road, Faulkner added, Caldwell's work "gradually grew
toward trash." Nonetheless, one critic, James Korges, says that a look
at Caldwell's best "will reveal what is now obscured by the very bulk
of his output: His is a solid achievement that supports the assertion
that he is one of the important writers of our time."

But Caldwell abstains from such literary gamesmanship, a posture
which may be a game in itself. Symbolism in his work? "I let the
professors worry about that. I'm a storyteller." His chances for literary
immortality? "How do you know? Nobody knows. You get too close
to it to judge." Did he know that Columbia University students had
picked him as one of the 10 greatest writers of all time? "Huh! It must
have been a joke."

Nor does Caldwell criticize other writers. In fact, he rarely reads
fiction. "You can't be a reader and writer, too. If I put in five or seven
hours a day writing, how can I have time to read?"

The New American Library, which has the rights to his paperback
sales, sends him 30 or 40 books a month. "My wife reads them all,
and once in a while, she'll say, 'Here's one you should read.'

"For the content, not the sex and sensationalism. Sensationalism—
it's a rat race. Somebody will come along tomorrow and have
something more sensational," says the most sensational writer of the
'30s. "The choice of words, the characters, the emotions, the
storytelling, that's what I look for."

Not only doesn't he read most novelists, but he also dislikes
meeting them. He and his wife first thought of moving to Sarasota,
"but there were too many writers, and tourists. I avoid writers. Writers
are real dull people. I know. I'm dull myself. Oh, you commiserate
about royalties, publishers and things like that, but what good does

that do? I like people in other fields—lawyers, doctors, TV people.
I'm good friends with Dan Rowan. I knew them, Rowan and Martin,
back when they were trying to get their start in New York, and I was
going around the coffee-pot radio stations—the 250 watters."

By this time, we have wandered into the family room facing the
swimming pool, and Caldwell is mixing drinks at the bar, pouring his
own out of a small glass jar, the kind that creamed herring comes in.
During a recent visit to the Mayo Clinic, the doctors talked him into
limiting his liquor intake, and so now Virginia measures the supply
each afternoon into the glass jar. "That way, I have no more than
that—*and* no less than that."

Behind the bar are row after row of liquor miniatures, souvenirs of
their frequent airline flights. Covering the walls are paintings collected
from around the world.

On weekends, they hop over to Key West, Vero Beach, Atlanta,
New Orleans, often as anonymous testers for the *Mobil Regional
Travel Guide*, sampling food at this restaurant or that. They do it to
help out an old friend who edits the guide. "I don't even use Mobil
gas," he says. "What brand do we use?" Enco, says Virginia, for the
free plastic glasses you get with a tankful.

Often, especially when a book is finished, they take longer trips,
occasionally tied to "those crazy things that writers get themselves
into." Judging the Miss Salad Bowl contest in Arizona. Serving on a
university panel "just to find out what the title meant. It was the
'Interdisciplinic Polymorphic Somesuch,' or something like that." Or
making the tour on the college lecture circuit: "I had to give them
their choice of two speeches. Actually, it was two titles and one
speech. How were they to know the difference?"

This summer, the trip was to Europe, where he served as the
American juror at the Cannes Film Festival. More nonsense. "I saw
32 films in 14 days, about two a day. That's more films than I've ever
seen in my life—and more than I'm ever going to see again . . . I lost
interest in the movies when the X-rated ones came along. They took
all the romance out of it. You've got to have romance in life, but it
was just sex. You might as well have stag movies."

What? Was this coming from the man who in the '30s wrote about
the aging lady preacher who bribed a young boy to marry her by
buying him a new car? Caldwell snorts, again shaking his head with
the wry grin. He does not answer.

It was after the success of *Tobacco Road* with its sex-starved lady preacher that life began changing quickly for Erskine Caldwell. Several times, in the late '30s and early '40s, Hollywood offered him contracts for screenwriting, starting at $500 and soaring to $2,500 a week.

But none of the Caldwell scripts were ever filmed. "The producer wanted me to do it his way. I wanted to do it my way. We had an impasse. Finally, I bought myself out of my last contract."

Those were the traveling years, too. He divorced his first wife, Helen Lannigan, by whom he had three children. In 1940, he married the world-traveling photographer Margaret Bourke-White, and together they covered the Japanese invasion of China, and the Nazi attack on Russia. In 1942, at the age of 38, he married a 20-year-old college senior from the University of Arizona, June Johnson, who later gave birth to his fourth child. He and his present wife, Virginia Merle Moffett, were married two minutes after midnight, Jan. 1, 1957, in Reno. "It was all planned," explains Virginia. "We decided to start the New Year off right."

It is dark out now, and Virginia says the dinner is ready. "Nothing special," she says, pointing to the free Enco plastic glasses. She and Caldwell give themselves carefully measured helpings of the chicken and rice casserole. Both are on diets, she explained, he because he just quit smoking. That was the work of the Mayo Clinic, too. The doctors demanded it. He went into a bar, had a quick couple of double bourbons and made up his mind. "I quit in five minutes, but now I always think I should be doing something with my hands. Striking a match, picking up the paper, something."

We sit there, eating in Dunedin, Fla., in 1972, and I mention the quirks of literary recognition. Like Nathanael West, barely recognized by the masses when he was writing in the late '30s, but now a cult figure whose *Miss Lonelyhearts* is mentioned as one of the century's great novels.

"Yes, yes," says Caldwell. "I knew Pep West." Time-warp. Of course, he knew West.

It was during the Depression, he says, and West was supporting his writing by managing the Sutton Hotel. It seemed that West was bothered that at night the hotel seemed dark and empty—an uninviting place for the weary traveler. So he began offering writers bargain rates to stay at the Sutton when they came to New York to visit their publishers.

Many, people like Saroyan and Caldwell, accepted the offer. But there was a catch. They had to agree to leave their lights on until midnight, and West occasionally ran out into the street to check on them, looking up at the carefully arranged checkerboard pattern of the lighted windows. Caldwell, alas, was an old-fashioned country boy who usually turned off the lights early and went to bed. West would chastize him in the morning, but they stayed friends, meeting together for lunch when they moved on to mutually disastrous screenwriting careers in Hollywood.

It is late, and Caldwell has had enough of all this crazy writer talk. He pushes back his chair abruptly and walks outside, sitting down by the edge of the pool, facing away from the dining table, looking out into the sky-lighting glow of the megalopolis night, perhaps thinking about his novel-in-progress, perhaps caught in his own time-warp.

For a while, Virginia and I talk about football, about the pre-Lombardi days of the Packers when she sat in Kezar Stadium and watched young Bart Starr get sacked all day by the red dog, as they called it then.

Caldwell comes back in. It is time to go, and as I leave their subdivision, I see first lights of the Little League field, then the starry flickers of the high-rise condominiums across the bay in Clearwater Beach. Tomorrow Erskine Caldwell will be in his study, writing his 50th book. Or, maybe, his 52nd.

Erskine Caldwell:
A Georgia Boy Returns Home
Helen C. Smith/1975

From *The Atlanta Constitution*, 7 October 1975, p. 5-B. Reprinted by permission.

Dignified Erskine Caldwell and his charming wife, Virginia, have December deadlines.

Caldwell, the author of 50 books including *Tobacco Road* and *God's Little Acre*, has promised his publisher the text for his annual book (that's about the rate he turns out books), a travel story of the land west of the Mississippi and east of the Rockies, or what used to be called the Louisiana Purchase.

Mrs. Caldwell is determined she will finish her first piece of needlepoint in time to give her husband a pillow for his 72nd birthday in December. It's only a year behind schedule, she confesses ruefully, as she shows the colorful apple design she is working on.

"The symbolism of this is that he's the apple of my eye," says Mrs. Caldwell to whom the author has been married almost 19 years. She is his fourth wife, and in addition to having her own personal December deadline, she is equally involved with her husband's new book [*Afternoons in Mid-America*] since she is doing the line drawings for it.

"I'm an artist by hobby," she says. "I'm piggy-backing on this book."

Mr. and Mrs. Caldwell are having morning coffee from pink-flowered cups in their elegant room (but not a suite) at the Fairmont.

"You bet," Caldwell answers succinctly when asked if the setting were not a long way from his childhood days first in Coweta County and then later in the Augusta-Wrens area, the setting for *Tobacco Road* and many subsequent stories on the poverty and ignorance of the deep South.

There was a time when the tall, white-haired, rather frail man would not have been welcomed in Georgia, would, perhaps, have been run out of town or tarred and feathered, a threat he has received several times in his life. His stories of the South were too raw, too shockingly real to permit him free passage.

But times have changed. He is welcomed now, he is honored, not only in Atlanta but in Augusta where he will be a special guest Thursday at Augusta College. Before then, he will participate in a seminar on Southern history at Atlanta University Tuesday; speak at Emory University Tuesday evening on the "Meet the Authors" program; and take part Wednesday in a seminar on the history of Southern literature at Emory University. He has also been seen on virtually every local talk show, and was the guest speaker at the Atlanta Press Club Monday.

A heavy schedule for a man just two months out of major surgery in which he had a half a lung removed. It had been his only good lung. He had lost half of his other one previously.

"I gave up smoking too late (he had smoked two packs a day for 40 years)," says Caldwell, who actually gave up the habit cold-turkey before he knew he had lung problems when the doctor threatened him with a heart by-pass for a blocked artery if he didn't stop. So far he's been able to avoid that operation.

"But I don't play tennis anymore. Let's let it go at that."

Though his hand shakes as he lifts the coffee cup to his lips, his penetrating blue eyes are right with every question. He is dressed almost severely in a black suit, socks and shoes, enlivened only by a conservative blue check shirt. He speaks slowly and softly.

The son of a Presbyterian minister, who moved around constantly and perhaps made $150 a year in salary, Caldwell was exposed early in life to the miseries of the persons his father visited in rural Georgia and other Southern states.

"He was always very concerned about their economic plight, even more than their religion," Caldwell recalls. "It rubbed off on me."

But he does not consider himself a social historian.

"I'm just a story teller," he says simply.

His stories used to shock people. They were often censored or banned (as they were in Georgia at one time), or kept on special shelves of the library for reference only, not to be taken out into daylight.

There are many critics, such as Calder Willingham who calls
Caldwell the "true myth-maker of the post-bellum South" in the
summer issue of *The Georgia Historical Quarterly* who feel that
Caldwell has been greatly overlooked in the literary scheme of things.
Willingham goes so far as to say that if Faulkner were worthy of a
Nobel Prize, how much more so is Caldwell, who reached a much
larger audience and in a more natural, less literarily self-conscious,
way than Faulkner.

One of Caldwell's highly revealing books, *You Have Seen Their
Faces*, with photographs by the late Margaret Bourke-White, the
famous *Life* photographer and Caldwell's second wife to whom he
was married for five years in the early '40s, has just been reissued by
Derbibooks, Inc. ($6.95). It is an incisive and sensitive statement
about the relation between the poverty of the people and the
depletion of the land in the Deep South.

Is it as valid today as when it was first issued in 1937?

"The human face changes very little," Caldwell says thoughtfully.
"It is stuck with itself forever. But there are different kinds of poverty.
Poverty isn't always hunger (as it often was in *Faces*). There is
poverty today in housing, in the urban slums, in the loss of stability.
There is a poverty of morals and customs as we go through a
transition."

The Great Depression, which was the setting of many of Caldwell's
best known books, made the South stronger in the author's
estimation. The South was hurt the worst in those dark, bleak days
because "it was strictly an agricultural empire."

Caldwell has not been able to find the house where he was born in
Coweta County some 40 miles south of Atlanta, but he has revisited
the Tobacco Road section of Richmond County several times.

"There were maybe a dozen Tobacco Roads then, each leading
from the tobacco fields to the Savannah River."

One road today in the area bears the name Tobacco Road, not to
the liking of those who live there who tried to get the name changed
but failed. The road has been black-topped.

Caldwell likes to see his works done on stage but he doesn't "care
too much about film versions."

"Film is inflexible. Once the picture is made, it is going to stay that
way."

Caldwell, who cut his writing teeth by being a cub reporter on *The*

Atlanta Journal for several years as a general assignment writer, claims such experience is "worth much more than any school of journalism, any course in creative writing."

His word of advice to any would-be writer is "Don't."

"I try to discourage him from writing. Then he has the inspiration to prove I'm wrong."

"A Writer First":
An Interview with Erskine Caldwell
Elizabeth Pell Broadwell and Ronald Wesley Hoag/1980

From *The Georgia Review*, 36 (Spring 1982), 83-101. Reprinted
by permission.

This year one of the grand old men of American letters,
Erskine Caldwell, will mark both his seventy-ninth—or is it
his eightieth?—birthday and the fiftieth anniversary of his
blockbuster novel *Tobacco Road*, a title that has perma-
nently entered the country's folklore. A persistent, prolific
writer, Caldwell followed up his 1932 achievement with a
succession of fictional and nonfictional portraits of the
hardshell rural South. Among the best of these are his
novels *God's Little Acre* (1933), *Journeyman* (1935),
Trouble in July (1940), and *Tragic Ground* (1944); his
masterful story cycle *Georgia Boy* (1943); and his social
documentaries *Tenant Farmer* (a 1935 tract) and *You
Have Seen Their Faces* (a 1937 photo-essay done in
collaboration with Margaret Bourke-White). A Georgia
boy himself, Caldwell has become very much a world
traveler since his early days in Coweta County. His more
than fifty books, many of which are set in the South, have
also transcended their roots, appearing in forty languages
and attracting well over eighty million readers.

The vicissitudes of Caldwell's literary reputation are
both complex and historically significant. His enormous
popular success, based largely on the perceived sensationalism of his books, waned when other more sensational books made his seem tame. However, his critical
acclaim has increased steadily in the past decade; and a
Caldwell revival now appears to be underway in American
universities, where his books have become standard fare
in many literature courses. Ironically, this new-found critical approval is based on many of the same stylistic extravagances that won him his once vast public following—
namely, his use of some of the techniques associated with
surrealism, black humor, and naturalism. At one time
valued by the critical establishment primarily as a social

commentator (a role that he all but disavows), Caldwell is now praised for his innovative melding of the fantastically grotesque, the perversely comic, and the grimly accurate in his fiction. But in the South, Caldwell's acceptance was long deferred. While the rest of the world savored his depictions of Southern hard times and their institutional causes, many Southerners took umbrage at such treatment, scorning their native son until well into the region's modern era of self-criticism. Like William Faulkner, who once named him as one of America's five best living writers, Caldwell found that his fiction had struck a nerve in his Southern theater of operation.

The following interview took place over a three-day period in June of 1980. Caldwell took time off from writing an autobiographical work, tentatively entitled "A Year of Living," to meet with us daily for two hours in the writing room of his Scottsdale, Arizona, home. Virginia Caldwell, an artist who has illustrated several of her husband's books during their twenty-five years of marriage, sat for a brief supplemental interview following our third session and since then has provided further background material in numerous letters. Seasoned travelers, the Caldwells left the day after our visit for a tour of the Canadian Rockies, journeyed to New England later that summer for Erskine's residency at Dartmouth College, and, most recently, made a January excursion to Detroit to watch the San Francisco 49ers ("our team for twenty-five years") play in the Super Bowl. Seated at his writing desk during each of our conversations, Erskine Caldwell answered all of our questions thoughtfully and deliberately, while sizing us up from behind the latest in a long line of manual typewriters on which he has produced his considerable body of work.

Mr. Caldwell, your readers think of you as both a Southerner and a Southern writer. Do you?

I consider myself an American who was born in the South. I say that because, although I recognize differences in dialect and styles of living among the various regions of the country, over all I've rejected the notion that I was some sort of regional character. When I was young, I had the good fortune to have parents who moved almost every year from one Southern state to another. But the fact is I've lived only about a third of my life in the South—twenty years to start

with and then eight years more, in Florida, in the 1960's and '70's.
For almost another third of my life, or close to it, I was in New
England. The other third, so to speak, has been spent in the West. So
I was never really a Georgian, a Floridian, or a North Carolinian. I
was always an American in that sense. I have had no great allegiance
to any one place, and that's true even today. I don't know how long
I'll be here in Arizona. Where I'll go next, I don't know.

*How would you characterize your attitude toward the South? Have
you perhaps had a love-hate relationship with this region?*

Well, that's something to ponder. As I was growing up, I did resent
the South. I resented its economy and its sociology. I resented the
lack of opportunity in general, and especially the fact that the black
people there were not accorded the same opportunity as the white
people. I happened to have grown up among black people in various
places, and I was unhappy that—economically and socially—they
were always second-, third-, and fourth-class citizens. On the other
hand, I would also say that, just like anyone who has a homeplace, I
have always had a deep regard for this region. I do not hate the
South. I have always liked the South and liked its people, even
though I had these qualifications because of some of the conditions
there.

Why did you move to the Southwest?

I came here to the western part of the country for the same reason
I went to New England when I left the South—to get a perspective
on life. By "perspective" I mean that you can look at something from
afar and find minute details you would not see if you were right on
top of it. You can live too close to a region to write about it. Each
move I've made, I made for that reason—purposely and, I think,
successfully. Also, when experiences are the basis of your writing, you
write about wherever you have been. So, if you live in different
regions, you have different experiences to write about.

But most of your writing has been about the South.

That's true. I was and probably still am prejudiced about that to a
great extent. I do prefer to write about the South. My reasoning—and
I guess my excuse, if I have to make an excuse for writing about the
South—is that I'm better acquainted with it than other places. I know
the territory, the people, the climate, the economics and sociology—
lots of things that a writer needs to know about.

You have lived in the West now for a number of years. Why not write about this region?

If I could live another fifty years, maybe I would. I'd go to Canada or Mexico or even back to the South, and there I'd write about the West. But right now I'm not prepared for it. Besides, the West is too big and expansive for any one writer. You've got the Indian culture, the Spanish culture, the Mexican influences—all combining to make it a diverse and complex region. It would take many writers to write about the West.

The years you spent in New England, especially Maine, produced many fine short stories but only one published novel, A Lamp for Nightfall. *Why is this?*

I suppose I didn't get to know the area well enough to do any more with it. The character of the people and of the state is very different from what I was used to in the South. So I was more or less forced to rely upon my Southern experience. I was too impatient to learn all I would have to know about New England in order to write novels about it. That one book, as you say, was the only novel I ever published about New England. I wrote another one, *Autumn Hill*, but it never appeared in print.

Do you see any striking parallels or differences between Southerners and New Englanders?

I've thought for years that the difference between the North and the South is that the people in the South are amoral, whereas the people in New England are immoral. New Englanders know better but they go ahead and sin anyway. Southerners don't know any better, and that's what makes them amoral. In other words, I think you have more license to sin in the South because all you have to do is go to church the next Sunday, confess, and have your sins washed away. Then you can start all over again. Religion is such a deeply ingrained characteristic of Southern life that it can take care of anything. Some Southerners act as if you can commit any sin as long as you go back to church and put a dollar in the collection. But in New England, you have a conscience to deal with, I think. When you do something wrong, something sinful, it sticks with you. You can't get rid of it just by going to church because church in New England does not absolve you of sin. In New England, the church is an intellectual institution, not an emotional one as it is in the South.

Your father was a minister in the Associated Reformed Presbyterian Church. Did his attitudes about religion influence you?

It could be that his attitude toward the profession of the ministry influenced me a great deal. You see, my father was interested in the whole field of religion more or less as a sociologist would be. He never relented from his idea that religion should involve a socialized, economic kind of life instead of just purely the worship of a God. He also thought that religion was being prostituted by money-making concerns, especially among some of the more evangelical ministers. In the South in those days, an evangelist would come into a small town along with a musician, someone who would act as his singing partner. He would arrange to take over a church for about a week; and, of course, he'd take up collections both before and after the meetings. At the end of the week, he would leave town with a lot of money in his pockets. Now, my father thought this type of activity was a religious fraud. Before I stopped going to church at the age of fifteen or so, my father would take me to these various denominations, especially to the more violent sort of evangelistic camp meetings—the Holy Rollers and whatnot. And from observing these meetings, I got the idea that this violent type of Southern religion was not for me. It was a little bit too farfetched, so far as I was concerned.

Farfetched religions play an important part in God's Little Acre *and, of course, in* Journeyman. *Is there a fundamental similarity between the religion of Ty Ty Walden, in the former, and that of Semon Dye in* Journeyman? *Perhaps in a shared emphasis on sexuality?*

No, I don't think so. Ty Ty's religion was his own personal, private affair; he was not trying to push it onto everyone else. Dye, though, was a salesman, a high-powered salesman of his evangelical brand of religion. I think that this is an important difference between the two.

Is there anything of value in the evangelical, emotional experience that Semon Dye brings to the town of Rocky Comfort?

Well, he brings a relief from the monotony of living; that's for sure. The emotionalism generated by his actions and his talk was a physical release for the people there. Dye was very adept at his profession. He was a real pro at arousing emotions. He knew exactly which button to push and when to push it in order to set the people off in a blaze of glory. I guess maybe he had to have some feeling for what he was doing; but how sincere it was, I don't know.

Is Semon Dye genuinely disturbed by his failure to convert Lorene, the prostitute?

That depends on what you mean by "disturbed." Having this opposition, this one failure out of his whole congregation, probably does bother him. It hurts his ego. Lorene was not easily taken in by his soft talk. What happens is that two people come together there and each is determined to have his own way. But Dye doesn't succeed in converting her; and, on the other hand, she does not really succeed in showing up his inability to convert her. I think the fact that Lorene provides a contrast, though, shows that there is a possible resistance to religion if you want to confront it. You don't have to surrender yourself to this fraudulent type of activity.

Fate of some sorts seems to function importantly in several of your novels. Do you consider yourself a fatalist or a determinist?

I think that my close association with the Presbyterian religion might have had some effect on me. As I understand it, the Presbyterians are predestinarians; they believe that what is going to happen is going to happen. I think that way myself to a degree. For example, I know I'm going to die, so I'm prepared for it. I'd say that I do have a slight prejudice in favor of fate being absolute, and maybe that belief influences me when I write. Of course, I know that a person has the ability to change his own life and to direct his own existence to some extent. But at the same time, I think, fundamentally, we are all people of nature and nature is going to get us one way or another. So I'm going along with nature.

In God's Little Acre, *was Will Thompson fated to die?*

I don't know whether he was or not. He was a headstrong young man who had a dream that he was going to get that mill started up again. I suppose if there hadn't been a strike, then something else would have come along that Will would have taken a definite stand for. He had a kind of determination that could be applied to any facet of life. It just happened in the book that he applied it to the mill.

But it seems that if the mill does not destroy him, then his brother-in-law Buck will. He can't win.

Well, that whole story got to be pretty complex. I had difficulty sorting it out myself as I went along because so many people were involved. Sometimes I regretted that I allowed so many characters to get into the act: [*laughing*] I couldn't control them all.

The men in God's Little Acre *are all more or less enamored of
Griselda. Is she meant to be some sort of ideal woman?*

Not necessarily. I purposely created three or four different
personalities among the women, from Darling Jill all the way through
to Rosamond. You may have admiration for one; you may have pity
for another. It depends on your own attitudes as a reader. But my
purpose there was to display these distinct personalities that you can
find in my town, your town, anywhere you go in life.

*Do you foresee any problems with this generation or future
generations of liberated women who read your books?*

No. I don't at all. Many of the women I've been associated with,
who have known me and my work, have been liberated for a long
time.

In two of your other novels about the South, Tobacco Road *and*
Tragic Ground, *the characters seem to be innately lazy and unwilling
to help themselves. But at the same time they are presented as
victims of economic oppression. Is this a contradiction?*

I don't think so. You see, the Lesters and the Douthits belonged to
a class of people that had completely lost the ability to survive. Many
years ago in several parts of the South, the poor whites simply lacked
the necessary elements of nutrition. When you're in poverty and
your sustenance consists of only one or two items—we'll say corn
bread and greens—your body is just not getting all that it needs to
function. And many of these people would not have even that much
to eat. In fact, some of them were forced to become clay eaters; they
would actually eat dirt to keep their stomachs from growling, to keep
from feeling their hunger. In the meantime, of course, the health of
the poor whites deteriorated, and they became susceptible to
whatever diseases came along. Often they contracted pellagra and
hookworm, both of which were very prevalent in the South of that
day. Now, pellagra and hookworm would not be apparent to the
naked eye. So what happened was that even though nothing
appeared to be wrong with these people, they had serious diseases
which resulted in habitual laziness. They really were not able to help
themselves.

*In other words, they do act shiftless and lazy, but this behavior is the
result of poverty and diet?*

Yes, exactly. They would try to overcome their inertia, but since they had no money for medical treatment they were unable to do so. They couldn't get rid of the diseases that caused their misery. The most they could do was try to alleviate it, like someone dipping snuff to kill the pain of a toothache. People could not afford to see a dentist, even if there had been one to see.

That explains the laziness, but what about the apparent moral depravity of a character such as Jeeter Lester, a man who will deny crumbs of food to his own starving mother?

When a person is subjected to a very severe beating in life, he might get the feeling that he has to protect himself first. Therefore, he's not going to give his wife or his mother anything to eat; he's going to keep it for himself. That might be one of the attitudes a person in such a defeated position would assume.

Many of your poor whites are at-times violent people. Is their violence, perhaps, also a response to their defeated position?

Oh, violence and cruelty have been part of Southern existence for a long time. I think personally that they're probably caused by the hardship of life itself. A person can feel that he is defeated and is unable to rise above his situation in life; he can feel at the mercy of fate. This would cause tremendous resentment. If a person has been shortchanged by his landlord, or if his landlord has taken something away from him, resentment builds up until he's got to find some kind of release for it. And just hitting the ground with a stick won't do it; he has to hit something animate. I've seen a person who had reached the limit of his endurance almost beat a mule to death with a stick. He'd been hurt and was trying to find some solace through displacement. Such a person is able to believe he exists only if he can hurt somebody or something in retaliation.

Many critics, among them Donald Davidson, the Southern Agrarian, have said that you exposed the South at its worst. In retrospect, do you think that you have slandered or distorted the South in your books?

I had no intention at all to try to make the South look worse than it was. But I never considered myself a spokesman for the South either. I think everybody has a right to give his own version of life, and I was just giving mine.

Then you believe your fiction portrayed the South as it actually existed?

Well, all fiction is a distortion. You have to shape, to add and eliminate. You cannot simply photograph a story; a story must be given variations of depth and color, of light and shadows. Every piece of fiction is a distortion to some extent because something has been omitted and something has been added. But I do not think that I distorted anything beyond recognition. You see, if you concentrate on one aspect of existence at the expense of something else, then you are exaggerating one phase and not paying much attention to another. A distortion in fiction might highlight something that is not a part of everybody's life but that does exist for certain people. A painter does the same thing. When he paints a landscape, he's not going to put in every blade of grass; he's going to suggest some grass. And the grass he suggests might be taller or thicker or more intense than the actual grass is. But you can then appreciate the fertility of this scene. That would be a distortion in painting. And I would call both of these distortions good distortions.

Why do you think the rest of the country has long found fiction about the South so interesting?

Because of the romance probably. In the time of the great plantations, the songs and legends of the South were romantic and generated a lot of outside interest. They portrayed people who had few hardships, who had servants to wait on them and were living a life of ease. Of course, the black people in the Old South suffered plenty of hardships, but they didn't count. Even today Southern writers still have some of this romantic tradition in their work—that life is easier, that the climate is better, that friendships are more lasting and so forth. These notions have been built up over the years to the extent that the Southerner himself still believes them today. He has great allegiance to the South because he thinks that Southerners are a little bit superior to the people of Vermont or Illinois, or maybe to those benighted people up there in Minnesota.

Much of your fiction and nonfiction about the South deals with race relations. Do you see any kind of solution to the racial problems in this country?

I think that the sooner there is amalgamation of the two races, the better off we will be. This seems to me to be the expedient thing to do. However, I don't foresee it in my lifetime, and I can't visualize one mixed color anytime in the near future. There may always be prejudice, within all races and among all races—between the Italians and the Spanish, the French and the Germans, the Arabs and the Jews. As far as the blacks and whites are concerned, I believe the ideal solution to the racial problem would be for the two races to become amalgamated as they are in Brazil. When I was in Brazil, many years ago after the war, I saw no racial distinction between the people there. Blacks and whites socialized and intermarried. I think this is the ultimate way that the two races could get along, but I don't know that it will ever happen in this country.

With your lifelong interest in race relations, did you become involved in the civil rights movement of the 1960's and '70's?

No. I had no contact with it, professionally or otherwise. Naturally, I approved of the attempt to desegregate the South because my sympathy has long been that segregation is wrong and should be terminated. So I watched with interest what went on. But I'm a writer, not a crusader. I leave the crusading to others.

In your nonfiction book In Search of Bisco, *you indicate that your own initiation into racial distinctions came about when you were not allowed to stay overnight at the home of your black friend Bisco. What prompted your father to take you home?*

Actually, I'm sure that my father's attitude would have been to let me stay. But I think my mother would probably have insisted that I be brought home immediately once she found out where I was.

What accounted for this difference in your parents' attitudes?

I think, basically, that my father was a practical person, whereas my mother was theoretical in a sense. He knew how to deal with the poverty and the prejudice that surrounded us; but she felt that she had no control over it, that she could not change it. Her response was to encourage me not to become too carried away with local life and local mores. She didn't want me to end up living my whole life in one small town as a butcher or a storekeeper or someone who delivered ice all day long. I listened to her and had great respect for her attitude. She had acquired an education and had become a teacher, so she was well aware of the shortcomings of these small Southern towns. She resented the ignorance that surrounded us very much. Her theory was that it is not necessary to have to end your life right here—there is something better than this. She encouraged me to try to find something beyond the horizon.

At one time you described ten novels that you had written about the South as a "Southern cyclorama."* What, specifically, did you mean by this term?

I saw those books as representative vistas, or visions, of the South. The thread I had in mind was not really a single theme but a process, you might say. I was just picking out various phases of Southern life to write about, of life as exemplified by the small-town politician, the schoolteacher, the boardinghouse keeper, by a colored brother and sister in one of those little Southern towns. I would say it was an attempt to cover the South in many of its different phases, including its social life, its religious life, and so forth.

Do you become emotionally caught up in the lives of the characters you create? Do you suffer and triumph with them?

No, not to that extent. I do get very close to these people, of course; but I don't live their lives for them.

When you explored the South with Margaret Bourke-White in preparation for You Have Seen Their Faces, *did you have a specific goal in mind or were you seeking what you've just called "representative vistas"?*

Well, for *You Have Seen Their Faces* I set out particularly to learn what was causing all the trouble in the agricultural South. And I discovered almost immediately that the basis of the economic difficulties of the people there was the sharecropper system. It was very obvious to me that if this system continued, the people would suffer. But fortunately things soon changed.

Yet despite the evils of sharecropping, it seems that in Tobacco Road *Captain John seals the Lesters' fate when he sells the land and puts an end to their life as his sharecroppers.*

Well, there must have been something he could have done to alleviate their situation, but you can't blame the landlord for everything that goes wrong. You see, it was the sharecropping system itself that was the real wrongful use of human life. It made a person an economic slave. The sharecropper had no hope of ever being able

---

The novels are *Tobacco Road* (1932), *God's Little Acre* (1933), *Journeyman* (1935), *Trouble in July* (1940), *Tragic Ground* (1944), *A House in the Uplands* (1946), *The Sure Hand of God* (1947), *This Very Earth* (1948), *Place Called Estherville* (1949), and *Episode in Palmetto* (1950).

to overcome his position in life. He ended up as an outcast, both
physically and socially.

You Have Seen Their Faces, *through its photographs and its text,
also portrays some problems in the South that seem more social than
economic, at least on the surface.*

Bourke-White and I witnessed many injustices during our travels.
For example, all over the South, every state had chain gangs. I've
seen them all the way from Tennessee to the Carolinas, to Alabama
and Georgia. I remember that the first time I saw one my reaction
was total abhorrence. I said to myself, "This is just not right; a man
should not be compelled to drag a chain and a heavy iron ball
around with him everywhere he goes." And my reaction was in no
way theoretical. It was practical, based entirely on observation—
here's a man in chains. Seeing these chain gangs was a turning point
in my life. I feel sure that if this condition of human bondage had
continued, it would have threatened American civilization. It's very
fortunate that chain gangs become obsolete when they did.

In your first book of nonfiction, Some American People, *you say that
"merely to see things is not enough," that "only the understanding of
man's activities is satisfying." How did these beliefs affect your
writing?*

When you're young, you're very curious about what goes on in
the world. Really, you don't even have to go out looking for material
to write about. The material is already there and it comes to you; it
forces itself upon you. Then you have to try to understand it and
form a judgment of it.

Did you hope that Some American People *would lead to the reform
of those things that you judged to be wrong?*

Oh, I might have made a few suggestions in that book, but now I
don't even remember what they were. I was mainly an observer
there, recording the difficulties in American life during the early
1930's, the time of the great Depression. I was affected emotionally
by my travels because what I saw taking place was not in keeping
with what I believed to be the American standard of living. And I was
afraid that the suffering I observed was probably only the initial stage
of something—something that should not be allowed to continue.
That book was written before the Depression had spread across the
whole country, when it was still being felt most in the populous

regions and in the manufacturing centers, such as Detroit. I suppose my attitude was that here is a major new problem in American life and there must be some action that can be taken to correct it.

You refer to yourself as an "observer," but in both of these nonfiction books the subject matter and the manner in which you present it clearly amount to a call for some sort of reform.
  I'm a writer, not a reformer. I've always considered myself essentially an observer, a bystander. Besides, these two books you mention are in a different category from my other writing.

In the early 1930's Marxist critics embraced your books because of what they perceived as a reformist aim in them. Later these critics became disaffected with your work. What happened? How would you characterize your relationship with the Marxists?
  Well, I never thought of myself as being in partnership with the Marxists at any time. I never, in all the years of my life, considered myself to be a Marxist, Communist, or fellow traveler. In fact, I don't belong to any political party because that way I feel free to vote for the man and the issue. I'm sure that especially in my early years I was willing to accept praise from critics of any stripe, and of course I did not like to get adverse criticism. But I never fell out with the Marxist critics because I was never in their camp to begin with. So whatever happened between us was their doing, not mine.

You've traveled extensively, not only in America but throughout the world. Have your observations of other countries influenced your views of America?
  I would say that I can understand American life much better by having had the opportunity to make a comparison, to observe social and economic and political differences between our country and others. Now, I don't purposely go looking for comparisons, but they're inevitable. For example, you can see how much better the peasant life might be in a given European country than in this country. Just compare it to the old days of the agricultural empire in the South, to the plantation system with its slave quarters and such.

Your answer calls to mind Tragic Ground, *in which Jim Howard comes home from the war in Europe a changed man. Apparently he has experienced something there that enables him to break away from Poor Boy, the Gulf Coast shantytown that drags Spence Douthit and others down. Just what did Jim Howard discover in Europe?*

Well [*smiling*], I wasn't there with him so I wouldn't know exactly. I would imagine that his experience in France showed him a type of civilization that he was not accustomed to back home but that he probably admired very much. Whatever he saw, it was a contrast to what he had known back in Arkansas or wherever, and certainly at Poor Boy. It made him want something better for himself, and so he got out. You see, the traditional French countryside is a very stable, solid environment in which to live. The work ethic there has something to do with this, I think. The peasant classes in Europe have a tradition of solid labor to rely on. They work hard, but they get something for it and they're proud of what they do. Their American counterpart has had none of that background and none of that training. I think the European peasant has been much better off economically and socially than his American cousins, at least until fairly recently.

You studied sociology and economics in college, did you not?

Yes, at the University of Virginia and at the Wharton School of the University of Pennsylvania. My interests as a student were not catholic at all; they were based primarily on those two subjects. At the University of Virginia I took an advanced field course in sociology, having to do with the eleemosynary institutions of the State of Virginia—the insane asylums, the poorhouses, and so on, even the prisons. I wanted to find out how these people got where they were and who was responsible for their condition. How did someone happen to get mutilated in a sawmill? Why were people in poorhouses, in prisons, in mental institutions? What reduced them to the position of being disadvantaged persons? And what I learned was that the answer to those kinds of questions is almost always economic, at least in part. I wanted to know about these things in order to write about them. I had to understand the sociology of life so that I could write about the ordinary person, the person whose affliction—whether poverty or physical disability or whatever—might make him a ward of the state someday. Even in my studies, I considered myself a writer first.

To further your writing, you apparently chose to study potential subjects for your own work rather than the literature produced by other writers. Do you not see a value to literature courses or to courses on the craft of fiction?

I classify people in two different categories—writers and readers. If you're teaching literature so that people will know how to tell what's good and what's bad, how to select their reading, well, that sounds okay. But if you're trying to teach writing, which is something else entirely, I don't think you'll succeed. [*Shrugging*] I'm just a writer, though. I don't read.

What about the Bible? One would suppose that, with a minister for a father, you would be quite familiar with it.

I've read parts of it, of course; but I never have read it all the way through. Perhaps I should have because, as it is, I'm sort of ignorant about the Bible. I've never studied it on my own; and, once my father gave me my leave of absence from churchgoings, I never attended Bible classes or Sunday School or any church services at all.

Many commentators have linked you to the tradition of Southwest Humor, as exemplified by Longstreet, Harris, Hooper, and others. Have you been an admirer of this group?

I hardly knew they existed. I can't recall his name, but there is one particular Georgia writer of maybe a hundred years ago who wrote little squibs of stories—one page, two pages, three pages long. I've seen them but I didn't read them; I don't even know what they're about. Now, several people have given me books of stories written in a vernacular or in dialect. They seem to think I should read these stories because that would inspire me to write similar ones. But why anyone would believe that I want to imitate a writer, any writer, is something I don't understand. I can't see it at all. So I just turn those books away—get rid of them. I only write like myself.

Your celebrated short story "Candy-Man Beechum" differs stylistically from almost all of your other fiction. It has, in fact, been called a prose folk ballad. Was this a particularly difficult form to work with?

Difficult? No, no trouble at all. I did it as an experiment, and I've found that experiments always have a certain ease to them—which is not to say that they're slight. In "Candy-Man Beechum" my experiment was to see if I could convey the sense of dialect, the feeling of dialect, by the rhythm of a sentence instead of by the sounds of speech. I wanted to prove to myself that rhythm is superior to dialect as a means of capturing Southern speech in fiction. You see, I have always had a dislike for dialect in stories. I think it's a very reprehensible kind of talk for a writer to use in his work.

Do you mean the graphic, phonetical representation of dialect on the page?

Yes. The reader should not have to decipher that sort of thing; it's too great an obligation to impose upon him. I've always felt that dialect should be outlawed for that reason.

Another of your works with a distinctive style is The Sacrilege of Alan Kent, *which has been described as a prose-poem. I wonder if this piece might have been a transition between your writing of poetry and your writing of fiction?*

It might have been, yes. Anyway, it was in that same era. What happened was that I was in the state of Maine then, trying to write fiction—or trying to learn how to write it. I would have written anything I thought might help me reach that goal because fiction was what I really wanted to do all along. *The Sacrilege of Alan Kent* was just one more experiment in that direction.

Did you give any thought to sticking with this particular form as something that you had pioneered?

No, I didn't view it in that light at all. I published the first part of *Alan Kent* in a little magazine in Boston called *Pagany*, and the editor there kept urging me to send him more and more of this same material. That was the only thing that encouraged me to write the next two parts. *Pagany* paid no money, though; and I was sure none of the bigger magazines would want this sort of thing. So in the end I had to do something different in order to make a little money.

You've obviously devoted your life to writing, but would you continue to write if you made no money at it?

[*Laughing*] That depends. Not now, I guess. Now I'd have to do something else to support myself. But in the days before I sold anything, I published probably fifty short stories in little magazines that paid no money at all. To me that was training, though; that was preliminary. I was willing to do anything to learn how to write because my expectation, or at least my aim, was that sooner or later a commercial magazine would pay me money for my stories—maybe *The Saturday Evening Post* or something. So I kept on sending out a short story every day, day after day, to these well-known magazines. It took a long time, but finally I got results.

Was there ever a time when you came close to giving up writing?

No, no. I would have been a failure if I had tried to go into any

other profession, I'm sure, because I would not have been happy with
anything else. You find many people in various occupations who
really are frustrated writers. They don't want to be doctors or lawyers;
they want to be writers. Well, I wanted to be a writer, and I think now
I was smart to jump right into it—not to try to go into some other
field that would be considered acceptable. I guess you could say that
I've been stuck with being a writer all my life.

You have written that Tobacco Road *began as a short story and
eventually worked its way into a novel. How did this transformation
take place?*

When I was living with my parents in Wrens, Georgia, there were
perhaps fifteen or twenty tobacco roads throughout that whole
region. I used to take trips with my father around the countryside,
and we would see the kind of life the people there were living. Even
then I was very interested in the fiction that could be written about
this part of the country. Later, I started scribbling and ended up with
a few characters in a setting. Then I think I probably had something
that might have been a short story in itself; but it was inconclusive,
and I was not satisfied with it. I could not tell everything I wanted to
tell in a short story, so I decided to ditch that idea. I began writing at
length about the subject later on when I lived in South Carolina.
After that I wrote some more of the book in New York, then went to
Maine and finished it. So in a total period of about a year, I suppose,
I wrote the book in those three different locations. But I always stayed
right with the region that I had started out with, which was a place in
Richmond County, Georgia, near my parents' home in Wrens.

*At what point do you usually know whether you're working on a
novel or a short story?*

Right from the beginning, as a rule. The novel and the short story
are quite different. I don't think the *Tobacco Road* sort of thing ever
happened to me again.

*You've said that you do not write with a plot in mind. In more
general terms, do you have any kind of a formula at all for writing a
book or story?*

Well, I would say that you build a story step by step up to a certain
point. When you reach that point, you cannot go any further. It's
important then to let the reader down right away, to jump off a cliff
with him—to do something to end that story on a high note.

Is the process of writing a disagreeable effort for you or something you look forward to?

It all depends. If it's going well, I want to get right back at it again. But if I'm having trouble—which does happen sometimes—why, then I wake up with a headache. [*Laughing*] Yes, it can be a real troublesome thing if it's not going well.

Over the years you've spoken many, many times before groups of university students and other audiences. Has this personal contact with the public been something of a welcome change from the isolation of writing?

Just the opposite. For a while I got caught up in yearly lecture tours, traveling around the country from Alaska to Puerto Rico, Boston to Los Angeles, back and forth, back and forth. I was under contract to do it—one-night stands, reading the same speech. But taking this job meant that for two or three months every year I had to drop my writing, even if I was working well at the time and wanted to continue. Lecturing like that is a very deadly occupation for a writer.

What about Dartmouth College? Don't you still visit there from time to time?

Oh, well, Dartmouth is a different situation. I've been there half a dozen times or more, anywhere from one week to six weeks. I speak to some classes. Students come in to talk about their writing or their difficulties in getting published. But what I do at Dartmouth is not part of a great, hectic lecture tour. It's a residency, and I'm much in favor of that.

Dartmouth also has a large collection of your manuscripts and first editions. Was it your decision to favor this particular institution?

Actually, there are three schools that have pretty good-sized collections—Dartmouth, the University of Georgia, and the University of Virginia. But Dartmouth's is the main one. Years ago, when I changed publishers to Duell, Sloan and Pearce, Cap Pearce asked me what I wanted done with my manuscripts once they were through with them. "I don't care what you do with them," I told him. I remember he looked at me and said, "Well, we're not just going to throw them into the ashcan." So he determined that Dartmouth had a good potential for accepting manuscripts. Since then, the library there has sent somebody around now and then to collect manuscripts and books. They've also bought some things at auction including, I think, the manuscript of *Tobacco Road*. Now they have quite a large display.

Your birth date has been variously listed as 17 December 1900, 1902, and 1903. Can you set the record straight?

Well, I was there at my birth but no one else who's still alive was. All I know about the year, month, and day of my birth is what my mother told me—December 17th, 1903. And I have always assumed that a mother knows more than a child about such things. You see, in those days the state of Georgia did not issue birth certificates. When the time came that I wanted to get a passport or something like that, I had to obtain statements from three people who had known me for at least ten years. They all tended to think I was born in 1903. But in order to make sure I was old enough to get a passport, or whatever it was I needed at the time, we put down 1902 as my birth-date. Even so, I consider myself to have been born December 17th, 1903. And one way or another, I think I'm lucky to still be living in 1980.

Malcolm Cowley, in And I Worked at the Writer's Trade, *describes his impression of your image as a writer. He says, in part: "Caldwell presents to the world, and to himself, the writing man as an ideal. . . . His only aim is to set down, in the simplest words, a true unplotted record of people without yesterdays. Past literature does not exist for him, and he is scarcely aware of having rivals in the present. As with Adam in the Garden, every statement he makes is new." Is this description—with its emphasis on experience, originality, and freedom from literary tradition—accurate, do you think? Do you recognize yourself, or perhaps your persona, in the words of this long-time admirer of your fiction?*

I have no personal image in my own mind, either about what I am or what I do. I don't even think of myself as a writer, by name. I would not try to create myself as a big man or a leader or anything of that sort. In my view I'm just a subsidiary character to the whole process of writing. The only thing that really interests me is what I'm trying to make—the story itself that I'm trying to get told. That's it.

The Art of Fiction LXII:
Erskine Caldwell
Elizabeth Pell Broadwell and Ronald Wesley Hoag/1980

From *The Paris Review*, No. 86 (Winter 1982), 126-57. Reprinted by permission.

Wearing the black socks by which he had said we would recognize him, Erskine Caldwell called for us at a motel in Scottsdale, Arizona. A large-boned six-footer who, in Wilkes-Barre, Pennsylvania, once played professional football, Caldwell is still physically imposing. His hair, which in earlier times earned him the nickname "Red," is now predominantly white; his eyes are an arresting pale blue. On the drive to his Spanish-style, single-story home at the foot of a desert mountain, he remarked precisely each traffic light, turn, and landmark so we could get out there on our own.

On the first afternoon we met with Mr. Caldwell in his red-carpeted study for exactly two hours. "I believe in rules," he declared, "and you said you wanted to go for two hours." The most prominent feature of Caldwell's study is his large wooden writing table, faced away from the window with its view of the backyard pool. Under the table, just a dunk shot away from the portable typewriter, rests a washtub-sized wooden wastebasket. An exercise bicycle, which Erskine says belongs to his wife Virginia, and she says belongs to him, occupies a corner of the room. Above it the wall is lined with Hogarth prints, purchased in London "when you could still buy them pretty cheap." In a bookcase along the opposite wall is a well-stocked library of dictionaries (he prefers the "old" *Webster's Collegiate* for its etymologies) and books on the English language. We did not notice that the bookshelves contained anything written by him.

With more than eighty million books sold to readers in nearly forty different languages, Erskine Caldwell is one of the most widely read literary figures of the 20th Century. His novel *God's Little Acre* has alone sold over fourteen million copies. His books have been made into three movies and three plays; the stage adaptation of *Tobacco Road* made American theatre history when it ran for seven-and-a-half years on Broadway. A versatile and pro-lific writer, Caldwell is the author of almost sixty books, including novels, short-story collections, autobiographical volumes, interpretive travel books, children's books, and photo-essay volumes (such as the recently reissued *You Have Seen Their Faces*) done in collaboration with the photographer Margaret Bourke-White.

In addition to *Tobacco Road* (1932) and *God's Little Acre* (1933), Caldwell's most celebrated novels are *Journeyman* (1935), *Trouble in July* (1940), and *Tragic Ground* (1944), all of which portray an impoverished, early-century, rural South that is both homeland and wasteland for its troubled and sometimes grotesque in-habitants. In a different genre and a different vein, *Georgia Boy* (1943), his genial short-story cycle about a small-town family enlivened by the antics of a quixotic father, is in many ways his best book and perhaps an American mas-terpiece. Caldwell's latest books are a reissuing of his seventy-five story collection, *Jackpot*, in a Franklin Library limited edition (Fall 1980), and the autobiographical *A Year of Living*, now in progress.

Erskine Caldwell was born in Coweta County, Georgia, in either 1902 or 1903; there is no accurate record of his birth. He spent his early years living with his parents in a household that moved frequently among the Southern states. On various occasions he attended Erskine College, the University of Virginia, and the University of Pennsyl-vania, but did not earn a college degree. Following brief stints at a variety of jobs and a term as a reporter for the *Atlanta Journal*, he moved in 1926 to an old farmhouse in Mount Vernon, Maine; there during the next seven years he served his literary apprenticeship. A thirteen-year mar-riage to Helen Lannigan ended in 1938. From 1939 to 1941 he was married to Margaret Bourke-White, and from 1942 to 1955 to June Johnson. He is the father of four children, from his first and third marriages. Since 1957 he has been married to his present wife, Virginia Moffett Caldwell, an accomplished artist who has illustrated sever-al of his books.

The first interview session begins rather stiffly. Cald-well's manner is formal as he addresses our questions carefully, in a firm voice still slightly tinged by a Southern accent. He speaks slowly and deliberately, pausing to formulate his replies and select the precise word he desires. His language, in general, is exact without sounding purposely elevated; and he uses an occasional slang term such as "chap" or "punk" as effective seasoning. Sitting behind his writing desk, he now and then toys with the typewriter carriage as we talk.

Interviewers: Mr. Caldwell, what first interested you in becoming a writer?

Caldwell: Well, I was not a writer to begin with; I was a listener. In those early decades of the century, reading and writing were not common experiences. Oral storytelling was the basis of fiction. You learned by listening around the store, around the gin, the icehouse, the woodyard, or wherever people congregated and had nothing to do. You would listen for the extraordinary, the unusual; the people knew how to tell stories orally in such a way that they could make the smallest incident, the most farfetched idea, into something extraordinarily interesting. It could be just a rooster crowing at a certain time of night or morning. It's a mysterious thing. Many Southern writers must have learned the art of storytelling from listening to oral tales. I did. It gave me the knowledge that the simplest incident can make a story.

Interviewers: How do you go about transforming such a simple incident into a story?

Caldwell: You get a kind of fever, I suppose, mentally and emotionally, that lifts you up and carries you away. You have to sustain this energy you've gotten to write your story. By the time you've finished, all your energy, your passion, is spent. You've been drained of everything.

Interviewers: Is this passion something that comes in a flash?

Caldwell: No. Things that come in a flash you have to hold suspect. If you rely upon a dream, you're going to be fooled. In the course of writing your story, you have to follow in sequence what your thoughts are.

Interviewers: But your thoughts have to start somewhere.

Caldwell: Well, you have an idea to start with, otherwise you wouldn't sit down at your typewriter. Whatever this idea is, that's the solid thing you want to work with. You can't wait for inspiration because it may never come.

Interviewers: Where do you get that first idea?

Caldwell: You see a school bus going along out there and you wonder where it's heading. Then you imagine a school, and a teacher. Well, who is this teacher? What is she like? Does she lead an interesting life? Then you recall some of the teachers that you had in the past. So it keeps on going and going.

Interviewers: You mention recalling teachers you had known. Would this experience be important?

Caldwell: Yes. Experience combined with imagination. You have to use your imagination to invent something better than life because life itself is dull and prosaic.

Interviewers: Would this inventing give you your plot?

Caldwell: No. I'm not interested in plots. I'm interested only in the characterization of people and what they do. I understand you can buy a pamphlet called "The Seven Basic Plots of Fiction." A plot is applicable to what's done in a mystery story, where the author knows in the beginning how it's going to end. I never know how anything is going to end. All I ever know is the first line, the first sentence, the first page. The work terminates itself without dictation from me. Signs and portents indicate in some manner that a conclusion is just around the corner.

Interviewers: Would this be true of your short stories as well as your novels?

Caldwell: Both are just a series of events and a cast of people that grow by themselves. I don't manufacture tapestries. I let the people say or do what's going to happen next.

Interviewers: Then your characters control you?

Caldwell: Completely. These are all entirely new people and that means they're unpredictable. You see, just like a child has to start from infancy to become a man, the character has to develop. You have a vision of some sort, maybe an insight into his appearance, but if you're true to what you're doing, he's telling you what his action's going to be and why he did it. If you let a person grow like that, little by little, you will have a character that is believable and maybe memorable to the reader.

Interviewers: But you must have some influence over your characters.

Caldwell: I have no influence over them. I'm only an observer, recording. The story is always being told by the characters themselves. In fact, I'm often critical, or maybe ashamed, of what some of them say and do—their profanity or their immorality. But I have no control over it.

Interviewers: But you do at least understand their motivations?

Caldwell: I'm not an oracle by any means. I'm often at a loss to explain the desires and the motivations of my people. You'll have to find your explanation in them. They're their own creations.

Interviewers: Among your characters do you have any favorites?

Caldwell: No, because I don't know that any of them are beloved in that sense. Some of them are reprehensible.

Interviewers: Which are your favorites among your novels, short stories, and books of nonfiction?

Caldwell: Well, if you have to pin a person down, I would say that I like *In Search of Bisco* in nonfiction, *Georgia Boy* among short stories, and *God's Little Acre* in the novel form. Those three strike me as being acceptable.

Interviewers: In *God's Little Acre*, is Ty Ty Walden's persistence in mining for gold on his land his faith or his folly?

Caldwell: It's a quirk of nature. There are people who get these tics. One person might get an idea to raise spotted pigs for no good reason at all. It will ruin his family life because the pig pens make a big smell right next to his house. His wife divorces him and so on. Now whether Ty Ty Walden got his tic through a dream or whether his father imbued him with it, somehow he got the idea that the land he owned had gold in it. In North Georgia, at a place called Dahlonega, they mined gold and minted gold coins. Well, that may have influenced him. Anyway, he was imbued with the idea that he had gold deposits and that all he had to do was dig until he could find them. Nothing would stop him.

Interviewers: Do Ty Ty's manipulations of the "God's Little Acre" that gives the book its title indicate his hypocrisy?

Caldwell: I think you would have to blame the author for that; I wouldn't blame Ty Ty. That was a literary movement to give variety, to give change, to have something happen in this story.

Interviewers: Would you admit to there being symbolism in your books?

Caldwell: No, not a bit. I wouldn't know how to inject it, and I

would probably abhor it if I found it. I think the whole object in the
search for symbolism in English and Creative Writing courses is just
to instigate a thought process in the students. The thinking is what
really counts in the end, I guess; even an average student can find
symbolism because you can't prove or disprove it.

Interviewers: Well, in your short story "The Growing Season," if
Fiddler isn't a symbol, who or what is he? Will you tell us?

Caldwell: Nope.

Interviewers: Does it matter?

Caldwell: It matters to the extent that it interests me to write that
way. I know who Fiddler is, or at least I think I do. I can't be positive
because it can go two ways. I won't even tell you what the two ways
are; that would help give it away. But, no, I guess it doesn't matter in
the end. The speculation is what really counts.

Interviewers: You've listed your favorites among your own
books. What have you admired by other writers?

Caldwell: I haven't read enough to know.

Interviewers: Do you expect us to believe that?

Caldwell: I don't make a pretense of that at all. Oh, I used to read
the Sears and Roebuck Catalogue, every year when it came out. But
I learned early in life that you can be a reader or a writer. I decided to
be a writer.

Interviewers: So you weren't influenced by any other writers?

Caldwell: Influence is a very tenuous matter. I try to avoid it in
every respect. I don't want to be influenced by anybody. If I were
being influenced by Shakespeare or Poe, let's say, I would be
second-rate at it. An imitation is always going to produce something
not as good as the original. The original, to me, is the only thing that
counts.

Interviewers: How do you feel about your many imitators over
the years, such as those satirized by James Thurber in "Bateman
Comes Home"?

Caldwell: Well, satire is a very legitimate field. I think you should
accept satirization easily, without being affronted by it. But imitation
seems to me to be a very low-down form of writing. Hemingway had
a great influence on fiction, and while in general that was all to the
good, he also had hundreds of outright imitators. I doubt that any of
them could do what he did as well as he could.

Interviewers: Like Hemingway, you also worked on a newspaper early in your career. Did this experience help teach you to write?

Caldwell: Yes. It was really good training because it compelled me to write something every day whether I felt like it or not. So in that way even writing obituaries helps fiction writing.

Interviewers: Was it working at a newspaper that got you in the habit of composing at the typewriter?

Caldwell: No. You might think so, but it didn't happen that way. My father had one of those great big old-fashioned Underwoods, and the first thing I ever wrote was on that typewriter. Since then I've always had to see what I'm working on right here before me.

Interviewers: Writing for a newspaper is a kind of on-the-job training. Did you also have any formal instruction in writing, perhaps at the various colleges you attended?

Caldwell: My most rewarding course at three different colleges was a graduate course in composition at the University of Virginia. It was conducted by a chap by the name of Atcheson Hench. I was only a freshman or a sophomore at the time, but I signed myself right in anyway. Life was too short to have to wait for four years. Hench let us write whatever we wanted to—poetry, short stories, nonfiction—and then everybody else would comment upon it. Hench wouldn't break my work down sentence by sentence or paragraph by paragraph. He left everything alone, which was very satisfactory to me. At the end of the course, he told me, "I had heard that you were not qualified for this course, but I watched you and I was satisfied. So, a lot of good luck to you."

Interviewers: Was this an early version of the creative writing courses that are so popular in colleges today?

Caldwell: No. It was not called Creative Writing; it was called English Composition. I fell out with the process when they invented the term Creative Writing. To me there is no such thing as creative writing. It's either good writing, whatever the subject, or it's not creative.

Interviewers: Does this mean that you don't distinguish between fiction and nonfiction?

Caldwell: That's right. It's not what you write, it's how you write it. Whether you want to base a work on facts or on imagination does not really matter. You can be a good writer in either field, or both.

The use of words is what makes writing, and in the end it's how well you do it that's going to count. Nonfiction can be just as appealing in a literary sense as a novel can be.

Interviewers: You said that Hench's was a composition course. Did you take any literature courses in college?

Caldwell: Well, I tried one English course and dropped out of it because the professor spent his whole time talking about Henry James or somebody of that caliber who was way beyond my comprehension. I also showed up for a graduate course called "A Study of Wordsworth." I remember that I'd been here for about half a term, I guess, when the Dean called me up to his office. He said, "I've received a question from the professor who's conducting the Wordsworth course. He wants to know how in the world you got into his class." I had told the professor that I didn't like either Wordsworth or his poetry, so he complained to the Dean. Anyway, I would say those were typical of my experiences with English courses in college. I think the problem was that my interest then had nothing to do with Wordsworth or Henry James but rather with the construction of a short story that had never been written before and that I wanted to write.

Interviewers: Did any of your college studies other than English interest you or help shape your writing?

Caldwell: Yes. Sociology and economics. I studied them because they are the basis of life. But I did not have what you'd call an intellectual interest in them as subjects. They were just a point of departure.

Interviewers: A point of departure?

Caldwell: I wanted to understand what life was, and why, so that I could write about it. But what I was writing in fiction was based much more on seeing life in action than on theory. For example, I really learned about economics by working in the basement of a ten-cent store in Wilkes-Barre and delivering milk in Washington at three o'clock every morning. And I learned about the hardships people were enduring by observing these things.

Interviewers: Yet some argue that your books present a distorted, rather than a realistic, view of the South. For example, they say that you exaggerated the plight of the Jeeter Lester family in *Tobacco Road*.

Caldwell: Many Southern people are not sympathetic at all to the story or to the condition of these people. They had not observed the extreme poverty, or, if they had, they paid no attention to it. When it was said to exist, they denied it immediately. Well, that's their privilege. But when I was living in Georgia with my parents, there were three or four different families from outside Wrens that would come in almost periodically, early in the morning. They would sit on our porch, begging for something to eat. From grandmothers to infants in arms, they would sit there all morning long, with somebody holding out his hand all of the time, moaning a little. So these things did exist. And I was always short-tempered with people who said they did not.

Interviewers: What about editors? Did they ask you to delete or change anything?

Caldwell: I've never encountered any situation where the publisher or editor has said, "This has to come out." In fact, they never change anything I write. At the beginning of my career Max Perkins, who was an editor at Scribner's, encouraged me to keep my attitude toward the integrity of writing. Since then I've never wanted anybody to tell me to change anything or to take anything out. And no one ever has.

Interviewers: Do you consider yourself unusually fortunate in having been left alone?

Caldwell: Yes, but after what Perkins told me I thought I deserved it, so I was not abashed at all. I had no doubts that I could handle it. I've never doubted that I can write what I want to write and do it the way I want to do it.

Interviewers: So no one advises you about your writing?

Caldwell: Well, I don't pretend to be infallible. When Virginia began helping me as an editorial assistant, I had to browbeat her to find some fault, to find what might be wrong with this particular word or that sentence. Victor Weybright, my publisher at New American Library, had cautioned her not to change anything I had written. So I had to educate her to be critical of my work, and now she's very strict with me.

Interviewers: Do you need isolation in order to write?

Caldwell: I do like privacy. In the old days in New York you could rent a room very cheaply, and I wrote several books in rented rooms because I had no distractions whatsoever. I could put a typewriter on the bed, sit opposite it in a chair, and write that way all day and night if I wanted to.

Interviewers: Do you ever have to overcome inertia to get yourself writing in the morning?

Caldwell: No, I wouldn't say so at all. Now, I might have the feeling coming in here that I don't know what I'm going to do. I might be worried about that. But I'll come in anyway and sit here until something happens. You see, it's something I wanted to do to begin with and so I'll still have that urge to see it through. I guess that talent is just a part of being a writer. You've got to have desire in order to make it all work.

Interviewers: Have you ever had any long dry spells?

Caldwell: No. You can always write something. You write limericks. You write a love letter. You do something to get you in the habit of writing again, to bring back the desire.

Interviewers: Do you do much revising as you go along?

Caldwell: I always have the biggest wastepaper basket in town, and it's full at the end of the day. I write three or four lines, don't like it, and in it goes. I found out early in life that there is no such thing as perfection or even close to perfection. Consequently, I discard constantly and try to do better with the next revision.

Interviewers: What is a good day's production for you then?

Caldwell: Oh, I might have two or three pages worth keeping at the end of the day. And that's a lot, you know; three pages is a lot. I probably write forty or forty-five total to get those three I can keep. And it is not unusual to sit at a typewriter all day and end up with nothing. But if you get up, you know you'll have nothing.

Interviewers: Is there much revising left to do after you've completed a draft in this manner?

Caldwell: Normally, yes. Now with *God's Little Acre* I dropped the sheets on the floor as I went and didn't pick them up until I had finished. Then I put them together and that was the book. No revision. But usually when a book is finished, I rewrite the whole thing anywhere from six to a dozen times because I'm never satisfied.

Interviewers: Do you add much in these subsequent drafts?

Caldwell: No. I might insert a description of a house or something, but you can overdo revisions. You can have too much fat and spoil what you should have lean. You have to know when to quit.

Interviewers: Do you read your books after they're published?

Caldwell: No. I open the books to see how the type looks. But once I've finished, I'm done.

Interviewers: Which of your books was the most difficult to write?

Caldwell: When you're young everything is easy, everything is smooth, everything you write is great. Every young writer feels that way. You don't have that backward look at it, that self-criticism. You have no judgment. But as you grow older, every book becomes a little more difficult because you're more critical of what you're doing. You reach the point where you know something is wrong but you're incapable of making it any better. So I would say the most recent two or three novels were probably the most difficult in that sense. The older writer is the one who has all the great trouble.

Interviewers: Do you think your writing has changed over the years?

Caldwell: Yes. Your attitudes and your style do change, in a progressive way, as you grow older. Whether there's improvement or not, at least there is change. Otherwise you'd be writing the same all the way through your career. You'd be writing Hardy Boys books or something. But when each work is a separate entity, there will be flux and change as you go.

Interviewers: As you look back upon your career, do you see it in terms of discernible stages?

Caldwell: Well, I suppose so. The first stage, of course, was learning how to write, which took eight or ten years during the twenties. Then after that was a period when I was able to make money by writing in a subsidiary way, in Hollywood and so forth. My most productive period was probably from 1950 to 1975. During that time I had the desire, the opportunity, and the material so I did not let up. From 1975 until the present has been my least productive period. You might say I've been recovering from the excesses of life. Now I'm back to normal, I hope.

Interviewers: Out of this long career, you say you spent almost the first decade learning how to write. Were you also publishing during this period?

Caldwell: The only way you can learn how to write is by writing;

but, yes, when you've written something, you do want to get it published. When I started writing, the little magazines would publish some of what I wrote, and that gave me the impetus to keep on writing. They paid no money; but because I was supporting myself in Maine, raising my own food, I was willing to stay with it for years and years if necessary until something happened. My first short story was published in the little magazine *transition* in Paris.

Interviewers: We've read that you devoted a year of your apprenticeship in Maine to writing poetry.

Caldwell: I think every writer has to go through the phase of writing poetry. That's almost mandatory. The lucky people, in my opinion, are those who overcome it and start writing fiction instead.

Interviewers: You gave it up entirely then?

Caldwell: Oh, sure, I learned my lesson. What gave me the courage to forget about poetry was a chap by the name of Louis Untermeyer. I had such admiration for him that I sent him some of my poems. He wrote to me and said that every young man is entitled to write poetry, but the sooner he gives it up, the better he's going to be as a man. So I took his advice.

Interviewers: He cured you?

Caldwell: Yes. And many years later when Untermeyer edited some children's books, he asked me to submit a book for his series. "I know you're out of poetry now," he said, "so perhaps you can write a good child's story."

Interviewers: And did you write one for him?

Caldwell: I did. *The Deer at Our House.*

Interviewers: Did you ever publish any of your poetry, either before or after Untermeyer gave you his advice?

Caldwell: No, but someone else once tried to. Just before Bourke-White died, a researcher visited her at the house we used to have in Darien, Connecticut. The two of them found some of my poetry stashed away under a window seat. This researcher threatened to publish it without my permission, but I told him he was going to get sued and arrested and maybe shot. Anyway, he's quieted down now and hasn't done anything about it.

Interviewers: Besides poetry, your apprentice period produced your first extended fiction, *The Bastard* and *Poor Fool.* How do you now regard these early novelettes?

Caldwell: As experimental, preliminary, amateurish, but I think necessary to make the transition from a brief short story to a novel. They were basically imaginary—an attempt to find out how to present imaginative ideas realistically. I am much in favor of what I did, but I would not do it now. You have to go through that stage just as much as you have to go through the poetry stage and get rid of it.

Interviewers: An early apprenticeship work that is rather poetic is *The Sacrilege of Alan Kent.* How does it strike you today?

Caldwell: It too was experimental, a little bit self-conscious maybe. It served its purpose at the time, but it was not traditional enough. It was not in the great tradition of fiction.

Interviewers: A recent French-English edition of *The Sacrilege of Alan Kent*, published by Galerie Maeght, was lavishly illustrated by Alexander Calder. How did this collaborative effort come about?

Caldwell: Well, Marcel Duhamel, who was my translator for many years, got together with Virginia in Paris one night and they decided to get this book done in an illustrated limited edition. Duhamel said, "Picasso will do it!" You see, Picasso was his neighbor at Antibes and he knew him very well. When I was visiting Duhamel, I met Picasso down on the beach one night and went to his house. We did not have a common language and about all we could do was smile, nod, and improvise gestures. During the hour, we had several drinks and passed comments via Marcel's interpretations. Picasso's parting handshake was warm and intensely firm and clinging. Anyway, Picasso put the book on his schedule but died before he got to it. Duhamel did not get discouraged, though. He just said, "Sandy Calder can do it just as well as Picasso or better. I'll get him!" And he did.

Interviewers: You mentioned a period after your apprenticeship in which you made money, in a subsidiary way, from your writing. Would you explain what you meant by this?

Caldwell: I was in a high salary bracket in Hollywood off and on, and I also had an interest in the Broadway production of *Tobacco Road* which ran for seven or eight years.

Interviewers: What did you think of Jack Kirkland's dramatization of *Tobacco Road*?

Caldwell: I would say that Kirkland's version is true and authentic for dramatic purposes. By that I mean he had to manipulate the story to create dramatic highlights for the stage. I had great admiration for Henry Hull, the actor who first played Jeeter Lester, because he played the part straight. But I objected to the actors after Hull who portrayed Lester, both on Broadway and in the touring companies, because they played principally to get laughs. Now Kirkland didn't like this either, but the producer was happy with the big box office and his authority was almost final.

Interviewers: What about the movie version of *Tobacco Road*? Did you like it?

Caldwell: Not particularly, no. It had good actors, good actresses, a good screen writer, and John Ford directing. It had everything in its favor. But then Darryl Zanuck came along and wanted a happy ending. So the characters go off to the poorhouse singing a folk song.

Interviewers: Did Zanuck's interference surprise you?

Caldwell: Not really. Movies were made pretty much under a studio formula. My agent told me that the movie of my novel *Claudelle Inglish* was so poor that I shouldn't even bother to see it. So I didn't.

Interviewers: What about the film of *God's Little Acre*? Were you any more satisfied with it?

Caldwell: Yes, because it was done independently, without any studio control. The studios were very union bound and might have toned down the part about the mill strike. Of course, I didn't have much to do with it except as an advisor here and there, but the freedom of an independent production was very interesting to me. At least nobody ordered a happy ending put on it.

Interviewers: You say you advised the producers of *God's Little Acre*. Did you ever take a more direct part in translating your books into movies or plays?

Caldwell: Well, *Journeyman* had a disastrous career for several weeks on Broadway. Then I came along and tried to doctor the script. I didn't succeed, though, and the whole thing eventually flopped. I never felt qualified as a dramatist because I had no training.

Interviewers: So you never attempted to write a complete play?

Caldwell: Oh, one of my misfortunes in life was that I wrote a musical for Broadway. About Mexican politicians. The principal actor, or singer, was to portray the President of Mexico. But this touched on a lot of toes in the State Department. Somebody there thought it might cause a diplomatic rub if we showed the President of Mexico chasing girls around the adobe walls and singing. So it never got produced. I don't think it was a very good musical anyway.

Interviewers: Did you give it a title?

Caldwell: Sure, sure. *The Strong Man of Maxcatan.* The script is in the Dartmouth College Archives, so maybe someday it'll get resurrected.

Interviewers: Were any of the movies you worked on in Hollywood particularly interesting to you?

Caldwell: Not especially. My early writing there was for a series of shorts called *Crime Does Not Pay.* Then I worked on *Mission to Moscow,* which was a propaganda film. The studio wanted me for it because of my experiences in the Soviet Union during the war. But I did not like the propaganda angle. After some preliminary writing on it, I asked to be relieved.

Interviewers: You said earlier that you need privacy when you write. Did working in a studio environment present any difficulties for you?

Caldwell: Yes. For one thing, in the old days in Hollywood you couldn't be a writer unless you could dictate your story to a secretary, and I never could dictate to anybody. So I had to go home at night to write where nobody could see me. I used to write in secret.

Interviewers: Did your Hollywood experiences help your fiction writing?

Caldwell: Not a bit. It was just a waste of time. It's impossible to write your fiction and work in the studio at the same time. I wasn't doing anything except hack work for five or six years. But, I needed the money and the longer you stay, the more they pay you.

Interviewers: How did you finally get out?

Caldwell: Saved enough so I could quit. In 1950 I quit cold and I haven't been back since.

Interviewers: Were you happy to get back to your fiction after the Hollywood years?

Caldwell: Very happy. After that deadly period I spent the next twenty-five years trying to catch up, to write what I had not had the opportunity to do. From 1950 to 1975 I probably wrote more stories, more novels, and more books of nonfiction than in any other period.

Interviewers: Which did you prefer, writing short stories or writing novels?

Caldwell: To me short-story writing is the essence of writing. I think a writer should always write short stories before he tries to write a novel. You have better control because a short story is concentrated into a small area. You also have better range because a short story

can be anywhere from one to fifty pages long. You can mold it much
better than you can a novel. A novel is a great, expansive thing. You
can't make a change at one point without affecting something
another fifty pages away.

Interviewers: But your short-story production seems to have
tapered off during the fifties.

Caldwell: Well, you're always going to like short-story writing
better than novel writing. But once you accomplish the short story
form, you're really stuck with it. So I wrote 150 and quit. Of course,
150 were probably only half of what got written. The other half I
threw into the wastebasket.

Interviewers: We have read that two of your novels, *The Bogus
Ones* and *Autumn Hill*, were never published. Do you have many
other unpublished manuscripts?

Caldwell: No, they go in the wastebasket. The two novels you
mention are the only ones I can recall that I completed but never
published. And they were not good enough to be published.

Interviewers: You said that your most productive period ended in
1975. What caused this?

Caldwell: The past five years have been sort of a fallow period
because I did too much traveling, going to Europe twice a year and
so forth. And I also took two years out to have cancer operations on
my lungs. I almost killed myself smoking cigarettes.

Interviewers: I notice you haven't smoked during this interview.
Did you quit completely?

Caldwell: Oh, yes. About six years ago. My doctor at the Mayo
Clinic told me I had to if I wanted to keep on living. So I crossed the
street to a bar and ordered a drink. I had two cigarettes left in a pack,
and I put both in my mouth and smoked them at the same time. I
haven't had one since.

Interviewers: Mrs. Caldwell said that you came close to doing a
book on President Carter.

Caldwell: What happened there was that just after Jimmy Carter
was elected President, the people at Dodd, Mead wanted me to write
a book about him and his hometown. It was supposed to be
illustrated with photographs. But there was no great money
involved—everything was more or less on "spec"—so I doubt that
we could have gotten the kind of photography we wanted. The idea
was interesting, I thought, but eventually it just evaporated.

Interviewers: Do you think the Carter family's Southern folksiness is authentic?

Caldwell: I think so. That menage is fairly typical of others that I have known, particularly in Georgia. My feeling about them is that they're just average, down-home Southern people in many ways. They're very close-knit, very friendly, and very outspoken. I've known many men like Billy Carter who drink beer all day and ride around in a pickup truck. In fact, I'd probably rather do a book on Billy than on Jimmy. He's more of a character.

Interviewers: Your new book, *A Year of Living*, has so far taken you a year and a half to write. Would you describe your daily writing schedule for that book?

Caldwell: Well, for this particular book I got into the habit of working twice a day. I am here at the typewriter at six o'clock with the lights on every morning and work until ten or eleven o'clock. Then from four until seven I'll be back at it again.

Interviewers: Did other books have different schedules?

Caldwell: Yes, I used to have all kinds of schedules. Years ago, in the state of Maine, I chose to write my book on even days and work outside on odd days. When winter came, I shovelled snow and slept a little during the day, then stayed up all night to write. Another early method I used was to take a trip to write a short story. I'd ride a bus, from Boston to Cleveland maybe, and get off at night once in a while to write. I'd do a story that way in about a week's time. Then, for a while, I took the night boats between Boston and New York. The Fall River Line, the New Bedford Line, the Cape Cod Line, all going to New York at night. The rhythm of the water might have helped my sentence structure a little; at least I thought it did. Those were all early methods, or schedules, of writing. Everything since then has been a little bit different.

Interviewers: Do you ever have several different writing projects going at the same time?

Caldwell: No, only one thing at a time. And I stick with it for six months, eight months, nine months, whatever it takes.

Interviewers: You have been an active writer now for almost sixty years. What motivates your continuous devotion?

Caldwell: Well, some people are addicted to singing to themselves. It's the same way with writing, I suppose. I write because it makes me feel good.

Interviewers: Do you worry about what the critics will say about a book?

Caldwell: Not at all. A critic is an egotist. "I am the judge," he says. He will wreck an author's work by tearing it apart and never getting it back together again. Of course, there are some good people in that field, but I just don't have much faith in what I call a critic. A critic is a superfluous commodity.

Interviewers: Is there any particular audience whose attention you do appreciate?

Caldwell: Well, in that sense you might say I write for the ordinary man in the street, the golden mean. If I'm appealing to that sort of person, I'm happy. For example, a couple of weeks ago Virginia and I were at the annual ceremonial of the American Academy and Institute in New York. Of course, the American Academy and Institute is a collection of very high-class intellects. Everybody's a big brain. On this particular occasion I was talking to Malcolm Cowley, I think, when a waiter came up with a tray of hors d'oeuvres. He was just a young punk, maybe a student at NYU working as a waiter. Anyway, he said, "Take one. . . . Now shake hands with me. You're the one person here I want to shake hands with." So I shook hands with the guy and took another hors d'oeuvre.

Interviewers: Why do you think your popularity as a writer has diminished until recently in this country but has remained steadfast abroad?

Caldwell: Fiction in America changes almost from one day to the next. We are still a very volatile civilization, whereas in an older country there is very little change except in a political sense. In America, fiction reflects current lifestyles, economic conditions, wars, lots of things. The interests of American readers change with the times. Especially here, writing has to be contemporary. But I don't know that any writer anywhere should consider his work immortal.

Interviewers: You don't sound very concerned with achieving a lasting popularity.

Caldwell: I have never been interested in popularity because popularity doesn't mean much. To be popular you have to be exploited.

Interviewers: What kinds of books are publishers exploiting today?

Caldwell: Well, they've gone heavily into what they call the Big Book, something 700 to 1,000 pages long. In recent years the American storyteller has been pretty well shunted aside by this blatant pressure to provide the best seller. There is no imagination being applied anymore in a storytelling sense. And the best seller itself is nothing more than a formula.

Interviewers: Do you plan to write any more fiction?

Caldwell: I've reached the point where I'm too critical of fiction right now. I'm too abashed by the trashiness of a lot of current fiction to enter into it. The great compendium of knowledge that goes into a James Michener book, *Centennial* for example, does not interest me. At present I don't see anything in between the trashy novel and the encyclopedic novel, so I'll wait it out. I think the novel's at a stage where something will surface between these two extremes. But what it will be, I don't know.

Interviewers: Could it be the journalistic novel, such as *In Cold Blood* and *The Executioner's Song*?

Caldwell: In my opinion that will be a very short-lived pattern. I think it is an attempt to find what the next phase of the novel is going to be. Of course, the Capote book was the first of that kind; then Mailer's came along. I've glanced at *The Executioner's Song* and parts of it seem to me to be purely extraneous to the story. The excerpts from newspapers, for example, are just a compendium of a lot of clippings. They had nothing to do with Mailer's writing at all. Well, to me that doesn't have much of a future.

Interviewers: Do you think storytelling itself will come back?

Caldwell: It will have to. It's inevitable that storytelling will come back because storytelling is the whole basis of fiction. That's where new ideas originate.

Interviewers: Mark Twain was one of America's greatest storytellers. In an interview a number of years ago you said you hadn't read any of his work.

Caldwell: I haven't yet. It's something to look forward to. I've heard so much about him.

Interviewers: You said once that you admired Sherwood Anderson's short stories.

Caldwell: Yes. In those days there were plenty of novels in existence but very few good short stories. What interested me about Sherwood Anderson were his short stories. I liked the brevity. I liked

the way he presented his people. His style was lean. It was not
cluttered up with superfluous adjectives and unnecessary paragraphs.

Interviewers: You have often been compared to Faulkner. How
do you feel about that comparison?

Caldwell: I don't know, because I don't know anything about
Faulkner's writing. I read one of his books, *As I Lay Dying*, which I
thought was a very fine exercise in writing. But I read it only to find
out what he was doing, and I don't know what he did before or
since. I met Faulkner a couple of times, once in France and once in
New York, but I was not well acquainted with him. The only subject
of conversation with him that I can recall was the difficulty of talking
to anyone in a foreign language when a person has the use of only
his native language.

Interviewers: Have there been any writers over the years with
whom you have been well acquainted?

Caldwell: Oh no. I don't mingle with other writers because it's a
bad class of people. My friendships have always been with the young
ladies of life.

Interviewers: What have you got against other writers?

Caldwell: They never talk about anything interesting, just about
themselves and their work. The only writers I ever got along really
well with were William Saroyan and a chap by the name of Pep West,
Nathanael West. I knew him in New York and in Hollywood. These
two were the only ones I had any great interest in knowing because
they did not talk about their work all the time. They talked about
cigars, anything.

Interviewers: But surely you knew other writers?

Caldwell: Oh, I've known a few more or less casually. I knew
Sherwood Anderson fairly well. Once when he was in Arizona he
spent a week with me in Tucson. I also got to know Steinbeck pretty
well, in Mexico and again in New York. Aside from those people I got
to know Theodore Dreiser slightly. He was another slave in
Hollywood when I was there. In fact, we both had the same agent.
Then Sinclair Lewis used to stop at my house in Connecticut on his
way to the country sometimes. But I would not say I ever had any
deep friendships with other writers.

Interviewers: Writers traditionally are notorious for having
difficulty sustaining marriages. Is divorce an occupational hazard?

Caldwell: Yes, and I'll tell you why. Whoever is not the writer in the family always gets the short end of the stick. That's because a writer has to be somewhat selfish. For example, I'm a retiring person in social life or in any other kind of life. I suppose you'd call me almost a recluse. I don't take days off. I work on Saturdays, Sundays, and holidays. Well, a woman can resent that, and eventually something is going to give somewhere along the way. Of course, once in a while there is a very even-spirited person who can take all this, and that's why some writers do stay married. But as a rule, no, they don't.

Interviewers: Have you enjoyed your fame and fortune?

Caldwell: Well, I'm happy to be able to live the kind of life that I've lived. But early in life I had a difficult time. Step by step I acquired marriages, and after each of the first three I was divided up. I lost three good houses—one in Maine, one in Connecticut, and one in Tucson. But I'm much smarter now. I put everything in Virginia's name, so I can never lose it. The car, the house, everything's in her name. So now I'm safe.

Interviewers: Do you have any superstitions about writing?

Caldwell: I have a red rug in my room. Wherever I've lived in life, I've carried my red rug with me. I keep it in excellent shape. I have it vacuumed; I have it dry-cleaned. We are sitting on it now, in fact. Why is it here? We have a very good carpet underneath. But I've got a reason for wanting it here. It's part of my life. Back in the early days I had to live on cold and splintery floors. There was a hardwood floor in Maine that was especially cold because the room I worked in was unheated. Now, an unheated room in a New England winter is sort of a difficult dungeon. Then, in South Carolina, I was confined to write for awhile in a rented room with a linoleum floor. The linoleum was cracked and it bristled with splinters. Anytime I didn't have my shoes on, I'd get a splinter in my foot. Well, as soon as I could afford to get a good rug, I bought my red one. And I decided then that I'd carry my red rug with me wherever I went.

Interviewers: And your black socks? You said on the phone the other day that we would recognize you by them, and I notice you've worn black socks every day.

Caldwell: On a Sunday I wear white socks. Thick white athletic socks for the outdoors. You should see me on a Sunday sometime.

Erskine Caldwell
on Southern Realism
Ronald Wesley Hoag and Elizabeth Pell Broadwell/1980

From *The Mississippi Quarterly*, 36 (Fall 1983), 579-84. Reprinted by permission.

In 1982 and 1983, two of the most celebrated and enduring fictional portrayals of Southern hard times marked their fiftieth anniversaries. *Tobacco Road* and *God's Little Acre* transform rural poverty and desperation into ribald, trenchant art. Their author, Georgia-born and Southern-raised Erskine Caldwell, is one of the best-selling writers of the twentieth century. Caldwell's nearly sixty books have appeared in forty languages and have sold more than eighty million copies. Best known for his writings about the South, Caldwell names among his major works the novels *Journeyman* (1935), *Trouble in July* (1940), and *Tragic Ground* (1944); the short-story cycle *Georgia Boy* (1943); the sociological tract *Tenant Farmer* (1937); and the photo-essay volume *You Have Seen Their Faces* (1937), done in collaboration with his second wife, photographer Margaret Bourke-White. Heralded as one of the first Southern literary realists, Caldwell brings to his craft some of the techniques of surrealism, black humor, and naturalism.

At the Arizona home he shares with his wife, Virginia, Erskine Caldwell made the following comments about his work.

Question: Mr. Caldwell, critics view your major novels of the 1930s as early realistic treatments of Southern life. Did you see yourself as a pathfinder in bringing realism to writing about the South?

Caldwell: Well, that's a curious thing. Many, many years ago I saw a headline in the *New York Times Book Review* that said "Realism Crosses the Potomac." It was an ad for Ellen Glasgow's *Barren Ground*, I think. Evidently hers was the first book of realism about the South to be recognized as such. Anyway, I was very much impressed that realism was crossing the Potomac for the first time at this stage of civilization. Because as far as life was concerned, realism existed there long before that. Now, as far as literature is concerned, realistic writing means writing that is based on life. I based my writing on the life I saw going on around me.

Question: Then your fiction is derived from real-life people and events?

Caldwell: To an extent, yes. You have to experience an incident in some way, or the germ of it, either by observation or by hearsay, in order to write about it.

Question: The climax of *God's Little Acre* occurs during a mill strike at Horse Creek Valley. Was the historical mill strike at Gastonia, North Carolina, the germ for this incident in your book?

Caldwell: That strike must have had some effect, I suppose. Reading about it and hearing talk about it might have caused me to wonder what would happen in Horse Creek Valley if they had a strike there. You see, the Gastonia strike concerned all the cotton-mill workers all over the South at the time. The mill owners were very worried about the whole thing too. Even when we went down to try to do the movie of *God's Little Acre* on location in Augusta, we were run out of town. The mill owners didn't want this film done because they were afraid of union reprisals.

Question: Did you also model the personal relationships in your fiction on interactions that you had observed? For example, in *Georgia Boy,* which you've said is one of your favorite books, the father, Morris Stroup, is childlike and irresponsible while his wife, Martha, has to be a mother both to her son and to him. Was this a typical Southern marriage, in your opinion?

Caldwell: Well, my own parents were not like that at all, but that was something I had noticed to some degree in other families. I wouldn't be capable of generalizing about humanity, though, in the South or anywhere else. I take only one person at a time. Martha was more dominant than Morris, certainly, but he was more animated than she was. In fact, I don't think there would have been any story at all without his animation. Just her role alone was not strong enough. When you write a story, you have to have a contrast between light and dark, high and low. These things have to be considered too, along with what you may have actually observed.

Question: Does humorous writing, such as that in *Georgia Boy,* require particular attention to these contrasts?

Caldwell: I would say, first, that I'm not a conscious humorist by any means. What can be humorous one moment can be very sad the next. It all depends upon the circumstances, and I don't think humor should be forced. I would say, though, that I am always very happy to recognize something humorous that does occur, because then I can exploit it to some extent.

Question: How would you do that?

Caldwell: I would give free play to what I want to emphasize. And emphasis, in my opinion, is exaggeration, like a highlight in a painting. If you notice, the *New Yorker* makes a great effort to impress a reader by underscoring certain words in stories. I resent somebody pointing out a word like that; to me that's abhorrent. To emphasize, I would rather exaggerate than underscore.

Question: In your fiction about lynchings, specifically *Trouble in July,* "Kneel to the Rising Sun," and "Saturday Afternoon," you apparently chose not to highlight the lynchings themselves. Why was this?

Caldwell: Because I never saw one myself. For me they happened offstage, you might say. I heard all the tales about them because people would take sides and argue for days. These lynchings were like a pebble dropped in a pond that makes waves; they sent ripples through the community. I think, also, that I would find the details about them too realistic. I wouldn't see any object in such descriptions. What led up to the lynchings and what resulted from them were what was important to me. The lynching itself would be incidental to the main story.

Question: Yet in other ways you highlighted realistic detail to the extent that you ran into trouble with censorship. What happened there?

Caldwell: If a character acts or talks a certain way, I've got to write him that way. When a censor comes along and says "You can't print that," well, he's destroying the character. A censor has no regard for the fictional character that has been created.

Question: Then you would prefer no censorship at all?

Caldwell: Censorship is always a mystery to me. At its worst, it was a stage in American life that I guess we're glad is over; but what we've got now is not really any more desirable. Any piece of trash, like X-rated movies, can claim freedom of speech, the First Amendment. Pornography is being written under the guise of literature. Now nobody's in charge of the store at all. I've always believed in having stop lights, in having some kind of order in the matter. But how you're going to do that, I don't know. Legally? Morally? I don't know.

Question: Did you believe in stop lights for yourself?

Caldwell: Well, in my schoolboy manner I started out being my own censor, and I resented anybody else taking over my job.

Question: What about your editors? Did they try to censor your work?

Caldwell: No, not a single editor ever changed anything I wrote. Not Max Perkins at Scribner's, or Marshall Best at Viking Press. When I went with the Three Musketeers—Duell, Sloan, and Pearce—Cap Pearce never changed anything. And no editor since then has tried to tell me what to write or what not to write. I have always operated on the premise that what I write has to please me, so I believe in doing my own censoring.

Question: Do you concern yourself with pleasing your readers also?

Caldwell: Whatever I accomplish as a writer I accomplish for myself, not for the reader. I've never worried about being a beloved author. I've never pushed my books at the reader.

Question: But you have been tremendously popular with readers.

Caldwell: Not because of anything I did; because of what the publishers did. Publishing is largely an economic situation, and the publishers are in charge of making a book into a best seller. This is even more true today. They make money by pushing a book as a leader; they dress it up so it will have mass appeal and then really hypo it.

Question: Do you think that similar promotions and manipulations affect the awarding of literary prizes such as the Nobel and Pulitzer?

Caldwell: Oh, I'm sure that there's campaigning involved in those things. And I've heard there's a problem with the Nobel because the judges more or less have to choose a winner from a different country every year to make the award politically acceptable. Of course, that way the best writing is not necessarily going to win. I suppose the Pulitzer might be more legitimate because they don't have these political subdivisions to consider.

Question: In terms of recognition, your own works are now undergoing a revival in colleges and universities across the country. Are you happy to see this taking place?

Caldwell: I think that perhaps the interest today in my works is in the method of treatment, the style that makes the clothing of the story, rather than in the content. Either that or maybe for some historical appeal. But I know that my books will never be contemporary again because what I wrote about was contemporary only at the time. I'm really not in any position to argue this, though, because I'm just a writer. I'm not a teacher or a critic; I don't have a critical mind.

Question: What is your latest publication?

Caldwell: The Franklin Library is bringing out a special edition of *Jackpot,* one of my earlier short-story collections that I like very much. It's been out of print a long time, and I'm very interested to see how it will be accepted after so many years. [*Ed. note:* The Franklin Library edition of *Jackpot* was published in 1980.]

Question: Do you have a writing project underway at this time?

Caldwell: Yes. It's a book called *A Year of Living,* which covers my activities and some of my thoughts during a cycle from New Year's Day to the following New Year's Eve. The "year of living" would be 1979. This volume is a combination of diary and recollections, written in the form of eighteen letters to a friend in Italy. In it I discuss a number of relationships that have been important to me. Maybe someday I'll do a final volume of personal recollections. That might be my next ambitious project.

An Interview with Erskine Caldwell
Michel Bandry/1980

From *Annales de la Faculte des Lettres et Sciences Humaines de Nice—Etudes Nord-Americanines,* 4(1982), 125-36.

This interview took place in Hanover, New Hampshire, on July 28, 1980. Mr. Caldwell who now lives in Arizona was staying at Dartmouth College for a few days. The Baker Memorial Library at Dartmouth has a unique collection of Caldwell's works and manuscripts, including his scrapbooks and his correspondence, and Mr. Caldwell was a guest-speaker in a program on writing. I wish to thank Mr. Caldwell and Mrs. Caldwell for their kindness and cooperation.

M.B.: Nearly all your books have a Southern setting and first, I'd like to ask you whether you consider yourself as a Southerner, whether you feel closely related to the land, to the people of the South.

E.C.: I suppose there was a time in life when I did think of being Southern-born, a Southerner and so forth . . . but I think I changed somewhere because early in life I went to New England and that gave me the idea that regionalism was merely a geographical condition and that the people who lived in a region, in a geographical region were the beneficiaries or the victims of their region, not by choice but by fate and I repudiated everything in life except being an American, and I left New England and I went West to California, very early, and in going to California by land you pass so many other regions, the so-called Midwest, the West, and finally you get to the Pacific Coast. Well, all those are regions too and these were people. These were not people to be identified by saying they were Westerners or Californians or anything. They were people, so everything now has in my mind for many years become one, and with the advent of the radio and the television the American speech has become one, because the people who listen to television or listen to the radio have achieved a common language or a common accent more or less, and it is very rarely that people will take the trouble of perpetuating their accents. Some will take pride in it, like in New England or way down in the South, in Louisiana or Texas, and so on, they take pride but for the most part people have lost their regionalism, so I'm saying that just to try and explain why I don't consider myself as a Southerner any more. I was at one time, but not anymore. When I was very young, I lived in all the states of the South.

M.B.: And then, you moved to Maine?

E.C.: Yes, I went there for the purpose of getting away from it, from the South. To get a kind of perspective.

M.B.: Was the kind of life you led in Maine more appealing to you because it was closer to the land, or because it was harder? You wrote in *Call It Experience* that you had to grow potatoes and to cut wood, if I remember correctly. . . .

E.C.: It was more intense, because I lived in a New England township as they would call it, which was a town but it was, say, a landed town, a farming type of township where everybody had a farm, where they lived in a place where whether there was a grocery store or not, they still had a farm where they grew potatoes or cut wood, and so I found a new type of life there which I had never had before.

M.B.: Did you already want to be a writer when you went to New England?

E.C.: Yes.

M.B.: So, you were looking for a new kind of experience?

E.C.: Well it was. . . . As I said, I was looking for a kind of perspective because I was not satisfied with what I had *read* by Southern writers and I stopped reading them and haven't read them since because to me they had falsified the life that I had known and had seen and lived myself and so I was unhappy with Southern writing if there was such a thing as Southern writing. So I wanted to go where I could look back from a distance and get a better perspective of what life was, by living with the people instead of reading books about people.

M.B.: Do you have a great interest in people?

E.C.: Yes, because I am still not a reader; maybe I read half a dozen books a year, and that's about all. I read newspapers, every type of them, and catalogues, and magazines and everything else. But that's journalism.

M.B.: To come back to the South. Many characters in your fiction are poor whites. Some of your early novels depict the miserable conditions of living of these people and you wrote non-fiction pieces like *Tenant Farmer* in which you exposed the causes of this misery.

E.C.: I was very close to it. I'd lived with it, just next to me so to speak, so it was out of pity more than anything else I suppose, because it seemed to be an injustice that some people would have something to eat there and that these people here would have nothing to eat. But they were human beings and why had it happened like this? So there must be some reasons for it and looking for the reasons, I could only deduct the fact that it was due to ignorance, to the lack of education, to the lack of opportunities of some kind, to ill health, all kinds of things, sociological things which combined with economic conditions, because in the Great Depression, there was an economic disaster and the effect became sociological—and that was all my whole feeling about it to know why it did happen. All was basically economic and the dire effect of it was the fact that children went hungry, children were uneducated, people died for lack of medical attention and so forth and so on, so those were the things that went into my feeling about the poor whites at the time.

M.B.: This was your feeling when you wrote *Tenant Farmer* and the text as well as the captions of the photographs of *You Have Seen Their Faces*. But what about the novels? It's not only pity—or is it?—which led you to write *Tobacco Road* or *God's Little Acre*. I have listed at least some twelve or thirteen novels which have poor whites as heroes.

E.C.: When I said pity, what I meant was sympathy. Without doubt I felt sympathetic in a way. In other words, they were not people to be rejected and to be ignored, because not only I had a story to tell but they had an appealing personality which had a great effect on me. What I was doing was just writing stories in the written word and nothing more. I had been living for it, you might say, looking for material. It was so obvious, you couldn't escape it, you had to write about what you were seeing. There was nothing else to write about that was of any interest to me because I knew nothing else to write about.

M.B.: So you consider yourself, first of all, as a story-writer?
E.C.: Yes.

M.B.: I know you have always firmly stated that your works of fiction were free from any ideological approach. And yet many writers in the thirties were influenced by Marxism; you were associated with Marxist writers; to many your early works appeared as an illustration of the need to change the economic organization of society. More than forty years later, can you tell me whether Marxism meant anything to you, and what?

E.C.: Well. . . People had an idea that I did have a purpose in mind, to popularize or to propagate communism, Marxism. It just happened that I had come along in a time, a climate, which was conducive to the same kind of feeling that Marxism was based on, I think. Marxism had come out of the autocratic society of Russia and there was a revolution. So the people who lived in the South as I did, in the agricultural South, were victims almost of the same thing. They were the victims of the plantation system which had come after the Civil War and the deterioration of life reduced them almost to the same level, I suppose, as that of the so-called muzhiks during the reign of Catherine the Great. It seems to me the origin of it was the same. But at that time, which happened to be my time, it had nothing to do with Marxism. I have been sympathetic to the idea of, not so much spreading the wealth or revolution, but the fact that there must be some economic reason why people suffer as they do and have done continuously, and whoever can find the correct solution for it is going to get my sympathy, my understanding, and my faith, because I am sure that many millions of people right now are living at that level of existence. In India for instance—that's a place that should be done with by some kind of revolution. Whether it should be a Marxist revolution, I don't know, it's not for me to say. But people in the South were in the same fix during the Depression. And they came out of it, they came out of the Great Depression by governmental rule, by the action of government. It was not a revolution but it was a democratic kind of thing that alleviated the hunger and the poverty. It can come back again and we could have another Great Depression; we'd have some hard time, I am sure. Throughout the country we still have poverty in the coal fields or things like that, but as a general rule I think the democratic process is still workable.

M.B.: When I said you were associated with Marxist writers. . . for instance you wrote articles for *New Masses*. What was exactly your connection with the people of *New Masses*?

E.C.: In those days and the days of *New Masses* . . . my participation was never official. I was a friend of one of the people associated with *New Masses* and this man was Mike Gold. Mike Gold was a very good friend of mine. He did not proselyte me, he did not try to influence me. We were writers. He liked what I wrote and I liked what he wrote. I was in New York during the period of the Great Depression. Several times I lived there in a cold water flat, cold water room, waydown in the Village. In those days living was very inexpensive. You might pay two dollars a week for a room, or three dollars. So that was my life in New York in those days of the Great Depression, and Mike Gold was an encouraging kind of person, encouraging in the sense that he liked what I was doing. He did not influence me in any way other than to encourage me. He was a young man, very young, my age, I suppose, at that time. He was the only person that had any association that I know of with *New Masses*. I wrote some book reviews, I wrote some articles not as a contributor to a cause but as a writer making a contribution to a magazine, and it would happen that *New Masses* might—well *New Masses, The New Republic, The Nation* were the three magazines that would publish what I would write, so for that reason I had a very close feeling towards Mike Gold, because he was a person who had a deep feeling for people, a deep feeling for writing about life, the economics of living, the sociology of living and he was just my kind of person.

M.B.: I asked the question because it has always been my understanding that you were not the kind of proletarian novelist the more militant writers of *New Masses* called for. I read this morning your answer to a question *New Masses* asked of some thirty authors in 1934. They wanted to know whether the Marxist criticism published in *New Masses* had helped those writers. Your answer was (I quote from memory) that criticism is about ninety percent soap suds and that a Marxist critic can work up just as much lather from a cake of soap as a capitalist reviewer. (Caldwell laughs). Do you remember that?

E.C.: Yes. But as I said, I also did write things for *The Nation* and *The New Republic* in that same period of time. They were more literary, they were not so pronounced political as *New Masses* was. They were more literary publications but they were liberal in the sense that they recognized the same principles of life that *New Masses* did. But I was never importuned, I was never asked, I was never invited to become a member of that society, the *New Masses* people.

M.B.: I hope I am not being too inquisitive about your political past but there is one more question I'd like to ask. A certain number of intellectuals or writers who had connections with leftwing journals were investigated later by the McCarthy subcommittee. Was that your case?

E.C.: No. My only association and my only knowledge of what McCarthy was doing was reflected in Hollywood, because in those days Hollywood was very sensitive, the management of Hollywood, the producers, they were very sensitive towards what McCarthy wanted and did not want. I was working on a film called *Mission to Moscow* which was the film I had to do on the Moscow trials which I knew nothing about but I was writing it anyway. I had the proceedings in English which I was using. But I knew nothing about the internal workings of communism as it was reflected by any communist party in America or McCarthy or anybody else. But I did know that I was once or twice cautioned not to admit and not to do anything that might reflect on McCarthy and his work because that's how sensitive it was to the management of the film companies. . . . But I was never connected with any committee of any sort. I was never influenced by McCarthy in any way. I knew about it. I was not among the people who were blacklisted because I did nothing to be blacklisted for.

M.B.: Well, I hope you'll excuse me for acting like McCarthy himself! To speak of the poor whites again, does the phrase "poor white" mean anything to you nowadays. In other words, are there still poor whites in the South?

E.C.: That's a very difficult thing to tell. Because the remnants of poor whitism, the poor white, still exists, but you see, times have changed so much, the economic, the social changes have been so drastic that you don't find the same elements now that you could find fifty or twenty-five years ago. The nearest thing to it is the Ku Klux Klan, for it is still in existence. There was something in the newspaper yesterday about the Ku Klux Klan in Chattanooga, Tennessee. So every once in a while it creeps up and comes about but you see that's a very isolated thing, it is very much of a minority. It's just the dying remnants of the old system. Now the poor white in those early days did belong to the Ku Klux Klan because for economics reasons it was

claimed that the Negro, the black man, was taking the poor white's
job away from him, which was true. The Negro, the black man, had
a stronger physique, he could stand the heat much better, he could
work longer hours and he did not complain. He was afraid to
complain you see. All right, so that more or less brought about the
revival of the Ku Klux Klan because the origin of the Ku Klux Klan
had nothing to do with that at all. It originated way back in the
carpetbagging days of the Civil War. That's when it originated but the
modern Ku Klux Klan played upon the idea that they could enlist the
poor white because they could tell him, if you join the Klan, we won't
let this black man take the job away from you and so forth. So the
Ku Klux Klan would intimidate the Negro and prevent him from
holding the good jobs and good wages. Now the poor white today
hardly exists because he is not poor anymore, because he has social
security, he has food stamps. So the poor white does not exist
anymore but the mentality continues, because the mentality resists
the enlightenment. It goes along with education and education has
been forced upon them, the white persons, whether they like it or
not. The Negro is getting an education. Colleges are full of black
people so the poor white has been forced to compete with the Negro
by going to college too, because he found out that the black man is
finding a job if he is a college graduate and the white man can't. So
now, they are in competition, education wise, and the economics of it
just don't exist anymore, but the mentality does and that's a physical
fact.

    M.B.: Talking of mentality. . . . We somehow have a picture of the
South as a land of leisure and easy relationships between white men,
even the poor ones. You know things like the crowd at the barber's or
the men loafing at the gas station. . . . Does this kind of easygoing
life still exist?

    E.C.: It's hard to answer that. It doesn't exist very much now. The
only closest thing to it would be Billy Carter's filling station. But that's
a very exaggerated set of course.

    M.B.: Are there many filling stations like Billy Carter's or is it a
kind of dinosaur from the past?

    E.C.: You see, all that has changed so much because now it's so
standardized. In the old days, an individual owned his own store or
filling station. Now he doesn't, because it's a chain, it's a franchise of
some kind, and he is just the manager, so he has no authority. So the

boss comes around, the inspector comes around and says "get rid of that and don't do this and don't do that." So he is afraid to let his friends collect around him. He is afraid for his job, of the influence that the outside might have on his own job. This life has changed so radically that it's almost a completely different civilization from what it was thirty years ago. The South has been contracted to a small area, it's becoming tighter and tighter. Right now. You used to think that the South was North Carolina, Kentucky, Tennessee, Texas and so forth. Now it's coming down to a small part, you have a band, a geographical band, Alabama, Mississippi, Louisiana, Arkansas, a very narrow band. That's the old South and it's still there in the rural area and the small town specially, because the small town is more representative of the old South or the new South or any part of the South than the country itself. The small town with a population of five hundred or one thousand people, maybe two or three thousand. That's the real South. That's where the tradition resists any change. They still resist and they still succeed in resisting the change.

M.B.: About the Negro. . . . Your works in the thirties and the forties did much to make people conscious of the hard lot of the Negro. In several of your short stories and novels—I am thinking of *Trouble in July* and *Place called Estherville* for instance—a young, innocent, defenseless Negro is opposed to a cruel white mob, and the Negro seems to be deliberately made an object of pity. I personally have a feeling that you felt at the time nearer the Negroes than the whites.

E.C.: Well, in my days, my knowledge of Negro life was limited, to some extent, because the people I came in contact with were usually servants or working men. But I trusted the Negro more than I trusted the white man. The Negro was always—I suppose you'd say—naive, but basically sincere and I have always had the feeling that you could trust the black man if he wanted to be trusted. That if he said he wanted to be trusted you could trust him, you could take his word for it, and I suppose I had a feeling of friendship because they were people who were not hiding anything, they were not hypocrites. They did not mind admitting that they would go to church on Sunday and that on Saturday they would shoot craps maybe; it was just a way of life, to be honest, with them. Of course, all that has changed in urban life. The Negro has changed a great deal. He takes up now the white man's skin, so to speak, all kinds of protecting devices, coming up with his heritage of trying to survive with the whites in urban life. So it is not in the cities like it used to be in the agricultural South, which is actually the home of the Negro in America. In spite of the fact that the Negroes have changed, I still have a good feeling of trustfulness, even now, with the Negro people I know. I know very few intimately, probably half a dozen I'd say right now. I still trust them. I am not suspicious of their motives. So I feel, er, very friendly.

M.B.: What was your purpose when you wrote *Trouble in July?* Was it the idea of exposing the evil character of lynching, or the way the white people were caught in a chain of events which ended in lynching, or was it simply that you had a story to tell?

E.C.: It was a combination of a lot of things because I had been in the environment of lynching in Tennessee, in West Tennessee where I lived in those days; also I had been in close touch with the environment of lynching in Georgia, and I had some feeling of the atmosphere of lynching in Carolina where I also lived, but Tennessee and Georgia were the places which influenced me, and this was a sort of combination of feelings about the attitude of the white persons towards the Negro. I had the feeling that the white man had hatred in his heart. I had a feeling that he had to find some excuse to hurt him in some way, and the greatest harm he could do to him was to hang him, not just to shoot him, but to hang him, to make a physical display of death, so that you could see him and so forth and so on. To me that was what influenced me in what I was doing about lynching in those days, the fact that there was a lot of latent animosity in the white man towards the Negro and it was a carryover, of course, of the fact that the Negro's background was that of slavery—not that he should continue to be a slave but he was out of slavery and he acted biggity—the word is biggity. To show that a black man could not act like a white man, you had to keep him in his place. You had the opportunity to do this when the Negro was suspected of looking at a white woman or following a white woman or what not—so that was the grand opportunity to gather all of the forces of this hatred that had been in a community or a surrounding community, to bring it together into a mob force and to extend that by lynching him.

M.B.: Have you been a witness, not to the lynching proper, but to the building up of this animosity?

E.C.: Not to the actual fact of it but only beyond the perimeter of it, to know that there was talk about that something had occurred

maybe ten miles away and there were waves of talk about it
spreading from this center to ten or fifteen miles away. You'd get the
lapping of its waves. You'd hear exaggerated accounts of what might
have happened and so these things spread out, and you'd hear these
things and some of the accusations were so blatantly absurd that you
couldn't believe it actually, but the person who was prone to believe
it believed it so that built up this feeling and you'd get swept up in it
and you wondered yourself: could this actually have happened? Was
the man guilty of what he was claimed to be? And the time came
when you felt helpless about doing anything about it. You did not
know the man, you were only an individual, you couldn't stop it, you
couldn't agree about it, so you only felt innocent and yet concerned
about something that was taking place somewhere out of the way.
This had occurred maybe five or six times in my life.

M.B.: You refer to it in *In Search of Bisco.*

E.C.: I had half a dozen experiences like that so they culminated in
one idea that I put into the book.

M.B.: Have you ever felt as a militant as far as the rights of the
Negro were concerned? Did you write this book with the purpose of
exposing the plight of the Negro?

E.C.: I didn't write it for any purpose of propaganda. I haven't
done that and never have, because the story to me is the only
important thing, and what the impact of the story is is what the reader
finds it to be, so the consciousness of the whole thing was the fact
that it was a story. It had to be told the way I had imagined it, I had
felt it, and I had put it together, and that's the way it had to be.

M.B.: One thing that has always struck me very much in your
books is the importance given to place, to the physical place where
the story is said to happen. Think of most of the titles of your novels,
*Tobacco Road, Tragic Ground, A House in the Uplands, Episode in
Palmetto,* to name but a few. Many novels start with a descripion of
place, as for instance *Journeyman* with the farm and the atmosphere
of stillness. How important is the idea of place for you?

E.C.: You can see these things, I can't. To me, my idea of writing
fiction, a novel or a short story, is to portray the characters; the
people and all the influences that have to bear on that
characterization are unconscious to me. I can't explain to you why I
want to talk about the landscape or the trees or the fishing or
anything about it, or the climate, or the thunderstorm or the rains. I

couldn't explain why. Because essentially what I am writing about is the people.

M.B.: Could we talk about your way of working? I know you are a great traveler. Do you do like Roderick Sutter of *Love and Money,* that is travel for a certain time, months maybe, waiting for the idea of a book, and then once you've started it go on writing till it's finished?

E.C.: I like to stay with it once I've started writing and do nothing else for the time it takes, five or six or seven months. Stay right at it and not do anything else, and when it's finished, after that I can go again. When I do go, I get the urge: I want to write something, so I know I have to go back home. So I am very pleased, and anxious to go back home.

M.B.: When you say "I want to write something," is it some kind of puritanical urge like "I have to work" or is it that you have the idea of a book and you must write it?

E.C.: You want to. You know how hard it is. Once you get involved, it's a terrible headache, it's a terrible pain, because you get so involved, you can't quit, you don't want to quit, you dislike what you are doing, you are not satisfied with it, you aren't happy with it, and so you do it all over again to try and improve it so that you be more satisfied, and the more you work at it, the more unhappy you get and so finally you say: "Well, this is going to be the last try. I'll do it one more time and I finish." So that you give yourself a deadline. That's what happens to me and . . . but once you've finished you are glad you did it, and then you want to go, and then something catches up with you. You may be waiting for, say, three or four or five or six months maybe, and then you say: "Well, I want to write a book" (laughs) and then you are not satisfied with you until you do it.

M.B.: In an interview published in *Studies in the Novel* in 1971, you said something about your way of working which I liked very much. You said you had to have a typed page which looked clean, that if you had an alteration to make in the page which you had just typed, you had to do it all over again.

E.C.: Well you see, when you're young these things come very easily and you think everything you write is perfect, you don't want to change a thing. If an editor says: "I don't like this, I am not satisfied at all with this page," you say: "Oh, forget it, send it back I don't want to change a word." When you are older you can see your mistakes, you know you are on with a mistake and you don't want to be writing it, and you find out that one word in here is wrong, that it is a completely wrong word, and you've got to take that out, and when you take that out, the new word you are going to substitute changes the rest of that sentence, or the rest of that paragraph so much that you have to change all that too. So you can't just stop with one word; you have to do the whole page as well.

M.B.: So the writer must be a real artist before anything else, like a painter, a musician . . .

E.C.: Yes, yes.

M.B.: Does he have a special role in society?

E.C.: I don't know. It depends on what he happens to be. He is an entertainer in some parts of the world, in some parts of it he is a propagandist, he is an opportunist in other places, he is a scandalwriter, he is a mercenary in other places, he can be a lot of different things. Now, if you are a D.H. Lawrence, *you are a writer,* in my opinion, because it seems to me, in my limited knowledge of reading books, that D.H. Lawrence was a man of letters as I would say. Whether he was a great writer, I don't know, that's not important to me, but the fact was he made writing appealing to me as a reader and he may have made me want to be a writer. I don't know, I already had the urge, but he may have encouraged me. So when you ask what is the role of the writer, he has many roles, it depends on whom he is going to influence. D.H. Lawrence influenced me, he encouraged me, not personally, just by reading some of his books. I judged what he was doing worthwhile, that it was worthwhile to be a writer, to do this, to achieve something which I'd like to do and so forth and so on.

M.B.: Apart from D.H. Lawrence were there other writers who influenced you?

E.C.: No, I don't know. I started from scratch. Let's put it that way. Not because I was influenced by other writers but because of the type of life I was living back in the thirties when I was in that college for the first time in Virginia. I discovered for the first time that there were so-called "little magazines." They were not *The Saturday Evening Post* or *Cosmopolitan* or *Collier's* or this kind of thing. I'd seen all that, it didn't interest me. I had read some of the stories in there and that said nothing to me. Then I found out that there was a different kind of writing. In the library at the University of Virginia, there was a room, a small alcove, just a table or something. And on this table there were dozens and dozens of magazines which I had never seen before but which had come to be called real magazines. There was *Contact* and *Transition* also which came from Paris; there was also out of Paris *This Quarter,* dozens of them. Here was writing that was being done and I had never known existed. It was so basically good, in my opinion, and none of it was like what I had read in *The Saturday Evening Post* and this kind of thing. It was disturbing me to know that this existed and I had never known it before. I read everything I could get. For that reason I ignored the older books, the so-called classics. And one day, one of those "little magazines" came on with a story, say, by Sherwood Anderson. To me that was the greatest event of the day, because I could see that Sherwood Anderson could write a short story, much better in my opinion than those you read in *The Saturday Evening Post* or *Collier's.* So that's what influenced me, those "little magazines," and I ignored, I still ignore the classics or contemporary novels of the time. And all I did and have wanted to do *ever* since is what I could do myself.

M.B.: You haven't written short stories for a long time now.

E.C.: No, I wrote one hundred and fifty and I quit. I decided that was enough for me and I had reached the point . . . You see, I used the short story as a learning device because it seemed to me the best way to learn to write a novel was of course to write a short story, I had to be able to write a short story, and I decided I had written enough and I could not improve myself in that field and that the next challenge had to be the novel.

M.B.: A last question. You don't read other novelists. Do you care at all about critics?

E.C.: Well, you see . . . I'll say about critics what I'll say about novelists. Other novelists can write and do anything they want; it doesn't interest me because I want to do it myself, I don't want to read what they have done. As far as the critic is concerned, what he feels about what I have done doesn't interest me. I did it the way I thought was the best way and I did it the best I could and his opinion doesn't interest me at all because I did it my way. In essence that's what I feel about other novelists and critics. Sure, they can do anything they want to do, that doesn't affect me at all, one way or the other . . . And, of course, there are many kinds of critics. In one time in my life, I was a book-reviewer. That's not being a critic. I have always had more respect for the book-reviewer than I do for the critic. . . . The book-reviewer tells you what the book is about and the critic tells you what's about himself. . . . (laughs).

Fifty Years Since Tobacco Road:
An Interview with Erskine Caldwell
Richard Kelly and Marcia Pankake/1982

From *Southwest Review,* 69 (Winter 1984), 33-47. Copyright ©
1984 Richard Kelly and Marcia Pankake. This interview first
appeared in the *Southwest Review.* Reprinted by permission.

On the evening of July 15, 1982, Erskine Caldwell and his
wife, Virginia, paid a visit to Wilson Library at the University of Minnesota for the opening of an exhibit celebrating
the fiftieth anniversary of the publication of *Tobacco Road.*
Austin McLean, curator of the Special Collections and
Rare Book Library, organized the exhibit and arranged for
the Caldwells to come from their home in Scottsdale,
Arizona for the occasion. The program, attended by more
than one hundred Friends of Special Collections, included
reminiscences by Edward P. Schwartz, a book collector,
founder of the Henry Miller Literary Society, and friend of
the Caldwells; a presentation by the author of a facsimile of
his 1929 broadside, "In Defense of Myself" (Palemon
Press), which was added to the Library's collection; and a
reading by Professor Göran Stockenström, Chairman of
the University's Department of Scandinavian Studies, of
the author's early story, "Country Full of Swedes."

The centerpiece of the evening was an hour-long interview with the seventy-nine year old Mr. Caldwell, which he
had agreed to in lieu of giving a formal talk. "I am not a
public speaker," he had modestly written to Austin
McLean, "and could probably not get a passing grade as a
conversationalist." In preparing for the inverview we chose
questions we hoped would allow Mr. Caldwell both to
entertain and enlighten those present—book collectors,
students and faculty, members of the general public—and
to talk about some aspects of his life and work not discussed in print before. We assumed that many in the audience—familiar with our guest for his enormously
popular *Tobacco Road* and *God's Little Acre*—would not
be aware that he has written fifty other books, one hundred and fifty stories, and that his work is increasingly the
subject of scholarship in the United States and Europe.

With the three of us seated at a small table before the group and a tape recorder running, Mr. Caldwell answered our questions extemporaneously and vigorously, commenting on such topics as his early life in the South, learning to write, his method of working, humor, screenwriting, favorite authors, little magazines, advice for young writers, Max Perkins, censorship, and the situation of blacks in the U.S. today. We are grateful to him for his generous responses to our questions and for allowing his answers (unedited by him) to be published. We would also like to thank Austin McLean for organizing the program and for inviting our participation.

Kelly: You've written eloquently about your father in *Call It Experience* and in *Deep South* and you seem to have absorbed some of your social consciousness from him. Could you tell us a little bit about your mother and what qualities you might have gotten from her?

Caldwell: Well, the reason I've never written much about my mother is because she once asked me not to—and so I haven't. But I suppose it would be all right if I said a few things about her here. She was a school teacher and I think it was probably that—her interest in education—that influenced me most. Then, as far as a career went, I didn't want to be a doctor, I didn't want to be a lawyer. I didn't want to be this or that, so the only thing left was to be a writer. That's what I ended up being, more or less, and I attribute that, fortunately, to my mother's influence because she had the idea that it was worthwhile to get an education. So I did the best I could to get an education, I suppose, to please her in a way. And I more or less became a tramp scholar, I went from one college to another, time after time. The reason I did that was I thought I could play football and so I more or less tried to improve my standing as a football player by going from a larger college to another larger college. And I ended up in my football career playing semi-pro football in the Anthracite League in Pennsylvania. So that's my whole background in education.

Pankake: What do you remember reading as a child?

Caldwell: I don't remember reading anything actually. The only book I ever remembered having or reading or looking at, I acquired when I was going to a lower grade school. I don't know what grade it was now, 5th or 7th or something, in Tennessee where we were living at that time, and the teacher had a test for her class. The test, I think it was based on Geography, was to point out what we had learned by studying Geography. Anyway, this was a kind of test all her students were eligible for in this lower grade school, and I happened to win the contest. I remember very well what the book was. It was called Gibbon's *Rise and Fall of the Roman Empire*. And that was so far above my ability to understand that I never finished reading the book!

Kelly: I wonder if you could say something about your early attempts at writing fiction and getting published. You mentioned somewhere, I think, a seven-year accumulation of rejection slips, which should be a great encouragement to anyone out there in the audience trying to write.

Caldwell: I think I had a normal career in those days of being an unpublished writer. I suppose I was no different than, let's say, another 10,000 or 100,000 would-be writers. Everybody has to have a rejection program in life in order to succeed. You can't succeed without being rejected to begin with because it's the only way you can learn. You've got to learn by failure. My career really began when I was working on a newspaper, as a newspaper reporter, and I was attempting to write short stories or write fiction at that time. I did not succeed after several years, so I left that field and went into raising potatoes as another avocation in the state of Maine, and it was there I continued my education, I suppose you'd call it. I was self-taught in that sense. And that was over a period of years—I think a period of 10 years altogether, probably, from the beginning to the end of my failure, and at the end of that time I did have a short story accepted and published in a little magazine. A little magazine, of course, is not a wide-circulation large magazine like *Cosmopolitan* used to be. But this was a little magazine, probably was mimeographed and only had 3 or 400 copies circulation, but it was *printed*. Anyway, that was my first publication, and I had this great big box full of rejection slips that I was keeping very assiduously, as inspiration, and so when I finished gloating over the fact that I had been published I took all these rejection slips I'd accumulated over the years and made a very fine bonfire with them.

Kelly: The first story you had accepted I think was "Midsummer Passion," and I remember reading somewhere that almost immediately after that you had about five more stories accepted. I wonder if you can identify any particular qualities that you were able to get into those stories that, say, were lacking in the earlier ones.

Caldwell: I think the only answer to that would be the fact that over a period of time you have to achieve some sort of ableness in constructing a story, because a story can be formless, completely formless, and have no sense of form at all, but I think you do learn, if you have any inclination to be able to learn, that sooner or later you're going to have to make this thing, this story, fit into a certain form. It has to have a beginning; it has to have a middle; it has to have an end; you have to have certain characters—the good boys, the bad boys, and so forth—those things constitute a story basically. I think any writer who is attempting to be a writer instinctively finds out that this is something he has to accomplish before he can get, he can achieve, publication. So to me, the whole idea of being a writer is completely in the hands of the writer himself. You can learn by example, you can learn by instruction, but in the end you have to do it yourself.

Kelly: One other question in that area—you said that in the early stage of your writing you made no attempt to break into the mass circulation periodicals—that you, rather, felt there was more to be learned from the little magazines, and I wondered what you learned from them, if there's anything you could tell us about what you might have gained in going that route and whether that would be a good route for writers today, as well?

Caldwell: The only answer I can see to that is this. A young writer has to have something to give or something to present; he cannot just be an imitator of an older writer. That's fatal; you end up being nothing. And to me, to be able to experiment with writing was the most important feeling I had of these so-called "little magazines," because there you could experiment. You had nobody hanging over you saying "Do it this way" or "Do it that way." You had no editorship to try to make you change something to fit someone else's conception. You were left entirely on your own. That was a great feature, in my opinion, of little magazines in that era. And by being able to experiment, I think, a writer, right now, today, a young writer, if he can find the means and the ways to experiment, I think he will achieve something much better than he will by trying to imitate what someone else has already done, because that imitation is fatal for a young writer. I don't know about the older writers, I'm not concerned about the old ones, but the young writers are the ones who should not fail. They should have this opportunity to experiment, and wherever they can find it, they should be encouraged. But of course these days you've great difficulty finding where you can do this in print. Because it has to be in print. If you don't write something and get it in print, it doesn't exist. It's still a manuscript.

Pankake: Your literary experiments served you very well. One aspect of your works that readers have enjoyed has been the colorful language—the earthy eloquence of southern whites and the vivid speech of the blacks or the talk of the Maine farmers. How did you convey such different speech, such different rhythms and dialects in your work?

Caldwell: I would have to answer that by saying that I was disinterested. I had no interest whatsoever in imitating dialect. You know, if you had read some of the early dialect stories written about Negro life, it was almost unintelligible to look at much less to pronounce or to get any sense out of because it was a phonetic kind of thing. It made no sense at all. To me, the secret (it isn't a secret but the essence of transmitting the ethnic life, we'll say, of the black people) is in the rhythm of their speech, not in their dialect, not in their southern accent, or in the western accent, or any accent. Accent means nothing. But the rhythm of their speech, I think, tells a whole story that you want to have on this character or these people you're writing about. And that rhythm, of course, goes with your place in life, with what you're doing. Are you doing manual work, are you digging ditches, are you driving a truck, or are you a lawyer pleading a case? All these things have different variations in rhythm, I think. At least to me they do. I can see that feeling of a person's occupation, his life work, whatever it is, in his way of speech, and to me, I think I always tried to transmit that rhythm, not the dialect of speaking.

Kelly: I understand that you are a great reader of dictionaries and that you once went through a *Webster's Collegiate* and crossed out all the words of more than four syllables. I wonder if you could say something about why you did that and about your practice of reading dictionaries.

Caldwell: To try to be facetious about the thing, I think, probably my main motive in crossing out the words of many syllables and of great length was because I couldn't spell them. I didn't want to be burdened with having to look up a word in the dictionary every time I wanted to use it because I'm not a very good speller. So I think that has something to do with it. But more than that it was my conviction that a simple word is much more effective than a long, compound word. You can compound a word to great length like the Germans do, which I would not adhere to for my point. To me, to use a simple word that derived from the origin—when you use a certain kind of dictionary, the older *Webster's Dictionary,* not the current ones, not the 3rd edition but way back in the 2nd edition, *Webster's Collegiate* or whatnot—you'll find the origin of the word, usually right in the beginning of the definition, where the pronunciation is, the accent marks, and so forth. They're always in there, whether it's Old French, Old English, Latin, Greek or whatnot—that gives you a key, an entré into that word that you're trying to use, and if you hit right, just right, you'll get the correct word every time, and it's going to be a very short word and it's not going to have any great compound length at all.

Kelly: You've tended, I think, to use shorter, simpler words in your fiction, and to allow yourself longer words in your nonfiction. Is that because you think there is really a fundamental difference—that the two forms require different vocabularies?

Caldwell: Yes, I think so. I know that's very true that I do that. I don't know whether I'm trying to impress people with my knowledge or what when I use a long word in nonfiction. I think that's a result of doing journalism because I've done much journalism in my life off and on. I did newspaper and magazine journalism, television, radio. In those kinds of things I think simply that you have to exert a little bit of, oh, boastful knowledge about something, so you impress them by the big long word. That could be true, I don't know. But I don't know any other explanation other than the fact that it comes out of journalism, whereas fiction I think is much different writing.

Pankake: Let's talk a little bit about the books of yours that people know best. Both in *Tobacco Road* and in *God's Little Acre,* important characters make fun of the church and of institutionalized religion. For example, Sister Bessie tells Jeeter that she's instructed Dude to preach his first sermon in the church against men wearing black shirts, and when Jeeter asks why, she says, "Preachers always have to be against things." Was your father shocked by this picture of religion that you put in these books, and did you have some other feelings about what religion was in the South and in people's lives?

Caldwell: Well, as far as my father was concerned, I don't think he was shocked by anything that I wrote because he knew more about life than I did. He was more of a sociologist than he was anything else, and he was very familiar with the bottom lines of existence, so that I could have learned from him, and I did learn from him, very much. Now the fact that he was a religious man in this sense, being a minister, I don't think had anything to do with the fact because he was also a teacher, a newspaper writer, in addition to being a minister. But his great interest in life was people—whatever people were doing, were saying, were living—that was his great interest. I think that, more or less, influenced me a great deal because I could see the origin of stories and fiction and anything else that is written. It has to come out of people's lives to start with. You can be a reporter as far as journalistic ideas are concerned, but you also have to be a creator, or inventor of stories, of life, because otherwise if you don't do that you're not creating fiction. You'll have non-fiction instead of fiction, and what we're trying to do as fiction writers, is to write something that does not exist, but may exist in the past or in the future. It may exist. But we can't go and put our finger on it and say there it is right there, and there he is, and so forth—that's non-fiction. So what I have always done is, more or less, to use the idea that you have to invent everything and to make it more lifelike than life is itself.

Kelly: I have to ask you a couple of questions about "Country Full of Swedes." One is that the narrator refers several times to the "back kingdom," and says he should never have left there, etc. I wonder if you could give us any clues as to what the "back kingdom" is?

Caldwell: That's just a figure of speech, in a sense. I lived in the middle of Maine, central Maine. North of that would be the forestland and all the occupation evolving around that—lumber mills and so forth. East of that is farming—potato country, where everything is flat and no trees. People who leave those two environments and come down to central Maine or coastal Maine leave something behind. They leave an old homestead or leave an old environment of some kind, and I have heard the expression "back kingdom." It also always applied to back home. Back home could either be in the North in the woods, or in the East in the potato fields. In this particular story I don't know where he came from or anything of the sort. It doesn't interest me and it doesn't matter, I don't think. But the "back kingdom" idea was that he was a newcomer, down in the more or less civilized part of Maine, so to speak, greater population and so forth, and the "back kingdom" was his reference to his former life.

Kelly: One other question on the story. I'm always interested in where ideas for stories originate and I'm wondering if you can remember where you got the idea for this particular story.

Caldwell: Well, I got it from a bunch of Swedes. I happened to be living in a rural community, in a township called Mount Vernon, in central Maine, and I was living there on a farm. The farms there were not very large, they were maybe forty acres, eighty acres, and so there were quite a few farms in the whole expanse of this road where I was living. I remember very clearly that down the foot of the hill from where I was living there was a house of Swedish people from Waterville who had been working in a paper mill for many years, came over and bought and renovated and added to and put a new roof on and built a woodshed and things like that and painted it yellow. That more or less originated the idea in my mind that these people were the prototypes of what I wanted to write about. So they were more or less based on actual existence. But I couldn't point out any one person who was in this story, for example. They had to be invented.

Pankake: Do you see, in retrospect, your works fitting into a tradition of Southern or frontier humor?

Caldwell: Frontier humor? I don't know—what is that?

Pankake: Oh, maybe a tradition of literature dealing with backwoodsmen, of dealing with violence in American life, of rather exaggerated characters?

Caldwell: Well, I thought what I was doing was being influenced by the environment in which I lived in the South, and maybe I lived in some of these regions that created or originated frontier humor. Of course there was violence, yes. But I lived in so many southern states, all the southern states I lived in at one time or another, and so I accumulated a lot of this feeling, I suppose, but it all happened to congeal into one local feeling. So I could not isolate my remembrances and say "This took place over here and this took place over there"—it's all just one complete picture to me. Now what the humor is I don't know. I think any agricultural region does generate a type of humor that you don't find elsewhere. You have backwoods humor, I suppose, or frontier humor. I suppose that's a legitimate kind of estimate to make of it. As far as violence is concerned, of course, that originated out of the Civil War, the aftermath of the Civil War, when there was retaliation against the black people, for being sprung out of slavery. I think that had a lot to do with it, for every opportunity that, you might say, every ignorant or perverse white person might have, if he could take advantage of a black person, he had the advantage he could take, because he was superior in having a white skin, as opposed to having a black skin. So you have violence accumulated like that, for many years—decades— you had lynching and that was violence. Now that's the only violence that I have ever witnessed. I only witnessed one lynching in my life. But I had read about and I had heard about—newspapers and word-of-mouth—many other instances of violence of that nature. So that did exist. Now my analysis is, as I said, that it was the result of the aftermath of the Civil War. And I'm very glad the Civil War got over with, we got rid of it, and now we don't have the same thing anymore, so maybe we'll never have it again in this country.

Pankake: Which of your works do you think is most successful?

Caldwell: That I have done?

Pankake: Yes.

Caldwell: In which sense?

Pankake: However you might define success, maybe achieve the ends that you were after when you set out to write that particular piece.

Caldwell: Well, that's sort of hard to say, because, you see, I don't consider any one thing I've done of any great value. I've written 50 books and 150 short stories, we'll say. To me it's a cumulative effect. That's what appeals to me in having accomplished this much, maybe. But to pick out one thing as my favorite or maybe better than anything else, I hesitate to do that because I have five children. So I would not say this is a better child here than this child here is. I like all the children equally well. I might be a little hard on one if he is not as obedient as this one is over here, but, at the same time, a story to me is something that a reader has to accept or reject, and not the writer himself. So I would not say that I like this, or this made more money, or this is of greater acclaim, or *that* I like better than anything else, no, I wouldn't say that. I'll leave it up to you.

Kelly: You eventually went out to Hollywood to do some screenwriting. I'm wondering whether there were any films that you worked on that turned out to be memorable, or that you especially liked.

Caldwell: Let's put it this way. I had several failures in life in Hollywood, off and on, because I used to go there in order to survive and to pay the rent back home. The only way I could do it in those days was to go there and work 13 weeks at a time. I had no great success whatsoever as a screenwriter in Hollywood. I never wanted success, all I wanted to do was to put in my time and get out and go home. That was my great ambition. But one thing I did remember having done was to contribute, in a small way, episodes to a series of what used to be called a two-reel film. Two-reel films were sort of like serials, and every week, or every month, there would be a new one. This series that I worked on for quite a few months was called "Crime Does Not Pay." These were episodes or case histories taken out of police files and then put into moving picture form, and it always ended that the crook was caught, apprehended and punished. That was the whole object, so I thought I was doing a good deed in life by trying to show that crime does not pay. But I was just one of many people who were writing on this serial. The other memorable film work I ever did did not turn out to be made into a picture after all. It was all wasted effort, since during one of my sojourns there for six months or whatever it was, I was assigned with another writer to write an original motion picture story for Clark Gable. Now Clark Gable at that particular time was a leading box office champion of Hollywood. There's nobody had a bigger box office than Clark Gable. Well, the studio thought that they were doing us a great favor, my friend and I, to be able to write a film story for Clark Gable. And we got so carried away with it that what we did was to make Clark Gable a lumberjack up in the Northwest woods. And we got so carried away with this idea that we brought him into town several times on a Saturday night, and that's where we got into trouble, because the Hays office, the censorship in those days, did not want this Saturday night lumberjack on the screen. So our picture was never made.

Kelly: You've often said that you're a writer and not a reader, and that when you read other writers you generally only read one of their books. But I'm wondering if you could name a few of your favorite books by other authors.

Caldwell: I can only remember people who are dead. I do not recognize anybody who's still alive. To me, the best writers are dead, and I think they always will be. In my early life, when I did try to keep up with everything that was being written, I remember very well being impressed by Theodore Dreiser, being impressed by Sherwood Anderson, by reading Ernest Hemingway, and later reading John Steinbeck. Now those four, to me, were the principal writers that I considered to be superior in fiction writing of that time, of that era. I don't know that they influenced me in any way. I don't think so. I was just interested to see what they were doing, because I happened to know all of them vaguely. In a small way, I did associate with some of them, and on the basis of friendship and curiosity, they came to be my favorite people. As I said, they don't exist any more, and who's existing today I do not know. I'll leave that to you and others.

Pankake: Perhaps we could talk a bit about how you write. When you're working, do you generally have a set schedule, to which you try to adhere?

Caldwell: Yes, just like you go to work in an office at nine and go home at five. I do the same thing. It was my habit, 9-5, seven days a week. I always started out with five days a week, and it graduated up to six days a week and then to seven days a week. I wish I had eight days a week, because there's not enough time. And then I experimented, in my early life, with different times of the day and night. In other words, in the winter, for example, I used to like to work at night, so from six or eight o'clock at night until five o'clock the next morning, the daylight ending hours, I'd try that. Other times I'd work the daytime. Other occasions I have experimented on the idea of doing physical labor on the odd days of the month and doing writing on the even days of the month. To me that was ideal because I had to do a lot of farming in my early life, cutting wood and raising potatoes, so working one day with your muscles and one day with your mentality was very suitable. I would recommend it. It keeps you fit, for one thing, physically fit.

Kelly: Could you tell us something about your method of writing, that is, once you get an idea for a story, what happens after that? Do you write it out in longhand first or on the typewriter and what sort of process do you go through in producing drafts of a work?

Caldwell: Well, it's a mysterious thing, I don't know how to describe it, and I wouldn't know how to tell somebody else how to do it. I only do it by hit or miss. I don't know how I'm doing it or why I'm doing it, just the inclination to do it this way, whatever it is I have in mind. Now if I have a theme or a subject or an idea—I might have nothing to go by except just that a truck driver is stopping to get something to eat at a diner, at a highway restaurant—that's all, so then your story might go from there. Or you might have a mental kind of picture that you dream up, or invent an idea that you want to present, but you have to accumulate the right kind of people to go with it because otherwise you'll have a failure, your stories aren't going to come off, so the important thing is not a plot. I don't know what a plot is. I couldn't use one. I wouldn't know what to do with a plot. The main thing is to have this idea and to see what they're going to do. And so you put them here to start with, and whatever, two people, five people, in this situation, let's say they're sitting in an airport—well, then you have to invent something to go with that. So that's where you do your mental sweating right away—if you get the right people, the characters. And then of course they have to be presented logically, they have to be presented faithfully, to write themselves. But you have to invent all these people, they don't exist. You've got to invent them. If they exist you're just doing a photograph—or a series of pictures.

Kelly: Do you do all of your work on the typewriter and do you get each page perfect before you go on to the next? That's what I've read.

Caldwell: No. You might do 10 or 15 drafts of the same story, of the same chapter, time after time. I'm talking about myself, not about what other people should do, or what makes you do it that way, but I have to do it over and over again. If I make one line wrong, after I read it over on the page, or if I see that one line is false, I want to scratch all that out and do it over again. Throw that in the wastebasket. Get rid of it, as fast as you can.

Pankake: Do you have any advice to give young writers, or aspiring writers?

Caldwell: No, I don't know what to say. I feel sorry for them. There's nothing worse than being a disappointed writer. Ten, fifteen years of it is all I could take. You see my weatherbeaten face, don't you?

Pankake: You've been an editor, in the long series *American Folkways,* and you've been edited. What is the proper job of an editor, and how can an editor help a writer?

Caldwell: Now in this particular case, *American Folkways,* there are about 20-25 volumes I had something to do with. My idea was not something that would be ordinarily editorship. In other words, I

had the idea for the thing, for the series. I would try to find the ideal
person for a region of the country, someone who had the ability to
write, and the knowledge and the inclination to write about this
particular field. If it was an agricultural region or manufacturing
region or urban region, whatever this particular thing was, this was
the person to be selected to write about that. Not only did he have to
have the ability to express himself, he also had to have the
knowledge, the background to write about it. And so that was my
only contribution, because once we got a manuscript, then I would
give it to somebody else to do so-called editing. In other words I
didn't correct spelling or anything like that.

   Pankake: Maxwell Perkins was one of your early editors. Did he
or did any other editors do anything that you think helped you in
your work?

   Caldwell: No. I had a great affection for Maxwell Perkins. He
more or less got me going, so to speak. I was writing short stories in
those days, and he was the editor of *Scribner's Magazine* in those
days, and I sent him two or three short stories, and he sent them
back, and I kept on sending him some more, and finally I guess he
got tired of sending stuff back so much, and he said he was going to
take some. So he did take two short stories, and I kept on sending
stories and stories, and he finally wrote me back and said, "Do not
send me any more short stories. I have finished publishing your short
stories. Write a novel." so I wrote a novel. He ordered me to write a
novel—I wrote it. He didn't say what kind of novel to write, he said,
"Write a novel, stop writing short stories and sending them to me. I
can't stand it anymore." So I wrote a book called *Tobacco Road,* and
I sent it to him. And he published it. I mean he accepted it and said,
"We're going to publish this book just as it is, we're not going to
make any changes, not a single word is going to be changed, it's
going just like it is," and it was. In other words, it was never edited.
Which is the ideal way, if you an get away with that.

   Kelly: I wonder if we could talk about censorship for a moment.
I've been doing a little research and discovered that in 1946 a St.
Paul patrolman's review of *God's Little Acre* caused the book to be
banned in St. Paul which led, of course, to subsequent brisk sales in
Minneapolis afterward. And I was stunned to find out it is still banned
in Massachusetts. Were you consciously attempting to take on the
censorship laws at the time when you wrote the book?

Caldwell: No, I was not trying to lure the censors into the idea of banning me or anything. I had no idea about it. I didn't know what censorship amounted to, it didn't bother me. And it still doesn't. The fact was, there was a wave of censorship . . . somewhere in the 40s, I guess, and it went not only in St. Paul and Boston, but many other cities. Detroit, for example, that was the place where the book was banned consistently for a while. And at the same time there was a play of *Tobacco Road* being played by road companies across the country and that also ran into a series of censorship cases. It got to be so common I just didn't pay any attention to it. I thought it was just a way of life. I didn't know there was anything unusual about being censored or banned or anything. So I just never paid much attention to it after that, and I still don't. I always have considered myself to be my own censor anyway, and I am capable, and just as qualified to be a censor as anybody else. I think I have been, and still stay with that theory, that I'm a good censor. And I'm not unhappy about taking that attitude; I'm very pleased with it.

Kelly: You've spoken out at times against sexual license in much of modern fiction, and I'm wondering where, if anywhere, you would draw the line in relation to the depiction of sex in fiction?

Caldwell: You mean at the present time?

Kelly: Yes, you've said in the past, I think, that you were somewhat dismayed at some of the license that's going on nowadays.

Caldwell: Well, yes, that's sort of what I was saying about being my own censor. I think every writer should have his own code of writing. For example, I think a writer should recognize that there are traffic signals out there, there's red, yellow and green. You don't go up to a yellow traffic signal and barrel through it, do you? If you do, you're nuts, crazy. It's the same thing with being a writer. You have an obligation to stop and wait for whatever it is. So I think a writer should be his own judge about this. I realize the fact that there are a lot of quickchange people in the business who will write anything to make a dollar. That's very obvious. It happens all the time. But to me that is not legitimate authorship. It's a sort of con game—it's like being a burglar, or something. Instead of working for a living, you steal your living, or whatever it is. I would not say this should not be printed, it should not be published, I wouldn't say that. I wouldn't go that far. Then I'd be a censor. But I would deplore that fact that this person did not have enough reticence, did not have enough literary ability to say the same thing in a reasonable way. That would be my criticism of a person who wrote what you might call salacious fiction or writing.

Pankake: We have quite a few more questions to ask you but we shouldn't keep people here all night long.

Caldwell: It's getting late, isn't it?

Pankake: Yes, it is, and so we'll have to limit ourselves. In your works you have a very respectful and sympathetic picture of blacks in the South. But it's a picture which reflects very badly on America in general. I'm thinking of stories like "The People Vs. Abe Latham, Colored," or "The End of Christie Tucker." Do you feel optimistic or pessimistic today about justice to blacks, and about the integration of blacks into American society?

Caldwell: Very optimistic right now, yes. I wasn't in those days because it seemed to be at a dead end. When those particular stories were written that was a reflection of a reality. In other words, not just pure fiction. In a sense it wasn't something that was made up out of nothing. This was a reflection of a social condition that existed. And I happened to have been living there, and having been part of it, and so I knew what was happening, and I had a resentment toward a social condition that made one human a second-rate citizen and gave preference to a white-skinned citizen over a black-skinned citizen. That was my feeling at that time. It still is. I don't think that's necessary anymore. There's always prejudice against a minority group, no matter what your origin is. For example, you may have a prejudice against Swedes, I don't know. But I do know that life itself, American life, has come to a point where I think we are much more intelligent and have much greater ability to assimiliate ourselves, our lives, than to pick out someone to give him a blacklisted name because he's a Methodist, or a Baptist, or a Catholic, or whatnot. That doesn't exist, I don't think. But if it did exist, I would be one of the first to want to oppose it.

Portrait of an American Primitive:
A Conversation with Erskine Caldwell
D.G. Kehl/1982

From the *South Atlantic Quarterly,* 83 (Autumn 1984), 396-404.
Copyright © 1985 Duke University Press. Reprinted by permission.

Erskine Caldwell, who observed his eightieth birthday in
1983, was interviewed by Professor D.G. Kehl in September 1982 in Paradise Valley, Arizona, where Mr. Caldwell now makes his home. The questions of the interview
were not prearranged. The interview was transcribed from
tape, with some slight editing, rearranging, and omission
of irrelevant matter.

Kehl: Mr. Caldwell, you've been one of the most prolific and
popular writers in American literature: 26 novels, 150 short stories,
various works of nonfiction—53 books in all that have sold over 80
million copies—and your works have been translated into fifty
languages. Yet you've never received much critical attention. Why do
you think this is so, and does it disturb you?

Caldwell: That's a question I would not know exactly how to
answer, and for this reason. You see, I do not write for critics or for
any kind of popular acclaim. I write for the reader, and to me that's
much more important than what anyone would judge my work to be.
The opinion of the reader is much more important to me than
anything else. Now, to go back even farther than that, you see, I write
for myself. I do not write for anybody else. . . . I think a writer who
sets out to win money, to win acclaim, to win popularity is in a
falsifying situation, because the writer should present himself, not try
to impress somebody else but to satisfy his own urge. Otherwise, why
should he be a writer? He could probably make more money doing
something else—in medicine or law or business or else being a
publisher, for example. So I think a writer is a person who should

write for himself and, after that, whatever falls into his hands is a gift of the gods.

K: Do you think the lack of critical acclaim might be in part due to the fact that your work seems to defy categorization and because so many readers seem unable to accept your work on its own terms?

C: Well, I don't know. I'm just a common ordinary writer. I'm not trying to sell anything; I'm not trying to buy anything. I'm just trying to present my vision of life. . . .

K: You've been referred to variously as a Realist, a Romanticist, a Naturalist, a Symbolist, a Social Critic, a Humorist, and probably a lot of other things we won't mention. Do you resent this labeling and pigeonholing? And what designation would you prefer?

C: I don't know. I'm a fiction writer. That's all I do know. In these years I say I'm a fiction writer; in the early years I was a journalist. So I do not characterize myself in any category. I wouldn't know what to say about myself other than the fact that I like to write fiction. I like to create stories. I like to imagine something and to write it because I do not actually, consciously write realism. To me, realism is something that is photographic, we'll say, something that's fixed, something unchangeable, something that exists like a rock or a tree. What I try to do in my writing is to create something that does not exist and try to make it real. To me, that's the ultimate aim of fiction: to create something that has never existed before. The word *novel* is something "new." In order to make something new, you have to create it. A novelist has to create. He cannot imitate nature; he cannot photograph nature. That would be false to his profession.

K: How do you react to being called a southern "mythmaker," as Calder Willingham has done?

C: Well, of course myth is something that may or may not have existed in the past. I may have created some character or some scenes that may have lingered on in memory and maybe that's the origin of myth. But a mythmaker—I wouldn't characterize myself as being a mythmaker. But that's all right for critics to say. I appreciate it, and it may be true.

K: How about "southern American folklorist," as Malcolm Cowley has suggested? Certainly folk stories, the oral tradition, have been a part of southern literature. Did you get a lot of stories from listening, maybe, to your father?

C: My material came from personal observation and living, because I lived all over the South in the early years, and it impressed me very greatly. Going from one town to another, from one state to another, because we were moving maybe every six months or a year so I would find a new environment. I would find new friends and new situations. Well, these things impressed me very much. It was a continual kaleidoscope of life. What probably made the greatest impression on me was not what somebody else said but what somebody else did. Observation for a writer is the most important of his assets.

K: Didn't you say that the idea for *Tobacco Road* came as the result of walking down the road and seeing a poor tenant farm family much like the Jeeter Lesters?

C: Yes, I did say that. In that particular element, at that particular time, it was such a common, ordinary thing to see people in that state of distress—economic, social distress. It was a common, everyday existence from morning to night wherever you went in East Georgia, where I was living at the time. It was a phenomenon that was existing side by side with the affluence in a county seat, we'll say, where you had more wealth, or in a milltown where people were working and had a job of some sort. So this agricultural era was to me the most, well, the most disastrous time of life for innumerable people. You see, that was a turning point from the sharecropper economy of the South to the corporate agriculture era, and the people who were living there were the ones who were caught in this transition, and there was nothing done to help them. That was before anything like public welfare existed; there was no social help. There were no welfare handouts, food, or money, so people were just destitute. So that's what I was writing about.

K: Do you consider yourself a Regionalist writer? Is place important in your fiction? H. Blair Rouse has said it is not, that *Tobacco Road* could have been set in California with little difference. Do you agree?

C: Well, of course place has influence on your environment, on your setting that you're writing against. The idea is to present people in their own environment wherever they may be. Now if you're writing about people in Louisiana, we'll say in Cajun country, you have a swamp element of life with great luxuriant backgrounds of growth of trees. If you're writing about mountain scenery, you have nothing but stark reality of trees and rocks. So every place you write

about has to have this background of some sort. So that's
Regionalism to me.

K: Or Local Color. Why do you think the South has produced so
many fine writers?

C: Well, I could be facetious about it and say that writers have
nothing to do in the South except to write stories, because they were
too lazy to do anything else. They didn't want to go out and work, so
they'd just sit down and write something about other people. You
see, in southern life there's a great fund of material. I did not know
other regions of the country as well as I knew the South. I did live in
New England for a long time, but in the South, for example, there
was so much activity. It was a country of violence for a long time; it
existed all the time. It had to be written about because it existed. The
same about what's called the romance of the South. The romance of
the South was very real. They did have magnolias. The odor of
magnolia blossoms was in the air. You could not escape it. So those
things did exist, and you had to write about it. That was part of the
material that you lived with.

K: How do you respond to Walker Percy's saying it was because
the South won the War?

C: I don't know that I would subscribe to that. I'd rather stay with
my own reason that writers had nothing else to do, because I know
myself I couldn't have made a living any other way. I could not have
succeeded if I had not had the urge to want to write about my life,
the life around me. And once I got that urge, then I wanted to write
about people elsewhere, in the whole country and the whole world.
And that took me out of the South, the urge to find something
beyond what I knew. Now what the War had to do with it, I do not
know.

K: Do you think the so-called southern renaissance is still going
on?

C: I don't think so. I think the national media—the television,
radio, and newspapers, all that, you see—are wiping out the
regionalism. For example, the southern accent is dying out. You do
find a little bit of it in Texas, but that's a big put-on, I think.

K: You've said that you divide the population into two camps, the
readers and the writers, and that you're in the latter camp. What
twentieth-century American writers *have* you read and whom
especially do you admire?

C: The whole fact is that all the good writers are dead. None of them are still alive. If you want to question that remark, I can say this: I think the early twentieth-century writers have usurped the privilege of writing. Now we can go back and start with Theodore Dreiser, Sherwood Anderson, Ernest Hemingway, Faulkner, Thomas Wolfe, and so on. You could name another dozen people like that. They were the ones who formed and formulated the whole concept of American literature in this particular century. I don't know that anybody else is making that same contribution now. I would hate to name one or two. I don't think I *could* name one or two that I think would be in the same category with the Dreiser, Hemingway, Steinbeck, Anderson, Wolfe contingent.

K: What about Robert Penn Warren? Eudora Welty?

C: Well now, you see we're talking about a very special thing now when you talk about a Robert Penn Warren. Robert Penn Warren is unique in American writing. He's a very astute critic as well as being a poet. He has a knowledge of writing that very few people have. I admire Warren very much. But to me he's not in the same category as a creative writer.

K: So you feel that there are no contemporary writers who come up to the stature of those early twentieth-century writers?

C: Well, I think contemporary writers have gone beyond that concept of what we call literature. I don't know what literature is, but whatever, it is. Because now you see the sensationalism draws the whole attention of publishers and writers and readers in a far different concept than I knew in my earlier existence as a writer. And I don't know that the motion pictures, the television, the constant pressure to make a best seller give the writer the opportunity or benefit of using his talent to the best advantage.

K: In your book *Call It Experience* you said you used to read the dictionary instead of novels and magazines. Do you still like to read the dictionary?

C: I read it every day. I have four or five around the house, one in every room, and I'm always looking up something. That's the writer's Bible, his handbook. If he doesn't like the dictionary, doesn't use the dictionary, I think he's at a great loss to try to be a writer. The etymology of a word is the great source of writing, because the meaning has to be traced back to its earliest definition and usually that takes you right back to the Greek or Latin. That's why you go to find what the word really means, and all the derivations that come out of this modern usage of that same word always reflect back to what were the Greeks thinking of when they used this word or how was it used or what were the Romans using this word for. And I like to carry that over and find out what we're doing with that particular word right now.

K: But yet your own style is simple, and you don't seem to use many unusual or big words. In fact, don't you say somewhere that you try not to use a word that anyone would have to look up in a dictionary?

C: Yes, but you see when you eliminate all that verbiage, all those syllables, then you get back to the original meaning of the word.

K: What lessons did your apprenticeship in journalism provide in the writing of fiction?

C: Primarily, I think journalism aided in the process of learning under the strict supervision of an editor, being constantly, constantly warned and told and threatened to cut out all of the unnecessary verbiage. What are you writing about? What are you trying to say there? Why do you have so many words here? Why don't you go ahead and tell us what you're saying, what you saw? That was the earliest indication that writing should be a very lean kind of recording. It should not be flowery words; it should not be long words; it should not be obscure words; it should be the plainest words you can use.

K: That relates to one of the principles of writing you've expressed: that the style grows out of the content, that one doesn't set out to be a "stylist," but that one has something to say and the style grows out of that. Is that your view?

C: Yes, because you see your content is the most important thing. There are, of course, such things as stylists. Usually they're essayists. Which is all right in that category. I admire that too. But when you're writing ordinary things in life, whether fiction or nonfiction, content is really what matters, because then that will dictate how you are writing it. You don't have to impose a style upon it. The style comes from the material that you're using.

K: How does the writing of your novels usually begin? Not with an abstract idea, does it? With a single image? An episode? A scene?

C: Well, I suppose I could only say that I write the first sentence first, the second sentence second and so forth. Now what instigates that, what prompts that first sentence is having seen something. It may have no bearing on what you're going to write, but it gives you an image of something in your mind and then it recalls something that might be imposed upon it. It might be a house on fire; it might be a man walking down the street; it might be a telephone conversation that you hear or something. Those kinds of things create a living image immediately if it's something you'd be interested in doing, and that's the only way I know how to start out writing something, because I would not know how to write something with a plot. I've heard of plots. A story has a plot, a novel has a plot, and so forth, but I would not know how to write a story with a plot. The plot has to come out of the material that you are going to present, to use. And that develops a plot, if that's what the word is; it develops *something*—a beginning, a middle, and an end.

K: Which of your novels is your own favorite? Which is vintage Caldwell?

C: That's so difficult to say. It's like saying, "Which of your children do you like best?" You like them all or you don't like any of them. The fact is that I would not want to pick out any one novel because I wouldn't want to slight some of the others. When each one was written, it was a very important process to me. I do have a favorite collection of short stories, if I may say so. It happens to be a collection of short stories called *Georgia Boy*. This was a whole series of short stories I wrote as the result of looking back at my early life and a playmate who happened to be a black boy, and he and I had quite a few experiences in our backyard where we lived at an early age. We were both of the same age, probably ten or twelve years old at the time. That was a sort of landmark as far as writing was concerned, because I wrote it purely for the fact that I wanted to go back and think about my early life and what it meant to me to live among black people. At that time there was a great furor in American life about integration and segregation and so forth, so I just went back to think about how my life was in the day when I had a black playmate.

K: Was that the same young fellow you wrote about in *In Search of Bisco*?

C: No, that was a different one. I always seemed to have some playmates and they seemed to turn out to be black boys.

K: Someone has said that especially a novel like *Tobacco Road* seems to be a sequence of episodes, which might reflect your skill as

a short story writer. Would you say that your strength lies in writing
the shorter episode rather than the longer, sustained work?

C: Well, I think the short story is the ultimate test of the fiction
writer; I think he has to be able to write a short story before he can
write a novel. In my case, I became enamored with the short story
because you can do anything with the short story. You can tell any
kind of story—long, short, or what not. You can tell it in two pages or
fifty pages.

K: What do you think is the secret of good dialogue?

C: To me, dialogue has to be rhythm. I'm not a musician; I'm not a
poet, so I don't know what that would mean in that kind of context.
But to me dialogue and writing itself, fiction writing, is a usage of
rhythm. I do not want and I do not try and I would abhor trying to
write dialect. To me, that is a falsity, because I do not think you can
carry out and carry over the inflection of speech by use of what you
have to do to words to make them into dialect. But the same thing
can be accomplished with rhythm. Now the rhythm of speech is very
important, and it's noticeable, too, if you pay attention to what a
person is saying. It gives you elation; it gives you a feeling of anger or
of humor, sympathy. All these kinds of things can be detected in a
person's speech. He might be telling a casual story or making a
casual remark, but if you are listening closely, you will find something
in that rhythm of his speech that would tell you exactly what he was
doing and talking about.

K: You mentioned humor. There has been a lot of comment about
the humor in your fiction. You've said it's not a matter of writing
comedy or tragedy but that life is both. Don't both come together in
the examples of so-called black comedy in your fiction?

C: Well, they're almost interchangeable, because there is comedy
in tragedy and tragedy in comedy. There's very little distinction
between the two; you can't have one without the other. You could
not have a readable novel of any interest if you tried to eliminate
tragedy from it or tried to eliminate comedy. You've got to be true to
your material, and life itself is a series of both. They go right together.

K: Do you consider yourself one of the pioneers of black humor?
I'm thinking, for example, of the description of the death of Jeeter
Lester's father in *Tobacco Road*. Jeeter and the other men are sitting
up with the body. They decide to go to town for booze and lock the
body in the corncrib. At the funeral the next day, a rat jumps out of

the coffin, and as the people file by they giggle nervously because half of the face is eaten away. That's certainly black humor, isn't it?

C: Well, it was not conscious on my part, no. I don't know that there was such a phrase or definition in those days. I suppose you could characterize it as that in the light of the present definition of "black humor." To me it's a perversity; I'd say it's a perversity, a kind of breakthrough. When there's a time of sorrow, there has to be a moment of levity of some kind. No matter what's going on—the most solemn moments in life, there can be some inadvertent movement or something that will change the whole thing. It may be a marriage or a funeral or a church service. Something like that can always happen that will change the whole tempo of these.

K: Isn't it also a matter of laughing so as not to cry?

C: Yes, sure.

K: Malcolm Cowley has said that there are really *two* Erskine Caldwells: one who is a social critic and one who is a fantasist and humorist. It has also been said that this dichotomy shows up in *Tobacco Road,* where the elements are incompatible, the novel being too comical for social indictment and too socially zealous for humor. *Are* there *really two* Erskine Caldwells—and two modes in the novel—and, if so, are they irreconcilable?

C: I suppose what my situation is, is being what I am. Now anyone can try to take me apart to see what parts are working or what parts are authentic or which might be fantasy or realism. But that has nothing to do with my life or my writing. I will accept the fact that a critic can give judgment on what I do and take me apart or find symbolism in what I do, but I have no such projection in mind. I do not know what symbolism is, for example. I have often heard that expression used—that a student is given the task of reading something of mine to find the symbolism of it. Well, I really am at a loss to try to find out what it is they are looking for.

K: Ty Ty Walden in *God's Little Acre* says, "There was a mean trick played on us somewhere. God put us in the body of animals and tried to make us act like people." Similarly, Jeeter Lester in *Tobacco Road,* referring to Ellie May's hare-lip says, "It was just meanness on His part." Is it valid to say that Erskine Caldwell has a "quarrel with God"?

C: Well, God . . . the word *God* . . . of course, I have no concept of what a god or the God or any god would be. That's something

that's imposed upon us, this concept that Somebody's had an
influence on us. Now life has an influence on people. So it's nature
itself that is doing these things, not God. . . . I would say nature gave
us a raw deal. I wouldn't say it was God's fault.

K: I was borrowing the phrase "quarrel with God" from Lawrance
Thompson, who applied it to Herman Melville. For example, in *Billy
Budd* Melville draws a parallel between Claggart, who is innately evil,
and the scorpion. What do you expect a scorpion to do but to sting?
It does what comes naturally. In one of your novels you have a
character say, "If you've got a rooster, he's going to crow." Aren't you
and Melville making similar points?

C: Well, I don't know the work you mention, but I suppose it's the
same idea.

K: At the end of a number of your novels, there is an act of
violence or a series of such—which seems to lead to a kind of
resolution or even a symbolic cleansing. Do you see a cleansing or
purging role of violence in your fiction, as we often see in the fiction
of Flannery O'Connor?

C: I don't know. You see, I think all the incidents of life either end
happily or unhappily. And when they are happy, nothing much is
going to happen. Now when they're unhappy, something's going to
burst out, and that's when you get your violence. You get mad at
somebody and you don't restrain yourself, and then you have an act
of violence. So that would be a natural outcome, it seems to me.
Now what the story was doing, it was probably leading up to this act
of violence, maybe unconsciously, I don't know. But I think if it did
occur, it had to be a natural resolution of what your story has led up
to. Now I don't think you'd find much drama or conflict in a story in
which everything was always nice and pretty and everybody ends up
happy thereafter.

K: Let's take a case in point. At the end of *Tobacco Road,* there's
the fire. Jeeter is burning off the sedge-grass, and it burns the house
down, killing Jeeter and his wife. The next morning Sister Bessie and
Dude find the bodies, and then Dude is going to try to work the land.
Now that's a remarkable change in the boy; throughout the novel
he's been a lazy . . .

C: Well, he's carrying on the tradition of his father.

K: Yes, but isn't it more than that?

C: He hasn't really learned anything. He's going to continue his family heritage.

K: Well, it's almost as if it took that act of violence to shock him into even that much action.

C: Well, I guess so. I don't know what my intention was at the time, but it seems to me that it would be logical to suppose that the whole incident was to bring out the fact that this was to be continued. This was not the end of the Lester family. They were going to have another generation doing the same thing over and over again.

K: As you look back on your career, do you have any regrets? What would you do differently?

C: Well, only technical regrets. I don't have anything moral or ethical to regret whatsoever. I do regret a lot of technical matters that I was foolish to indulge in or be taken into. I've had a lot of bad experiences with publishers, for example.

K: Thank you, Mr. Caldwell.

A Good Listener Speaks
Kay Bonetti/1983

From *Saturday Review,* 9 (July-August 1983), 8-11. Copyright
© 1983 *Saturday Review* magazine. Reprinted by permission.

Erskine Caldwell is the author of more than forty-five
books. His works have been translated into at least forty
languages and have sold over 65 million copies world-
wide. His first novel, *Tobacco Road,* published in 1932,
immediately stirred both praise and controversy because
of its earthy depiction of poverty-stricken Southerners.
The book was adapted to the stage by John Kirkland and
ran eight years on Broadway (1933-1941). In 1933 Caldwell's second novel, *God's Little Acre,* was published and
firmly launched his career.

Ever the wanderer, Caldwell has lived and worked in all
sections of the country and served as a foreign correspondent in Russia, Spain, Mexico, and Czechoslovakia. Now
80, he lives in Phoenix, where this conversation took
place.

SR: Where did you get your strong sense of social justice?

Caldwell: I think it derived from the fact that I grew up in the
agricultural South, fifty or sixty years after the Civil War. The
remnants of that society still existed. There was the imposition of the
white person upon the black person, which was the aftermath of
slavery. It became so violent that, during my early life, lynching was a
summer pastime all over the South. Tuskegee College had a whole
department devoted to statistics regarding lynching. I grew up with
this inhumanity by the white against the black. I had a lot of contact
with the black people; my playmate was a black boy, a "yard boy"
we called him. When you are friendly with somebody you abhor any
injustice that person might have thrust upon him. A Negro might not
have been working fast enough for the white boys, so they would
beat him with an ax handle. What could the poor fellow do? He

244

couldn't fight back, he'd get lynched. The people in charge of political life put the black people on chain gangs. Chain gangs have died out now, but for many years, if the road commissioner needed some work done on his highways, he wouldn't pay money to do it: the chain gang would supply the work force. If a black man bumped a white man on the street he was liable to be put on the chain gang the next day.

SR: But not everybody saw that as being wrong, and you were vilified and criticized for writing about this.

Caldwell: Oh, nobody liked being told about it, because they wanted to keep the chain-gang institution well manned. So if you criticized that, they said you were not true to the white race. Anybody could have seen the same things I saw and had the kind of response I did. I just lived all over and saw a great variety of it.

SR: Do you think your father and mother were an influence?

Caldwell: Well, my father was a sociologist more than anything. He had a great feeling about injustice, especially poverty. He introduced me to the people he knew, who make up the characters of *Tobacco Road*. He would take me and show me people who were in dire distress.

SR: Were you writing to try to change those conditions?

Caldwell: No, that would have been propaganda. I could have written about it as an essay for somebody to interpret, but I did not write to influence. What influence came out of it was the fact that somebody read it and had the same feeling I had that this should be changed. I was not the one to change it.

SR: You said recently that your beginning as a writer was more a question of learning to listen than of learning to write. Would you elaborate?

Caldwell: Anyone learning to be a writer has to have a background, or foundation, of life itself. You can't learn from a book what another person is or is not. You have to hear life as it is lived. When I wanted to learn something in my early days I was a listener, never a talker. That did me a very good turn, because I'm still not a talker, I'm a writer. I don't even read other people's books to any great extent.

SR: Did you hear stories when you were growing up, and did this have any effect on the kind of writing that you attempted?

Caldwell: Probably my formative years were between the ages of

10 and 17. We lived in a number of Southern states and every year we'd move to a new place. Even though life was different in every subsequent move, the texture of life was about the same. I was fortunate enough to live in small towns. There would be two or three stores, a post office, a sawmill. I learned a lot by just listening. Storytelling achieved its ultimate height just before the agricultural empire was broken down and the South became industrialized, which happened after World War II. Around the stores and shops— that's where storytelling actually flowered. Anyone who was exposed to that had to be influenced. I was, to a great extent. I did not try to imitate or transpose storytelling into written form. I wanted to create my own, but I had to have the background, to know the kind of people and the kind of life they lived, and that was what contributed to what I have written.

SR: Do you feel you have an ear for the rhythms of speech?

Caldwell: I do not try to write the dialect of the people, because it's such a tedious kind of thing, and if you look at it on a piece of paper it's just a conglomeration of misplaced words, misspelled words, and it doesn't mean anything. The rhythm of speech is the important part of trying to translate dialect into ordinary language. I try to find the rhythm of speech rather than imitate sounds in print.

SR: You have said that journalism gave you your schooling in writing. Would you elaborate?

Caldwell: Journalism in the broadest sense is relating the events of the day. You have to write every day to be a journalist. It's the best thing that I know of for anybody trying to be a writer. The thing to do is to learn a journalist's way of work: get up early, stay at work all day. Don't sit around waiting for inspiration. You must be prepared in case it does come, so you can use it.

SR: You have said that if you're going to be a writer you can't be a reader. Why do you think that's true for you?

Caldwell: That's difficult. People will look at you askance and say, "What's the matter with you? Are you illiterate?" I have to admit that I'm more interested in what I'm writing than in what someone else has written. Not that I feel in competition or am jealous. If you are going to just be a critic and read other people's books, trying to emulate them, I don't think you are going to succeed.

SR: Some self-taught writers say that they wonder if having studied under another writer would have saved them time, grief, false moves, and stories they threw away.

Caldwell: I was sort of a tramp scholar. I went from one college to another all over the country and never graduated. My education was the variety of life that I encountered: delivering milk at 3 a.m., working at a 5-and-10 store in the basement. These experiences contributed to my understanding of life, and the way I wanted to write. I found out that I didn't want to be a milkman all my life. I wanted to write stories. I approve of education, but it just was not for me.

SR: In those early years when you were teaching yourself to write, were you conscious at the time of just how experimental those stories were?

Caldwell: I did a lot of experimental writing. Of the 150 short stories I've written, I doubt if more than two or three are written in the same manner, style, background. Everything had to be a little bit different with me, otherwise I was bored. I didn't have any hard and fast rules in the beginning. I wanted to create something that would interest me, not you, or any other reader. I write for myself. There are millions of readers. Every reader is different: how are you going to write for the reader? I have to please myself. After I'm pleased, then I'm willing to let someone else have a go at it.

SR: Did you ever sit down at any point in those early years and go back over what you had written to see what you'd learned?

Caldwell: No. I never look back. It's always looking forward to new ideas, new locales, new thoughts. I do not read what I have written unless I'm imposed upon to read for a recording, things like that. But I do not read for the amazement or amusement of myself. Once I have finished a short story or a novel I am through with it. I don't even want to read the proof. I let somebody else do that. Actually, I'll probably write a short story ten or fifteen times before I'll let it be finished. By that time I will have exhausted all my capacity to improve it.

SR: Character is one of your strong points, even in your short stories. Was this something you were striving for?

Caldwell: I write about people. To me that's the important ingredient: what his influences are on his surroundings and how his surroundings influence him as a character, and how he is deviating from the norm.

SR: Many think *Georgia Boy* is your best book. This collection is very different from your other books in that the stories in it are all related. How did you come up with this form?

Caldwell: It was written over a period of seven to ten years. I wrote it during a period when I was traveling, and I probably wrote some from as far away as the Soviet Union, when I was a journalist. I know I wrote some when I moved to Arizona the first time and got out of the chain gang of Hollywood. I had no idea I would write enough to make a book. Once I got started I would always have another idea. There was no progressive thought, no beginning or end, just a collection put together of everyday existence and events.

SR: You have said that the short story is the form for you. Why is that?

Caldwell: I like the short story because you don't have to conform to the commercial idea of a novel, which must have so many pages. A short story can be one page or fifty.

SR: Is the novel a harder form in which to work?

Caldwell: It's more demanding in the sense that you are compelled to spend more time doing one theme. The novel is subject to being too long for the subject matter. I have always tried to write a novel no more than 200 to 250 pages. I have been asked by publishers to write a big long novel, but I don't want to. I stick to the briefest way you can go.

SR: A lot of readers have commented on the mode of repetition that you use. "Handsome Brown and the Goats" is a good example, because if you analyze why it is so uproariously funny, one of the keys is the repetition by Handsome Brown that his arches are hurting him. Is this repetition something you were conscious of?

Caldwell: Yes, repetition is necessary; it's like refrain in music. If it's pertinent, adaptable to your idea, then it's an important ingredient in making a point, so long as it doesn't get monotonous or too obvious.

SR: One of "those professors" that I know you are so unfond of has written an essay about your stories in which he talks about this technique. He refers to stories like "Candyman Beecham" as prose-poem ballads. Are you comfortable with that interpretation?

Caldwell: It was written with the rhythm of speech. The whole thing started with that idea. The dialect emphasized the life of the black man who was happy-go-lucky, half-free from white domination. The rhythm of it was the essential part of the story. I wouldn't know any other way to write that particular story. I don't know about the "ballad."

SR: Did you, or do you, have a sense of how much ahead of your time you were?

Caldwell: I had no recognition of that. I didn't know what the times were; I only knew of the time I was living in. It never occurred to me to find out if I was with it, ahead of it, or behind it. I was writing about contemporary life as I observed it.

SR: Your stories are full of a keen sensitivity to all kinds of injustice, but you deal particularly well with those issues that concern women.

Caldwell: That's just the same general feeling that I have about people and life. I don't consider anyone superior to others, whether they are Democrat or Republican, black or white, man or woman. I don't have any prejudices.

SR: People tried to ban your work. How did you weather this?

Caldwell: I didn't see any difference between what I was writing and what somebody else was writing. I didn't consider that I was doing something that I shouldn't. I just thought it was natural to make a story as compelling as possible.

SR: Did it make you angry or bitter?

Caldwell: No. You have to accept criticism. People will say you are illiterate, don't know how to tell a story, have no plot, that your characters are reprehensible. If you are going to take criticism very seriously, then you will stop writing anything. You're not going to get 100 percent approval. It's the same thing with censorship—a matter of opinion.

SR: Despite the fact that your publishing history was very prestigious in those early years, accompanied by awards such as the Yale Review Prize and the O. Henry Prize, critical opinion began to turn against your work. What did you think these people were saying that was particularly mistaken?

Caldwell: I think they were unfamiliar with what I was writing about. The language I used in the stage version of *Tobacco Road* upset a lot of people because it was something that was not done in those days. The poverty was known, but nobody wanted to look at it. They knew people were hungry, ragged, but they didn't think it was a good idea to show it in public. Most of the critics were isolated from life, living in their own little vacuum. The critics who wrote these reviews weren't familiar with the lives I was writing about, so they thought it was exaggerated. Well, it was. Everything has to be

exaggerated in fiction and on the stage. You can't put down life
verbatim or it would be too dull. You have to pick out the highlights
and the lowlights. They took the idea that what I was doing was
sensationalism.

SR: You engineered the American Folkways project, in which you
found writers to write books about their regions.

Caldwell: That was a moonlighting job that let me travel around
America. Between writing my own books I'd have a month or two off
and would be traveling somewhere, so this was suited to my way of
life. Over five to six years we finally accumulated a library of about
twenty-five volumes. These were people I had known or who had
been recognized. I'd go to see the person and talk with him on the
kind of writing he would produce; then I would select him and the
publisher would give him a contract. The book would be sent to me
and I'd look at it and pass it on to the editor.

SR: Was your motive to travel?

Caldwell: No, my motive was to promote the regionalism of the
country. I've always been a regional writer, and I think the best
writing is regional. To write about the Cajuns of Louisiana, the
Mexicans along the Rio Grande, the Indians of New Mexico, to me
that is regionalism and what I wanted to do was to bring out these
various sections of life in America, because every part of the country
is different—at least, until we got radio and everybody tried to lose
their accent. So we're losing our Southern accents, and our New
England accents, because everybody tried to talk like Walter
Cronkite.

SR: Do you think that writing is by necessity a very solitary thing
that cuts you off?

Caldwell: There have been instances when people would get
together to form a school of writing. In the old days it was in
Greenwich Village. Everybody would meet and praise each other's
work. It never appealed to me, and in order to avoid it I didn't know
very many writers. The fewer writers you know, the easier it is to
avoid being caught up in that mishmash of literaryism which to me is
a very deadly kind of existence.

SR: Yet, you were friends with William Saroyan and Nathanael
West. What was different about them?

Caldwell: They were free-minded people who didn't follow the
crowd or belong to a certain group. They did not write by formula.

They were very creative; you've got to be creative if you're going to be a fiction writer, otherwise you're just a hack. And Saroyan was no hack, by any means. I admired his ability to withstand the pressure to conform.

SR: William Faulkner named you, along with himself, as one of the five finest contemporary writers in America. He praised you for your plain style. Is this a phrase that you feel comfortable with?

Caldwell: I never think in those terms. I'm just an ordinary writer, I'm nothing special; so I don't have to have that kind of appreciation. I can do without it. All I'm interested in are the books that I've written. I'm just the writer. The books speak for themselves.

Erskine Caldwell's Little Acre:
A Portrait of the Irascible, Maverick Author at Home
Kent Biffle/1983

From the *Dallas Morning News,* 6 November 1983, pp. G 1,6.
Reprinted with permission of *The Dallas Morning News.*

"Polyester."

Big-boned, rockslide-rugged Erskine Caldwell doesn't cuss much, but the scorn in his lifted voice double-damned the word.

"Polyester" is his contemptuous term for most of today's fiction. "It's shoddy stuff," said the author of *Tobacco Road, God's Little Acre* and more than 50 other books bought by more than 80 million readers.

"Formula writers and pornographers," growled Caldwell, the creater of lusty scenes that half a century ago were commonly called scandalous and carefully dogeared both by protesting puritans and passionate pubescents.

In the eyes of admirers of Caldwell's work, however, there exists a wide artistic arroyo between his treatment of sex as basic to realism— at least as basic as, say, winter turnips—and the unabashed pornographers' increasingly strained exercises aimed nowadays at titillation of increasingly jaded readers.

"These formula writers and pornographers are in a competition. Each novel must be more sensational than the last one. Their stuff isn't from natural wool. It's not natural cotton. It's not natural silk. It's polyester."

He voices suspicions that much fiction today is being formulated by computers. (And some is.) A literary purist to a point, he rejects all fictive formulas and contrived plots.

In a sunny sitting room opening onto the pool where he swims, the author, who, with passing years, has achieved the appearance of an ancient Roman senator, explained, "Someone told me long ago that there are seven plots for fiction. You simply choose one or a variation and write a novel.

"Hearing that, I promptly threw out plots. I have no plot in a story. I wouldn't know how to write a novel or a short story with a plot. If I knew what was going to happen in a novel, I'd be too bored to write it. I write page No. 1, first line, second line, next paragraph. I go on from there to see what's going to happen."

What happens, on a good day, is that his characters begin performing and take over the story. On a bad day, well, his wastebasket is a spacious, sawed-off, wooden barrel. While more than 150 of his short stories have been published, a like number have gone into the barrel. A couple of novels have gone into it, too. On a bad day, any hungry writer probably could find subsistence in that barrel. Caldwell is a tough critic of his own work—and that of others.

"Unfortunately, everybody *thinks* he can write—even people without talent. They become mesmerized by their own verbiage. That becomes a sort of screen. They always think they've written something great. But they can't see through that screen. They can't see the junk. You have to be more objective than that. You have to have deeper feeling. That's where original talent plays a part. The best thing that can happen to an aspiring writer is to be born with talent."

He said he spent eight or 10 years learning to write. Few editors are much help, he is convinced. His favorite was the late Maxwell Perkins. "He never changed anything I wrote."

Unsurprisingly, given his views, Caldwell, a college dropout, blasts creative writing courses. He rarely bothers to read the works of other writers or re-read his own. He read one William Faulkner novel—*As I Lay Dying*—and liked it. He said he has never read a book by Mark Twain, although he likely will get around to it. Early in his career Caldwell divided the world into readers and writers.

During his newspaper days, including a tour at the *Atlanta Journal* where Margaret Mitchell (*Gone With the Wind*) was writing feature stories while he wrote endless obits, he began reviewing books for a Sunday column. Sometimes he would tackle 15 or 20 a week. "That was a lot of reading," he said. And some weeks there wasn't a good one in the bunch. He believes he may have suffered early burn-out on bad books. He doesn't read for fun.

"I've never catered to academic life. I used to lecture a couple of months each year, usually to departments of English or classes in creative writing or such. I soon found out that the professors had ideas different from mine. And they didn't want their students to become particularly interested in my way of writing."

But academics still welcome him to their campuses. His books and their stage and film adaptions are highly regarded by scholars and cultist fans. It's no oddity that one can scarcely find a book by Caldwell in his big, airy house in an economically upscale valley outside Phoenix. The reason is that there are major Caldwell collections at three universities.

In Dallas this week, Caldwell, the dropout, literary maverick, the quintessential Southerner who has lived most of his life outside the South, will appear at Southern Methodist University's Ninth Annual Literary Festival. He will read from his writings Friday at 8:30 p.m. in McFarlin Auditorium.

Apart from his steamy opinions about modern fiction, Caldwell is an affable man, although a private one. For the most part, he avoids the company of most other writers because "all they talk about is themselves or their writing." Caldwell isn't like that. But perhaps because of his background in journalism, he tries to be a willing interview subject.

"I've already had my 80th birthday party," he announced, grinning broadly. It was in France last month, although he won't really become an octogenarian until Dec. 17.

Le Ministre de la Culture, Republique Francaise, dubbed him "Commandeur de l'Ordre des Arts et des Lettres." He depended on his petite, French-speaking wife, Virginia, to translate fully the meaning of the green-ribboned gold medal with which he was decorated. He'd received a grand honor, the order of the Commandant of Arts and Letters.

"There was a gathering of 500 Frenchmen in Nice," he said. "They all sang *Happy Birthday* in English with a French accent." Each held a lighted candle during the singing. Among the guests were playwright Eugene Ionesco and novelist Anthony Burgess.

"It was beautiful," said Virginia Caldwell. Her husband enjoyed it all except when they showed John Ford's movie version of *Tobacco Road,* a film Caldwell detests because Hollywood distorted the story. "Instead of the tragic ending I wrote, that film showed Jeeter Lester's relations, after they had lost their farm, headed for the poor house happily singing folk songs and hymns."

Since even the French cannot canonize a literary saint without a devil's advocate, severe questions were in order in Scottsdale.

Is Erskine Caldwell even sure that Dec. 17 will be his 80th birthday?

"I'd have a difficult time proving it," he laughed. "The State of Georgia had no birth records in those days."

Is he, in fact, legitimate? Wasn't his first book, in 1929, titled *The Bastard?*

"Well, I had a father and a mother," he roared with laughter. "My father was a preacher of the Associate Reformed Presbyterian church. He married everybody who came along, and he must have married himself."

Speaking of marrying everybody, hasn't Caldwell been married four times?

True. And being multi-married isn't a profitable habit, he conceded.

"After each of the first three I was divided up. I lost three good houses—one in Maine, one in Connecticut, and one in Tucson. But I'm much smarter now. I put everything in Virginia's name, so I can never lose it."

Why all the marriages? Is Erskine Caldwell *that* disagreeable, *that* hard to live with?

"Well, sure, I'm hard to live with. I don't like to talk about the other people or about my complaints or what the circumstances might have been. But certain things exist in a writer's life that aren't conductive, in my view, to stabilized living or peaceful existence.

"I don't like to talk about it because two of these people are still living. (Photographer Margaret) Bourke-White is dead."

His first marriage, to Helen Lannigan, ended in 1938 after 13 years. He was married from 1939 to 1941 to Margaret Bourke-White. In 1942, he wed June Johnson. That union lasted until 1955. The father of four is rather proud (or relieved) to point out that his 1957 marriage to Virginia Moffett Caldwell has lasted well.

Although he still drinks wine, Caldwell was forced to give up ardent spirits by a doctor's warning. He didn't quit cigarettes until it was too late to save half of each of his lungs.

Like John Steinbeck and others who wrote with sympathy for the poor, Caldwell eventually drew political criticism from conservatives who labeled him a pinko. He admits that during the Great Depression, when dabbling with communism was almost fashionable in intellectual circles, he did associate with a few Greenwich Village communists—but always because of common interests that were literary rather than political. "I even submitted stories to the *New Masses,* but I don't recall that any were ever published."

Caldwell's politics aren't complicated.

"I have always been in favor in a presidential year of voting for the party that isn't in. I'm always in favor of kicking out the people who are in the government and putting in some fresh ones who might do better."

Erskine Caldwell appended this note to his entry in *Who's Who*:

"I am fully aware that my life has not been without fault and error; even so, in my present state of mind, I would hesitate to change anything in the past were I given the opportunity to do so. My reason for declining an opportunity to change the past is that I am satisfied with myself."

Erskine Caldwell at Eighty-One:
An Interview
Marilyn Dorn Staats/1984

Erskine Caldwell, the Georgia-born preacher's son who grew up to shock his elders with tales of sex and violence in the Deep South, is now eighty-one years old. Once America's most popular fiction writer, he was largely deserted in the late fifties by readers who left him for more sensational fare. Critics who admired him primarily for his depictions of poverty, ignorance, and social injustice in redneck Georgia turned their attention to more topical grievances.

But today, when Big Macs have replaced wormy turnips in the hungry mouths of those living on paved Tobacco Roads and rural dreamers are designing Cabbage Patch dolls instead of digging for gold on God's Little Acres, there are signs that Erskine Caldwell may yet be recognized as one of the important writers of twentieth-century America.

A Caldwell revival is occurring in college classrooms across the country, and some in the literary establishment are agreeing with William Faulkner's assessment of Caldwell as one of the top five writers of his time. His use of grotesque comedy, exaggerated characters, stark settings, and primitive violence is being reappraised as "stylistic extravagances associated with surrealism, black humor, and naturalism." Others identify Caldwell's fiction as belonging to the tradition of Southern myth and folklore, of frontier humor.

Always esteemed in Europe, Caldwell recently received the first Writers of the World *L'Ordre des Arts et des Lettres* from the French Government and was acclaimed as being the sole survivor of that extraordinary group of American writers consisting of Caldwell, Faulkner, Hemingway, Steinbeck, and Dos Passos.

Now cured after two operations for lung cancer in the past six years, Erskine Caldwell continues to write from his desert home out of Scottsdale, Arizona, and to travel extensively throughout the

United States and Europe with Virginia Caldwell, his artist wife of twenty-seven years.

He is currently working on a diary, "impressions of a lifetime of travelling in different parts of the world." A collection of twenty-two short stories about race relations called *The Black and White Stories of Erskine Caldwell* was published in 1984.

A tall, thin man (his nickname is "Skinny"), he seems stronger and younger than his years. During the following interview in his Arizona study, he kept his arms folded across his chest and occasionally swung his knees wide and back together again rapidly, like a small boy impatient to be done with it. Courteous and shy, the one time he was startled by a question ("Are you a deeply spiritual writer?") he leaned forward in his chair and gave the interviewer a stern look of disapproval before settling back to answer.

Staats: Fifty-two years have passed since *Tobacco Road* was published. What are the grandchildren of old man Jeeter doing today?

Caldwell: They're either on welfare, living on food stamps, or they might be high-powered executives in Atlanta, Georgia. Who knows? That's the gamble in life. What is another generation going to develop into? It can be industrious, or it can be slovenly and lazy. How do you know?

Staats: Someone has written that Faulkner was saddened by the conditions in the south he wrote about and that Caldwell was outraged by them. Have your economic and political feelings changed since then? Have you now moved more toward the center?

Caldwell: I was living in that era in which the whole South was a sharecropping system. I saw the hardships of it, the difficulties, the changes that should have been made. And, of course, it was all tied in with segregation. The two together were a great handicap. I was opposed to segregation and I was opposed to the sharecropping system, having lived with it myself. I thought I had the privilege and the right to criticize them. They're nothing for me to criticize now, because they don't exist. I'm not outraged by anything these days because the only thing now is politics, and I'm not concerned with politics.

Staats: You have not been pleased when critics have seen you as primarily a crusader on social injustice, but to what extent should an artist concern himself with the social and political problems of his time?

Caldwell: They're part of life. A writer writes about anything that has to do with a living person. Of course, you can become a fanatic on any subject—religion, politics, social service—but that has nothing to do with the writer. He must select his own material. If he wants to be a missionary and go out into the world and influence people with propaganda, that's his business. But I don't consider that a field for a writer.

Staats: The Southern writer often writes about characters who are victims of their society and yet must be held responsible for their own actions. Your Deep South characters are certainly victims, but they seem too primitive to be capable of making value judgments. Do you agree?

Caldwell: Well, the primitive society has been subjected to very little outside influence, and therefore it only knows what it exists in, and that might be a vacuum. The primitivism of people is inherited. You cannot get away from it. It becomes part of the genes of life and what people are going to do. Are they cruel? Are they kindhearted? Are they law-abiding? Whatever they are, they have some instincts, some characteristics that they express without any great pressure from other societies or from other examples of living.

How you behave has to do with your training. What your education was. Your inheritance. The influences. If you never knew the difference between right and wrong, how would you know what to do? I don't know how you can blame a person for not knowing. He's not born with that feeling, no more so than an animal, a dog, or a cat knows the difference between right and wrong. You can train a dog to do something right. And you can train him not to do something wrong. The same with a child, a person.

Way back in the early days of the South, for example, lynching was a normal pastime. Now it is not. Times change. People change. The influences that go about it change.

The influence that was the great savior of the South was education. There's no doubt about it. At the same time was the industrialization of the South and the abandonment of agricultural empires. When there was no longer any demand for human labor on the farm, the children did not have to stay home from school. They could go get their education.

Staats: Many readers have admired you for your ability to show your downtrodden characters' sheer animal will to survive. Do societies have that same will? Do you see the South, for example, having a will to survive with most of its "Southernness" intact?

Caldwell: I don't think there's a criterion for society itself to do this or do that. Society is a collection of different ideas. The Old South relied upon living by tradition, but being "superior" socially (peons or slaves or poor whites had nothing to do with the plantation society, which was a different level of life). The South was economically deprived. Wealth accumulated in the North with industrialization in the mills of New England where all the cloth was made, all the shoes were made, everything was made.

When you think you're a little bit inferior, I suppose you become defensive. "Yankee" became a term of derision. It still may be a little bit. Of course, the Yankee was no different, basically, from the Southerner. Both came from the same origin which was England or France or the Huguenots and so forth. But the South had a chip on its shoulder for a long time. I think it's been gradually removed. I think now, for example, Atlanta is just as representative an American city as, say, Denver, Colorado. Fifty years ago, Atlanta was looked upon as being way deep South in the backwaters.

Now, no more. Now we're all equal. Now we're *all* Yankees.

Staats: You've said that every novelist should invent his own style. How would you define your style?

Caldwell: My style? I have no style, per se. I could not describe it. My style is in simplicity. It has to show itself in its simplest form to convey the deepest feeling. Fiction writing, or poetry, I suppose—I'm no poet, but I imagine the poets have the same feeling I have about fiction prose—has to exhibit and reveal feeling. It's not the mere words. They mean nothing. It's the feeling that is conveyed by a combination of words. That's the style I try to use. I do not want to be characterized as a "stylist."

Staats: What is the difference between Erskine Caldwell as a novelist and Erskine Caldwell as a short-story writer?

Caldwell: My first inclination as a writer is to write short stories. To me, the short story is much more of a discipline than a novel. The short story has to reveal so much, in such a small extent or length, that you must reveal what you are trying to express much more closely, much more deeply. A novel can run for a thousand pages and say nothing. A short story has to say something in five or six or eight pages.

Staats: You certainly use humor in your writing. Can you define how you use it in your work?

Caldwell: Humor and tragedy, or comedy and tragedy, go hand in hand in my opinion. Everything in life is susceptible to one or the other, and there is no difference in my mind between them. It's all the same. It just depends upon your circumstances. What could be a funny joke at one point would be a very sorrowful event at another. It might be the same happening. Humor is something that is derived out of life itself, just as tragedy is derived out of life itself. There are humorous incidents, I imagine, in nature. I imagine nature could laugh at a lot of things that happen out in the forests, in the fields, if it had the expression to do so.

Staats: Do you consider yourself a deeply spiritual writer?

Caldwell: Spiritual.

Staats: Spiritual in the sense. . . .

Caldwell: Religious? Religion itself is, in my opinion, a propaganda organization, just like Communism is a propaganda organization. The Christian concept is to go ye out into the world and save every creature—whatever it is, I can't quote the Bible correctly. I'm not a religious writer by any means. The spirit of something is what I call "emotion." I'd rather be characterized as an emotional writer. That's the reaction, the human reaction, to an event or situation. That's the emotionalism I carry over into exuberance or sorrow or a lot of different things.

Staats: Ty Ty Walden in *God's Little Acre* said "There was a mean trick played on us somewhere. God put us in the bodies of animals and tried to make us act like people." Does Erskine Caldwell say that too?

Caldwell: I can't elaborate on that too much; it's just the way people attribute that feeling to God. If there were a God, I don't know how He would react to that Himself. The fact that people are inheritants of animal nature cannot be denied, unless you want to go into a long argument about the divine creation and so on, which, of course, I do not subscribe to. I do believe we all probably sprang from some kind of a fish or something in the old days. To me, the idea of there being anything divine about human beings has no basis of acceptance.

Staats: Some critics have accused you of being disdainful of your characters, of not sympathizing with them. Of laughing at them. Could you reply to that?

Caldwell: I don't know how to answer other than to say I have to attribute to characters what their actions or what their words reveal about them. If I suspect a character is insincere, or antisocial, or whatever, I'm going to be influenced by that fact. I probably *would* disdain him.

Staats: Another critic has written that you believe all women are either presently or reminiscently sex-crazy, while most men are supine idiots. Would you care to comment on that?

Caldwell: I don't think it's necessary to comment on that, because it's not in my doctrine. That's his opinion; it is not mine.

Staats: Other critics have compared your fictional world to a dream world, in which there is a yearning, a compulsion in your characters that is similar to what one feels in a dream. Do you agree?

Caldwell: If you listen to what other people say, you'll hear anything.

Staats: But your characters do have an exaggerated quality, a kind of mythic quality. . . .

Caldwell: The best characters are never real. They are created. Invented. If you make your characters so-called "lifelike," you're just photographing. You're depicting nothing more than that, in my opinion.

Staats: Do you care what critics say about your work?

Caldwell: No. I'm sometimes interested in what they say, but it does not influence me. Praise, for example, can be insincere. If you're going to believe that insincerity, then you are hurting yourself. It can go either way. Anybody who tries to impress the public by saying this writer is not worth reading, he's vulgar, he's pornographic, or whatever it is, then in my opinion he's a propagandist. If he says, this is the greatest writer who ever lived, who's going to believe him after reading something this writer has written? So I wouldn't believe in either school. The kind that says a book's not worth reading or the kind that says this is a book everybody should read. Why should you read it unless you select it yourself?

Staats: Do you write for any particular kind of reader? An ideal reader?

Caldwell: I write for myself. I am the reader. Anybody else who comes along is welcome to read what I am reading. I have to please myself to start with, because I consider myself the best critic of my work in existence, much better than anybody else, no matter what his reputation.

Staats: What do you want to be remembered for in your work?

Caldwell: Nothing in particular, other than the fact that I would like to think that I'd had a good influence on other writers. I had the feeling when I was trying to write that I was unwanted. No one would publish my short stories. I finally broke through the barrier to the extent that eventually my short stories began to be published, but it took a lot of persistence, eight or ten years of it, more or less. I hope maybe I might influence writers to stick with it rather than to give up very easily. Because it's so easy to give up these days unless you make a lot of money. The pressure's so great, you give it up and do something else. I think a lot of talent is lost that way.

Staats: Have you any close disciples who have been successful that you know of?

Caldwell: No. No. No. Every generation has its own story to tell in your place. That's it. A writer belongs to his own age. Young writers depict their own times. At twenty, you have the opportunity to present your own process, your own era, your own vision of the world. At forty, fifty, sixty, you're writing about your youth. Your attitudes haven't changed as much as your years.

Staats: In their primitive innocence, many of your Deep South characters seem to take death almost as an incident, like scratching an itch. They don't react to it as I would react. Is death not a fearsome thing to you?

Caldwell: No. I cannot get excited about it, or worry about it, or feel about it. It's an inevitable occurrence. Like you expect the sun to rise tomorrow morning, you should expect to die sometime. When it's going to be is like a game of chance. It's a dice game. You never know.

Staats: Life is very much a game of chance to you?

Caldwell: There are so many different factors applied to a person, you never know what's going to happen to you next. You may have a good job today working in a bank, and then, for all you know, the next week you're going to lose that job. The bank may fold, or consolidate, or you might be charged with stealing some of the bank's money. I don't count on anything for sure in life. It's a chance, yes. It is. As long as you're alive, you're all right. Once you're dead, you don't know about it anyway. So there you are.

Staats: Are you optimistic about the future of society?

Caldwell: No more so than I know by inference. Every civilization in the past has gone through a certain course of events and that civilization has reached a peak, and from that point on, the civilization has floundered. Sometimes it's wiped out. We know what happened to the Roman Empire. Right now, the Communist system of the Soviet Union is attempting to do the same thing, conquer the whole world and subject it to its empire. Maybe that's the next great step in civilization, the culmination of the Soviet Empire. But we won't be here when that happens. We may become subjected to it, but we won't be here to see its ending. So, no. I don't think there's anything to be optimistic about. We're going to live and die as a civilization.

Staats: You've written over fifty books, been read by eighty million people. Do you still have a compulsion to write?

Caldwell: No. It winds down as you go. When you're very young, you have twenty-four hours in which to write. You use every hour of the twenty-four, because even when you are asleep, you are mentally writing something. You dream it or something. That youthful exuberance becomes more calm as the years go by. Now I can skip a day or two and have no qualms at all about skipping. I just build up and up until the steam gets to a nice head again, and then I want to write something.

Staats: There seems to be a resurgence of interest in Erskine Caldwell. For people who have not read you, are there any specific books that you would recommend they start with?

Caldwell: [*Smiling*] No. Tell them to read all fifty. Then they can choose the one they like best.

Interview with Erskine Caldwell

Edwin T. Arnold/1986

The following is an edited version of an interview I conducted with Erskine Caldwell on 2-3 March 1986 at his home in Paradise Valley, Arizona. The interview is published for the first time here with the permission of Mr. Caldwell.

Arnold: Much has been made of the fact that you moved around so much during your childhood. Do you think there were any negative aspects to that situation, such as the lack of a definite home place?

Caldwell: Well, I'm satisfied with the way it was for this reason: I don't think I could have accomplished what I did if it had been otherwise. The varieties of experiences dictated the course of my life. I attribute my ability as a writer to the fact that people—their aspects, their exclamations, their activities, their lives, social and political— varied from place to place. What I experienced was living, seeing, observing varieties of life. I don't know if I missed something by not having a stable family life. But the life I had, had a lot to do with the characters that I created, because it gave me an insight into these personalities, to be able to know why they act as they do. And I couldn't write in any other way than I have written, because I would not have known what I know, and I could not have infused my fiction with the various elements of these characters or characteristics. I think that, for the most part, my life was conditioned by the fact that I did not consider anything as stable or stationary or unmovable. And by that I mean that life was fluid, I was fluid, I was moving all the time, or most of the time, and I considered life itself as movement. The environment was constantly changing, from one scene to another, and this contributed to the kind of story that I wanted and tried to write. If I had not let myself loose, feel loose in a sense, I don't think I could have created the kind of stories I was trying to write. I think I would have been too handicapped.

Arnold: What about your lack of a formal education?

Caldwell: Well, I was deprived, some people would say, of an

education. That also had a lot to do with my insight, I think, because I
had to get my education out of the thin air, so to speak. And, of
course, that was a handicap. I still feel handicapped, because I am
not an educated person. I'm more of a primitive person than an
educated person. But what resulted from that particular situation was
a fortunate experience: I was able to get an education that was not
prescribed. I can think of many instances where I discovered the
principles of learning by accidently coming upon a certain book or a
certain poem or a certain story that enlightened me to the extent that
I thought that I was making a great discovery. Of course, I *was*
discovering, but everybody else had already done so because they
had been guided in their educational process whereas I was going on
my own and I had to do it accident by accident. Whether there was
good result, I don't know, but it suited me and it still suits me and I'm
very glad that my education came about the way that it did. I never
graduated from anything. I had one year of kindergarden, and I
didn't graduate because the instructor said I spent all my time
watching the girls play.

Arnold: Where was this?

Caldwell: This was in Staunton, Virginia. So I was asked to leave
the kindergarten because I wasn't conforming to the education rules.
But, you see, along the way my mother was teaching me. I don't
know when she began. I really don't know when it ended, except
that she permitted me to enter grammar school, grade school, and so
she gave up the privilege of instructing me, turned it over to the
public authority. I don't know exactly what grade I went in to, but it
was over my head anyway. However, I put in two years at this school
as a student, my first two years of education as a student other than
for my mother. But by that time I had acquired a lot of interesting
theories about life. I couldn't spell. I couldn't read very well. I
couldn't do anything very well even when I was forced to, let alone
when I had to feel my way. When I went into the public school
system, then I had to go back and learn how to read and how to spell
and so forth. And that was very good. But I was so far behind that I
never caught up. By the time I had reached the age of fourteen or
fifteen, living in Wrens, Ga., I was six feet tall, and when you fit into a
class of first-year high schoolers and you're six feet tall, you feel a bit
awkward because all the other students are much younger and
shorter. You feel out of place. The superintendent of the school felt

that I was too tall and that I might create a disturbance among the
younger and smaller students, and so he put me up in the Junior
Class, the third class, instead of the first class. So I found myself in
the third year of high school without any first or second year of study.
And I floundered. Of course, I wasn't really interested in the studies
anyway, and by the time I got into the fourth level, I was completely
waterlogged so to speak; I couldn't float and I sank right down. By
that time I had realized that life was more than a small town, and I
had decided to go and find a better life than I would have achieved
there. But of course I didn't graduate from high school—had no
units, didn't pass anything. I did finally manage to get into this
Presbyterian college [Erskine College] with the help of my father. It
was decided that if I could get in there, I would go. I thought I would
try it, knowing that I would never achieve anything where I was. But
Erskine was really not what I wanted, and I soon set my sights on the
University of Virginia. I had a very good impetus to go there, because
my mother was a Virginian, and she thought that the University of
Virginia was the only worthwhile place to go.

Arnold: Before you went to Virginia, you did some traveling
around. For example, you have described a number of times in your
writing—*In Search of Bisco, Call It Experience*, and other places as
well—your experiences in Bogalusa, Louisiana, when you were
placed in jail for nine days. You recount the story in almost a
humorous way, but it couldn't have been funny at the time.

Caldwell: Well, at the time it happened, it was unreal. I had never
been in jail before. It was a new experience to be put behind bars. I
had seen other people behind bars. I had an acquaintance early in
life in Wrens, a black yard boy. We were very friendly, and he used to
get put in jail, and I would go to see him. I would shine shoes at the
jail for a nickel, spend thirty or forty or fifty minutes shining shoes for
a nickel just so we could talk. And sometimes I would go down to the
chain-gang camp on Sundays and spend a whole afternoon talking
with the convicts. So I had some experience from the *outside* of a jail.
The only difference in my situation was that my colored friend wore a
ball-and-chain, and in my case, since I was in a very elevated kind of
jail, I did not have to wear a ball-and-chain and I was free to walk
around as much as I wished. I thought I was in a very good situation.
Of course, I wanted to get out, but I was not exactly unhappy there.

Arnold: You have described yourself as an "in and out student" at the University of Virginia from about 1923 to 1926. But during this time you also lived in Pennsylvania and in Washington, D.C., and you attended classes at the University of Pennsylvania.

Caldwell: The University of Pennsylvania in Philadelphia.

Arnold: In March of 1925 you married your first wife, Helen Lannigan. Her father taught at the University of Virginia, is that right?

Caldwell: He was the athletic director and he coached track.

Arnold: You were married in Washington on March 3rd. Later, you withdrew from the University of Virginia and moved to Atlanta to work on the *Atlanta Journal*. There, as you note in *Call It Experience*, you met Hunter Bell, who had a great influence on you. How did this journalistic experience affect your writing style?

Caldwell: It taught me to be concise, not to try to impress the reader of the newspaper with unfamiliar words. That newspaper style helped regarding simplicity, and the simplicity led to formulating a literary style that was as precise as possible. So that newspaper work was my opportunity to learn to write fiction, because I had been trying to write fiction and had never succeeded, and I thought that once I had mastered a journalistic type of writing, then I could transfer that into what I wanted to do. It took a long time, but I did it in some respects.

Arnold: The other two names that you mention from that period of time are Margaret Mitchell and Frances Newman. Was Frances Newman working on the paper at that time?

Caldwell: Frances Newman? No, she was the friend of a friend of mine, the reporter Frank Daniels, and I used to get all the news from Frank. He would tell me what she was doing and what she said and what she was criticizing and so on. And so any influence she had on me was, you might say, second-hand, because it came through Frank Daniels. He would tell me what she thought about certain writers and books, and so that was the main influence I got out of her.

Arnold: You've mentioned her book *The Hard-Boiled Virgin* in *Call It Experience*.

Caldwell: Yes. That was one of the first books I'd ever read in which I learned that people could tell a story in that language.

Arnold: And Margaret Mitchell: what impressed you about her?

Caldwell: Well, Mitchell was a feature writer for the *Journal*. She had a chair and desk in the same building, the same floor, as the City Room. The only time I would see her was when she would come to see the editor and would be standing there talking to somebody and I would happen to overhear her say something. And so my association with her was very brief, but I did know that she was working on this particular book *Gone With The Wind* because Frank Daniels had heard about it and would say that she had finished such and such a chapter of the book. That's how I kept up with the progress of the book.

Arnold: You admired her willingness to give up her job to dedicate herself to her writing. You followed suit very shortly thereafter, although in your case it was a much riskier business, I would think.

Caldwell: Well, you accept the risk when you're young. It's only when you get older that you count the risk.

Arnold: How did your wife Helen respond to this move? Was she supportive?

Caldwell: Oh, yes. She was young, too, so she was all for it. No difficulty there.

Arnold: So you moved to Mount Vernon, Maine, in order, you've said, to get away from the South so you could write about the South.

Caldwell: Yes, for the perspective, for the distance.

Arnold: According to letters written at the time, you felt that in order to consider yourself an authentic writer, you had to get your work published and be paid for it. Do you still believe that? Do you not believe that there are any great unpublished writers out there in the world?

Caldwell: No. Because if you haven't published anything, what is there that exists that can be read? You don't expect the writer to go around handing out his manuscripts for the world to read. It has to be in print to be considered the work of a writer. If you're going to be a writer, then that's your profession. I can tell you that you have to pay your way through life in your profession, whatever it is. We don't go through life living on inheritances. Writing is production, and money is a symbol of what you have produced. You have to have some kind of active symbol to show that you have produced something and that what you have produced is accepted by somebody else who thought it was worthwhile enough to pay for it.

Arnold: So that being paid well for your book is part of the business of being a successful writer?

Caldwell: Well, I don't say that every writer has to be or wants to be a businessman, but—if you go out here and grow a hill of turnips or squash or corn, whatever, and you produce that product and you take it out on the side of the road and put it on a stand and wait for somebody to come by, you expect them to pay you for it. You don't take it out there to give it away. You expect to be paid for your toil and your effort.

Arnold: In a letter to your parents in 1929, you expressed great discouragement over your failure to achieve publication. Did you ever think about just giving up?

Caldwell: Oh, no. When you're young you don't think of those things. You have great ambitions, and you just sweat it out. You read a book or you read a review at some point, and somehow that would appeal to you and you would think, "That must be the kind of writer I wish I could be" or "I wish I could write a book as good as this book review says this book is." You get a lot of hope just from the fact that someone has written a book that is acclaimed—not necessarily a best seller or anything like that—but the fact that it gets good critical responses. It serves as an inspiration to a writer to try to achieve something of his own similar to that, not necessarily a replica of what has been done. Just the fact that these things can be achieved is the influence that has been so important to me, instead of trying to slavishly imitate somebody else's work. I have always avoided other people's work when I thought maybe I might be influenced by it. That was the principle I have taken and I've stuck with it and I'm glad I do it because I don't want to, and have never wanted to try to imitate somebody else. To me it had to be original.

Arnold: In 1929, shortly after the letter I mentioned, "Midsummer Passion" was accepted by *The New American Caravan*.

Caldwell: Yes. It's a very interesting thing. You see, that story had various titles. Every time I would send it out to a magazine and it came back, I would change the title and send it out again. I had sent it out to, oh, six or eight different magazines under that many titles, and under two of those titles the thing was accepted. One was the title "Midsummer Passion" and another was "July." Anyway, "July" was published in *transition*, a little magazine in Paris. A few weeks later *American Caravan* came along and accepted the same story under a different title. And so that one story did have a world-wide travel before it settled down, but always under a different title.

Arnold: Alfred Kreymborg was the editor of *The New American Caravan*, and he put you in contact with Erich Posselt, who was editor of The Heron Press, which published *The Bastard*, your first book. That was not the original title of the book, was it?

Caldwell: Well, he selected it. I don't know if I had a title or not, I may have, but he said, "This is going to be the title." That was during one of our trips in his taxi cab office. He didn't have an office in an office building. Every time I met him we would get in a taxi and ride up and down Fifth Avenue and discuss various editorial and business matters.

Arnold: This was a very impressive and elaborate publication. It was illustrated, published in a limited edition of 1100 copies. How did this publication come about? You were just beginning to have your stories published; you certainly weren't well-known.

Caldwell: I don't know. I didn't have an agent at that time. You see, I used to take the night bus down from Maine to New York. It was very inexpensive; it cost two-fifty or three dollars and you didn't have to spend a lot of money eating or anything. Anyway, I used to take manuscripts down to try to find somebody to publish them and to try to find an interested agent. And Kreymborg I guess had maybe taken that story, whatever the title, and I guess he suggested or said, "Do you have any other manuscripts?" And I think what happened was that I said, "I have a novelette right here" and he said, "Well, here's a chap who might be interested." And so I got in touch right away with this Erich Posselt, a German chap, and he said, "Sure, we want to publish this." To my surprise it came out in a very expensive edition for those days—I think for five dollars—heavy paper, very good sewn stitch and cloth binding, limited edition. As soon as it came out, Posselt said, "I know you've got another manuscript. I'm too busy doing something else, I can't publish it, but my friend over here will." And his friend was a fellow by the name of Alex Hillman. I had given this second work the title *Poor Fool*. So I gave this to Hillman and we signed a contract. Then I came to find out that he did not intend to pay any royalty. I inquired around with somebody else and they said, "Oh, Hillman. Well, his grandmother has your money and she lives in New Jersey and she won't give it up"—that kind of a story. So I never got any money from Hillman or *Poor Fool*.

Arnold: So you didn't make any money off *The Bastard* or *Poor Fool*?

Caldwell: No.

Arnold: In *The Bastard*, some of the early scenes take place in a

cotton mill. Do these scenes come from your own experiences? I
believe that you worked for a time in a cotton mill in Wrens.

Caldwell: Well, it wasn't a cotton mill, a spinning mill; it was for
getting cottonseed oil. What we did was de-lint the seed, then crush
the seed and make oil. I would shovel the cottonseeds. But, of
course, I was familiar with cotton mills also, because there were
cotton mills in Augusta and across the river in South Carolina. I used
all the cotton mill scenes in *God's Little Acre.*

Arnold: James Devlin, who has written a critical study of your
work, says of these two books that they "hint at a disturbed state of
mind in the author." They are pretty nightmarish and frightening
books when one reads them today.

Caldwell: Well, you have to realize that back then, what I was
trying to do was *create* a different world, and I had to *imagine.* I was
not duplicating life. I was not photographing life. I was not writing
about real people. I had to invent people for my fiction. And when
you have that philosophy or that ideal in mind, especially in the
beginning, you're liable to go to an excess. You have to learn to
control your imagination. I had started out on the premise that I was
going to *create* stories; I was not going to imitate life but I was going
to *make* life that had not existed. You see, fiction is something that
does not exist until you create it—otherwise it's not fiction. So my
philosophy has always been, since the beginning, that in order to
create people you have to eliminate the process of realism to the
extent of using photographic impressions, photographic images. You
want to *make* something that has not yet existed but now it does exist
because now you have made it. So, these two books, if you consider
them to be on the wild side, I'm sure the reason is because with
unbounded imagination we can imagine anything. In this case it had
to *relate* to people in Georgia I had known, for these people in my
book were people that I had *made* and cultivated and put into the
form of living characters. I'm sure the psychologists could explain
why I have gravitated toward certain characters, for example, the "big
woman." You know, that it says something about my views toward
the matrix, the mother in life. The bigger the woman, the stronger her
influence, I suppose, for the good or for the bad. But I can't explain
where these characters come from. And I don't want to.

Arnold: You also wrote around this time another novel which was
never published called *The Bogus Ones.* Guy Owen described it as
an autobiographical story of an artist in a materialistic society.

Caldwell: That's so far back in my memory that I cannot see through the dimness of it. I don't remember the story or what I was trying to do. It was another experiment, I'm sure, and an unsuccessful experiment since it wasn't published. But as I've said, I was always experimenting in those days, nothing was certain in my mind except the idea of avoiding traditional writing. I was trying to start out fresh, as if I had never read a book or no one had ever written a book. Everything was new and unique.

Arnold: In 1930, "The Mating of Marjory" and "A Very Late Spring" were accepted by Maxwell Perkins for *Scribner's Magazine*. Soon after, you applied for a Guggenheim Fellowship and you wrote your parents in March of that year that your ambition was to write a novel that would win the Pulitzer Prize. That must have been a very heady time when you were beginning to be published and had set your sights on these goals.

Caldwell: Well, of course, a time like that in your youth, you have to have aims and ambitions. But in your youthful ignorance, you don't realize your limitations. You don't realize until after the fact that you're not going to do all the wonderful things that you have dreamed. That comes later, and it's a part of growing up. Of course, I would never write a letter like that later on because I would know better. It was my youth speaking at that time.

Arnold: It was that same summer of 1930 when you built a big bonfire and burned a lot of unpublished stories and other manuscripts.

Caldwell: You reach a point where you look back and realize that everything you write is not perfect. So I guess I wanted, in a sense, to start over, to put the poorer stuff out of sight. Maybe that was overreaction.

Arnold: You've described Maxwell Perkins as an editor. What was he like as a person?

Caldwell: Well, he was very down-to-earth. He was a simple Vermont farm boy who had made good in the big city. He never seemed very complex to me. He used to complain that people came to New York and tried to become New Yorkers instead of what they actually were. He used to tell writers to stay out of New York. If you're living in Illinois, stay in Illinois and write about it. Don't try to write about New York. That's not where your knowledge, your roots are. And he was not addicted to any kind of pretense. What impressed me about his individuality was that he liked to wear his hat in his office. He had a sort of gray fedora hat, not turned up, which he wore in his office. And I remember on one occasion in his office, he was walking around with his hat on, and he had on new tan shoes, and they were the brightest tan shoes I had ever seen. They were new, and evidently they hurt his feet because every so often he would stop and rub his shoe against his heel. I remember that so well. I wanted to ask him why he didn't buy some shoes that fit him well enough that he could wear them without hurting his feet.

Arnold: In 1930 you returned to Georgia, to Wrens and Augusta. There, as you have written, you were reminded of the poverty and hopelessness and degradation of the local tenant farmers and sharecroppers, and this experience inspired you to write *Tobacco Road*.

Caldwell: That's right. I had been away so long from that environment, and so when I went back, it was quite a shock. When you compare that with what I had experienced in Maine, it was like returning to another world which I had rather forgotten. It brought back a lot of memories of the inhumanity of the Georgia chain gang, for example: all these black people shackled, ball and chain, in their striped suits, sweating it out. I remember my father saying that he deplored the system of convict labor, but that he also deplored the fact that contractors, who were building the roads, used mule power in a way that was also inhumane. He took me once to a construction site where the convicts worked. They didn't have tractors in those days, and so all the hauling and grading and everything was done by mule. In the heat of the summer, we would sometimes walk to the site. My father probably knew what was happening and he wanted me to see it. One day they were hauling dirt up and down, up and down an embankment, and one of the mules fell down in the heat, from prostration, and the contractor foreman had the convicts come up to the mule that was lying down in the way, struggling to get up. He had them take a large scoop they were using to make the road, and he had them scoop up the mule and push it, dump it down over this embankment so that the dirt would then pile on. They would take these mules that had fallen due to the heat, and they would bury these mules alive, and then put a fresh mule in their place. And that was one of the things that came back to me when I came back this time. The same thing was happening. The same kind of poverty was still existing among the people, as well as the inhumanity. To me that was something that needed to be addressed. I couldn't think of anything else to do except to write what my conscience told me about these people who were suffering. I thought other people could help somehow, either by medical aid or by food—something. What else could I do but write about it?

Arnold: It was a conscious protest.

Caldwell: Yes. Of course, it changed very rapidly during the administration of Roosevelt. I think he was the first one to recognize that these people had to have assistance, that they were at the end of their rope.

Arnold: You have said about the book *Tobacco Road* that "there was never any doubt in my mind about the outcome of the novel from that time [the time you began] to the time I finished the first draft of it three months later." When you speak of the "outcome" of the book, what exactly are you referring to?

Caldwell: Well, the conclusion of the story. I wasn't talking about the reception, whether it would be successful or not. The ending seemed distressing to me. It's the same thing all over. That's the way it was historically, until the Roosevelt era. Then it changed. But that's what I wanted to show.

Arnold: You finished the first draft of the book in April of 1931, and then you finished the second draft by the end of July. Were there only the two drafts of the novel?

Caldwell: Well, I can't say for sure. I rewrote all the time, and this is pretty far back in my memory.

Arnold: Did your wife Helen read these drafts and make comments on them?

Caldwell: Oh yes, she would read them and make corrections, correct my spelling and so forth. She would help make them acceptable for the publisher. I wouldn't dare to write a book without having someone read it before I sent it to my publisher, to catch my mistakes. Yes, Helen did that.

Arnold: *Tobacco Road* was published by Scribner's, but at first it was not particularly successful.

Caldwell: No. It got fairly harsh reviews.

Arnold: Scribner's had an option on your next two books. The next book was what you call your New England novel, *A Lamp for Nightfall*, which was not published until many years later. By the way, was that the title in 1931?

Caldwell: Yes. What happened there was that Perkins read it and made no comment. And he gave it to somebody else—I don't know who—and that person didn't want to publish it. Now, in the meantime I had gotten an agent, Maxim Leiber, and Max used that book as what he called "fishing bait." He went to Viking and he offered them another book; he didn't offer them the New England book. What they got turned out to be *God's Little Acre*. And so *A Lamp for Nightfall* was never submitted, or if it was, I didn't know anything about it. Now I'll have to get ahead of myself to say what happened to the book. When I left Viking Press to go to Duell, Sloan and Pearce, they offered to publish it along with my American Folkways series. They would do anything I wanted. Then Little, Brown bought out Duell, Sloan and Pearce, and along with their purchase came all my books, and among them was this book. So it finally got published under Little, Brown.

Arnold: At Viking you worked with Marshall Best.

Caldwell: Yes. He was a good friend. When I went there, I had no money. The hotel prices were pretty steep, several dollars a night, and Marshall would almost beg me or urge me to stay at his apartment. He had a big cot which he would fold out and I would sleep on it. And then in the morning when Marshall would go into the office, I would stay behind and have breakfast. He was very considerate of me.

Arnold: As an editor, what kind of comments would he make on your typescripts? Did he deal much with the story itself?

Caldwell: No, no. I can think of only one editorial comment he made on my work. I had written "to make short shift." He said, "No, no, that's wrong, you can't do that." He said, "That's called 'shrift.' " So I changed it.

Arnold: Well, I know that on the typescript of *Journeyman*, for instance, which was published by Viking, there is evidence of at least two hands at work there making editorial comments and suggestions. I assume one would be Marshall Best. Would the other be Helen?

Caldwell: I would imagine.

Arnold: What about Harold Guinzberg?

Caldwell: Well, he was more in the business end of the business, and I had nothing to do with him. He and Mark Spiegel ran that part of the business. He was cordial. I was invited to his house for dinner, but it was not the same feeling that I had with Marshall Best.

Arnold: In 1933, after you had published *Tobacco Road* and *God's Little Acre*, you did some Hollywood work, at first in Louisiana on location with the director Tod Browning. Is it true that you replaced William Faulkner as screenwriter on this film, *Louisiana Lou*.

Caldwell: That's what I heard.

Arnold: And after a few weeks in Louisiana you went on to Hollywood to work for MGM. What was the whole Hollywood experience like at that time?

Caldwell: Well, there was a great deal of glitter my first time there—I made five or six trips all in all, but that was my first impression. It was unreal, like Christmas. Remember now, I was really just a country boy from Georgia, Maine, whatever, and I was out there and I had no knowledge or feel or admiration for the highlife of Hollywood, which in those days was very high, comparatively speaking, because of the monetary difference. The secretary who signed me in at personnel was a very wise, streetwise, Hollywood girl who had come there from some other place. Her name was Ruth Carnell. She found out that I was staying at a sort of run-down hotel. And I said, "Well, it's ok; it's inexpensive; it suits me." And she said, "Anybody in your position, making $250 a week, should have a Cadillac convertible and you should live in the Garden of Allah." The Garden of Allah was a high-priced residential hotel in Hollywood, Beverly Hills, with wet bars and all kinds of things, big chambers, the works. So that sort of sobered me right away, and I realized that the Hollywood highlife that writers lived was not for me, and I never changed my opinion while I was there.

Arnold: One of the things you worked on after the *Louisiana Lou* project fell apart was a script for Howard Hawks. I believe that was *Roughshod*, a lumberjack story.

Caldwell: Well, that was one I worked on with a collaborator. Harry Behn, a good chap, and I were assigned to write an original story for Clark Gable, so we went right to work on it, but nothing ever came of it. Next I was assigned to write a serial for MGM called *Crime Does Not Pay*, two-reel episodes based on police records.

Arnold: In a letter to Helen you mentioned that you hoped to have the chance to work with Ernst Lubitsch on a Miriam Hopkins film. You seemed very excited at the possibility.

Caldwell: What happened there was that I was assigned to work on this story—I don't remember the title of it—on a sound stage, and the director wanted the dialogue changed. And so I was one of the first people to be called in to write this new dialogue. Now the picture was set in the South. There was an antebellum house, tall columns, and Miriam Hopkins very comfortably sitting in a swing. I don't know what exactly the story was about, but I was told to bring myself up and offer some suggestions as to what she could say in this particular situation. They told me, "She's mad; she's angry. Her suitor is an hour late. And here she is, sitting in a swing, waiting, waiting, waiting. And so what does she say?" I stood there and thought about it and *they* stood around waiting on *me*. I had no idea what they wanted. So I said, "Let her say, 'Aw, shoot!' " Well, then I was gone. They had no more use for me.*

Arnold: Also in your letters to Helen you indicated that you were disgusted with some of the other screenwriters in Hollywood who were unsympathetic to the social plight of the poor during this time. You said that these people had sold out for the easy money.

Caldwell: Certainly Hollywood was not particularly sympathetic to the laboring people, with rare exceptions. I mean, the place was full of immigrants working in these people's gardens while living in substandard housing. Many of them were illegal, I imagine. They had no leverage, and they were there as waiters to the rich. I had not known Spanish or Mexican people before that time, and their situation was very much as it was in the South. I was struck by that similarity, certainly. And many of my fellow screenwriters were considered, and considered themselves, radicals. But they took the money.

Arnold: Maxim Leiber, your first agent, was himself politically radical.

Caldwell: Yes. We had met at a party given by *The New American Caravan*. We introduced ourselves, and he wanted to know if I was represented by any agent, and I said no, so he handed me a card and he became my agent. When this UnAmerican Activities Committee came into existence, Leiber was involved in some way. I never knew what his involvement was, but when they started taking depositions, overnight he got out of the United States and went to Mexico. The first thing I knew was I got a letter from him

---

*There is no Lubitsch-Hopkins picture from this date that fits Caldwell's description. However, Hopkins did star in *The Story of Temple Drake*, based on William Faulkner's *Sanctuary*, which was released in 1933. Caldwell claimed never to have read *Sanctuary*; the only Faulkner book he ever referred to was *As I Lay Dying*.

saying he's doing business as usual down in Mexico and he felt that I would have no objections. So I got my lawyers and they got in touch with him and somehow got him to sign a release that he would give up his interest in my properties that he had been involved in, that he would accept only a 5 percent commission on everything derived from that period of time. My new agent, James Oliver Brown, had to accept 5 percent himself. That was the understanding, and the paper was signed. But then about two years ago Leiber wrote saying he wanted a full accounting of my earnings to the present day, that I owed him money and he wanted it sent to Mexico. It finally came to the point that he said I owed him interest and that he would sue and maybe we could settle out of court. My lawyer told him that he had signed a release, showed him the paper, but we had to go through all of our records, find all the cancelled checks, everything.

Arnold: You've called yourself a "sociologically-minded writer" interested in economic and social truths but not politics per se. Still, as a young man you were liberal in your ideals; at least that comes through your letters and, of course, your stories as well. What about now?

Caldwell: Well, I'm conservative now. I am much older, and one becomes more conservative as one becomes older, just as one is more apt to be radical as a young man. That is the natural state of things. Years ago I saw much that needed to be changed; I was against the status quo. But I believe in order. So in that sense I am conservative, yes.

Arnold: In 1933, the New York Society for the Suppression of Vice brought charges of obscenity against *God's Little Acre*, resulting in a landmark court case. How did you defend yourself against these charges?

Caldwell: That was the Greenspan decision, wasn't it? I don't think I actually testified except maybe in a written statement perhaps. A large number of people did testify or wrote in support of the book. I do remember that. And we did win, of course. The decision was an important one.

Arnold: It was also about this time that Jack Kirkland wrote the dramatization of *Tobacco Road*. How did Kirkland come to suggest this?

Caldwell: Well, I guess he read the novel and found out who my agent was, and they signed the papers. We gave him the rights to write and produce the play on Broadway, and after that I paid no attention to it. Kirkland went off for six months or so, and I never heard anything about it. Shortly after that he came back, and I read in the papers that they were going into rehearsal. That was the first I knew that he was actually going to do it. I was so indifferent about the whole thing that I didn't go to opening night.

Arnold: What sort of a person was Jack Kirkland?

Caldwell: Oh, he was a nice Arkansas farm boy who made good. He enjoyed the good life, and he had a number of successes. He was a good chap. His problem was that he always fell in love with whatever actress was playing Pearl in *Tobacco Road*; he always married them. Well, that's an exaggeration.

Arnold: The play was more comic than the novel. Maybe that's not right: The play is not as tragic as the novel.

Caldwell: Well, look at it this way. There are several different versions of the play, and each one was created by a different actor who played Jeeter Lester. The first actor to take that part was Henry Hull. Henry Hull was not a comic actor. He was a classic actor, and he did not play for laughs. He played the role precisely as the material dictated. And he succeeded to the extent that he was able to bring out any humor that existed in Jeeter without sacrificing any of the serious nature of the character. After Hull there were three or four other actors—James Barton was one—and they played for laughs, made up lines. But the play was not a comedy. My theory is that tragedy and comedy co-exist, to the extent that you cannot have tragedy without an awareness of the other side of tragedy. But the others played it strictly for laughs, so much so that the play just became a kind of *event*. For example, I heard that one night Groucho Marx came to see the play and decided to take over the role. At the end of the first act, Marx went back stage and put on Barton's makeup. Then he came on stage and walked through the whole thing imitating the business, and there was a lot of laughter. I don't know if that's true or not, but it shows you what had happened to the play, which was meant to be a serious play.

Arnold: The next novel you published was *Journeyman* in 1935. Did you have any political ideas in mind in creating the character Semon Dye, who is certainly a demagogue, a kind of Huey Long or Eugene Talmadge?

Caldwell: Well, no, except, you see, when I grew up in the South I was often surrounded by politics and politicians, because Georgia has always produced that quality of demagogue politicians. And I always related evangelistic religion with politics. To me they were one in the same. So Semon Dye, in my opinion, could either be a senator or a preacher: he would be the same character, whatever role it was. I had no other motive than that.

Arnold: What does the term "journeyman" mean to you?

Caldwell: Well, the dictionary meaning would be that he is an expert at different callings, at different professions—an expert carpenter, an expert plumber. So this was a man who was an expert preacher.

Arnold: Or con man.

Caldwell: Or con man.

Arnold: He's presented in terms of the devil in many ways. When his car pulls up, he's enveloped in this cloud of stinking smoke.

Caldwell: Well, the whole terminology I used in the book draws a connection between the preacher and the devil, I think. He's an expert at winning souls, but I suppose you could win souls for the devil as well as for God. He is a well-trained preacher at what he preaches.

Arnold: There was a limited edition of *Journeyman* published by Viking in 1935 and then a revised edition published in 1938. In comparing the two, I would think that the changes in the revised edition were mostly to make it not quite as sexually explicit.

Caldwell: Harold Guinzberg's idea was that this was a censorable book, and he was afraid that it would be charged with obscenity, and that's why it came out in a limited edition to begin with. But then, when it was accepted, I suppose, by readers, he decided to try it again in a general trade edition. Whatever Guinzberg was afraid of, I guess that was changed for the trade edition. But I don't remember it that clearly any more. I'm sure that I accepted suggested changes and made them myself. I know I would have had to approve them.

Arnold: Yes, according to the evidence in the material I've seen that seems to have been the case. Someone would suggest a change and you would write "O.K." or would revise passages or delete.

Caldwell: It's a book I like.

Arnold: You were also publishing collections of short stories in the 1930's, such as *Kneel to the Rising Sun* in 1934. Would you select the stories and arrange their positions in these collections?

Caldwell: Yes, I would choose the stories, but they would usually be included in the order in which they first appeared in print.

Arnold: But, for example, in *Kneel to the Rising Sun*, the last story in the collection is "Kneel to the Rising Sun" itself. Did you see that as the strongest story in the collection, since you gave the story's title to the collection? Were you pointing your readers in a certain direction?

Caldwell: Well, I suppose I could visualize that that was where that story belonged, for whatever reason. It was a good choice as the final story. I would not say, however, that I had some sort of *thematic* idea in mind by placing the stories in certain positions. At least not consciously.

Arnold: I noticed in your typescripts at Dartmouth that for some books you wrote down a whole list of names and then went through and chose the ones that you wanted for that book. Is that your standard practice?

Caldwell: Well, it's a phonetic kind of thing to me, I suppose, because a person's name has a great meaning to what he is and to what I am writing about him. And so the sound of his name has much more importance to me than the spelling or the characteristics or the derivation of his name. It is something you pull out of the air, I think, but it must seem suitable for the character that I'm trying to create. I would be at a loss to write about this character if I were not familiar with the name or if I did not like the name or if the name did not have a good *ring* in my ears when I say it out loud. I have to hear it with my ear as well as see it in print. So these names come to me. Whatever the story is, I choose out of a whole conglomeration of names—not choose so much as eliminate, when you come right down to it—the ones that seem to me to be the most suitable and appropriate characteristic of this person. The same way with place names. I'm very much interested with place names, because that sort of characterizes the scenery, the terrain, the geographical location. So I am very particular about place names and the characters' names.

Arnold: So that in a book like *Journeyman*, "Rocky Comfort" and "Semon Dye" and "Clay Horey" are all wonderfully expressive names. I suppose we could read symbolic meaning into them.

Caldwell: Well, yes, in that particular instance it seems to me that I arrived at it very quickly that these were the only suitable place name and character names that would be appropriate to the story I was trying to do.

Arnold: I have not mentioned *The Sacrilege of Alan Kent*, which was written in the late 1920's but which you published in book form in 1936. That was a very different kind of writing for you, a very expressionistic writing. Why did you not continue in that style?

Caldwell: I don't know. You see, when you're young, you have all of these very wild ideas about things. You try not just to be different but to find new ground, so to speak, new area. I had given up trying to write poetry, as every young man should. *Alan Kent* came out of that experience, you see, because I realized that I had no ability as a poet while I still had the inclination to write poetry, so the transition from poetry to prose occurred, I think, at that point. And so as a result I wrote this novelette or whatever you want to call it, with the idea that I would be writing poetry in the form of prose. The result was not poetry and it was not exactly prose, but it was a transition from poetry to prose. And that work was my farewell, you might say, to the idea of being a poet.

Arnold: Do you consider *The Sacrilege of Alan Kent* as having a plot?

Caldwell: Well, you see, everything anybody writes is, I suppose, autobiographical to some extent, but you have to go beyond the actual biography of a character to write something of any value. So what I was trying to do was to use my limited experience as a person to write *idealistically*, I suppose you might say, or *imaginatively*— living in an imaginary world but using my realism of life as a basis and from there springing out and beyond realism or the actuality of my life, trying to project myself into another world. You do have to have, I think, a basis of realism no matter how idealistic you are or whatever your motive is in writing, and *Alan Kent* was my considered result.

Arnold: In the late 1930's you moved back into journalism. You did *Tenant Farmer* and articles for the *New York Post*, but the first major work you did was *You Have Seen Their Faces*. You have said of that book that you wanted to show "that the fiction I was writing was authentically based on contemporary life in the South."

Caldwell: I wanted to show that it was based on the actual existence of people. Because, you see, there was a lot of controversy or adverse criticism during the run of the play *Tobacco Road*. Critics liked to try to find something wrong with what I was doing or what the play or the novel did or said. It was a very popular pastime to take a shot or two at the play as being untrue. And of course the critics in the South had a field day, especially the Fugitives in

Nashville. Donald Davidson and the others were campaigning at that time for the reinstitution or the re-establishment of the Old South. Of course, my writing was directly opposed to their theory, and so I wanted to set out to show that this was life as it actually was, that it was based on authentic observations and findings as a writer. And so I did that book purposefully to try to counteract what I considered to be adverse, unfair, unwarranted, unprincipled criticism, especially among Southern critics and Southern politicians.

Arnold: Max Leiber introduced you to Margaret Bourke-White.

Caldwell: Yes. What happened was that Leiber approved of the idea of doing this book. I told him that I needed a photographer. He said, "We'll find one." So we had a list of people, and he accidentally or purposefully found an opportunity to talk to Bourke-White before he spoke to any other photographers on the list. She immediately accepted the idea, very eagerly so as I found out later, and I was very pleased and elated. I didn't know anything about her work particularly except that she was highly recommended. So we started out to do this book, and she contributed a great amount of enthusiasm and ability and technique to the final result.

Arnold: In *Call It Experience* you refer to a "Sally" who started off with you.

Caldwell: Well, that was an assumed name, a pseudonym. I didn't want to use Ruth Carnell's name at that time, and so I just had to do it that way.

Arnold: In *You Have Seen Their Faces*, you supplied the text, which consisted in part of imaginative monologues such as, you suggest, some of these people photographed *might* have spoken. Do you consider the work to be fiction or nonfiction?

Caldwell: Nonfiction.

Arnold: Even though you are creating words, putting them in their mouths.

Caldwell: Yes. In other words, I was trying to use the impressions I would get or had already gotten from people in certain situations, like landowners or prisoners or field workers or whatnot. And I was trying to use that as the material for my interpretation. So you can call that fiction if you want to, but it was based on prior experience with the people I was dealing with.

Arnold: In 1939 you left Viking and went to Duell, Sloan and Pearce.

Caldwell: Those were the three Rover Boys, we'll call them, all three of them about the same age and all with some experience in publishing. They came from different locations and got together. Sam Sloan was the money boy. Charlie Duell was a very good executive for the company, and Cap Pearce was an editor who'd been at Harcourt, Brace. He was a very clever chap. Now all three of them are dead, and I miss them very much. But Cap Pearce was one of the best editors I ever had because he never did anything. He'd just say, "O.K., let's put this in print." Of course, he would correct a misspelling or suggest a rephrasing, but he never told me what to write or what not to write or how to do it, so he and I got along very well. It was very unfortunate that they had to sell out to Little, Brown. When they did, they lost their identity. Soon after that they started dying off anyway. So I guess it was inevitable.

Arnold: The books you did with Margaret Bourke-White, with the exception of *You Have Seen Their Faces*, were published by Duell, Sloan and Pearce. Of the four books you did with her, do you have a favorite?

Caldwell: Well, I sort of liked the Czechoslovak book *North of the Danube*. I thought it was very appropriate for the time and the situation, and it was my first introduction to life in middle Europe. I was very pleased with what came of that.

Arnold: The first novel you wrote after your marriage to Margaret Bourke-White was *Trouble in July*. You have said that you don't think much about symbolism when you're writing, but in this book there are images that seem symbolic. For example, where did the image of the Negro and the rabbit come from? Sonny, the man who is lynched, has taken the pet rabbit and put it under his shirt as he flees from the lynch mob. Why have the rabbit escape from his shirt at the moment of his lynching?

Caldwell: I don't know what prompted that at all. I had almost forgotten all about that. It was just one of those things you reach out and get, I suppose, when you're thinking about a person and what would be suitable for him to do or what might illustrate him to some extent, to bring him to life, to make him human. Those things to me are just so unconscious that I just can't explain them.

Arnold: You also started doing the *American Folkways* series around 1939. How do you feel about that series now?

Caldwell: Well, of course it didn't get very much circulation. We

did too many books too rapidly, I think. I jumped at the opportunity
for Duell, Sloan and Pearce to start this series, and they agreed to do
four a year. I had been turned down by Viking Press, and I was so
elated with the idea that it ran away with me, and I did it too rapidly, I
suppose, with too many people involved. I couldn't pay too much
attention to the preparation and reading of manuscripts and revising.
All that had to be left to Cap Pearce. I think it would have been a
much better series if we had cut it down in half and maybe spread it
out over a longer period of time.

Arnold: In 1940 you also published *Jackpot*, bringing together 75
of your stories. You wrote short introductions for each of those stories
and created a character, a Professor Horatio Perkins, who appeared
in those introductions as an obvious shot at critics, especially
academic critics.

Caldwell: I guess I was using this character to embody my feeling
about the stolid kind of scholarship that was too conservative and not
opened to what the writer was trying to do. I don't think I had in
mind any idea of satirizing the college professor or teacher. It was just
to embody my frustration, my displeasure with the kind of criticism
that was being peddled about the country.

Arnold: In 1941, you and Margaret Bourke-White went to Russia
and were there at the beginning of the Russian-German War. There
you made broadcasts for CBS Radio; you wrote for *Life* magazine
and the newspaper *PM*. But this work is not often mentioned. Do you
feel that you have been properly recognized for what you did at that
time?

Caldwell: Well, you see, in those days communications were not
as important, not taken as seriously, as today. When television came
along, it changed the whole picture of communication. If that had
been a television age, I think it would have been much different. But I
didn't want any more attention than I was getting. I did most of my
activity for CBS radio twice a day, three o'clock in the afternoon and
three o'clock in the morning. I spent most of my time with that rather
than newspaper correspondence. And there were very few
correspondents there. There were two permanent ones, Henry
Shapiro and Henry Cassidy, from UP and AP, and I came to be the
third. Others were clamoring and knocking on the borders trying to
get in, but they could not get an entry visa. Some of them, NBC and
so forth, were down in Turkey waiting, and so I had the radio field to

myself. I was the only person there on the radio beat, so I was very well satisfied with what I was doing. But there was nobody else there to compete with anyway.

Arnold: When you returned to America, you went back to work at MGM on the film *Mission to Moscow*.

Caldwell: You see, the reason they hired me was because I had been in Russia during that time, and they thought I could contribute something original. Probably I could and did. But what happened was that Roosevelt pushed that film as a propaganda organ or vehicle, because he was selling the American people on cooperation with the Communist Party, the Communist government, and he had to overcome a lot of resistance against America helping the Russians in any way. My part was to be a propagandist. I was not that enthusiastic about Joseph Stalin, because in Moscow I had heard unofficially that he was a cut-throat who would think nothing of exterminating a whole group of people if he thought they were going to oppose him in any way. I disliked trying to build up Stalin as a symbol of the Communist Party, because I was not a Communist myself and I did not subscribe to Communism. There were the two opposing factions in Hollywood among the Communist sympathizers and fellow travellers. One was the straight Communist Party line faction and the other was like a Trotskyite faction. Well, I wanted neither side, and so I bowed out of any association with these people. And of course they had infiltrated the whole Hollywood system. So I was more or less boycotted, I was shunned. I finished my chore, which was to write a synopsis or treatment for the filming, and then I got out and left, happily so, long before the film was finished. In the meantime, the elements at work had prevailed to the extent that they demanded that my name be taken off the film credits as one of the writers, and so I never had any credit for the contribution that I did make. But I did not oppose it, I did not resist it, I did not complain. I was very happy to get out and leave the whole thing behind.

Arnold: At Dartmouth there is also a screenplay you wrote dated 1942 of *Look Homeward Angel*. Who were you doing that for?

Caldwell: That was for an independent producer. I had left Hollywood and was living in Tucson at that time. My Hollywood agent, Al Manuel, had this offer from this independent producer for me to write a treatment and possibly a screenplay for *Look Homeward Angel*. I took it on, but I was working in, you might say, a vacuum. I had nobody to talk to about the film. The producer came only once, and I think that was the end of that, and I didn't want to go back to Hollywood to work on it. I spent maybe three or four months with this thing, and finally I just had to give it up because I couldn't quite figure out what kind of film they wanted to make.

Arnold: In 1943 you published *Georgia Boy*, which you have said is your favorite collection of stories. Some of these stories were written while you were in Russia, I believe.

Caldwell: Well, I wrote them in various places around the world, some in China, for example, when we were on the way to the Soviet Union. I had started writing these episodes—so I call them—before leaving the United States, and I just continued because I had the whole book in mind and wanted to do a whole, book-length series. And so I used any opportunity I could get—when we were waiting around for transportation in Chungking, China, for example—to work on these things. I don't know how many I wrote abroad—maybe two or three or four. Then I came back and finished off after we got back.

Arnold: Why is it your favorite?

Caldwell: I don't know. I just thought the incidents were interesting—to me. I'm not interested in the reader's reaction, you see. They interested me, and I was captivated with the idea, and so I stayed with it. Actually, they were not in any way autobiographical. It was all imaginary creation, speculation. Of course, but there are a lot of surroundings that *implied* that these things had happened. There was enough realism in the whole series of episodes to make it believable and interesting to me. I had this feeling by association with the black boy in the book. It was a human kind of feeling I had of friendship. I had no instinctive feeling about racism as a boy. To me it was just a natural occurrence—one person was white and one person was black. I guess I still have that feeling.

Arnold: The book really has a kind of warmth to it that is not often associated with your work, but you went from it to your next novel *Tragic Ground*, which is a return to the very harsh, although at times comic, kind of book.

Caldwell: Well, I suppose that book was a reaction for me toward *Georgia Boy*, because *Tragic Ground* was contemporary to the time, whereas *Georgia Boy* was a book of recollections. But *Tragic Ground* was something that was happening that particular month, that particular day, that particular year. This was just about right in the middle of wartime fervor in American life. I'm an amateur sociologist. One of my favorite subjects at the University of Virginia was sociology, and of it all the most important was the field trips the class would take to various institutions. I became very interested in the lives of people who were living in a deprived situation. Even the deaf, dumb and blind institutions and the poor house farms or the insane asylum or the state penitentiary or the local jail—they all made a great impression on me. That came out in this book.

Arnold: You are often criticized for your portrayal of women, I think unfairly, because it seems to me that the women in your novels are often stronger and more admirable than the men. Starting with *A House in the Uplands* in 1946, women become the main characters of your novels. Even the titles of the books—*Jenny by Nature, Gretta, Claudelle Inglish, Annette*—indicate the switch from the male character as your protagonist to the female. Why did the switch take place?

Caldwell: Well, maybe because I began to have a lot of personal experiences with women. There was quite a large turnover there, you know, as far as being married was concerned, so maybe that had something to do with it. You become disillusioned as time goes on, so you start reflecting about it, and maybe that leads to creation of female characters.

Arnold: What you have in a number of those books are women who are trapped by society, who feel they are being forced by society to act in a way that they don't want to act.

Caldwell: I think it's obvious that women are, to a great extent, victims in a male dominated society. Even to the extent that feminism is in ascendency, that does not alleviate the fact that women are still more or less second class citizens, not in the sense of responsibility but in the sense of personal freedom.

Arnold: It is about the time you're writing books about racism, books such as *Trouble in July*, that you also turn toward women as your main characters. Do you see the second subject as an extension of the first?

Caldwell: Yes, I guess it would be.

Arnold: In *A House in the Uplands*, you have the old judge, Judge Lovejoy, say at the end of the book, "The way to handle the colored is to stop treating them the way Grady Dunbar treats them and let them go to school and get an education and earn their living like the rest of us." Now that is in 1946. What kind of reactions did you get because of proclamations like that in your books?

Caldwell: Well, of course, you always look to the critics for that kind of an answer, and in those days they would really tell you off, that you were a traitor to the South, to the institutions of her heritage. Or else the critics would say that I was trying to write propaganda for the black race and it should be ignored, and that the book was not very interesting anyway. I always had hanging over me the threat of "communist." I was charged in many instances of being "Un-American," without their coming out and saying the other thing. I was not a good American citizen, I was not a good Southerner. But it meant nothing to me. I didn't take the reviews very seriously. I was too busy thinking about my next book.

Arnold: Do you think such charges kept people from treating the books in terms of their stories, their characters? That they hooked onto an idea at the expense of the fiction?

Caldwell: Well, you gain a certain kind of a reputation. I think if critics hammer, hammer, hammer at you over and over, sooner or later it's going to have a great effect on what the average reader will feel about a particular writer. So I think that had a great deal to do with it.

Arnold: It also struck me as I was reading the books during this period, for example *The Sure Hand of God* or *Gretta* or *Love and Money*, that the main character is often struggling with loneliness. This was just after your divorce from Margaret Bourke-White and your immediate marriage to June Johnson, which was not a happy marriage. Were your personal experiences being reflected in these books?

Caldwell: Well, I don't know about loneliness, maybe that was one of the emotions, but maybe it was just dissatisfaction with life in general. Because when you are burdened with the feeling of being dissatisfied with your existence, it has a great effect on your writing, I'm sure. It wasn't conscious at the time. You have found the overtone of it, to an extent. When you question me, I will say that I was living a life of not complete satisfaction over this period of time. What that had to do with the writing are the results that you find. It wasn't planted there; it wasn't done purposefully. It was just a sympathetic feeling that came into my writing, I suppose, from my plight. I didn't get along very well with June in those days because I was very unhappy about her isolation. It is something I had to write about in this autobiography [*With All My Might*], her addiction to psychiatry, psychoanalysis. It was not only a financial strain, it was also a burden to live with someone who could not or would not live what I would call a normal existence or a normal life, associating with the rest of the world.

Arnold: When did you sign with The New American Library?

Caldwell: That was during the time of Duell, Sloan and Pearce. Signet was just beginning then. A chap by the name of Victor Weybright and another chap by the name of Kurt Enoch got together in New York and started this company, The New American Library. I guess they just reached out to see what they could get everywhere, and my books were available. There were no paperbacks at that time. So they made a deal with Duell, Sloan and Pearce and began publishing as fast as they were available. I got along very well with Weybright for many years until finally we had a showdown and a blowoff toward the end, which I regretted very much. Of course, he's dead now, so it can't be changed. It didn't work out between us, and I haven't been very happy since. This was over a period of twenty years, you understand, and maybe isn't very important. I am *now* beholden to New American Library because they have a lifetime ownership of some of my books, and I don't get along too well with all the new changes of ownership—it's always a new turnover. So I have no dealings with them even though I'm beholden to them and I have to live with them. It sort of hurts my feelings that I got suspended high and dry, I would say, just hanging up there kicking my feet and can't touch ground as far as they're concerned. But it's just one of those publishing things that can happen to you.

Arnold: The only novel that I'm aware of in which you discuss the business of publishing and writing is *Love and Money*, in which the main character, Rick Sutton, is a writer. Is it autobiographical?

Caldwell: [*chuckles*] Well, to some extent. There is a basis for some of the story, I suppose, for some of the characters. There is some sympathy involved.

Arnold: In the book, the writer Sutton goes to visit a friend, Rob Mizemore, who is a critic. Mizemore says, "Rick, you have a driving urge to be a storyteller in the written word, and that's why you will write novel after novel whether they are worth writing or not. The question then is this: Is it better to write a poor novel than not to write a novel at all?" So I'll address the question to you.

Caldwell: [*laughter*] Is there no answer in the book?

Arnold: Well no, there really isn't.

Caldwell: Too bad. [*chuckles*] Well, you do the best you can, of course. Every writer would, I think, say that. If he has the urge to be a writer, he's going to write, and he's going to do the best he can. Whether he's a serious writer or a frivolous writer or a popular writer or a scholarly writer, I think he'll keep on doing what he wants to do or has an urge to do, regardless of any criticism or any results. The writer is always working in a void, so to speak, a void to which there is no exit and no access for the outside world, so you never know what's happening *out there*, among the readers, whether they like what they read or dislike. But you have to keep on working at what you're doing in your own way because that's your life. So there's no escape from it. You have to be in retreat, keep a stiff upper lip, and do the best that you can.

Arnold: In *Love and Money*, Rick is searching for an ideal woman who constantly evades him. When he has the chance to make love to other women, he refuses.

Caldwell: He is not going to be content with a substitute. He wants the real thing, in his mind.

Arnold: But he doesn't get her.

Caldwell: No, but you should always strive to get what you want, you know. You always strive for perfection or achievement. So that doesn't matter. The whole basis of the story is that he will not quit or be diverted from his goal.

Arnold: Is this, then, your version of the artist's search for the impossible, the ideal? The realization that you can never capture the ideal?

Caldwell: But you never know you can't. You always hope and expect that some day you will capture that ideal. You don't give up. You still have that urge and that desire to continue your search until you reach your ultimate goal.

Arnold: So that's why you always write one more book.

Caldwell: Exactly.

Arnold: Standard criticism holds that the books that you wrote starting with *A House in the Uplands* through the mid-1950's or so were not as strong as the ones written in the 1930's. Would you agree with that judgment?

Caldwell: I really don't know if there was a falling off in retrospect. You're acquainted only with the most recent work, I suppose, and you don't compare it to the past. Otherwise you'd be *imitating* yourself in some way. I think you always hope that what you're doing *now* is just as good or better than what you did last year.

Arnold: How much are the books of this period, like *Episode in Palmetto, The Sure Hand of God,* and *Jenny by Nature,* meant to be social comedies?

Caldwell: That's exactly what I think they are, because the characters in them are influenced by, made by, their environment. The environment is what dictates their course in life. It all goes back to the fact that it's the writer's experience that dictates the course of his characters. I wanted to touch all the bases as much as I could out of my experience, and 95 percent of my experience was always in small towns, small rural communities. So I wanted to describe southern life in a rural environment and show what those influences had upon the people I was dealing with.

Arnold: The novels of the 1960's such as *The Last Night of Summer* and *Annette* are once again very violent. The characters are terribly punished for their actions. Why the angry, moralistic tone in these books?

Caldwell: Well, that's probably just the evolution of a writer. I don't think anybody remains the same. Also, I think that this was the time of my recognition of the growing violence in life, in society. Violence was evolving into terrorism in the '60's. This was the time of the assassinations, so there was plenty of evidence of it. And, you see, in the 1960's, lynching as a pastime, as an outlet of emotions, had more or less disappeared. When I was growing up, lynching was an ordinary event in the South. It was violence on a massive scale, because a lot of people took part in it, as observers mostly. But that disappeared, and what took its place, I think, were these individual acts of violence—one upon one, so to speak, rather than a hundred people against one. I had not recognized these kinds of individual acts of violence happening before, not to that extent, so I thought there was a trend, I suppose, in this direction of terrorism.

Arnold: Which of all the novels do you consider among your better books?

Caldwell: Well, of course, you have to go back and do a lot of reflection to decide. But, for example, I like the books in the middle

era. To me they were the most important, the most interesting ones at
the time and upon reflection. For example, to me *Tragic Ground*
might be considered to be of lasting interest. I wouldn't say it was one
of the best or one that I *liked* the best or anything like that, but I do
think it was an interesting book in that era, and I do think that that
era did bring about three or four books that I still consider interesting.

Arnold: Would you name some others of them for me?

Caldwell: Well, *Gretta*, for example.

Arnold: Which is not often ranked among your best.

Caldwell: No. But Virginia liked it so much that one night in Las
Vegas she was playing dice next to Elizabeth Taylor and came over to
me and said that we should try to get her to play Gretta. But we
didn't follow up on it.

Arnold: So, *Tragic Ground, Gretta*—any more come to mind?

Caldwell: Well, don't push me to say which I think are the best,
now. I won't say that. Just which are the most interesting.

Arnold: That's fine.

Caldwell: Oh, *A House in the Uplands, Episode in Palmetto,
Summertime Island*. Yes, I would consider them in that category.
That's three. That's enough. Now look, I won't decry any of my
books. As a matter of fact, I like them all. Otherwise I wouldn't have
done them.

Arnold: Why no more novels after *Annette*?

Caldwell: I don't know. I had been doing a lot of traveling in
those years; I guess that had one thing to do with it. And I didn't
want to go back into journalism, so I was just sort of treading water,
because when you get to one point you hesitate to do what you had
done before. I didn't want to imitate anything or to compete with
anything I had done before. So I was just treading water.

Arnold: That's hardly accurate. You turned to more personal
recollections such as *In Search of Bisco*.

Caldwell: Well, yes. That was close to journalism but not exactly
journalism.

Arnold: Were you at all reacting against the state of modern
literature? You have referred to it as "a noxious stew of vulgarity."

Caldwell: To me, writers today take advantage of the fact that
there is no censorship to see how far they can go, to what extreme
they can go, not for the sake of writing but for the sake of shock. And
I don't know what the end results are going to be because my
sampling of current writing is not very inspiring.

Arnold: But the criticism you are voicing has often been applied to you over the years.

Caldwell: Oh, but I'm different. I'm not in that category. I do it for the sake of writing, not for the sake of shock. I don't write for money and I don't write for shock.

Arnold: But there are shocking events in your writing.

Caldwell: Yes, and that's inescapable *if* I have the freedom to do it. And, of course, I approve of that freedom. But I don't misuse it just for the sake of trying to make money by writing a book that would be shockingly scandalous.

Arnold: So you would consider yourself to be a very moral writer.

Caldwell: Yes, definitely. I am.

Arnold: In honor of your election to the American Academy of Arts and Letters in 1984, Richard Wilbur, in his presentation, said, "Though his characters are driven, deluded, and luckless, there is no cruelty in his treating them as he does with the greatest comic gusto. This is because he celebrates in them the crazy solidarity and the will to assert in the midst of every privation the basic appetites of life." Do you think that assessment captures what you've done?

Caldwell: Oh, in a way. That's his poetic explanation of it, his estimation. He's an accomplished poet and he can say things like that. I would have to say it differently, but he's entitled to that, and I appreciate it.

Arnold: If you could say it differently, how would you phrase it?

Caldwell: [*laughing*] Oh no you don't. I don't speak in praise of myself, so I wouldn't say it.

Arnold: Without praising yourself, how would you describe your accomplishments?

Caldwell: Well, it's one man's individual expression of an invented, created existence of life.

Arnold: This election was quite an honor, but you've told me before that you really aren't concerned with how you will be remembered.

Caldwell: And I'm not. Have you ever known anybody who made any comment about his existence after he had died? Well, I won't be making any either. As for other people, that's their right and privilege, but it's all immaterial to me. Once you're dead, what is there to be concerned about? Whether you leave a good impression or a bad impression, it doesn't matter to *you*. The same thing with what you've written. If you've written something good, why, that's going to exist. If it's not good, then it won't last. That's the way it is.

Arnold: But your children will be here, and your children's children.

Caldwell: Well, I'm not too concerned about my offspring. I have the theory that they should be on their own to start with and live their own lives and not rely upon me to support them, to help them in any way out of the ordinary. I do want them to always know that I exist and that I'm their father, of course. And I think I have received a certain amount of respect from the children. They know they have to achieve their own future. Each person is responsible for his own future.

Arnold: So it is finally a question of will, the will to achieve.

Caldwell: Yes. You see, I didn't expect to have any great inheritance, I didn't expect to have any great fame, I didn't expect to have anything except the pain of living. I did expect that. Not the ecstasy but the pain of living. So, you see, I'm very comfortable with my agnostic way of existence because I don't expect anything except the pain of living.

Arnold: So has your life been, in some ways, a pleasant surprise?

Caldwell: Well, every once in a while you have the feeling, yes, maybe I have accomplished something, but I don't have the conceit to feel that I should get more than I've got, should be more famous than I am or richer than I am. I'm simply very satisfied with what life has brought my way.

Erskine Caldwell: The Final Chapter
Charles Trueheart/1987

From *The Washington Post*, 1 March 1987, pp. G1, G6, G7. Copyright © 1987 The Washington Post. Reprinted by permission.

Erskine Caldwell has earned the right, at the age of 83, to dislike a few things.

One of them is social injustice, a theme to which he has clung in his books, most memorably in his best-known novels of the early 1930s, *Tobacco Road* and *God's Little Acre*. Another is "propaganda," a term Caldwell uses to shrug off everything from literary theory to public relations. Also on the list are editors, publishers, professors and autograph collectors.

Having made his own way in the world, he maintains an air of stubborn dignity, suffering the demands of literary achievement and human company only to a point. His devotion has been to his work, not to his image or reputation.

"I'm not going to talk about anything unless I'm asked, because I have nothing to say," Caldwell announced a few days ago from a big green armchair in the study of his suburban *hacienda*. Even at the end of his life, his big shoulders and long limbs and beaked nose suggest prowess, and a single conviction: "The only thing I have is my books."

"Only" is hardly the word. Erskine Caldwell's 55 books, published in 43 languages, have sold more than 80 million copies, according to the meticulous records kept by Virginia Caldwell, his wife of 30 years. His latest book, an autobiography called *With All My Might*, has just appeared. "I was convinced it was about time to do it," he explained, with a quick flash of the eyes that said: Leave it at that. Lung cancer may make this interview one of his last.

In the 1930s and 1940s, Caldwell was a publishing phenomenon, a best-selling author and a record-setter in the infancy of the mass-market paperback. As late as the 1950s, his publisher could claim that he was the world's best-selling novelist; his audience was and is

global—about a quarter of his books have been sold to readers
overseas.

The novels were not just widely read. They made news. With their
blunt depictions of oppression and squalor in the Depression South,
and their daring (for the time) passages of ribald humor, *Tobacco
Road* (1932) and *God's Little Acre* (1933) immediately ran afoul of
God-fearing citizens, protective judges, see-no-evil newspaper editors
and many of Caldwell's fellow southerners in general. Adapted for
the stage, *Tobacco Road* played on Broadway for seven years, a
record at the time, and yet another bitter pill to those who blamed
Caldwell for giving their part of the country a bad name.

Though time and fashion have muted the judgment, Caldwell's
work was deemed by the critics of the '30s and '40s to be on a par
with William Faulkner's. Faulkner himself, asked in 1946 to name the
five contemporaries whose writing he most esteemed, put Caldwell in
the company of Thomas Wolfe, Ernest Hemingway, John Dos Passos
and John Steinbeck.

Now Erskine Caldwell has stopped writing. These days, in the
vigilant company of his wife, he husbands the time and energy that
remain to him. Referring to his current regimen of chemotherapy
treatments, he offered a blunt colloquialism that managed to carry
the gentlest irony and surest wisdom: "They take the life out of you."

The voice was still strong, gruff and inflected with the grit of his
East Georgia childhood. But the blue eyes were pale and watery, the
weathered hands trembled in each other's grip; from time to time,
Caldwell's head sank to his chest in weary distraction.

His doctor told him recently that the chemotherapy treatments
weren't going well, and asked what he wanted done. According to his
wife, Caldwell said, "I want a miracle." For this doggedly self-reliant
man, it could not have been an easy thing to confess.

Three years ago, after Erskine Caldwell celebrated his 80th
birthday, Virginia Caldwell collected the congratulatory messages and
arranged them in two massive leather-bound volumes.

Among those writers who paid their respects were Wallace Stegner,
William Styron, John Updike, Robert Penn Warren, Richard Wilbur,
Malcolm Cowley, Peter De Vries, John Hersey, Shirley Hazzard and
Saul Bellow, who told Virginia her husband should have received the
Nobel Prize.

Norman Mailer wrote, "One of my first literary heroes, and always one of the best." (In December 1984, Mailer and Caldwell were inducted together into the nation's most exclusive intellectual society, the American Academy of Arts and Letters.)

"In the 1930s," Kurt Vonnegut wrote, "you and a handful of contemporaries pulled off a revolution in American literature. . . . If, without older brothers and sisters of your sort, persons my age had had to conduct such a revolution for ourselves, I wonder if we would have had the guts or brains to pull it off."

Mention Erskine Caldwell to supposedly well-read younger people today, however, and the reaction tends to be squinted eyes, a desperate scan of murky mental files.

Bring up *Tobacco Road*, though, and everyone nods in relief and recognition. It is more than a book. Tobacco Road is a place, set distinctly in time, and everyone knows what it looks like.

"The land was desolate," Caldwell recalled, describing the novel's setting 10 years after its publication. "Not far away across the fields were several tenant houses, shabby and dilapidated, two-room shacks with sagging joints and roofs. Around the buildings were groups of human beings. The children were playing in the sand. The young men and women were leaning against the sides of the houses. The old people were merely sitting. Every one of them was waiting for the cotton to mature. They believed in cotton. They believed in it as some men believe in God . . .

"But it had failed them, and there they were waiting in another summer for an autumn harvest that would never come."

The despair of these people mired in the Depression South moved Caldwell deeply. "The sharecropper subsistence was choking people to death," he remembered in Paradise Valley. "You knew it was medieval. It was not 20th century. You can't have hungry people starving, children crying for food, without having some kind of feeling for it."

But *Tobacco Road* was not just documentary—not just "propaganda," as Caldwell would have it. Jeeter Lester and his family, its central characters, are antic grotesques, laughing and flirting and scrapping on doomed terrain. The comic dimensions of the story helped make it palatable to Broadway audiences.

The writer Ralph Ellison, in his long birthday letter to Caldwell, recalled his own reaction to the play. "There, in a darkened theater, I was snatched back to rural Alabama. When Jeeter Lester and the horsing couple went into their act, I was reduced to such helpless laughter that I distracted the entire balcony and embarrassed both my host (Langston Hughes) and myself. . . . I became hysterical in the theater because by catching me off guard and compelling me to laugh at Jeeter you also forced me to recognize and accept our common humanity."

Though Caldwell has a deft comic touch as a writer, in person he is taciturn, and he does not willingly reflect on his literary skills.

"I have no secret," he said. "I like to be a silent witness. I like to listen to what they're saying. It's an introduction to something . . . And what is it? It's not what you see and what you hear, it's what you don't see and what you don't hear."

The small-town stores and barbershops of his youth, he allowed, trained his eyes and ears. "It was a very contagious atmosphere, impregnated with a lot of possibilities. You'd listen to one story, and you could imagine a story yourself that might be a little bit better than that, or more exciting."

Caldwell wrote a memoir once before, in 1951, *Call It Experience*. But that, he said, was a "literary autobiography." (He pronounces it *auto-bee-ography*.) The new one is a "biological autobiography."

Over the years, Caldwell's books have been published by, among other major houses, Scribner's; Viking; Little, Brown; and Farrar Straus & Giroux. *With All My Might* carries the imprint of Peachtree Press, a small house in Atlanta that accepted the book after some larger publishers quibbled with the manuscript.

"I was not impressed by any comments I got, do this and do that and so forth," Caldwell explained. "Everybody wants to be an editor." Especially editors. But Peachtree Press "gobbled it up in five minutes. [The editor] said, 'I'm not going to read it, I'm going to publish it.' "

With All My Might takes swift strides, beginning with Caldwell's Southern boyhood as the son of an itinerant Presbyterian preacher. The young man's formal education was skimpy—a few semesters of college—but his learning was profound as a cottonseed shoveler, a YMCA driver, a baseball scorekeeper, a short-order cook, a poolroom attendant, a Kresge's stockroom manager and a Chinese tourist's bodyguard.

In the 1920s, Caldwell moved to Maine to devote himself full time to writing fiction. He survived in part on the sale of books sent to him for review by *The Charlotte Observer*; his first wife, Helen Lannigan, even opened a bookstore stocked entirely with his review copies.

By 1931 his stories had begun to appear in literary magazines of the day, among them *Scribner's*, edited by Maxwell Perkins, who agreed to publish *Tobacco Road*—without changes, much to Caldwell's satisfaction—the following year.

It was Perkins who gave Caldwell a piece of advice he embraced with a vengeance—not to talk about your writing. "Talk, and you dissipate your enthusiasm and much of the spirit will disappear from what you write later," Perkins said. He also advised Caldwell not to live in New York, and Caldwell never did.

The appearance of *Tobacco Road* and *God's Little Acre*, both of them commercial and critical sensations, quickly enhanced Caldwell's fortunes. During the 1930s, he was earning $2,000 a week from stage royalties on *Tobacco Road* alone.

His prominence as a voice for the dispossessed earned him the swift embrace of the American left, but the clutch made him uncomfortable.

"I felt like a stranger," he says. "I was not one of them. The left in those days was always associated with communism. Today, left is just being a dissident. That's the way I grew up, I guess, being a dissident. So it was just natural for me to gravitate toward the life of people who were being harmed in some way . . . But communism didn't interest me at all."

Caldwell's literary success emboldened him to try new forms of expression. In fact, from the mid-1930s until after World War II, he produced very little new fiction.

Instead, and in keeping with the contemporary vogue for documentary works, he wrote a number of nonfiction books describing the lives of ordinary people, beginning with *You Have Seen Their Faces*, which served to substantiate his fictional assessments of destitution in the South. Similar books followed, drawn from his observations of Eastern Europe, the Soviet Union and the United States from coast to coast.

His collaborator on all four of these volumes was *Life* magazine photographer Margaret Bourke-White. Their extended travels in the late 1930s put an inevitable strain on Caldwell's marriage, which ended in 1938. Soon after he and Bourke-White were married.

The famous writer and the famous photographer made a dashing pair. But Caldwell, for all his past itinerancy, yearned for routine and domesticity. Bourke-White was a hard charger, and according to her biographer, Vicki Goldberg, was frustrated by Caldwell's long silences and moodiness. Before long, she chose to put her career ahead of the marriage—and, more to the point, ahead of Erskine's. They were divorced in 1942.

After the war, Caldwell returned to a prolific rhythm of writing fiction, turning out a book a year for many years. The Hollywood screen writing stints that had engaged him from time to time in the '30s and '40s no longer held their attraction. His disaffection with movies can be traced in part to his disgust at the 1941 screen adaptation of *Tobacco Road*, which substituted a cheerful ending for the bleak conclusion of the novel and play.

By this time, he was married again and had settled in Tucson. He continued to write, and to travel extensively, tending to his literary business with agents and publishers in Europe. His books from this period did not, in the critics' view, measure up to his early work, but they continued to be popular, especially in Europe.

By Caldwell's account, his third wife was not a happy woman. "Deeply absorbed in the throes of psychoanalysis" and attached to her analyst, June Caldwell refused to travel with him, or to move away from what Caldwell found the confining environment of Tucson. In 1955 they were divorced, and Caldwell decamped to Phoenix.

Erskine and the fourth Mrs. Caldwell, Virginia, celebrated their 30th wedding anniversary on New Year's morning. With a sparkle in her eye that defies the melancholy circumstances, Virginia called it "a record."

After their wedding, the Caldwells lived in San Francisco and Dunedin, Fla., before settling in Arizona 10 years ago. Their stucco house sits in the shadow of Mummy Mountain, in this verdant enclave between Phoenix and Scottsdale.

The house is festooned with paintings, many of them Virginia's work (she has illustrated two of Caldwell's recent travel books), others acquired on their foreign trips. Collecting art overseas is not just a family habit; in some countries the only way Caldwell can collect royalties and avoid export taxes is by purchasing native works of art.

Virginia Caldwell, a vivacious dark-eyed woman of 66, seems to deflect any hint of gloom that might attend Erskine's struggle with cancer. "He has such willpower," she says, and she speaks for both of them.

When they first met, at a literary dinner party in the hunt country outside Baltimore, Virginia Fletcher expected the famous writer to be "conceited." She wore an old dress and arrived late—"I wasn't going to kow-tow to anybody." But she was charmed by his unassuming manner, and still is. "He likes Chevrolets and blackeyed peas, but he's sure complex inside."

After they were married, she said, she worked "with conscious effort" at bringing Caldwell out of his shell, and believes she "restored a lot of the confidence he had lost" with his broken marriages.

Virginia is the unofficial and highly energetic curator of the Caldwell enterprise. Her bulky diaries of their appointments and travels, she says, are for tax purposes, but they are in fact albums of their life together—invitations, ticket stubs, clippings, doodles, labels from champagne bottles, business cards, jotted notes of hairy airplane rides and luxurious hotel rooms. Caldwell manifestly is in her debt for the assembly of the latter part of his autobiography.

By his own admission, he has not been an easy character to live with. (Bourke-White, according to her biographer, said he looked "like a man who never laughed," and referred to his icy silences as "the white plague.")

In his autobiography, Caldwell recorded the "accusations" he has heard directed at his person over the years, that he was "hardheaded, perverse, single-minded, stubborn, selfish, and took delight in inflicting mental cruelty on other persons by insisting on having my own way without compromise."

Asked to elaborate, he shifted uncomfortably in his armchair and said:

"When I was having domestic trouble, I did not hesitate to get out of it. I was not a nice guy. I considered my job more important than anything else. But I had to take a stand, selfishly, not thinking of anybody, just myself."

The only family that remains is his four children (three from his first marriage and one from his third) and Virginia's son by a previous marriage. "We don't encourage visits," he said. "They learned at an early age to be on their own. It's a very healthy way to live, from my point of view, because we're not obligated and they're not obligated."

Even if his family doesn't intrude, his public does. Caldwell gets letters, as many as a dozen a day, and with Virginia's assistance, tries to answer most of them.

He is asked to autograph his books, or to sign index cards, which makes him suspicious ("what they do is trade them"). Sometimes writers want his comment on current topics—the Iran arms scandal, for example. He refuses: "It's too obvious."

Most, however, are fan letters.

From Katonah, N.Y.: "I am a young aspiring writer. I have written my first novel and am preparing to write a second. I believe my presence is very sorely needed in literature today. That's why I am writing to you—I need the support of my kindred spirits of the pen."

From Rome, Italy: "I have found your private address in the Christensen's Ultimate Movie, TV and Rock Directory. If you result in this directory this must mean . . ."

From Palic, Yugoslavia: "Excuse me, please, when I disturb you. My name is Laszlo Magyar. Do you remember me?"

Responding to the mail may be a nuisance, but it is the kind of attention Caldwell values most. Virginia recalled that when they were checking out of their hotel in Reno after their wedding night, the porter noticed the name tag on Caldwell's suitcase. "May I just shake your hand?" the porter said. "I've enjoyed your books so much." Later, in the taxi, Caldwell turned to Virginia and said, "I would rather have a comment like that than the praise of all the great critics."

Erskine Caldwell will not second-guess himself; his self probably wouldn't let him anyway.

"I would not willingly consent to relive my life for the purpose of rectifying the mistakes I have made," he writes at the end of his autobiography. "I accept my own failings together with the knowledge that my writings and I must exit with all our imperfections to the end of my time."

Sitting in his study in Paradise Valley, Caldwell put it another way. He said his approach to the world has been "take it or leave it."

He illustrated the point. "Let's say I write a short story, and I send it to a magazine. And then word comes back that they'd like to publish it *if* I consider a new opening, a new beginning. I say, forget it. I'm not rewriting a short story for any editor or publisher. I'm writing for myself."

He illustrated the point again, accidentally and with the pungency of his best stories, when the conversation turned to politics. Asked about the presidential potential of Arizona's young ex-governor, Bruce Babbitt, he reckoned it this way:

"If he'll grow up enough. He's probably still pretty juvenile. Probably still washes his own socks. As I do.

"That means," said Erskine Caldwell, with a nod, "he's his own man."

Index

A

American Academy of Arts and Letters,
196, 295, 299
The American Mercury, 146
Anderson, Sherwood, 92, 133, 142, 144,
147, 197–98, 217, 228, 237;
Winesburg, Ohio, 142
Associate Reformed Presbyterian Church,
16, 84, 164, 255
Atlanta, Georgia, 13, 46, 87, 157, 258,
260, 268
Atlanta Journal, 3, 13, 17, 27, 46, 52, 87,
106, 150, 158–59, 180, 253, 268
Atlanta Press Club, 157
Atlanta University, 157
Atoka, Tennessee, 16
Augusta, Georgia, 201, 272, 274
Augusta (Ga.) College, 157

B

Babbitt, Bruce, 305
Babel, Isaac, 92
Barton, James (as Jeeter Lester), 20, 280
Behn, Harry, 277
Bell, Hunter, 268
Bellow, Saul, 298
Best, Marshall, 203, 276
Bogalusa, Louisiana, 267
Bourke-White, Margaret (second wife), 8,
12, 18–22 *passim,* 26–31 *passim,* 33,
69, 154, 158, 160, 170, 171, 180, 190,
200, 255, 284, 285, 286, 290, 301–02,
303
Brown, James O., 49, 279
Browning, Tod, 277
Burgess, Anthony, 254
Burke, Kenneth, 98

C

Calder, Alexander, 191
Caldwell, Caroline Bell (mother), 15–16,
84–85, 169, 219, 266, 267
Caldwell, Erskine, awards to, 249, 254,
257; biography, 12–13, 16–19, 27–28,
34, 52–53, 58–59, 84–86, 106, 109,
150–51, 157, 178, 180, 219–20,
245–46, 255, 265–69, 300–02; and
cancer, 157, 194, 255, 257, 297, 298,
302–03; on censorship, 5–6, 34–37,
40–41, 48–49, 77, 115, 157, 202–03,
227, 230–32, 279, 281; on his
characters, 3, 7, 53, 182–83, 201, 202,
262, 272, 282, 295; on Civil Rights
Movement, 100–02, 169, 214; on Civil
War, 226, 236, 244; on Communism,
24–25, 120, 144–45, 172, 208–10,
256, 264, 287, 290, 301; on "creative
writing" classes, 13, 92, 96, 98, 116,
185, 253; on critics and criticism,
13–14, 98, 120, 172, 196, 209, 217,
233, 241, 249–50, 262, 283–84, 286,
290; on Czechoslovakia, 8–10; on
death, 263–64, 295–96; on democracy,
10, 23–25, 80; on use of dialect, 48,
131, 174–75, 222, 240, 246, 248; on
dictatorships, 23–25; on economics, 12,
68, 72, 75, 77, 79, 115–16, 173, 207,
208; and editors, 42, 125, 126, 187,
203, 229–30, 276, 285, 286; on
education, 12–13, 16, 46, 68, 69–70,
77–78, 79, 83, 84–85, 101, 116, 173,
185–86, 211, 219–20, 247, 259,
265–67, 268; on emotional stability of
writers, 55; on experience, 53, 83,
118–19, 128–29, 132, 143, 162, 163,
186, 234–35, 247, 272, 293; on
fascism, 8–10, 23–25, 49; on fate, 165,

263–64; on decline of fiction, 97–98,
100, 133, 197, 252, 294–95; definition
of fiction, 118–19, 142, 168, 201, 224,
234, 272, 283; on elements of fiction,
3, 59–60, 182, 229, 239, 252–53; and
football, 13, 17, 85, 150, 219; genres:
children's stories, 50, 190; nonfiction,
43, 97; novel, 43, 112–13, 194, 248;
poetry, 43, 116, 190, 283; short story,
42–43, 45, 92, 97, 112, 193–94, 217,
221, 240, 247, 248, 260–61; on the
Great Depression, 207, 208, 209, 256;
on Hollywood, 18, 44, 89–91, 107,
136, 144, 154, 155, 191, 192, 193,
210, 226–27, 254–55, 277–78,
287–88; on humor, 11, 20, 123–24,
127, 146–47, 174, 201–02, 225,
240–41, 257, 261, 280; on
industrialization, 73, 201, 246; on
journalism, 13, 46, 59, 85, 86–87,
91–93, 116, 130, 142–43, 158–59,
185, 223, 238, 246, 253, 268–69,
270–73, 294; on the Ku Klux Klan,
210–11; on learning to write, 46–47,
87–88, 106–07, 114, 115–17, 130–32,
142–44, 146, 150–51, 175–76, 181,
185–86, 189–91, 216–17, 220–21,
238, 245–46, 268–69; 270–73; on
lecturing, 177, 254; on listening,
245–46, 300; and "little magazines,"
106, 116–17, 120, 130–31, 140, 175,
190, 216–17, 220, 221; on lynchings,
12, 14, 20–21, 72, 79–80, 202,
213–14, 226, 244–45, 259, 285, 293;
manuscripts of, 177–78, 281, 282; on
marriages, 149, 198–99, 255, 290–91,
301–03; on miscegenation, 74–76,
139, 168–69; on motion pictures,
32–33, 39, 44, 89–91, 153, 192, 193,
210, 226–27, 277–78, 287–88; on
New England, 143, 163–64; on the
Nobel Prize, 141–42, 158, 203; on
originality, 37, 96, 118, 184, 221–22,
270, 272, 273, 293; on paperback
books, 81–82, 291, 297–98; on
southern penal system, 73, 171, 245,
267, 274; physical description of, 5, 7,
8, 11, 15, 17, 31, 32, 38, 52, 66,
104–05, 149, 156–57, 179, 252, 258,
297, 298; on pirating of books, 49–50,
81, 148; on plantation system, 66,
67–69, 208, 260; on politics, 23–25,
56, 107, 120–21, 172, 208–09, 256,
258, 278–79, 280–81, 301, 305; on
pornography, 54, 77, 133–34, 202–03,
252; on poverty, 19, 58, 67–68, 83,

84, 86, 93–94, 95, 148, 158, 166–67,
187, 207, 208, 210–11, 235, 245, 249,
274–75, 283–84, 299; on propaganda,
32–33, 48–49, 193, 214, 245, 261,
287; on publishing industry, 35–36,
96–100, 125–27, 129–30, 197, 203,
276, 284–86, 291; on Pulitzer Prize,
203, 273; on racism, 10, 12, 45, 66–80
passim, 82, 100–02, 139, 162,
168–69, 210–11, 212–14, 226, 239,
244–45, 258, 288, 289–90; on his
readers, 20, 21, 40, 41–42, 50–51, 59,
65, 94, 105, 110, 121, 129, 196, 203,
226, 233, 247, 262–63, 292, 304; on
his reading, 16, 64–65, 85, 91, 92,
106, 108, 118, 132–33, 142–43, 152,
184, 206, 219–20, 227–28, 246, 253;
on regionalism, 13, 35, 48, 95–96,
136–37, 205–06, 230, 236, 250; on
religion, 52, 54, 78–79, 84, 121–23,
145, 163–65, 174, 223–24, 241–42,
261, 281; use of repetition, 127, 248;
reputation of, 56, 117–18, 146, 151,
152, 158, 160–61, 196, 203–04, 234,
241, 257, 263, 290, 295–96, 304; on
reviewers, 99–100, 110, 217; on
reviewing books, 88, 106–07, 132,
253; on Russia, 23–25, 27, 28–31, 62,
93, 144–45, 193; sales of books, 36,
38, 52, 81–82, 88, 103, 148, 160, 179,
180, 200, 233, 244; on sensationalism,
34–35, 36, 65, 94, 132, 144, 152, 250,
294–95; importance of setting, 214–15,
235–36, 282; on sex, 53, 54, 66–67,
74–78, 104, 114–15, 135–36, 149,
153–54, 231; on simplicity of style,
111, 260, 268; on slavery, 69, 213,
226; on smoking, 154, 157, 194; on
sociology, 46, 115–16, 173, 289; on
the South, 3, 12, 13–14, 20–21, 35,
47, 61–62, 66–80 *passim*, 82, 83–85,
87, 100–02, 104, 121, 139, 142, 158,
160–78 *passim*, 186–87, 200–02,
206–14 *passim*, 235, 244–45, 246,
258–60, 283–84; on southern writing,
143–44, 200–01, 206–07, 236; on
storytelling, 3, 39–40, 58, 106, 110,
134, 138, 152, 157, 178, 197, 207–08,
234, 246; on symbolism, 111–12,
183–84, 241, 285; on television, 97,
205–06; on tenant farming, 69–71, 73,
170–71, 207, 235, 258, 274;
translations of, 21, 49, 81, 103, 148,
160, 233; on traveling, 16–17, 43–44,
60, 62, 64, 108, 114, 137, 139, 150,
153, 154, 161–62, 173, 194, 235, 245,

Caldwell, Erskine, (continued)
246, 250, 257–58, 265, 267; on
violence, 12, 61–62, 79–80, 167,
225–26, 242–43, 293; as war
correspondent, 93, 108, 154, 286–87;
on women, 53–54, 74–78, 166, 249,
289; on words, 45–46, 63, 111,
222–23, 237–38; on World War I, 150;
on World War II, 23–25, 62, 72,
286–87; on writers, 13, 50–51, 54–55,
63, 89, 91, 96, 104–05, 106, 107–08,
119, 133, 139–43, 152–53, 154–55,
159, 173–74, 198, 216–17, 227–28,
233–34, 236–37, 250–51, 253, 254,
292; on writer and social reform,
13–14, 20–21, 40, 55, 101–02, 107,
138, 139, 166–67, 171–72, 241, 244,
255, 258–59, 274–75; on writing as
business, 49, 55, 56, 81–82, 88, 108,
134, 138–39, 149, 152, 153, 269–70,
292; on writing process, 11–12, 13, 17,
21–22, 38–51 passim, 52, 53, 56,
62–63, 110–14, 119, 123–25, 127–29,
135, 146, 148, 149, 176–77, 181–84,
187–90, 195, 215–16, 228–29,
238–39, 247, 253, 264; works:
Afternoons in Mid-America (travel
book), 156; All Night Long (novel), 28,
32, 33; All-Out on the Road to
Smolensk (nonfiction), 23, 27, 31, 33;
American Earth (stories), 53, 88;
American Folkways Series, 47–48,
229–30, 250, 285–86; Annette (novel),
289, 293, 294; Around About America
(travel book), 64; Autumn Hill
(unpublished novel), 163, 194; The
Bastard (novel), 3, 4, 151, 190–91,
255, 271–72; The Black and White
Stories of Erskine Caldwell, 258; The
Bogus Ones (unpublished novel), 194,
272–73; Call It Experience
(autobiography), 84, 86, 132, 134,
206, 219, 237, 267, 268, 284, 300;
"Candy Man Beechum," 79, 174, 248;
Certain Women (stories), 38, 47, 92;
Claudelle Inglish (novel), 38, 192, 289;
Claudelle Inglish (film), 192; Close to
Home (novel), 100–01, 102, 124;
"Country Full of Swedes," 218,
224–25; "Crime Does Not Pay" (film
series), 18, 33, 193, 227, 277; Deep
South (nonfiction), 103, 219; The Deer
at Our House (children's story), 190;
The Earnshaw Neighborhood (novel),
149; "The End of Christy Tucker," 232;
Episode in Palmetto (novel), 170, 214,

293, 294; Georgia Boy (stories), 44–45,
55, 148, 160, 180, 183, 200, 201, 239,
247–48, 288; God's Little Acre (novel),
8, 12, 15, 20, 21, 28, 34, 38, 39, 40,
45, 50, 58, 59, 77, 81, 83, 87, 88, 103,
109, 148, 149, 156, 160, 164, 165–66,
170, 179, 180, 183, 188, 200, 201,
207, 218, 223, 230–31, 241–42, 244,
252, 261, 276, 277, 279, 297, 298,
301; God's Little Acre (film), 38, 39,
44, 192, 201; Gretta (novel), 47, 289,
290, 294; "The Growing Season," 184;
Gulf Coast Stories, 92; "Handsome
Brown and the Goats," 248; A House
in the Uplands (novel), 38, 45, 70, 170,
214, 289–90, 292, 294; "In Defense of
Myself," 218; In Search of Bisco
(nonfiction), 82, 169, 183, 214, 239,
267, 294; Jackpot (stories), 21, 180,
203, 286; Jenny By Nature (novel),
75–76, 289, 293; Journeyman (novel),
20, 38, 160, 164–65, 170, 180, 200,
214, 276, 280–81, 282; Journeyman
(play), 192; Kneel to the Rising Sun
(stories), 8, 281–82; "Kneel to the
Rising Sun," 202, 282; A Lamp for
Nightfall (novel), 163, 275–76; The
Last Night of Summer (novel), 58,
61–62, 134–35, 293; Look Homeward
Angel (screenplay), 287–88; Louisiana
Lou (screenplay), 277; Love and
Money (novel), 119, 215, 290, 291–92;
"The Mating of Marjory," 17, 273;
"Midsummer Passion," 3, 220, 270;
Mission to Moscow (film), 32–33, 193,
210, 287; Molly Cottontail (children's
story), 50; Moscow Under Fire
(nonfiction), 27, 33; "My Old Man,"
21; North of the Danube (photo-essay),
8, 9, 19, 28, 43, 285; "The People Vs.
Abe Latham, Colored," 232; Place
Called Estherville (novel), 45, 47,
74–75, 170, 212; Poor Fool (novel),
151, 190–91, 271, 272; Roughshod
(screenplay), 227, 277; The Sacrilege of
Alan Kent, 175, 191, 282–83; "Saturday Afternoon," 79, 202; Say, Is
This the U.S.A.?, 28, (photo-essay);
Some American People (nonfiction),
171–72; The Strong Man of Maxcatan
(musical), 193; Summertime Island
(novel), 103, 135, 294; The Sure Hand
of God (novel), 170, 290, 293; Tenant
Farmer (nonfiction), 160, 200, 207,
283; This Very Earth (novel), 170;
Tobacco Road (film), 192, 254–55,

302; *Tobacco Road* (novel), 6, 8, 15, 17–18, 21, 28, 38, 39, 42, 45, 56, 58, 59, 67–68, 83, 87, 88, 103, 109, 110, 120, 125, 126, 148, 151, 152, 153–54, 156, 160, 166–67, 170; 176–77, 178, 180, 186, 200, 207, 214, 218, 223, 230, 235, 239–41, 242–43, 244, 245, 252, 258, 274–75, 277, 297, 298, 299, 301; *Tobacco Road* (play), 5–6, 7, 11, 18, 20, 21, 28, 35, 39, 81, 89, 141, 149, 151, 180, 191–92, 231, 249, 279–80, 283, 298, 299–300; "Tracing Life With a Finger," 3; *Tragic Ground* (novel), 38, 72, 160, 166–67, 170, 172–73, 180, 200, 214, 288–89, 294; *Trouble in July* (novel), 12, 20, 49, 148, 160, 170, 180, 200, 202, 212, 213, 285, 289; "A Very Late Spring," 17, 273; *The Weather Shelter* (novel), 135, 139, 148, 149; *The Wicked Woman* (screenplay), 18; *With All My Might* (autobiography), 291, 297, 300, 303; *Writing in America* (essay), 104; *A Year of Living* (unpublished autobiography), 160, 180, 195, 203; *You Have Seen Their Faces* (photo-essay), 8, 19, 28, 43, 69, 70, 158, 160, 170–71, 180, 200, 207, 283–84, 285, 301
Caldwell, Helen Lannigan (first wife), 4, 87, 154, 180, 255, 268, 269, 275, 276, 277, 278, 301
Caldwell, Rev. Ira S. (father), 12, 15–16, 17, 83–84, 85–86, 145, 150, 157, 164, 169, 176, 223–24, 245, 267, 274
Caldwell, June Johnson (third wife), 154, 180, 255, 290–91, 302
Caldwell, Virginia (fourth wife), 38, 46, 49, 50, 64, 66, 67, 74, 80, 81, 104, 125, 148, 151, 153, 154, 155, 161, 179, 180, 187, 199, 200, 218, 254, 255, 258, 294, 297, 298, 302–03, 304
Cannes Film Festival, 153
Cantwell, Robert, 140
Capek, Karel, 9; *R.U.R.*, 9.
Capote, Truman, 197; *In Cold Blood*, 197
Carnell, Ruth, 277, 284
Carter, Billy, 196, 211
Carter, Jimmy, 195–96
Cassidy, Henry, 286
Charlotte Observer, 106, 301
Chicago, Illinois, 5–6
The Children of Sanchez, 95
Christians, Mady, 18
Chungking, China, 28, 288
Clemens, S. L. (Mark Twain), 92, 197, 253

Cohen, Octavus Roy, 131
Collier's, 216, 217
CBS Radio, 108, 286–87
Columbia University, 152
Conrad, Joseph, 131
Contact, 217
Cosmopolitan, 216, 220
Coweta County, Ga., 15, 156, 158, 160, 180
Cowley, Malcolm, 98, 140–41, 178, 196, 234, 241, 298; *And I Worked at the Writer's Trade*, 178

D

Daniels, Frank, 268, 269
Darien, Conn., 7, 15–22 *passim*, 26–27, 190
Dartmouth College, 109, 161, 177–78, 193, 205, 282, 287
Davidson, Donald, 167, 284
Davies, Joseph E., 32; *Mission to Moscow* (book), 32
Devlin, James, 272
De Vries, Peter, 298
Dilling, Elizabeth, 144; *The Red Network*, 144
Dodd, Mead, 195
Donald, E. P., 96
Dos Passos, John, 140, 149, 152, 257, 298
Dreiser, Theodore, 13, 133, 144, 198, 228, 237
Duell, Charlie, 285
Duell, Sloan and Pearce, 12, 21, 28, 36, 177, 203, 276, 284–85, 286, 291
Duhamel, Marcel, 191
Dunedin, Florida, 120, 149, 150, 302

E

Eisenstein, Sergei, 30, 33; *Alexander Nevsky*, 30; *Peter the Great*, 33
Ellison, Ralph, 299–300
Emory University (Atlanta, Ga.), 157
England, 27
Enoch, Kurt, 291
Erskine College (Due West, S. C.), 16, 180, 267
Ethridge, Mark, 86

F

Farrar, Straus & Giroux, 82, 300
Faulkner, William, 13, 21, 54, 56, 80, 91,

Faulkner, William, (continued)
    92, 133, 140, 141–42, 144, 149, 152,
    158, 161, 198, 237, 251, 253, 257,
    258, 277, 298; *As I Lay Dying,* 91, 92,
    118, 133, 142, 198, 253
Fitzgerald, F. Scott, 149, 151
Ford, Charles Henri, 140
Ford, John, 192, 254
Fugitives, the, 283–84
Fuller, John, 67

G

Gable, Clark, 227, 277
Garden of Allah, 277
Gastonia (N.C.) mill strike, 201
Geer, Will (as Jeeter Lester), 20
The Georgia Historical Quarterly, 158
Gibbon, Edward, 106, 220; *Decline and
    Fall of the Roman Empire,* 106, 220
Glasgow, Ellen, 200; *Barren Ground,* 200
Gobi Desert, 28–29
Gold, Mike, 145, 209
Goldberg, Vicki, 302
Graham, Billy, 122
Guggenheim Fellowship, 273
Guinzberg, Harold, 276, 281

H

Harcourt, Brace, 285
Hardy, Thomas, 131
Hawks, Howard, 277
Hazzard, Shirley, 298
Hemingway, Ernest, 4, 21, 56, 91, 133,
    141, 149, 151, 152, 184–85, 228, 237,
    257, 298
Hench, Atcheson, 185, 186
Henning, Edgar, 7
Heron Press, 271
Hersey, John, 298
Hillman, Alex, 271
Hitler, Adolph, 8, 9, 23, 24, 25, 30, 62
Hopkins, Miriam, 277–78
"Horseplay Hill" (Darien, Conn.), 15,
    19–20, 22, 26–27
Hughes, Langston, 300
Hull, Henry (as Jeeter Lester), 6, 7, 20,
    191–92, 280

I

Ionesco, Eugene, 254

J

James, Henry, 186
Jarrell, Randell, 127
Joyce, James, 4; *Ulysses,* 4

K

Kelly, Mayor Edward H., 5–6
Kennedy, John F., 56, 76
Kent, Rockwell, 27, 145
King, Dr. Martin Luther, 78–79
Kirkland, Jack, 20, 191, 192, 279–80
Knopf, Alfred, 99
Korges, James, 147, 150
Kreymborg, Alfred, 270, 271
Krutch, Joseph Wood, 98

L

Lawrence, D. H., 216
Leiber, Maxim, 276, 278–79, 284
Lewis, Sinclair, 198
"The Liberated Theatre" (Czech theater
    group), 8–9
Life magazine, 108, 158, 286, 301
Little, Brown & Company, 82, 276, 300
Long, Huey, 280
Longfellow Square Book Shop, 3,4
Louis, Joe, 10
Louisville *Courier-Journal,* 86
Lubitsch, Ernst, 277–78

M

MacArthur, Douglas, 24
Macon *Telegraph,* 86
Mailer, Norman, 197, 298–99; *The
    Executioner's Song,* 197
Malraux, André, 95
Manuel, Al, 287
Marx, Groucho, 280
Mary Baldwin College (Virginia), 85
Maugham, Somerset, 18
Maupassant, Guy de, 143
Mayo Clinic, 153, 154, 194
McLean, Austin, 218, 219
McLeod, Norman, 140
Melville, Herman, 242; *Billy Budd,* 242
Mencken, H. L., 46, 146; *The American
    Language,* 46
Metro-Goldwyn-Meyer (M-G-M), 18, 32,
    90, 277, 287
Mexico, 16, 18, 24, 278–79

Michener, James, 197; *Centennial*, 197
Miller, Henry, 54, 56
Mississippi Oral History Program, 138
Mitchell, Margaret, 253, 268–69; *Gone With the Wind*, 253, 269
Monroe, Marilyn, 54
Mount Vernon, Maine, 7, 11, 13, 18, 28, 47, 87, 88, 94–95, 141, 180, 190, 195, 206, 225, 269

N

Nabokov, Vladimir, 76; *Lolita*, 76
The Nation, 209
Nevsky, Alexander, 30
The New American Caravan, 3, 28, 270
New American Library, 82, 152, 187, 291
The New Masses, 145, 208–10, 256
The New Republic, 209
New York City, 11, 87, 89, 126, 140, 145, 154–55, 187–88, 209, 250
The New York Post, 283
New York Society for the Suppression of Vice, 77, 279
The New Yorker, 202
Newman, Frances, 268; *The Hard-Boiled Virgin*, 268
Nietzsche, Frederich Wilhelm, 146

O

O'Connor, Flannery, 242
Otis, Elizabeth, 82
Owen, Guy, 272

P

PM (newspaper), 18, 108, 286
Pagany, 175
Peachtree Press, 300
Pearce, Cap, 36, 177, 203, 285, 286
Pearl Harbor, 23, 24
"People's Culture" (Czech book guild), 8
Percy, Walker, 236
Perkins, Maxwell, 42, 46, 88, 100, 125, 126, 145–46, 151, 187, 203, 230, 253, 273–74, 276, 301
Picasso, Pablo, 191
Pollinger, Laurence, 82
Posselt, Erich, 270, 271

R

Radio City Music Hall (New York), 11, 87

Random House, 99
Roberts, Oral, 122
Rockefeller Center, 87
Roosevelt, Franklin D., 275, 287
Rose, Charlie, 89
Rouse, H. Blair, 235
Rowan, Dan, 153
Runyon, Damon, 136

S

San Francisco, Calif., 38, 302
Saroyan, William, 89, 136, 146, 147, 155, 198, 250–51
Sartre, Jean Paul, 94
The Saturday Evening Post, 131, 216, 217
Schwartz, Edward P., 218
Scottsdale, Arizona (Paradise Valley), 179, 257, 302
Scribner's, 42, 125, 126–27, 187, 203, 230, 300, 301
Scribner's Magazine, 17, 46, 88, 125, 151, 273
Selwyn Theatre (Chicago), 5
Shapiro, Henry, 286
Silver City, Nev., 19
Sloan, Sam, 285
Southern Methodist University, 254
Spiegel, Mark, 276
Sports Illustrated, 140
Stalin, Joseph, 287
Staunton, Virginia, 266
Stegner, Wallace, 298
Steinbeck, John, 21, 54, 91, 133, 140, 141, 198, 228, 255, 257, 298
Stevens, Charlie, 86
Studies in the Novel, 215
Styron, William, 298
Sumner, John S., 77
Sutton Place (see Nathanael West), 89, 154–55

T

Talmadge, Eugene, 280
Taylor, Elizabeth, 294
This Quarter, 217
Thompson, Lawrence, 242
Thornhill, Arthur H., 82
Thurber, James, 53, 184; "Bateman Comes Home," 184
Tom Swift and the Electric Cannon, 106
transition, 3–4, 140, 190, 217, 270
Tuskegee Institute (Alabama), 244

Twain, Mark—see Clemens, S. L.
Twentieth-Century Fox, 90

U

U. S. House UnAmerican Activities
    Committee, 278
University of California, 17
University of Georgia, 85, 177
University of Minnesota, 218
University of Pennsylvania, 16, 173, 180,
    268
University of Southern Mississippi, 138
University of Virginia, 13, 16, 17, 106,
    109–10, 115–16, 130, 173, 177, 180,
    185–86, 267–68, 289
Untermeyer, Louis, 43, 116, 190
Updike, John, 298

V

Vietnam, 94, 95
Viking Press, 8, 77, 127, 203, 276, 281,
    284, 286, 300
Virginia Reel, 110
Vonnegut, Kurt, 299

W

Warner Brothers, 32, 90
Warren, Robert Penn, 237, 298
Welty, Eudora, 237
West, Nathanael, 89–91, 149, 154–55,
    198, 250–51; *Miss Lonelyhearts,* 89,
    154
Weybright, Victor, 82, 187, 291
White, Oak Georgia, 15, 16, 150
Wilbur, Richard, 295, 298
Wilkes-Barre, Pennsylvania, 17, 53, 85,
    150, 179, 186
Willingham, Calder, 158, 234
Wolfe, Thomas, 140, 151, 152, 237, 298
Wordsworth, William, 186
Wrens, Georgia, 16, 176, 187, 266, 267,
    272, 274
Wright, Richard, 74; *Native Son,* 74

Y

Yordan, Philip, 39; *God's Little Acre*
    (film), 39

Z

Zanuck, Darryl, 192